JOHN·IVTH
E^L of LOUDOUN
COM^{DER}in CHIEF in
the N AMERICAN PROVINCES.

LORD LOUDOUN
IN NORTH AMERICA

By

STANLEY McCRORY PARGELLIS

ARCHON BOOKS
1968

Copyright 1933 by Yale University Press
Copyright ©1961 by Stanley McCrory Pargellis

Reprinted 1968 with permission
in an unaltered and unabridged edition

[YALE HISTORICAL PUBLICATIONS: STUDIES VII]

Library of Congress Catalog Card Number 68-16333
Printed in the United States of America

PREFACE

THIS book is neither a biography of Loudoun nor a history of his campaigns. It is the story of the high command which he held. Loudoun exercised the usual commander in chief's authority over various branches of his army and in addition had duties and powers in regard to the civil governments of the North American colonies. This second aspect of his command is the more interesting and important. The basic factor in British colonial policy in the early years of the Seven Years' War was a traditional belief that the colonies should bear the chief burden in men and costs of their own defense. Loudoun's task was to persuade them to work in unison, and he had to concentrate his attention as much on that as on fighting the French. For Americans raised a violent objection, not to assuming a share in the war, but to assuming it under the conditions and according to the formula which Great Britain imposed. Their antagonism was based on the fear that a standing army threatened the free working of their colonial institutions and was to reappear even more markedly in the 60s and 70s when Gage was commander in chief. The parallel with the attitude of the seventeenth-century House of Commons towards the army is easily recognizable. That colonial antagonism, growing in strength during Loudoun's career, seemed to the ministry of William Pitt vast enough to threaten the success of the war. So Loudoun was recalled; and the idea of a commander in chief who should be more than a military officer was forgotten until Canada had been won.

Loudoun left an extraordinarily complete set of papers, a record of everything of importance he saw, thought, and did. This collection, known as the Loudoun Papers, is now in the Henry E. Huntington Library at San Marino, California, and it has been my privilege to examine it in detail. I am grateful to the officials of the Library for giving me access to the documents and for permitting me to print excerpts. My friend Captain R. B. Haselden, the Curator of Manuscripts, has arranged the collection in the most convenient form for use. He knows an incredible number of things, and was, and is, most generous in drawing on his stock to meet my every request. I should like also to thank Miss Norma Cuthbert of the Library staff for her assistance.

It is a privilege to record His Majesty's kindness in permitting an American historian to use the valuable collection of Cumberland Papers in the Royal Archives at Windsor Castle. I am indebted to the present Countess of Loudoun, both for the memory of a pleasant visit at Loudoun Castle, and for permission to reproduce for the first time a portrait of the fourth Earl. The officials and staffs of the Public Record Office and the British Museum have been most helpful, as every American student who has worked in London attests, and I am glad of this opportunity to express my appreciation of the kindness of the staffs in the Yale and Harvard University Libraries, the Connecticut and Massachusetts Historical Societies, and the State Archives at Hartford and Boston. An appointment as Sterling Fellow from Yale University enabled me to acquire abroad material without which I could not have completed and rewritten this study, originally submitted as a doctoral dissertation at Yale. My warm thanks are due Professors U. B. Phillips, Wallace Notestein, and L. W. Labaree of Yale University for helpful suggestions and advice. Finally, to Professor Charles M. Andrews, who from first to last has guided, criticized, and encouraged this work, I must record an inestimable debt.

S. M. PARGELLIS.

Cape Porpoise, Maine.
  September, 1932.

CONTENTS

Preface v

List of Illustrations ix

Chapter I. Colonial Defense before 1756 . 1

Chapter II. Administrative Tangles . . 45

Chapter III. Provincial Troops . . . 83

Chapter IV. Recruiting the Regular Army . 104

Chapter V. Shirley and Oswego . . . 132

Chapter VI. The Temper of Colonial Assemblies 167

Chapter VII. Quartering 187

Chapter VIII. Military Union of the Colonies–I 211

Chapter IX. The Campaign of 1757 . . 228

Chapter X. Military Union of the Colonies–II 253

Chapter XI. The Administration of the Army 279

Chapter XII. Loudoun and Pitt . . . 337

Bibliography 366

Index 379

ILLUSTRATIONS

John, fourth Earl of Loudoun, painted by Allan
Ramsay (Reproduced by kind permission of the
Countess of Loudoun, from the original in Lou-
doun Castle) .   .   .   .   .   *Frontispiece*

Plan of Oswego in 1756, by Patrick Mackellar
(Reproduced, by permission, from the original
in the Royal Library of Windsor Castle)
Facing page 150

Map of the Frontier Line in the Middle Colonies,
1754–1758, showing the principal forts and
settlements .   .   .   .   .   *Following index*

CHAPTER I

COLONIAL DEFENSE BEFORE 1756

To the honor of Colonel Townshend who fell at Ticonderoga in 1759 his mother erected in Westminster Abbey a proud inscription, enrolling him among those "immortal Statesmen and Commanders Whose Wisdom and Intrepidity, In the course of this comprehensive and Successfull War, Have extended the Commerce, Enlarged the Dominion, And upheld the Majesty of these Kingdoms, Beyond the Idea of any former age." These words strike a new note in British history; through them breathes for the first time the spirit of Empire. For commerce and dominion are, or may be, distinct; the one looks towards immediate gain, the other towards future development. So little did the idea of empire influence opinion throughout most of the so-called Second Hundred Years' War with France that ministers who might have taken Quebec and North America with as much ease as Venables and Penn took Jamaica seldom considered the suggestion twice. Pitt's cabinet of 1757 was the first deliberately to undertake to bring under the British flag vast stretches of wilderness. His predecessors would have thought such aims disastrously expensive, impolitic, and visionary.

The main lines of British foreign and commercial policy before 1750 show clearly enough where official attention was directed. As diplomatists ministers were not interested in colonial conquests. They were concerned with preserving the Whig settlement of 1689 against attacks of the Stuarts, aided by France; with the maintenance of a balance of power in Europe, and especially in the Low Countries; and, after the accession of George I, with the safety of his electorate of Hanover. For these objectives they declared war, or preserved with Walpole an unexpected peace. Their volumes of correspondence are charged with papers on the kaleidoscopic diplomatic scene; the minutes of their cabinet and inner cabinet meetings show constant vigilance over successions of foreign crises; their biographies, whatever they may omit, dwell on their skill in guiding the ark of England's honor through the floods of Spanish trickery and French deceit. In this greatest of games the colonies counted for little. In time of war British troops fought on the Continent; they were too few to fight also in the New World. In the intervals between wars any daring show of force in the colonies might have aroused a hostility that would endanger the security of British alliances and the peace of Europe. Schemes for taking Canada were sometimes broached but rarely considered. They were too ticklish. They were also too dull, in comparison with the dangerous joys of outwitting a Fleury or an Elizabeth Farnese.

British commercial policy likewise had little in common with schemes for the mere enlarging of dominion. Ministers were adherents, yet not too violently, to the tenets of mercantilism, for it was a fact increasingly patent that England's greatness depended upon her navy and upon her wealth, and both were served by trade. Commercial interests had to be preserved and extended, particularly in the North American and West Indian colonies. But it was commerce, and not land, that was to be extended. In the eyes of the mercantilist permanent acquisition of new territory was futile unless such territory either directly aided the creation of a favorable balance of trade or protected existing colonies and trade routes. Every territorial gain which Great Britain made in North America before 1750 played a definite role in the mercantilist scheme of things. Possession of Newfoundland kept the French from profiting in the fisheries; possession of Nova Scotia and Georgia gave to the long, narrow strip of continental colonies a safeguard from attack at its vulnerable extremities. Further than that no ministry would go. Conquest of the St. Lawrence and Mississippi valleys promised scanty commercial return. For only the fur trade, already well supplied by the Hudson's Bay Company and the New York outposts, would profit from British control of the interior. The fact that thrice during actual war ministries sent expeditions against Quebec does not prove the absence of a consistent policy. The abortive expeditions of 1693, 1711, and 1746, carelessly planned and inadequately supported, were poor efforts to cripple in the New World that French power which seemed omnipotent in the Old. They were launched rather for diplomacy's sake than for empire's. The third one, for instance, was a desperate and avowed attempt to get something with bargaining power at a peace conference to offset the victories of Marshall Saxe. Leaders of opinion, whether in high office or in trade, if the expedition of 1746 had chanced to be successful and they had seen England permanently saddled with half a virgin continent, would have deemed it a more damaging blow to their delicately balanced commercial system than any that France might have dealt. For that system was year by year increasing its profits, while empire remained an extravagant venture.

The real problem of colonial defense, before Pitt's time, had nothing to do with empire. It was negative, the protection of already existing colonies whence came England's treasure in trade, the holding of what England had. On the continent, with which alone we are concerned, it meant the discovery of some means whereby in time of peace local Indian attacks could be beaten off, and in time of war with France or Spain a capable military force could be created and concentrated in threatened areas. The same problem has always confronted the nation with distant dependencies. Great Britain never reached a satisfactory solution.

Why did ministries before the middle of the century fail to settle the problem of colonial defense? The easiest answer is that it never became imperative enough to force a solution. The continental colonies were a narrow strip bound to England by the sea-lanes of commerce and separated from French and Spanish possessions by a wide belt of hinterland which none except Indians inhabited. The safety of the sea-lanes demanded no more attention than the maintaining of a navy devoted to the traditions of Blake and Clowdisley Shovell. From the hinterland stretching to and beyond the mountains the ministry fancied it had little to fear as long as white settlers kept away and left in undisturbed possession Indians faithful to British interests. So ministers did not encourage western expansion, though, as is shown by their attitude towards Governor Hunter's settlement of Palatines in New York, Thomas Coram's proposed colony between Nova Scotia and the old Province of Maine, and Sir William Keith's design for a new plantation beyond Virginia, they did not actively oppose it. To keep the Indians their allies, especially the great tribes of the Five Nations whose friendship Governor Dongan of New York had won in 1684 and with whom the covenant chain had been strengthened in 1701 and 1726, was an objective well worth the trouble. When gained, and the ministry considered the alliance an accepted fact for most of this period, the Indians became "our frontier guards, always ready to defend our out-settlements and to make war upon any other Nation whenever we require them to do it.'"[1] Ministers were inclined to discount constant reports of the dangers from French activities along the interior lakes and rivers. For with the navy upon the coasts, and loyal Indians upon the backs of the colonies, there seemed to have been reached a stable security.

There is a second reason, far more complicated, for the failure of ministries to find a dependable means of protecting the colonies. Though Indian allies might serve in peace, in time of war, against the trained troops of France or Spain, some more disciplined and unified force was needed. How was that force to be raised, and how supported? On the face of it this question seems to admit the simple answer which James Oglethorpe in 1736 gave to Sir Robert Walpole: "there were but two ways of defending our Colonies from the French and Spaniards and their Indians, the one by forming a regular and warlike militia, the other by keeping a body of regular troops."[2] By militia Oglethorpe understood not only the old military system of the colonies, the true militia, the entire population permanently organized in companies and regiments, but also provincial troops raised by vote of a colonial assembly for a limited period and paid and supplied by that body. By regular troops he meant British regiments of the line, on the British establishment, and therefore paid by parliament. But in practice the distinction was by no means as clear as that. For it was possible also to have colonial troops formed in the American fashion with American officers, but paid from England; to have regulars sent from England, but paid from colonial revenue; to have British regiments with British officers on a regular establishment, but with the rank and file consist-

[1] Board of Trade to Newcastle, Aug. 20, 1730, Public Record Office, C.O. 5: 4, no. 42.

[2] Historical Manuscripts Commission, *Diary of the first Earl of Egmont*, II, 340.

ing wholly of Americans; and to have a mixture, a British commander in chief, some British, some American officers, Americans in the ranks and charges divided between assemblies and parliament. All of these methods were tried, and all of them met opposition either from England or from the colonies.

Let us consider these methods in detail, examine their merits and shortcomings, and why they failed. For they exhausted the possibilities; there was no way to provide for colonial defense except by one of these schemes, or some combination of them. They were therefore the precedents before the ministry at the outbreak of the final Seven Years' War, and from them was formed the plan upon which that war was undertaken. There are five schemes.

The first, in true mercantilist fashion, left everything to the separate colonies. Though the mother country might send occasional gifts of ordnance, the assemblies in those colonies adjacent to the one attacked were expected to take the initiative in assisting their neighbor with men and supplies. In the force so created both officers and men, of course, were American, and the sole commander in chief, if indeed there was one, held a separate commission from every colony which had troops in the field. In most cases New York province, nearest to and most accessible from Quebec or Montreal, was the principal object of French attacks, but the regions of Maine and the Carolinas also saw Indian wars, sometimes instigated by French agents. In six different wars such provincial troops of the several colonies did what they could to protect their frontiers. That they did not do more was because of a jealous and suspicious sectionalism. The governments in America, differing from one another in race, religion, social structure, political form, and economic interests, were intensely particularist. A sole example of the results of that jealousy will suffice; it could be multiplied many times. When the governor of New York, in and after 1691, bespoke aid from his neighbors against the vigorous action of Count Frontenac of Canada, he received nothing but excuses of remarkable ingenuity: they had their own frontiers to defend; they considered the Five Nations ample protection for New York; they did not see how the safety of New York determined their own safety; they did not believe in fighting; they had already sent more than they could afford; they would not furnish troops unless other colonies furnished them too; they would not allow their men to be under the command of a governor of New York. Impatient with such jarring animosities and selfishness, the Crown intervened, commanded the colonies to aid New York, and named the quotas according to which each was to furnish men and money. But neither then nor later did compliance follow. The capture of Louisbourg by the New Englanders in 1745 was the only instance in this whole period of a successful colonial enterprise. There was little in that expedition to show that it was more than a flash in the pan, a happy accident arising from a combination of peculiarly favorable circumstances. In general the colonies by themselves could not be trusted to look after their defense.

Still clinging to his dictum that the colonies should bear the costs, the mercantilist developed out of their failure to do their duty a second and obvious scheme. It was the most revolutionary colonial project ever conceived by the merchants and ministers of the Stuarts, and if it had succeeded it would have settled the problem of defense once and for all. For the mercantilist was prepared to scrap existing colonial governments altogether, and to erect a supergovernment which should exercise supreme military and civil control over the entire continental area. In such

a state local differences would give way under the leadership of a governor general to unified command; provincial
troops drawn from all sections would take post at threatened areas; military expenses would be defrayed from a
common colonial treasury. This state came to represent
the ideal; it provided uniformity in civil administration
and the enforcement of the acts of trade, and it constituted a self-supporting, efficient, military unit. But a
variety of causes prevented the accomplishment of the
dream. Once only, for a brief period, was any state set up
which approached the ideal model. The Dominion of New
England, as enlarged in 1688, included the Five Nations
and the principal passes into French territory; it united
the colonies affected by French attacks under a civil and
military commander in chief whose four regular companies of foot were combined with provincial troops; both
were to be paid from local revenues. But Andros's administration was too abrupt a departure from the independent government to which the people of New England
were accustomed to become permanent. The Revolution
of 1689 proved that a union of colonies for defense had to
be accomplished by less drastic means. For the next
thirty years the Board of Trade vainly tried to discover
such means. It was blocked by the existence of corporate
and proprietary colonies whose charters removed them
from direct royal control, and whose legal rights were
defended in England by influential noblemen in the House
of Lords with economic interests at stake as proprietors.
If such governments could have been reduced to the
status of royal colonies, the board would have recommended the creation of such a federation as was in force
in the Leeward Islands, with a governor general enjoy-
ing supreme military power and control of Indians, assisted by lieutenant governors in separate provinces. It
advanced that scheme in the most statesmanlike docu-

ment it ever produced, the famous representation of 1721, the real credit of which belongs to John Locke's original proposal of 1696.[3] But the bills introduced into parliament to level colonial governments to a standard pattern did not pass, and negotiations with individual proprietors for the purchase of their claims met with only partial success. The one enduring gain was an opinion from the attorney general in 1694 that the Crown might in an emergency appoint a captain general over the troops of private colonies. In 1697 Lord Bellomont was named governor of New York, Massachusetts, and New Hampshire, and by virtue of this opinion captain general of the forces in Connecticut, Rhode Island, and the Jerseys—a faint replica of the Dominion of New England. But he held the post during a brief period of peace when there was no need to demonstrate the advantages of union; at his death factional politics and jealousy between New York and Massachusetts brought it about that no successor was appointed. Before 1721 the chief stumbling blocks in the way of union seemed to be the constitutional ambitions in the colonies themselves, sectional antagonism, and the interested opposition of lords proprietors.

After 1721, though this same opposition is still heard, another somewhat surprising factor enters into the story of colonial union. The mercantilist himself became persuaded that perhaps his idol had feet of clay. The bursting of the South Sea bubble showed him the danger in toying with colonial speculative schemes; it was much safer to let matters take their course. Jeremiah Dummer's *Defence of the New England Charters* offered un-

---

[3] *Calendar State Papers, Colonial, 1696-1697*, §286. This paper of 1696 bore the signatures of the entire board, but Locke's authorship is attested by a letter to Lord Townshend from William Popple, the board's secretary, July 20, 1720, Historical Manuscripts Commission, *Eleventh Report*, Townshend Papers, p. 296.

rebutted arguments that trade would increase best if the private colonies were left free. And most important of all, it was realized that colonial assemblies would not of themselves support the costs of a military union under a governor general, and that if the only other solution were adopted, the levying in the colonies of a parliamentary tax for the purpose, trade in some mysterious fashion would be harmed. How to find a tax that would not affect trade? On that shoal the fine craft of colonial union, launched with so much vigor in the preceding century, rested for nearly thirty years. Lord Townshend, who as Lord President of the Privy Council and one of the Lords Justices in 1720 encouraged the Board of Trade to prepare its great representation, was the last statesman to concern himself actively with it. Though under Walpole many schemes for taxing the colonies were advanced, among them that of Martin Bladen, a capable member of the Board of Trade, and although Walpole's opposition in parliament tried to force the question of colonial security to the front,[4] no minister seriously considered the idea. It was not until 1748 that the question was reopened by Governor Shirley of Massachusetts, to whose opinion the ministry, and especially Bedford, assigned weight. He proposed that uniform acts relating to military affairs be framed in England for colonial assemblies to pass, and that a parliamentary tax be levied to support a fort and a British garrison in New York. That proposal was the prelude to another series of efforts to solve the problem of unified defense by laying the charges on the colonies. Such efforts, as they developed, were eventu-

[4] In 1735, when the House of Commons demanded all representations from the Board of Trade relating to the state and trade of the colonies and the dangers from French encroachments, Newcastle, then a secretary of state, thought it inadvisable to lay before the house the representation of 1721 and carefully withheld it from the mass of documents submitted. British Museum, Additional Manuscripts 33,028, f. 340.

ally to cost England her colonies, and do not concern us here. But when one realizes the magnitude of the slowly accumulating forces which were to separate England and her colonies, sees how closely tied to the problem of defense these forces were, and appreciates the grandeur of that ideal state of the mercantilist which would have counteracted many of them, one can scarcely give to the ideas of its opponents the same cogency that Walpole gave. By his persistent refusal to support Townshend and the Board of Trade during a period when a long peace offered ample opportunity for making the changes they suggested, Walpole more than any other single man was responsible for bequeathing unsettled to the ministers of the last half of the century the question of colonial defense.

Since the colonies neither voluntarily nor under a compulsory realignment of their forms of government could be made to bear the charges, ministries had reluctantly to approach parliament. The third, fourth, and fifth schemes for maintaining a force in North America all laid the costs, or the greater part of them, on British taxpayers.

The third one was that named by Oglethorpe to Walpole as the direct alternative to provincial troops, the sending from England of British regular regiments. Such troops might serve for a brief period, to return to their base when war was over, as was the case with the single company which accompanied Nicholson in 1710, the seven regiments with General Hill in 1711, and the two regiments which garrisoned Louisbourg after its capture in 1745. Or they might be stationed in permanent garrisons, as the 40th regiment in Nova Scotia, Nicholson's independent company and later Oglethorpe's regiment in South Carolina and Georgia, and the four independent companies of New York. In theory this scheme of maintaining trained troops in forts at critical points was perfectly sound. But the actual number of men employed—these three widely separated corps contained only fifteen hundred men altogether—was too small to do any effective work and too unimportant to merit a supervisory system which should promote its efficiency. The men were cruelly neglected.[5] At the same time they cost in 1741, to choose a convenient year, no less than £32,407, a sum great enough to cause the ministry considerable misgivings. It was impossible to get parliament to increase the numbers, though that suggestion was repeated for sixty years. Governors of New York continually asked for reinforcements; the Board of Trade, in 1720, recommended the construction of a line of forts and the dispatch to Nova Scotia and Carolina of eight battalions of foot;[6] and in the opinion of such persistent promoters as Archibald Cummings, the collector at Boston, Sir William Keith, once governor of Pennsylvania, and Governor Ogle of Maryland, the safety of the colonies could be assured only by British troops and a permanent establishment. The answer to all such proposals was the old one: the colonies should live of their own.

Under the fourth scheme, which was born of the necessities of war when British troops were needed in Europe, soldiers were raised in the colonies but were paid in whole or in part from England, and under some direction from British officers. The plan was expensive, but the mercantilist expected to spend money in wars that advanced or protected his interests, and it may be consid-

[5] S. M. Pargellis, ''The Four Independent Companies of New York'', in *Essays in Colonial History.*

[6] Report of the Board of Trade to the Lords Justices, Aug. 30, 1720, Public Record Office, State Papers 43: 65. This proposal was made under Townshend's influence, at the same time that the board was beginning work on its representation of 1721. Both the king and the Lords Justices approved the recommendation.

ered in general as the most successful way of creating
rapidly a unified force at a desired point. The general
procedure was simple. An advance agent from England,
or some trusted official in the colonies, supplied with
money or credit and assisted by a handful of British subalterns, supervised early in the season the raising, drilling, clothing, and provisioning of American soldiers with
their American officers. At the appointed time, this army
was to unite at a rendezvous with a British regular force
and both were to be under the command of a British general. Colonial assemblies were asked for as much as could
be got from them, sometimes the costs of provisioning,
sometimes the whole of the charges before the British
commander arrived. But the British government was prepared, if worst came to worst, to foot the bills. Thrice
during Queen Anne's War this scheme was employed,
and though of the three British commanders in chief—
Thomas Wetham in 1709, Viscount Shannon in 1710, and
John Hill in 1711—only Hill managed to reach America,
in each year colonial troops were raised with the coöperation of the agents from England and were waiting. Again
in 1740 Newcastle, with more careful attention to detail
than is usually associated with him, planned to raise for
service in the West Indies an American regiment of four
battalions. He sent to America in June the adjutant general of the expedition, William Blakeney, who carried
£8000 in specie, arms, clothing, and blank commissions in
the British army for all the captains, all the ensigns, and
half the lieutenants in the proposed regiment. The other
thirty lieutenants, to aid American officers in drilling
the men, were selected volunteers from the British
army, "sober, pretty, handsome, young Gents" of good
family. The privates were promised English pay, arms,
clothing, food, and a share of the booty; the only expense
assemblies were to have was the victualling and trans-

port of the soldiers to their West Indian rendezvous. If they refused, governors by secret instruction were allowed to draw on the commissioners of the navy. Under such conditions men of good standing in the colonies clamored for commissions, and private soldiers readily joined. Blakeney's chief worry was in accommodating his limited supply of arms and clothing to the numbers demanding them; in September six companies had to be broken for want of equipment. He treated Americans with understanding and tact, and tried to "spread a love of the Service among them". Wise in recognizing the nature of American egotism, he counselled for expediency's sake a just deference to it. By the middle of December, 1740, over three thousand Americans, officers and men, from every colony north of South Carolina, had reached Jamaica. The success of this scheme encouraged its repetition six years later. The ministry in 1746 contemplated the invasion of Canada by two expeditions, one to proceed by sea against Quebec, the other by the Lake Champlain route against Montreal. Newcastle ordered that colonial troops engaging in both these expeditions should serve under their own officers, should have British pay from their enlistment, should be clothed and armed from British funds unless colonial assemblies would defray that charge, should receive their proportion of booty and a fat bounty for enlisting. Such liberal terms encouraged men in every province north of the Carolinas; by the end of the summer seventy-five hundred men had been voted, half again as many as the ministry expected, and fifty-five hundred of them were in the field. Not one of all these expeditions attained its object, for Nicholson's capture of Port Royal in 1710 with his one regular company and a small colonial force was not a part of the original more ambitious plan. Hill in 1711 wrecked his fleet in the St. Lawrence; Vernon and Went-

worth in 1741 frittered away their force in the West
Indies and angered Americans by forcing them to serve
nearly two years as sailors in the British fleet; and General St. Clair, in the summer of 1746, after vainly trying
to get away from England, saw his strength diverted, on
August 22, to an abortive attack on Port l'Orient on the
coast of France. These failures, joined with the constant
criticism by army men of American officers and with what
seemed the insatiable greed of colonial governments for
British funds, tended to blind the ministry to the real
merits of the scheme. Only a few saw that under this
arrangement Americans, without a thought of their local
differences, could be made to join eagerly in a service
which connected them directly with the British army and
might, as in 1740, bring them British rank.[7]

The fifth scheme was an effort to correct the evils of
the fourth as the ministry saw it. That unconventional
and unsupervised method, with every colonial assembly
and every individual liable to submit a bill, was too dear in
comparison with the effectiveness of the force produced.
If money was to be spent on Americans in the British
army, let them enroll in regiments definitely established
and with definite and limited sums allotted. When, therefore, Governor Shirley and Sir William Pepperrell were
rewarded for their part in the capture of Louisbourg by
the colonelcies of two regiments to be raised out of the
New Englanders stationed there, those regiments were

[7] For the expeditions under Queen Anne see W. T. Morgan, ''Some At-
tempts at Imperial Co-operation during the Reign of Queen Anne,'' Royal
Historical Society, _Transactions_, 4th series, X, 171-194; ''Queen Anne's
Canadian Expedition of 1711'', _Queen's Quarterly_, XXXV, 460-489; _Society
of Colonial Wars in Massachusetts_, 1897, pp. 81-144. For the Cartagena expedition, Public Record Office, C.O. 5: 41; State Papers 44: 184; and
British Museum, Additional Manuscripts 32,693. For St. Clair's expedition,
G. A. Wood, _William Shirley_, chapters XIV-XIX; C.O. 5: 36, 45; C.O. 42:
13; State Papers 42: 98; and _ibid._ 45: 5.

intended to have a permanent place in the British army.
Men did not enlist in them for an expedition, but for a
period of years, the duration of the war, or for life. Nor
were their officers to be the men under whom they had
served at Louisbourg; less than half the commissions
were sent blank for the colonels to use in rewarding men
who raised companies. Most of the other officers were
British, strangers whom the Americans disliked and distrusted. The inevitable result was that most colonials
stubbornly refused to enlist and neither of the regiments
was ever completed.[8] In 1748 both were broken. The les-
son to be learned from this experience, compared with,
for example, Blakeney's, should have been clear. Americans would gladly join an American regiment in the British army; they would not enlist in a British regiment
disguised with an American colonel. If, as was actually
suggested, the British government could have broken
with army tradition and created a New England regiment
on the British establishment, a New York or Virginia
regiment, made them permanent, offered to Americans
of "character and substance" the opportunity for a
career in the army, and promised to American rank and
file even the poor rewards of a British private, it would
have had in time a force capable of managing colonial
defense. But that idea was palatable neither to army officers nor to the House of Commons which would have
borne the charges.

The student of colonization and empire in any country
will recognize how universal are the principles laid down

[8] In the academic controversy as to what person first had the honor of
suggesting that Highland soldiers be enlisted for service in North America
from among the Jacobite adherents of 1745, some attention, perhaps, is due
Sir William Pepperrell, who, on June 24, 1746, wrote to Newcastle asking
that two hundred of the "Rebell prisoners, who may have been unwarily se-
duced", be sent over for his and Shirley's regiments, Public Record Office,
C.O. 5: 45, f. 15.

in these five methods of conducting colonial defense, and how difficult it is to choose the best and the cheapest. Great Britain, in her first attempt at governing dependencies, without the wisdom of experience to guide her and without the driving incentive of necessity to compel a settlement, had to face as varied and as stiff an opposition as can be found in modern history. For at home there were the great and insurmountable convictions of those men who were reaping the most commercial benefit from the colonies that as little as possible should be spent upon them; the unwillingness of lords proprietors, often backed by the legal immunity of a seat in the House of Lords, to forego their special and private interests in the New World; and the traditions of the military service which could not bring itself to admit, for the sake of policy, inexperienced Americans to share in its privileges. In America there were eleven colonies, each one exhibiting an intense local pride both towards its neighbors and towards any attempt of Great Britain's to alter its form of government or to dictate the purposes for which its funds should be spent; that same pride caused individual Americans to distrust British military methods and to refuse their coöperation in any military enterprise which did not give them a sense of equality with British soldiers. How to fit any method of defense into these difficulties remained after the middle of the century as much of a problem as before.

The years between the close of the War of the Austrian Succession and the beginning of the Seven Years' War have not been chosen arbitrarily as a dividing point in the story of colonial defense. They marked a fundamental change in the general situation. After 1750 that belt of unsettled territory dividing French and British possessions and inhabited by friendly Indians was no longer able, by its comfortable presence, to lull British ministries into paying only a casual attention to the colonial problem. For in Nova Scotia and in western Pennsylvania expanding French and British settlements had come into direct contact. By their settlement on the River St. John and their construction of forts on Chignecto Isthmus the French isolated Nova Scotia from other British possessions so that it no longer served as a barrier. They also threatened the British lumber and fur trade, and gave themselves a better outlet to the Atlantic than the twisting and dangerous St. Lawrence. "In one word several of those great commercial Advantages and national views" which England had hoped to gain from the possession and settlement of Nova Scotia "will be not only lost to Great Britain, but transferred to the power of France."[9] On the upper Ohio a trading company of British and colonial merchants had been authorized by Governor Gooch of Virginia in accordance with instructions from England to make a settlement and build a fort for the greater security of the other colonies and for the extension of Indian commerce. Into this same region the French had penetrated. In the midst of this critical situation, the Indians, "our frontier guards", so long "a strong barrier to the Northern colonies", repudiated their alliance of seventy years. They began to deal with the French; in 1753 the Mohawks left a conference with Governor Clinton of New York declaring that the covenant chain was broken. These new factors constrained the ministry to face squarely consideration of new measures of defense.

Before we consider what those measures were, and what plan was finally chosen, it will be wise to emphasize the general considerations which influenced the ministers

---

[9] Representation of the Board of Trade to His Majesty, Dec. 7, 1753, from the Cumberland Papers in the Royal Archives at Windsor. Bedford to Governor Cornwallis, Aug. 17, 1749, C.O. 324: 37, p. 513.

of this period. Their own predilections, the domestic political situation, and the particular diplomatic issues uppermost at the time, all had importance in shaping, in 1754, the scheme adopted.

In the first place, there is no reason to conclude that the statesmen of this period were any more attracted by the idea of empire than their predecessors had been. Both they and the merchants to whom they listened thought it still a fantastic thing. Ministers had no illusions as to the value of territory west of the settled areas or any desire to possess it for its own sake. Though an occasional merchant might describe to them in flowing terms the fertility of the Ohio valley—its vines, mulberries, timber, stone quarries, mines of copper, silver, and gold, its furs, cotton, flax, and indigo[10]—or expatiate upon its value for pasturage and dairy-farming,[11] those merchants whose opinion had more weight did not advocate expansion but the maintenance of Indian friendship and the construction of a permanent line of forts, lest the French hope of a "universal monarchy" lead to the "Destruction of the British Nation thro' the Conquest of these Your Majesties American Colonies", and reduce England to the stature of a small nation like Sweden or Holland.[12] Ministerial pronouncements of opinion follow that same idea. That unjustifiable encroachments threaten to cut off all communication with or support from the Indians, and that England must send a force to prevent attempts against her colonies, was the tenor of Newcastle's summary. In the instructions to the Lords Justices the point

[10] An undated plan for the conquest of the Ohio valley, 1754 or 1755, Public Record Office, Chatham Papers (hereafter cited as G.D. 8), vol. 97.

[11] Peter Collinson to Newcastle, Additional MSS. 33,029, f. 378.

[12] Alderman Baker's Thoughts of the Expediency and Manner of supporting a Regular military Force on the continent of North America, Oct. 1, 1754, Additional MSS. 32,737, f. 16; Memorandum from Mr. Hanbury, undated, probably August, 1753, C.O. 5: 7.

emphasized was the "Preservation and Security of the Navigation and Commerce of Our Subjects" and the "Safety of Our Colonies, and Preservation of Our Rights and Possession in those parts." The cabinet council of 1754 which learned of the destruction of the Ohio company's fort, "whereby all Intercourse with the Indians would be cut off, and such Advantage be gained by the French as would endanger all the Northern Colonies, and tend to the total destruction thereof, and of their Trade", was concerned above all with defending the frontiers and "causing the French to retire." The most startling evidence of the ministerial state of mind appeared early in 1755, when the leaders were willing to negotiate an agreement with France whereby the English would adopt as their western boundary a north and south line drawn through what is now eastern Ohio, and the French would limit their activities to the west of a line drawn south from the mouth of the Miami river to the head of the Wabash and down that river to its mouth. The territory between was to remain neutral, with its Indian trade open to both. Forts within the area were to be demolished and free access to lakes and rivers permitted traders of both nations.[13] Among those in authority only Lord Halifax, the first lord of trade and plantations, showed traces of future imperialism. He objected to the creation of a neutral strip as a yielding to France on that question which was the basis of the principal British rights in North America, the Iroquois lands granted to Great Britain at the Peace of Utrecht. He held out stoutly for the retention of all lands to which Great Britain had claim, and distrusted the French assertion of right to all territory draining into the Mississippi.

---

[13] Points agreed upon in a cabinet council as a foundation for negotiations with Mirepoix, the French ambassador, Feb. 20, 1755, Additional MSS. 32,996, f. 34.

They will have completed their favorite plan, and will be in possession of near two thirds of the very best unsettled Land on this side the Mississippi and the St. Lawrence, while Great Britain will not only lose near one-half of the Territory to which it is indisputably entitled, but in case of a future Rupture will find it extremely difficult to keep the other half.[14]

Pure mercantilist considerations, then, impelled the ministry as a body to defend only what was valuable, as cheaply as possible.

To such a general policy the diplomatic situation lent additional support. In 1754 an overt attack on undeniably French territory in the New World would have begun a new European war, and the ministry was anxious to avoid an open breach until Continental allies could be found to guarantee the safety of Hanover. Otherwise France, easily occupying the electorate, could demand as the price of its surrender either what gains Great Britain might have made in America or an acknowledgment of French claims there. Newcastle was unwilling to declare war until Spain avowed herself neutral and an ally to guard Hanover was found in Frederick of Prussia, who was frightened into signing a treaty, early in 1756, by England's negotiations with Russia and Austria's acceptable overtures to France.

The political situation in England likewise encouraged the adoption of a cautious policy. Henry Pelham's death in March, 1754, left a ministry in which the leaders, Newcastle, Hardwicke, and Granville, were peers. No capable person was available to conduct the ministry's business in the House of Commons except either Henry Fox, the secretary at war, or William Pitt, the paymaster general. The former in Hardwicke's eyes was tainted by his close

14 Lord Halifax upon the French encroachments in North America, Aug. 15, 1753, Additional MSS. 33,029, f. 96.

association with the king's son, the duke of Cumberland, captain general and head of the army; while the king himself would have nothing to do with Pitt. Neither man would accept the leadership of the House of Commons without either some share in the distribution of patronage or a responsible voice in the determination of policy. Newcastle therefore fell back on the attempt to run the house with a nominal leader only, but he feared that with both Fox and Pitt in opposition he could not afford to introduce any such critical measure as a demand for a large grant for an expensive American war. A surplus of a hundred thousand pounds was available and any measure undertaken for the defense of the colonies had to come within that figure.[15] So from whatever point of view ministers regarded the threatening colonial situation, whether as mercantilists whose chief concern was the protection of existing sources of wealth and not territorial expansion, or as diplomatists who had to maintain a European peace, or as politicians whose motto must be economy, they were driven to adopt a cheap, defensive policy.

That policy, until June, 1754, concerned but two points: the construction of a fort at the forks of the Ohio, to which the ministry was prepared to contribute money if necessary, cannon, and a garrison of regular troops; and the urging of colonial assemblies to undertake their own defense, to assist their neighbors in case of hostile action on the part of France, and to join a general conference for the cementing of the ancient alliance with the Five Nations. These were well-tried mercantilist doctrines: a fort and garrison in territory directly threatened by France as was the case of Nova Scotia and the West Indies; a barrier of friendly Indians; and for the rest the

---

[15] Points for consideration with the Lord Chancellor, Sept. 11, 1754, Additional MSS. 32,995, f. 319.

burden to lie on the colonies. The chronology of the various orders which together make up this policy show the reluctance, and even the indifference, with which the ministry gradually approached the point where some more radical decision was necessary.

In March, 1753, the Board of Trade passed on to the Privy Council Governor Dinwiddie's account of the hostile attitude of the enemy, and recommended that thirty four-pounders be shipped to him for use in the fort he was planning to build in the contested area.[16] In May the Ordnance Board objected to sending the cannon until it knew the size and needs of the fort, and the Board of Trade undertook to write Dinwiddie and find out.[17] In August, on the receipt of Dinwiddie's letters of June stating that the French had driven English traders from the upper Ohio and were building a fort (Fort Le Boeuf) of their own, an inner cabinet met at Mr. Pelham's, ordered the ordnance forwarded at once, and instructed all governors, in case of hostilities, to summon assemblies, point out the need of mutual assistance, and engage them to grant such supplies "as the Exigency of Affairs may require."[18] In September, on receiving the minutes of the disastrous conference between Governor Clinton and the Mohawks, the Board of Trade instructed all colonies to appoint commissioners to a general conference to restore the covenant chain. In January, 1754, Holderness

16 *Acts Privy Council, Colonial, 1745-1766,* §206.

17 Report to Committee of the Privy Council on a report of the Ordnance Board, May 10, 1753, C.O. 5: 1367, f. 31.

18 Halifax to Newcastle, Aug. 12, 1753, enclosing Dinwiddie's letter, Additional MSS. 32,732, f. 450. I have found no minute of this cabinet meeting, the first devoted to the American situation, but clear references to it are in Holderness to Newcastle, Aug. 27, 1753 (Additional MSS. 32,732, f. 546), and in Granville to Newcastle, Sept. 23, 1754 (Additional MSS. 32,736, f. 567). Holderness to American Governors, Aug. 28, 1753, *Maryland Archives,* VI, 3.

ordered a South Carolina independent company[19] and two of those of New York, still incomplete in numbers and equipment, to garrison the forts Dinwiddie was building. On June 18, a cabinet council determined to allow Dinwiddie the use of the royal revenue arising from the tobacco duty, some £8500, and to send him £5000 in specie, to be used in gratuities to the Indians and for paying and provisioning the regular garrisons in the forts.[20] A week later news came that Dinwiddie's fort had been destroyed by the French. The sum was thereupon increased to £20,000, half in specie and half in credit, and Governor Sharpe of Maryland was appointed to command until a general officer should be sent out.[21]

By June it was clear enough to the ministry that the colonial assemblies would not aid Virginia in the manner asked by the secretary of state's letter the preceding August, and that some further step was necessary. When letters came from Governor Shirley, telling of his expedition to build forts on the Kennebec river and urging, in forceful terms the necessity of some form of colonial union, a cabinet council sat expressly upon his recommendation. It unanimously approved his Kennebec project, and it instructed the Board of Trade to prepare a plan for a general concert of the colonies "in order to prevent or remove any Encroachments upon the Dominions of Great Britain."[22] That plan, submitted by August

[19] The three South Carolina companies had been formed out of Oglethorpe's regiment when it was broken in 1748.

[20] Minute, Newcastle House, June 18, 1754, Additional MSS. 32,995, f. 276.

[21] Minute, June 26, 1754, Additional MSS. 33,029, f. 124. Sharpe was commissioned as lieutenant colonel of foot in the West Indies, July 5, 1754, State Papers 44: 189, p. 13.

[22] Minute, June 13, 1754, Additional MSS. 32,995, f. 266. Those present were Hardwicke, Granville, Newcastle, Holderness, Halifax, Anson, and Robinson.

9, was the first the board had drawn since 1721. It defined as its objects the creation of a permanent fund of colonial money for building and maintaining a line of forts and for treating with Indians; machinery whereby a commander in chief appointed from England in charge of such forts, forces, and Indians might draw upon that fund; and a method for raising and paying troops to meet the emergency of an invasion. Such aims have a familiar ring about them, and represented no departure from past points of view. But the noteworthy point about the board's scheme is the extreme care, for which there was no official precedent, taken in every particular to make the union one imposed by the colonies upon themselves, and infringing as little as possible upon their rights of self-government and freedom of action. It was, in fact, only a series of suggestions which provincial commissioners might use as the basis of their own "general Convention", and the legality of the plan they framed would derive from the acts of the various assemblies to which it would be submitted before it received royal approbation. The board took especial pains to limit, in its suggestions, the powers granted to a commander in chief. He could normally draw upon any colonial treasury only for funds assigned by commissioners as the quota of that colony; before he could employ an increase in forces or funds to meet an actual invasion, a general meeting of commissioners was necessary to apportion among all the colonies whatever sum the invaded colony named as needed to cope with the enemy. The reasoning that influenced the board to draft so cautious a proposal, so inoffensive to colonial susceptibilities, seems clear. Any other scheme, requiring the intervention of an act of parliament either to levy a tax upon the colonies or to reduce to a uniform royal pattern the four chartered governments which still remained in North America, would have raised opposition not only in the colonies, but also in the House of Commons, from which the ministry for political reasons tried to keep all American matters. No other plan that involved a permanent revenue for colonial defense except this one could have been based upon the royal prerogative alone. Confronted with the same dilemma which had wrecked all projects of union from 1689 to 1721, the board compromised as best it could with the particularism of the colonies, the convictions of mercantilists, the political ambitions of a ministry of peers trying to govern without interference from the House of Commons, and the need of some stable form of colonial defense. One need go no further back than the suggestions of Shirley in 1748, mentioned above, to find the basis on which it worked. But before the ministry, its members spending the month of August in the country, could deliberate as a whole upon the board's scheme, news came on September 4 that Washington had met the French in a hostile action at Fort Necessity and had been defeated. Immediate action became imperative.

There followed three weeks of frantic discussion before the ministry decided what form that action should take. On September 15 Newcastle so far sunk his distrust of the duke of Cumberland as to invite his opinion of the military points at issue. By that decision there entered into an active part in the government of Great Britain a member of the royal family, possessing to the fullest extent the confidence of the king his father, backed by the enthusiastic admiration of an army on whose improvement he lavished vigilant care, and with parliamentary supporters who could honor in his person rather than the king's the Hanoverian dynasty. Thenceforth Cumberland sat in nearly every important inner cabinet on American affairs. His dominating personality, his balanced judgment, and his forcefulness in thought and speech combined with his high rank to give him a commanding influence in any discussion which dealt with troops. For the next two years he more than any other single man determined the details of Great Britain's policy of colonial defense.

During the three weeks of discussion Cumberland and the ministry debated three points: a union of the colonies; the employment of American troops under British pay; and the sending of British troops under a British commander in chief. They reached no conclusion on the first. Everyone disapproved of the Board of Trade's plan. Hardwicke thought that any convention reached by the colonial commissioners ought to be approved by the ministry before it was sent to colonial assemblies for them to accept or reject, and that the governor, council, and assembly of any invaded colony ought to be empowered to decide upon the proportion of aid which their neighbors should give. Charles Townshend, who was consulted as knowing more about the colonies than any man in English politics, objected to the whole basis upon which the board's scheme was drawn. He argued that the colonies would never agree upon a plan of "reciprocal expense"; that even if commissioners framed a plan, colonial assemblies would either refuse to pass acts of supply or would insert further encroachments upon the prerogative in their acts permitting a commander to draw on their treasuries. Any effective plan of union should come from an act of parliament along the lines of the bill of 1710 framed to compel New York to provide a permanent revenue. William Murray, the attorney general, thought these objections of Townshend's unanswerable. Newcastle feared the dangers of giving colonial assemblies additional leverage to increase their powers; there were "ill consequences to be apprehended from uniting too closely the northern colonies with each other;

an Independency upon this Country being to be apprehended from such a Union.''[23] When Cumberland was
first confronted with the plan, he thought that ''some
great Person of quality and distinction, after the manner of the Spaniards'', should be sent to America to carry
a plan of union into execution and to have under him the
military commander in chief. This proposal the king immediately rejected, for the only man to fill such a post
was Lord Halifax, who would make impossible conditions.[24] Further consideration of a plan of union was then
tacitly shelved until the immediate danger of French
encroachments should have been removed by military
force.[25]

But what form should that force take? Provincial assemblies had refused to furnish troops for Virginia's defense. Which of the alternatives left, American troops
paid by Great Britain or British troops sent from England and Ireland, should the ministry choose? In general
it favored the former, but each minister had a different
notion about details. Halifax, again basing his proposal
on Shirley's success in raising a force for the Kennebec

[23] Conference with the Speaker, Sept. 9, 1754, Additional MSS. 32,995,
f. 309.

[24] There is a hint that Lord Albemarle, the titular governor general of
Virginia and ambassador in Paris, had some designs upon a post in America.
He offered at this time to repair to his government if the king so desired.
Robinson to Newcastle, Sept. 22, 1754, Additional MSS. 32,736, f. 563.

[25] The famous Albany Plan of Union, which had been drawn up by the
commissioners sent to Albany to cement the covenant chain with the Indians,
arrived in England late in October. Since it did not meet with the approval
of a single colonial assembly, it carried no further weight than the sanction
of the leading colonials who had framed it. In the eyes of Dupplin and of the
Board of Trade the conference had not redressed the Indian situation, its
chief task, for it made the management of Indian affairs and the strengthening of the frontier dependent upon its plans of union, which had to be laid
before assemblies and parliament to become effective. Dupplin's notes on the
Albany plan, Additional MSS. 33,030, f. 344.

expedition, thought that any number of men might be raised by order of the Crown. Charles Townshend went a step further in a detailed memorandum; he suggested regimenting all the independent companies in the colonies and raising there another regiment, to be officered by Americans of character and rank, but to be paid from England.[26] Murray would not stop with that; he proposed raising twenty thousand men in the colonies, under British half-pay officers and commanded by a British general. Lord President Granville emphatically agreed with Murray's principle. Their vehemence had due effect upon the great twin brethren in the ministry, for Newcastle and Hardwicke embodied the same idea in their formal resolution:

That, in the present Situation of Affairs in North America, It seems advisable to send a Commanding Officer of Rank, with a Number of Half-Pay, or other Officers, with Money, Arms, and Ammunition; and Directions to concert with the proper Persons at Virginia, etc., upon the Measures to be taken, for the Defence of His Majesty's Colonies, and dispossessing the French, from the Settlements made, or Possessions taken, on any Parts of His Majesty's Dominions there.[27]

Since Dinwiddie had specifically asked for British troops, there was talk of sending the Highland regiment, the 42d, and of raising additional Highland independent companies; but the king bluntly refused to part with a British regiment for service in America.

The ministry, therefore, was slowly agreeing upon the plan tried in 1711, 1740, and 1746: a British general, some

[26] Scheme for the improvement and employment of His Majesty's troops in North America for the defense of Virginia, Additional MSS. 32,736, f. 515.

[27] Points for consideration with the Lord Chancellor, Sept. 11, 1754, Additional MSS. 32,995, f. 319.

British officers, American rank and file, with the Treasury footing the bills. Such an outlay could be kept within the limits of Newcastle's hundred thousand pound surplus. But upon the important point, whether British half-pay officers would aid Americans in drilling troops, or whether they would be regimented with them to the complete or partial exclusion of American officers, the ministry had formed no decision.

Cumberland settled that point himself. After a week's study of the situation and after discussing it with the king, who eagerly agreed to his son's proposals, Cumberland named Braddock as the general officer, and suggested that instead of half-pay officers two regiments in the Irish army, which on their peace footing of three hundred and ten men were over-officered, be sent to be recruited to full strength in the colonies. He suggested also definite operations, against the French forts at Chignecto, Crown Point, and on the Ohio. Such directness contrasted favorably with the ministry's indecision, but it also resulted in the discarding of the only means of military coöperation between Americans and British which had ever been a success. Not by recruiting British regiments in the colonies had Blakeney fired Americans with enthusiasm.

An inner cabinet meeting at Cumberland's apartments on September 26 adopted the main outlines of a plan, and when Cumberland and Fox pushed forward preparations in a manner that seemed to Newcastle and Hardwicke too recklessly extravagant and too threatening to the peace of Europe, a second meeting on October 9 was called to settle certain details.[28] Other details were arranged, sepa-

---

[28] T. W. Riker, ''The Politics behind Braddock's Expedition'', *American Historical Review*, XIII, 742. For the meeting of September 26, Newcastle to Murray, Sept. 28, 1754, Additional MSS. 32,736, f. 591; for that of October 9, Additional MSS. 32,995, f. 328.

rately and without consultation, by the War Office, the Admiralty, and the Treasury.

The plan, hereafter for convenience called the Braddock plan, was, as one might expect, a compromise. Like the expeditions of 1711 and 1746, it was designed as an expedition with definite objectives and was not meant to become a continuing method for carrying on a war. There was no war; ministers in general earnestly desired to avoid one; and they expected in time to create a union of the colonies to provide for future emergencies. Braddock, therefore, was given a commission as commander in chief of all forces raised or to be raised in North America, couched in the customary terms which permitted a commander on distant service to exercise military authority within the limits of the Mutiny Act, to sign warrants for pay, and to promote to vacant commissions. The troops over which he was to exercise authority were meant to be few: seven British regiments, seven independent companies, and detachments of the Royal Artillery. Of these, three regiments were the permanent garrison of Nova Scotia: the 40th (Hopson's), which had been in the province for nearly forty years; the 45th (Warburton's), one of the two regiments sent to Louisbourg in 1746; and the 47th (Lascelles'), which had arrived from Ireland in 1750, two hundred and ninety privates with a hundred and thirty women and fifty children, to become part of the settlement of Halifax.[29] The seven companies were the permanent garrisons of New York and South Carolina. Two other regiments, the 44th (Halkett's) and the 48th (Dunbar's), were sent from Ireland for Braddock's expedition. It was Cumberland's idea that they should recruit in the colonies four hundred and twenty men each, but when Anson, the first lord of the Admiralty, pointed

[29] *The Northcliffe Collection*, p. 72.

out emphatically how scarce recruits were in America, the king agreed to increase them by a hundred men each drafted from Bockland's and Bury's regiments in Ireland.[30] The supplying of the men then needed to complete their numbers to seven hundred and thirty each was left to the colonies. To save expense these regiments were left on the Irish establishment, the Irish parliament paying the costs of the original number and the British parliament the charges of the augmentation. The other two regiments were the 50th (Shirley's) and the 51st (Pepperrell's) which had been broken in 1748. They were ordered re-raised in the colonies, a thousand and forty men each; of their eighty officers, twenty-three only were their colonels permitted to appoint in America.[31] To this pitiful remnant Townshend's and Murray's splendid schemes for an American army had shrunk; that the cabinet included it at all was a concession to Granville's stubbornness. Besides these regular troops there was an independent company of rangers on the Nova Scotia but not the regular establishment and a handful of local provincial troops in Virginia and perhaps Maryland. By inclusion of these also under Braddock's command, he superseded Governor Lawrence of Nova Scotia, the governors of New York and South Carolina, and Sharpe, as commanding officers in their respective districts. But of other provincial forces not a word was said during the preparations of 1754. The total cost for a year—including general staff and hospital charges, ordnance supplies,

[30] Newcastle to Hardwicke, Oct. 2, 1754; West to Newcastle, Oct. 11, 1754, Additional MSS. 32,737, ff. 24, 103; 27 *House of Commons Journal* 87.

[31] Names and Services of Shirley's and Pepperrell's officers, Additional MSS. 33,029, f. 281. Thirteen of the officers named in England were half-pay from the previous establishment of the regiment; one was a lieutenant of rangers in Nova Scotia, and one was Shirley's son. The others were half-pay officers from other British regiments or from additional forces raised in the previous war.

and transports—was estimated at £100,664 15s. 2d.[32] As close as that did Newcastle think it wise to limit expense to avoid possible trouble with the House of Commons.

For the other charges which would attend the expedition recourse was had, as a last resort, to the Board of Trade's plan of union. They were thrown upon colonial assemblies. Governors were asked to collect supplies of provisions, to provide wagons and quarters when necessary, and to assemble three thousand men for drafting into the four British regiments, the 44th, 48th, 50th, and 51st. They were also to persuade their assemblies to contribute as much as possible to a common fund, "for the Benefit of all the Colonies, Collectively". Braddock alone would administer it, and its chief purpose was to defray the costs of raising the American recruits. But since Anson doubted the willingness of colonial assemblies to contribute to such a fund, Braddock was privately instructed to draw upon the paymaster general for recruiting or levy money and was assured that his bills for other charges would be met if necessary.[33] It was also in accordance with the Board of Trade plan of union that Braddock was given supervision over all Indians and authority to appoint proper persons to superintend them both in the north and the south.

The Braddock plan, in brief, comprised a British commander in chief over regular regiments of the British army, composed of a nucleus of British soldiers recruited to full strength in the colonies, supported by voluntary financial aid from colonial assemblies, and devoted to

[32] Additional MSS. 33,030, f. 332. This figure of course omits the regular establishments of Nova Scotia and of the New York and South Carolina forces.

[33] Braddock's general instructions are in *Pennsylvania Archives*, 1748-1763, p. 203, and in Winthrop Sargent, *The History of the Expedition against Fort Duquesne in 1755 under Major-General Braddock*, Appendix I, p. 393. The private instructions are in C.O. 5: 6.

specific objectives. The next February, after some control
of the House of Commons had been assured by bribing
Fox with a seat on the cabinet council, but not in the inner
cabinet, to support the ministry's interests, the Braddock
plan was further developed. All regiments in North
America were ordered recruited to a thousand and forty
men each, the common fund to defray the costs if possible; and Shirley's eager insistence was met by allowing
him to raise two thousand New Englanders for a year's
service in Nova Scotia. Under their own officers but paid
from England, this force was the unique instance during
the war of men raised according to Townshend's ideas
and the plan of 1746. These two additions meant another
four thousand men to be supported by parliament.

The objectives of all these troops were settled in November. Though Newcastle and Hardwicke tried to limit
them to the French forts on the Ohio, Cumberland's
broader campaign plans were supported by the king, by
Anson, and, as Newcastle learned, by Pitt, who thereby
showed that his influence in the House of Commons would
not be thrown against an aggressive American policy.[34]
As finally arranged, the 44th and 48th were to march
against Fort Duquesne; the 50th and 51st against
Niagara; the four together, later in the season, against
Crown Point; and the Nova Scotia regiments against
Fort Beauséjour on the Chignecto isthmus.[35] Cumberland

---

[34] "For, as to the Fond of the affair, the Expedition itself, I mean as consisting of the several parts, I never apprehended that would be altered, considering the *great Person* [Cumberland] with whom it was concerted. I remember it was allways so during the late war. Your Brother frequently threw
in objections, and struggled a little, but such as was the opinion of that
great Person, such was the King's, and that finally prevailed." Anson to
Newcastle, Oct. 13, 1754, Additional MSS. 32,737, f. 147.

[35] The original plan was for the 50th and 51st against Fort Beauséjour,
and Braddock's regiments against Fort Duquesne. By the end of October
Cumberland had included the Crown Point scheme, to be undertaken by the
50th and 51st; the Nova Scotia regiments, with perhaps aid from New Eng-

knew nothing of the difficulties of campaigning in the
American wilderness; what information he had been able
to gain minimized the strength of French forts and discounted the labor of cutting roads.[36] To him, as to everyone, it seemed that the force finally arranged, on paper
ten thousand men, was more than enough to defend
British interests.[37]

The campaigns of 1755 demonstrated the fatal weakness of the Braddock plan. Colonial assemblies refused to
play the merely contributory, coöperative part assigned
them. They assembled few recruits to be drafted into the
British regiments; they voted little money to form a common fund; they supplied few provisions and no wagons.
Braddock found that he had to pay at an exorbitant rate
for nearly every item in his preparations, and when his
expedition finally began its arduous march over the mountains, it was being supported almost entirely by British
funds. So little did it conform to Newcastle's hopes for
economy that the charges for wagons alone were estimated by Sir John St. Clair, the deputy quartermaster

land, to attack Fort Beauséjour. In November reports from Lieutenant-
Governor James DeLancey of New York, Thomas Pownall, and Halifax on
the vital importance of Niagara, control of which would cut French communications, influenced him to include that objective also. These plans are in
the Cumberland Papers. Braddock's secret instructions, which give the final
plan, are in *Documents relative to the Colonial History of the State of New-
York*, VI, 920 (hereafter cited as *New York Colonial Documents*).

36 ''An Account of the French forts in Canada and upon the Lakes'', by
John Desieure, a quondam matross in the Royal Artillery, servant to an Ohio
Indian trader, escaped prisoner from Louisbourg. ''Different Routes in
North America'', 1754, a report which gives distances only, with few re-
marks on roads. The ''road'' from Wills Creek to Fort Le Boeuf, it states,
was made by Indians and traders. Cumberland Papers.

37 ''It is taken for granted, that this summer's campaign will make
Major General Braddock Master of the *Ohio, Niagara, Crown Point*, and
St. Johns, as he is already of *Beau-Sejour* and *Baye-Verte*'', begins a project for the campaign of 1756, dated August 11, 1755, Additional MSS.
35,909, f. 208.

general, at nearly forty thousand pounds sterling. It may be remarked incidentally that as a British expedition Braddock's almost succeeded. Its defeat at the Monongahela on July 9 can be ascribed to military reasons, unconnected with the failure of colonial assemblies to support it. For since over half the men in the British regiments were either Irish drafts, the worst soldiers in the Irish army, or raw American recruits who had joined in April, the force was undisciplined; it was unnecessarily divided into two sections for the sake of speed; and on the morning of the 9th precautions against surprise which had been scrupulously followed before were unaccountably relaxed.

In place of supporting the Braddock plan, the northern assemblies undertook on their own initiative to put a wholly provincial army into the field, under the command of a general of their own choosing. They were persuaded to that course by Governor Shirley, whose American career was largely made up of projects not authorized from England. Since this provincial expedition of 1755, designed for an attack on Crown Point, was already well under way when Braddock met a council of governors at Alexandria in April, it was perforce accepted as a part of the general campaign plan and given a formal but meaningless approval by the commander in chief. But since Shirley, following Cumberland's plans, continued his expedition against Niagara, there was presented the spectacle of two separate commands in New York, one of them under the control of provincial assemblies, the other under a general selected by the Crown. A clash was inevitable. William Johnson, the provincial commander, had been appointed by Braddock, acting on instruction from England, as superintendent of northern Indian affairs. Between Shirley and Johnson there developed over the control of the Indians a quarrel so violent that the former felt compelled, in the interests of his campaign, to destroy the unity of Indian management in New York and to appoint his own agents. New York province was far too poor to provide transportation facilities for two armies; Shirley and Governor Hardy became bitter enemies when the latter was unable to meet the general's demands, while Johnson's failure to march against Crown Point was largely due to the shortage of supplies and provisions. Shirley paid the heavy expenses of the Niagara expedition out of British funds; the warrants which he and Braddock drew in 1755, exclusive of the pay of the troops, amounted to a hundred and twenty thousand pounds.[38] Robert Monckton's capture of Fort Beauséjour, in an expedition wholly supported by British funds and dependent in no way upon aid from colonial assemblies, was the only clear-cut success.

As an attempt to induce voluntary support from the colonies, the Braddock plan failed in 1755 because colonial assemblies were unwilling to vote sums of money the disbursement of which they could not control; as a military enterprise, it failed chiefly because of the inadequacy of the supply and transportation services. In the autumn, therefore, the ministry again approached American affairs with the old alternatives before it. Should it try to force through parliament an act for taxing the colonies, the proceeds to pay expenses already incurred and to provide a fund for the construction of permanent forts and garrisons? Halifax insisted that such a course alone would prove adequate.[39] Or should additional regulars be sent to the colonies, and steps taken to utilize in some new way the vast man-power there? Cumberland was for send-

[38] Declared Accounts of Thomlinson and Hanbury [the money contractors], Audit Office 17: 592: 190.

[39] Hints from Lord Halifax relating to a Tax in North America, Oct. 31, 1755, Additional MSS. 32,996, f. 265.

ing over immediately a general officer to concert with governors "that he may not meet with those unforeseen and unexpected Retardments"; for sending also another regiment, and perhaps raising further regiments in the colonies. But Newcastle, following the same line of opinion as the public press, doubted whether British troops, in view of Braddock's disaster, could be relied upon, and whether the principle ought not to be adopted that "Americans should fight Americans".[40]

Such sharp divisions of opinion were further complicated by the diplomatic and domestic situation. In the autumn of 1755 Newcastle's ministry of peers was dependent for its next step upon the mercy of the House of Commons. Whatever it did in American affairs, whether an act for union and taxation of the colonies, or appropriations to meet expenses, would need the house's approval. There was a more pressing question. Though the ministry had committed England to a colonial and naval war by the hostile orders given the fleet in the summer of 1756, it knew how futile was the expectation that France would limit the war to that narrow sphere. France would play her trump, her army. She would attack England through Hanover, to the defense of which a ministry that depended upon royal favor had to pledge itself. Continental allies had to be purchased for that, and subsidies appropriated by a House of Commons notoriously antagonistic to such measures. Newcastle's chief worry was the bolstering of the ministry's strength in parliament without lessening his personal control. When his overtures to Pitt had been refused, he fell back on Fox, who, shortly before parliament opened, was given the seals for

[40] Considerations of what may be necessary to be done, Aug. 25, 1755, Additional MSS. 35,415, f. 55. A convenient compilation of press opinion is in N. D. Davis's ''British Newspaper Accounts of Braddock's Defeat'', *Pennsylvania Magazine of History and Biography*, XXIII, 310-328.

the southern department and the conduct of business in the House of Commons. The adherents whom Fox brought to the ministry's support assured a majority.

For four months, then, the ministry marked time in American affairs until the temper of the House of Commons was gauged. After Braddock's death the Lords Justices sent Shirley a temporary appointment as commander in chief, "to command until the King's pleasure be known". During the remaining months of 1755 everything waited upon the major domestic difficulty. Not until the Christmas recess was it considered expedient to approach the problem.

It was then so late that, though plans of colonial union were being still discussed in the public press[41] and had a place in ministerial minds,[42] the imperative need was to remedy the evils which had attended the 1755 campaign. The inner cabinet of January 7, called especially to discuss American affairs for the first time since 1754, based its deliberations upon the reports from various persons in the colonies and upon its own analysis of the causes of disaster. All the letters from America agreed in asking further aid from the mother country: Hardy and Dinwiddie wanted an able experienced British general and more regular regiments; Shirley asked for arms and supplies; the assemblies of the New England colonies wanted shipments of ordnance and a grant of funds to relieve their debts. DeLancey of New York wrote a letter highly commended by the ministry for its clarity and force; it argued that New York should be the storehouse

41 *Gentleman's Magazine*, November, 1755, p. 501. *Monitor*, Dec. 8, 1755, quoted by W. T. Laprade, "The Stamp Act in British Politics", *American Historical Review*, XXXV, 736-7.

42 "Whether any scheme relating to the northern colonies, should be laid before the Parliament this session", Jan. 4, 1756, Additional MSS. 32,996, f. 348. WM to Pitt, Nov. 16, 1756, G.D. 8: 95.

and center of operations, that taking Fort Duquesne was
but the cutting off a toe, that the strengthening of Oswego
was the primary need in the west. Halifax's diagnosis of
the situation dwelt upon the unhappy consequences of the
divided command in New York and the need of a single
unified expedition against Crown Point; the impropriety
of Shirley's remaining longer in command, since his unfortunate dispute with Johnson had alienated the Indians; the need of a royal storehouse of provisions, paid
for by the Crown and under a general's directions; more
regular reinforcements, including perhaps a battalion or
two raised in the Highlands; the appointment of Johnson
as colonel of the Indians by royal commission; and finally,
"no Harmony nor Union in the Conduct of our Affairs to
be expected, but by a General to be sent from Home as
soon as possible", who should convene a council of governors and deputies of the assemblies to fix the quota of
men to be furnished by each province.[43]

Halifax, the imperialist, went much further than the
Braddock plan. His ideas should be borne in mind, for the
ministry was to veer around to them. But at the moment
they were too much of a surrender to colonial assemblies
to be palatable. In advising the use of provincial troops
Halifax ran foul of Cumberland's notions of military
effectiveness, and his scheme for erecting provision magazines at the sole expense of the Crown hurt Newcastle's
sense of economy.

The decision of January 20, therefore, conformed far
more closely to the Braddock plan than Halifax's proposals.[44] The initiative displayed by the northern colonies
in 1755 in raising an army of their own was acknowl-

---

[43] Lord Halifax's Paper, Jan. 7, 1755[6], Additional MSS. 32,996.

[44] Minute, the Duke's apartments, January 20, 1756, Additional MSS.
32,996, f. 352. Present were Cumberland, Hardwicke, Granville, Newcastle,
Holderness, Halifax, Anson, Sir Thomas Robinson, and Henry Fox.

edged; the inner cabinet approved the Board of Trade's recommendation to grant them a hundred and twenty thousand pounds as a bounty and recompense. But Cumberland did not intend that gift to encourage the raising of future armies. No authority was given governors to put another provincial force into the field, though it was decided that if practicable two thousand New Englanders, as in 1755, should sail to Nova Scotia to release the regulars there for service in New York. Instead, the colonies were asked to provide recruits, not only for the regiments already in America but for completing to full strength two new regiments to be sent from England and for raising four new battalions of a thousand men each. They were also to send provisions to Albany for the army. But for use until provincial supplies arrived a quantity of beef and butter was ordered shipped from Ireland. To ensure that the commanding officer should meet with as few constitutional difficulties as possible, it was decided to send to New York a lieutenant general "with every power civil and military that can legally be given him", together with two major generals to serve under him. Finally, Sir William Johnson in the north and Edmund Atkin in the south were to be commissioned as superintendents of Indian affairs under the command of the general.

The details of the manner in which these decisions were worked out belong to later chapters. As the war in America in 1755 was fought upon the plan formed in September and October, 1754, so the war for the next two years, with some alterations, was to be fought upon the plan framed in January. The same difficulties which had attended British operations in America since the seventeenth century—unwillingness of colonials to coöperate with British forces except on their own terms and the constitutional ambitions of colonial assemblies to attain

complete control both of the sums they voted and of their
own troops—were to reappear again. That clash between
British conceptions of colonial importance and the colonies' ideas of their own worth is as much the key to the
early years of the Seven Years' War in America as to the
whole of colonial history.

Various names were suggested for the chief command
in America: Lord Tyrawley, Sir John Mordaunt, Lieutenant General Cholmondeley, Lord George Sackville,
Lord Loudoun, Lord Panmure, Colonel Conway, Colonel
Cornwallis, Colonel Abercromby, and Lord Howe. Out of
this curious list, which ranged from Tyrawley, one of the
ablest men in the army, to Abercromby and Howe, whose
chief claim to consideration at this time was Newcastle's
political indebtedness to them, Cumberland selected John
Campbell, the fourth earl of Loudoun, a lowland Scot.
Some political reasons can be found for his appointment.
Loudoun, as one of the sixteen representative peers of
Scotland, was closely attached to the powerful duke of
Argyll, and therefore, as with all Argyll's followers,
voted consistently with the ministry. Since he had been
seeking a place in America for some time and had been
suggested as early as 1752 for the governorship of New
York,[45] it was a gracious gesture to Argyll to appoint him
to this high post. Loudoun was likewise friendly with Fox
and Halifax. With Newcastle his ties were not close, for
there still remained some of the bad feeling created in
1731, when on the death of the third earl of Loudoun Newcastle lent his support to the election of Lord Crawford
as a representative peer instead of to the young fourth
earl. But Cumberland was primarily concerned with Loudoun's abilities as a soldier and organizer. His previous
military career, while empty of brilliant exploits, had been

---

[45] *New Jersey Archives*, 1st series, VIII, part 1, 93.

varied enough to bring most aspects of the military profession within his experience. As a young man of twenty-
two, he had entered the Royal Scots Greys in 1727, had
become a captain in the 7th Dragoons in 1734 and five
years later captain in the 3d Foot Guards with the army
rank of lieutenant colonel. After the battle of Dettingen
he had served in Flanders as aide de camp to the king.
During the Jacobite rebellion of 1745 he had raised and
acted as colonel of a regiment of loyal Highlanders, had
served as adjutant general to Sir John Cope and later as
commander of the North of Scotland. Since 1749 he had
been colonel of the 30th regiment of foot, on the Irish
establishment. Moreover, his rank and personal qualities
and tastes seemed to commend him as a fit person to deal
with Americans. He was rich enough to support the dignity of a high command with appropriate style. His rank
was high enough to inspire respect in the colonies as it
did in England.[46] He was often described as "amiable";
he moves through the pages of the Whitefoord letters as
a family friend whose judgment in delicate private matters was respected.[47] His success with Scottish Highlanders, more democratically minded than Englishmen,
the ministry might justifiably expect to be duplicated
among the "levelling" opinions of northern colonials.
Loudoun had broad tastes for a man of his narrow military training. In Ayrshire, soon after he came into the
earldom in 1731, he had busied himself with the construction of good roads and the building of substantial bridges,

[46] Loudoun's warrants in America bore the resounding title: "His Excellency John Earl of Loudoun Lord Machline and Tarrinzean etc etc etc,
one of the Sixteen Peers of Scotland; Governor and Captain General of Virginia and Vice Admiral of the same; Colonel of the Thirtieth Regiment of
Foot; Colonel in Chief of the Royal American Regiment; Major General;
and Commander in Chief of all His Majesty's Forces raised or to be raised
in North America."

[47] W. A. S. Hewins, ed., *The Whitefoord Papers* (1898).

following the example set by General Wade in the north. He was deeply interested in the prevailing fad of the time, botany; he adorned the extensive grounds of Loudoun Castle with all manner of trees and shrubs imported from the various countries where he served, England, Ireland, Holland, Germany, Portugal, and America, and dexterously combined his major interests in life by planting the spacious avenue approaching the castle in the form of his regiment drawn up in review, a tree to a man, with officers in their proper places. He was styled "the father of agriculture in that part of Ayrshire", and in February, 1738, was elected a fellow of the Royal Society. Throughout his whole career he kept alive his curiosity for a number of things with which the military profession customarily has little concern.

Loudoun was not selected hastily, or because he was the only man available for the post. His qualities and experience seemed to fit him especially for it. Nor did the command he was to exercise have a purely military function. Based as it was on long experiment with colonial defense and more particularly on the deficiencies of the Braddock plan as revealed in 1755, it was a positive attempt on the part of Great Britain to unite the colonies for military purposes.

CHAPTER II

ADMINISTRATIVE TANGLES

AT the same time that Cumberland was choosing Loudoun the French minister of war was notifying the Marquis de Montcalm that the king had selected him to lead troops in Canada. The centralized system of France enabled all preparations for Montcalm's departure to be completed by the end of March; he embarked at Brest on April 3 with two battalions, and lay at anchor in the St. Lawrence on May 11. Loudoun did not sail from Portsmouth until May 20, and did not reach New York until July 23. He faced in 1756 that most disastrous of handicaps in a campaign, the handicap of time.

Why should it have taken so long for Loudoun to get away? The cabinet of January 20 had mapped out with commendable clarity the things to be done. Some of them were customary routine; some were a little out of the ordinary. They were neither too many nor too difficult to keep a government which pretends to some degree of efficiency, as most modern governments do, from dispatching them with expedition. But efficiency was sadly lacking in the administration which kept Loudoun tied to his house in Privy Gardens. As one follows the fate of each of the many orders issued in connection with American preparations, one is led to the conclusion that the chief reason for delay is not to be found in the personal shortcomings of any minister, but in the character and the methods of the great departments of state. The secretary of state's office, the Admiralty, the Treasury, and the War Office possessed an independence of judgment

and of action left them from the time when the king in
person, who once supplied the unifying force, ceased to
exercise the chief responsibility in matters of policy or
administration.[1] Responsible in theory to the king alone,
in practice they often tended to be responsible only to
themselves. Some unity of policy was achieved by the device of the cabinet or of the inner cabinet. But to work
well that device required the presence of a single man
such as Walpole who possessed the confidence both of the
king and of the two houses of parliament, and could
therefore restrain department heads from exercising too
independent a judgment. In 1756 the elements which Walpole had gathered together to produce his "system" were
distributed. Newcastle's control in the House of Lords
was assured, but the influence which his patronage gave
him in the House of Commons was contested by Fox, who
was in the government, and by Pitt, who was not. Fox
with justice believed that he held the seals of the secretary of state for the southern department in his own
right and not as Newcastle's lieutenant. The confidence of
the king was likewise divided, but if any person possessed
more of it than another, that person was Cumberland.
Personal friendship drew Cumberland and Fox together.
A cabinet so composed of men with conflicting personal
ambitions, the most forceful of them without any direct
dependence on parliament and therefore feared by those
whose manipulations made parliament the guarantor of

---

[1] See Miss Doris M. Gill, "The Treasury, 1660-1714", *English Historical
Review*, XLVI, 680, and Mark A. Thompson, *The Secretaries of State, 1681-
1782*. The War Office differed in origin from the chief departments; in 1756
Cumberland may be said to have represented it in the cabinet, while Barrington, the secretary at war, represented it in parliament. Both had access to
the king, but Barrington took no decisions without Cumberland's cognizance.
The Ordnance Board likewise occupied a unique position. Marlborough, the
master general, was responsible neither to parliament nor to the cabinet, in
which he had no seat, but to the king alone.

their power, found it difficult to agree on policy. They
tended to reflect their dissension in the conduct of their
separate departments.

How cumbersome was the ordinary routine of administration, even when department heads had agreed upon
definite measures, can be seen in the execution of those
decisions of the cabinet of January 20 which required
only standardized procedure. Two things approved by
that cabinet involved old, customary processes: the sending to North America of two regiments from the Irish
establishment, augmented on paper to full strength; and
the providing from Ireland of a small quantity of beef
and butter for immediate use in America. Matters began
briskly enough, with the secretary of state acting as the
mouthpiece of the king to the Admiralty and the Ordnance Board, and the secretary at war taking the initiative in the strictly military side. After Cumberland had
selected the 35th and the 42d, Fox wrote to the lord lieutenant of Ireland to send them to Plymouth; wrote to the
Admiralty to convoy them from Ireland, to purchase the
Irish beef and butter, and to provide at Plymouth the
transports to take them to America. The Admiralty,
either under its own hand or through its capable secretary, Cleveland, ordered Captain Hughes at Plymouth
to convoy the transports from Ireland, instructed the
Victualling Board to purchase the beef and butter, and ordered the Navy Board to contract for the necessary transports at the rate of two tons a man and to see that they
were properly fitted with beds, victualled, and washed
down with vinegar. The Navy Board, in turn, ordered its
agents to survey in the Thames ships which could quickly
be put in condition for fitting at Deptford. On the other
hand, the secretary at war procured the sign manuals to
the colonels of the two regiments authorizing the augmentation to full strength, and for the payment of baggage

and forage money to the officers. He wrote to the apothecary general to prepare chests of medicine for the use of the augmentation; to the secretary to the Board of General Officers to arrange for a survey of patterns of their clothing; to the paymaster general to advance a portion of one month's subsistence to enable them to purchase camp necessaries; to the secretary to the Treasury to lay before the Treasury the request for the ultimate issue of that one month's full subsistence; to the commanding officer of the Plymouth garrison to disembark and quarter the troops on their arrival; and to Fox to procure the sign manual to the Ordnance ordering the issue of arms for the augmentation. These letters were written, and the sign manuals prepared, by January 30, ten days after the inner cabinet meeting.[2]

Their execution involved considerably greater delay. The simple matter of transhipping the Irish beef and butter, which reached Plymouth by March 20, threatened to cause an altercation with the Treasury. The acts of trade forbade importation of provisions from Ireland and made them liable to seizure by customs officials. The Admiralty did not content itself with informing the Treasury that in this exceptional case the food was destined for North America. It got the support of an opinion from the attorney general, ordered the Navy Board to prevent seizure and the commanding officer at Plymouth to see to it that transhipment was made in midstream, no nearer to shore than the low-water mark.[3] As for the 35th

[2] Fox to Admiralty, Jan. 24, 1756, Ad. 1: 4120; Admiralty to Captain Hughes, Jan. 24, Ad. 2: 76; Admiralty to Navy Board, Jan. 24, Ad. 2: 219; Admiralty to Victualling Board, Jan. 30, Ad. 2: 515; Sign manual to Otway and Murray, Jan. 29, W.O. 26: 23; Barrington to West, to the apothecary general, to Darlington and Dupplin, to Robert Ince, and to Fox, Jan. 27, W.O. 4: 51; Warrant to Ordnance Board, Jan. 29, S.P. 44: 189.

[3] An open printed letter to Newcastle from Britannicus, March, 1756, declared the importation contrary to 32 Charles II, c. 2, and prejudicial to dairy and grazing counties in England. Additional MSS. 32,864, f. 115.

and 42d, the lord lieutenant of Ireland disliked to part with them. He feared that the Irish parliament, which had recently authorized an increase in the Irish establishment to twelve thousand men, would be bitter if asked to support regiments, not for the protection of the British Isles, but for North America. Because the 44th and 48th, already in America, were being partly paid from Irish funds, the 35th and 42d were put upon the English establishment after their arrival at Plymouth.[4] They reached their destination early in March and were quartered. But until they had actually arrived in England and until the date of their going upon the English establishment was determined, the Treasury could issue them no advance subsistence for the purchase of camp necessaries. Barrington wrote the paymaster general for one month's advance on March 15; the Treasury, acting on the paymaster general's memorial, ordered it the 18th. Three months additional advance was ordered by the Treasury on March 30. Though the regiments could not be equipped with their mess outfits until these orders passed, both they and the Irish provisions were ready in March and waited upon the transports.

The Navy Board contracted for the transports on February 3, the *Essex* of 600 tons, the *Stafford* of 602, the *Charlton* of 393, the *Longeville* of 294, the *Fortrose* of 246, the *Sidenham* of 269, and the *Sarah* of 207. By February 19 they were all at Deptford ready to begin fitting, with the exception of the *Longeville*, which was not ready until March 3. Since they were to sail in company under

[4] Newcastle's argument to the lord lieutenant was that Ireland should bear the cost of the regiments because she had interests of her own in America and because her coasts were defended by the British fleet which cost England between three and four million pounds, Newcastle to Devonshire, Feb. 16, Additional MSS. 32,862, f. 3. The opposition in Ireland at this time was led by the speaker, who was finally bought off by the gift of an earldom and a fat pension.

convoy, one tardy ship delayed all. By March 13 four of
them were at Gravesend, their fitting finished, and the
Charlton was on demurrage in the Downs. On March 16
twenty men of the *Stafford's* crew were impressed by a
man of war, and since she was at least a week behind the
others a new ship, the *Wilmington,* 637 tons, just arrived
from New England with masts, was substituted. On
March 19 fourteen of her men were impressed. On both
March 17 and 19 the Admiralty issued orders for preparations to be completed with all possible speed, the first
time they had written the Navy Board about these transports since January. The 20th saw the ships in the
Downs, where they waited until March 26 before a peremptory order from the Admiralty to the commanding
officer there got them a convoy to Plymouth. They were
beating down the channel before it was noticed that
though they had been fitted with berths they had no beds;
the Navy Board promised to have a thousand and forty
beds at Plymouth before April 10. The ships reached
Plymouth April 5 and 6, the *Wilmington* still short-
handed. She was supplied from vessels in the harbor.
Beds were installed by April 11, the day that saw the
regiments embarked, but the camp necessaries had not
arrived and the transports sailed on the 15th without
them.[5] From the day the cabinet had decided on the measure it had taken over twelve weeks to get a thousand and
forty men stowed on six transports and off to America.
The chief blame, perhaps, belongs to the Navy Board,
but it was really the entire system that was at fault.
There were too many ill-fitting cogs in the machine. The
clash between the Treasury and Admiralty over the Irish
provisions, the misdirected zeal which took seamen from

---

[5] The transport book for this period has survived, Admiralty, Navy Board:
259. Other correspondence is in Admiralty, Navy Board: 246, 2188; Admiralty 2: 515, 516.

one important service to supply another, and the curious oversight in the matter of beds, approach very close to absurdity. But of more interest is the revealing light which this analysis throws on administrative methods. The system did not allow for foresight; it was a hand-to-mouth performance. Once Fox or Barrington had set an affair in motion it passed from his supervision, and each succeeding repetition of his original order, as it was copied and transmitted by one clerk after another, grew fainter and fainter. This absence of coördination will be seen again.

Some palliation of such a performance can be found, it is true, in the rather unusual circumstances under which these preparations were made. American affairs became of small significance to a ministry faced during these same weeks with the threat of invasion from France. One must remember that men like Newcastle had lived most of their lives in terror of a combined French invasion and a Jacobite rising. The news of January 27 that a large army was at Boulogne only confirmed fears harbored since the autumn, when Boscawen and Hawke returned with weakened ships and sickly crews, and the French navy, for the moment, seemed superior. From the Hague, from Madrid, and from Newcastle's secret sources of information reports continued to pour in during February of Belle Isle's hostile preparations. An army of fifteen thousand men and a fleet so enfeebled by long service abroad that it could produce in January only fourteen ships of the line for the western squadron, and could muster in March only half crews on forty-six ships of the line, constituted England's insufficient defenses.[6] Born of the fear of invasion were the timid orders to

6 A review of naval strategy from March, 1755, to the declaration of war, Additional MSS. 33,047, f. 65. This long document is a defense of the ministry in the Byng affair.

Admiral Osbourn of the western squadron commanding him to return to Spithead after convoying the East Indian trade past Ushant; the impressment of seamen in Ireland, the search for deserters from the navy and the execution of the laws against vagabonds, all of which culminated in March in a general press; the attempt to pass a militia bill through the commons; the perfecting of schemes of defense for London and the south coast; and most important for American preparations, the effort to put into effect the treaty with the Netherlands, by which, if another nation were the aggressor, England could ask for six thousand Dutch troops. Transports for the six thousand were ordered January 31; they were given priority in preparation. They arrived at the Hague on March 2 to embark the men that Holland never intended to furnish, and on March 15 they were sent back, empty, to England. They were then kept in readiness to bring over the Hessians and Hanoverians, who arrived in May. In requiring the Navy Board to provide transportation for the mythical Dutch defenders of England, the ministry interfered with the equipping of ships for the defenders of America. But even with due allowance for the threat of invasion, such routine business might have been handled more expeditiously.

Two other decisions of the cabinet of January 20, to give Loudoun extraordinary powers, and to raise in the colonies a regiment of four thousand men, broke new ground. Having no precedents to follow, the departments might justifiably be expected to mark time.

To form into a document the cabinet's vague words on Loudoun's authority—"every power civil and military that can legally be given him"—was the first thing of its kind in the history of British relations with the colonies. Fox's first idea is indicative of the lengths to which the military opinion in the ministry was willing to go. As early as February 5 he sent a draft of a warrant for a commission under the great seal to the attorney general, asking him to make alterations if necessary. In this warrant Fox, not content with granting the commander in chief a military authority coextensive with that of the governors, completely annulled the governors' military powers: ". . . and it is our further WILL AND PLEAS-URE, that you do insert a clause or clauses, constituting and appointing the said John Earl of Loudoun, General and Commander in Chief over all our Forces, Regular or Provincial, or distinguished by any other Name, that are, or shall be raised or employed, in any of Our Provinces, Colonies, Towns, or Places . . . from Newfoundland to Georgia, both inclusive: and also Commander in Chief in all Military affairs in the said provinces and colonies; And you are to insert a clause, revoking or superseding, so much, and such parts, of our commissions to Our respective Governors of the said Provinces and Colonies in North America, whereby We have appointed them Captains General within their several Governments, respectively, as shall be necessary for the Purpose above mentioned: And for so doing, This shall be your Warrant. . . .'" Such a commission was deemed legal enough, for the Crown could do as it liked with royal colonies and by the attorney general's opinion of 1694 could in time of war appoint a military commander in chief over the troops of private colonies. But because Fox was persuaded that it would defeat its own objects by rousing the jealousies of royal governors and by antagonizing those colonies from whom great aid was expected, such as Massachusetts, Connecticut, and Pennsylvania, the commission in its original form was dropped. The whole month of February was spent in discussing how Loudoun

---

[7] Fox to Attorney General, Feb. 5, 1756, S.P. 44: 136, p. 345.

might exercise an equal amount of authority without raising colonial apprehensions. John Rutherford and Staats Long Morris, whom Shirley sent to England to plead his cause,[8] and Thomas Pownall, who argued Johnson's cause, were called upon for their opinions.[9] Young William Johnson of Connecticut, a son of Dr. Johnson of King's College, New York, thought the conflicting testimony of these three agents the chief cause of ministerial uncertainties. ''There has been so much perplexity in their different accounts that the ministry have been really at a loss what to believe, or how to act; for since Pownall came whose character and accounts are much the most relyed upon, they have, 'tis said, chang'd almost all the measures they had before taken, and Morris, finding

[8] C. H. Lincoln, ed., *Correspondence of William Shirley* (hereafter cited as *Shirley Correspondence*) II, 368, 428. Rutherford was a former captain of a New York independent company and a member of the New York council. Staats Morris was nephew of the governor of Pennsylvania. While in England he fell a prey to the wiles of the Dowager Duchess of Gordon, became her husband, and through her influence rose to high rank in the British army.

[9] That Pownall did not go to England solely in Johnson's interest is clear from *Sir William Johnson Papers*, I, 803-6, 833, 834, 853, 886. Governor Morris actually considered him an excellent person to carry Shirley's dispatches, *Pennsylvania Archives, 1748-1763*, p. 395.

Pownall was one of the rare men of talent in the eighteenth century who deliberately undertook to acquire a knowledge of the colonies to use as a stepping-stone to political preferment in England. He went down from Cambridge University in 1744, and during three years in the office of the Board of Trade learned the British side of colonial administration. In 1753 he accompanied Sir Danvers Osborn to New York as private secretary. After the governor's suicide he made it his business, though ''not employed as a Commissioned Servant of the Crown'', to acquire as much information as possible, and to keep an eye open for his own advantage. As such a free-lance observer he accomplished a good deal. At Albany in 1754 he proposed to the commissioners the need of building vessels on the Lakes (*Documentary History of New-York*, II, 616), and ''by his Care to collect Materials as well as compiling them has gott form'd & published a map of that Part of America where the Present seat of Action lyes which map is more Correct & actually precise than any thing yet extant.'' This was Lewis Evans's *General Map of the Middle British Colonies* (1755), dedicated to Pownall. Pownall's account

Shirley's side the weakest, began to turn about and contradict many things which he had before affirmed: however I believe his character is too well known, as a great story-teller (to say no worse) to be able to do much good, or harm.'"[10] Loudoun's own ideas of the powers he would like can be gleaned from a letter to him from the earl of Balcarres, with whom he had discussed the affair. After congratulating Loudoun upon his alacrity in accepting the responsibilities of public service, the earl added: "I shall be glad to hear ere you goe, you have solid marks of their favour, and of being well sustained, and vested with necessary powers over these enthusiastic saints and independent sinners. The English are the only nation, who ever parted with a million of their people, without taking some measures to preserve their subjection. You will deal with them (if needful) as I observed you did Lt. Crawford att the crop, you gave him the severest correction with the softest smiles. . . . You have the benedictions of an honest old farmer.'"[11] Cumberland, Fox, and Loudoun were agreed in thinking that the commander in chief

of himself is in the appendix to the 1770 edition of *The Administration of the Colonies.* His ability to theorize on the nature of government is well seen in a plan sent in 1755 to his brother John, one of the secretaries of the Board of Trade. In it he laid down "Considerations of the Methods and Nature of Settling a Colony on the Lands South of Lake Erie", and analysed the kind of settlers wanted, their land system, and form of government. He ended with a prophetic observation, "This would also be in Time the Center of the Manufactures of this Continent which if the English do not possess and make so the French will." The central point of his colony was the site of the present city of Cleveland. This document, with accompanying map, is among the Loudoun Papers in the Henry E. Huntington Library and Art Gallery, San Marino, California, numbered, respectively, 716 and 740. Reference to this collection will hereafter be made by the library catalogue mark LO.

10 William Johnson to William Samuel Johnson, March 31, 1756, William Samuel Johnson Papers in the Library of the Connecticut Historical Society, Hartford.

11 Balcarres to Loudoun, February 16, 1756, LO 825.

ought to have fairly extensive powers, a fact to remember in interpreting the meaning of the commission finally passed.

This same month a dispute between factions in Pennsylvania politics reached London offices, and added a further complication to the discussion of Loudoun's powers. A liberal group in that colony seized the opportunity to make Quaker reluctance to prosecute an active war the lever for gaining control of the assembly. They or their agent, Ferdinand John Paris, petitioned the king and the secretary of state.[12] Willing to take the unprecedented step of calling in parliament to settle their grievances, they submitted to Fox ''a bill for the better defence and Preservation of His Majesty's Dominions'' which prohibited any man from sitting in any colonial assembly unless he took the oaths and subscribed the declaration. No conscientious Quaker, of course, could take the oaths. This eagerness on the part of colonials to invite parliamentary action may have suggested to the ministry that Loudoun's authority could be strengthened without arousing too violent an opposition; Cumberland, Fox, and Newcastle paid great attention to the Pennsylvania affair. Newcastle met four London Quakers on March 5. Representing the old, not the new group, they acknowledged that something should be done to remedy Pennsylvania's lack of preparedness, suggested a dissolution of the assembly by act of parliament, and undertook to answer ''for their people declining being chose in the next assembly''.[13] But about the same time either these Quakers or Thomas Penn presented Cumberland with infor-

[12] *Acts Privy Council, Colonial, 1745-1766*, §304; C.O. 5: 1274. The petition to Fox, with the proposed bill, is in the Holland House papers; Lord Ilchester very kindly permitted me to make a copy.

[13] Minutes about the Quakers, Newcastle House, Additional MSS. 32,996, f. 368; W. T. Root, *Relations of Pennsylvania with the British Government*, ch. X.

mation to prove that the situation in Pennsylvania was not as bad as reported, that sixteen companies of soldiers were posted at twenty-two frontier forts and towns, and that every man had properly heard the articles of war and taken an enlisting oath. Before any unusual new measure could be approved the terms of Loudoun's commission had been settled and the Royal American Regiment established to draw most of its recruits from the Germans in Pennsylvania. The ministry contented itself, therefore, with pushing through parliament an act for the enlistment of indentured servants, to apply chiefly in that colony, and with urging upon Thomas Penn the appointment of a military man as governor. Cumberland himself, after apparently considering Pownall, recommended William Denny, who had served in Flanders; Penn gladly acceded, and Denny received a commission as lieutenant colonel in America only.[14] By this compromise Penn saved his rights and the colony its self-government, but how unsatisfactory the settlement was Denny's subsequent difficulties showed. The whole affair served to complicate and therefore to delay the promulgation of Loudoun's commission.

Early in March the commission took its final shape and by March 17 passed the seals. Skilfully worded, it sought to accomplish the same ends as Fox's first suggestion and to lodge complete military authority in the colonies in the hands of the commander in chief. "We reposing especial trust and confidence in your prudence courage and loyalty HAVE constituted and appointed and by these presents do constitute and appoint you to be General and Commander in Chief of all and singular our Forces employed or to be employed in North America, TO HAVE

[14] Pownall's Reasons for declining the Government of Pennsylvania, *Pennsylvania Magazine*, XIII, 441-446. From its context the document should obviously be dated 1756.

HOLD EXERCISE and ENJOY the said office during
Our pleasure together with all the powers authorities
Rights and Privileges thereunto belonging SUBJECT
however to such restrictions Limitations and Instructions
as We have Given or shall hereafter from time to time
give under Our Royal Sign Manual AND We do hereby
charge and require all the Governors Lieutenant Governors Deputy Governors and Presidents of Council of Our
respective Colonies and Provinces of North America and
all other Officers Civil or Military within the same to be
aiding and assisting to you in the exercise of this command And in case the said John Earl of Loudoun should
by death or in any other manner be disabled from exercising the said command Our Will and Pleasure is that
the same with all authorities rights and privileges contained in this Our Commission should devolve on Our
. . . Major General Abercrombie or on such other officer
bearing Our Commission as shall be next in Rank to the
said Major General Abercrombie. And we do hereby authorize and empower the said Major General Abercrombie or such other Officer to take upon him the said Command in as full and ample manner as if he was provided
with a particular Commission for that purpose IN WIT-
NESS whereof We have caused these Our Letters to be
made Patent WITNESS Our self at Westminster the
Seventeenth day of March in the twentyninth Year of
Our Reign.' "[15]

This brief commission represents the greatest extent
of authority which the British government ever tried to
exercise over the colonies as a unit. That authority was
deceptive in that it was not defined, as Pownall later saw
so clearly. "The general words which made it up mean
nothing, or suppose everything, when a justifiable oc-

[15] Public Record Office, G.D. 8: 95.

casion, or perhaps a colourable pretext calls for the exercise of them.'"[16] Early in May the superior dignity of the commander in chief was reasserted in a sign manual order of precedence which authorized him to take the first and highest rank on every occasion where he met with governors.[17] No mere form for ceremonials, this warrant was intended to emphasize further the divorce in military matters between the professional soldiers and the civil governments.

But while Loudoun's commission represented a considerable extension of authority over that enjoyed by Braddock and Shirley, the instructions which limited it were couched in the same general terms as Braddock's. By them Loudoun could correspond with governors and if necessary visit their provinces in person on the subjects of recruiting, quartering, raising the common fund, distributing Indian presents voted by the assemblies, impressing carriages and providing necessaries, transport and victuals; he could call governors to a council of war to determine campaign operations, or in emergencies. His commission charged and required governors to assist him; his instructions ordered him to aid and assist them in aiding him. The commission represented the revised Braddock plan; the instructions, as the words regarding the provision supply and the common fund attest, were the Braddock plan itself. One might explain this difference as a further instance of ministerial disagreement: the cabinet as a whole approved the instructions; Fox probably drafted the commission and it never got formal approval.[18] Or perhaps routine again was to blame; since all instructions required a long time to prepare, the

---

16 Thomas Pownall, *Administration of the Colonies* (1765), pp. 55-63.

17 *Pennsylvania Colonial Records*, VII, 472.

18 Minute, May 6, 1756, Additional MSS. 32,996, f. 419. Loudoun appeared in person at this meeting.

phrasing in more precise terms of the delicate nuances of the commission would have taken weeks and might have reopened the controversy. Whatever the cause, the two documents set a trap into which the wariest commander might fall. If he followed the implication of his commission, he might be held to have interfered in civil government beyond the words of his instructions; if he did not, he might rightly have been accused of failing to do his utmost in promoting colonial unity. The path that Loudoun would follow could have been foreseen; his friends were Cumberland and Fox, and Cumberland's mind alone he knew intimately.

Though it appointed him commander in chief under the great seal, the commission of March 17 gave Loudoun no powers over the army. A separate military commission under the signet and sign manual, in the same words as those which constituted Braddock's and Shirley's sole authority, was deemed necessary. Such a commission was issued as late as April 15, though on April 2 the king signed a much briefer document authorizing the holding of courts martial, in words incorporated into the general commission two weeks later. To finish these four documents required a disproportionately long time: the discussion began in January; one commission passed by March 17; the military commission, April 15; the order of precedence and the instructions, May 7. To how considerable an extent the delay was caused either by the novelty of the contents or by the differences in the cabinet and not by the routine alone of business offices, may be seen from a comparison of the time required to prepare Loudoun's commission and instructions as governor general of Virginia. Early in February he learned that the honor would be given him. It had been vacant since Albemarle's death, and though various names were suggested, Halifax believed the post ought no longer to be a sinecure. Bestowal of it upon Loudoun served many purposes: it made him of equal rank in civil matters with any governor in America; it added to his dignity and his emoluments, for he made with Lieutenant Governor Dinwiddie the same bargain as his predecessor and received annually the sum of £1665; it seemed to make the office a little less a sinecure, for the fiction was preserved throughout Loudoun's career that he would normally execute his duties in Virginia unless by chance he should be "absent from his Government, and engaged in the King's Service, in some other Part of America." The Board of Trade submitted its representation and draft of the commission on February 10; the Privy Council approved it on the 16th; the following day the *Gazette* announced the appointment. On March 15 the instructions were ready, and two days later Loudoun attended at St. James to take the oaths. This Virginia affair was ordinary routine and five or six weeks a usual length of time for it. More than twice that time was needed to reduce to documentary form a definition of Loudoun's major office.

Another decision of the cabinet of January 20, to raise four battalions in Pennsylvania and adjacent colonies, was also much easier to make than to put into effect. That scheme, which was to develop into the Royal American regiment (later the Sixtieth, the King's Royal Rifle Corps), had been long brewing. It would seem to have been the concoction of one James Prevost, a Swiss soldier of fortune whose military career on the continent had ended in such abrupt disaster that he was compelled to seek employment elsewhere. As Pitt rightly put it in the House of Commons, "The nation would not have been blessed [with the scheme], if by a fortuitous concurrence of circumstances Prevôt had not been going an adventurer to America, and had not found his way from Brest hither; and if, after all, he had not taken it into his head to have

a regiment.'"[19] In the previous October, when the ministry, faced with the outbreak of war and a possibly hostile
parliament, was willing to consider any means of getting
a capable reinforcement in America, Prevost appeared
with a providential suggestion. It was to raise a regiment
for American service from among the deserters of the
five hundred odd regiments in Germany.[20] But he soon
altered his plan to include the Germans of that populous
colony prevented by its Quaker assembly from active par-
ticipation in the war. So much did the scheme appear both
to solve the Pennsylvania problem and to satisfy the need
for more troops in America that the king provisionally
authorized him to pick up Protestant Swiss and German
officers on the continent. He was to promise them from
fifty pounds for captains to twenty for sergeants, send
them to America to recruit, and be himself the colonel of
the regiment. There was no money available at the time
to meet such promises. For since by the Act of Settlement
foreign officers were incapacitated from holding British
commissions, the legality of the whole affair depended

[19] Walpole, *Memoirs of the Reign of George II*, II, 171. Prevost was captured on the seas at the same time as Governor Lyttelton of South Carolina.
Two years later Loudoun picked up some rumors of Prevost's early career
from a French officer, a deserter. In the 1740s he had tried to get a French
commission but the subalterns in the regiment of his choice represented, as
was their custom, that he was not a fit person to be an officer. Not to be
denied, Prevost acted for a time ''as a lower sort of sundry,'' finally got his
rank and was put in charge of the sick. His captain, perhaps to get him out
of the way, supplied him with funds to recruit in Switzerland, where he met
a Dutch officer also negotiating for men. Prevost thereupon sold to the Dutch
the recruits he had raised for the French, recruits who actually cost him
nothing, said Loudoun's informer, for they were all deserters and in danger
of being hanged. This account is from the Loudoun notebooks in the Huntington Library, vol. 5, New York, Jan. 18, 1758. Hereafter they will be cited
as Huntington Manuscript (HM) 1717.

[20] Reflections on the present state of North America, Additional MSS.
33,029, f. 345. The document is in a foreign hand and phrasing, but is unsigned.

upon an act of parliament which was not yet passed and
the Treasury therefore flatly refused to advance Prevost
funds. Nevertheless he trustingly departed for his favorite recruiting grounds, and by March, at a total commit-
ment of £2500, had succeeded in gathering together
some ninety commissioned and non-commissioned officers,
among them Henry Bouquet, Frederick Haldimand, and
Augustin Prevost. Thus far Cumberland was the plan's
chief backer. Others were doubtful; both Fox and Newcastle listened to the strenuous protests of colonial agents
and feared lest foreign officers and the arming of German
settlers stir up a dangerous discontent in the colonies.
But in December, after the House of Commons had
demonstrated its pliability, they decided to go through
with the scheme. Barrington was instructed to introduce
a bill, and the Treasury signed a warrant to Prevost for
a thousand pounds, taking his bond and that of two London merchants. Having so committed itself, the cabinet of
January 20 had no scruples in increasing Prevost's original regiment to one of four battalions of a thousand men
each. Barrington introduced his bill early in February
authorizing the commissioning of a limited number of
foreign Protestants as officers in America only. There
was bitter debate. Bollan, the Massachusetts agent, petitioned against it, and Pitt, using it as a weapon against
the administration's military policy, affected to see the
entire Act of Settlement tottering to its fall and England
ruled by foreign armies. It did not go up to the Lords
until February 27 and did not receive royal assent until
March 9.

The fact that the bill was not yet through the Commons
in February did not deter Barrington from getting the
sign manual authorizing the raising of the regiment, from
issuing instructions for the Board of General Officers to
inspect the clothing patterns, and from asking the Ord-

nance Board, through Fox, to provide drums and hal-
berds from the Tower.[21] He expected the arms to be
supplied in America out of the ten thousand stand
shipped to Shirley that spring. But until the bill passed,
no commissions could be issued to the officers waiting in
England and the Treasury could not order payment to
them as British officers. They had received only a part of
the sums promised by Prevost and could not equip themselves or sail until the whole was paid. On March 26
Loudoun appeared before the Treasury to urge the issue
of six months subsistence to cover that charge. But the
scrupulous Treasury fancied to see an illegality in paying
officers who only held their British commission after the
passage of the act from the date of the establishment of
the regiment, fixed as December 24, 1755. The board appealed to the attorney and solicitor general, and got a
blunt reply to the effect that the Treasury had no business to know that foreigners were enrolled in the regiment, that its responsibility began and ended with the
issue of funds to the paymaster general, who passed them
on to the colonel and agent, the really responsible parties,
and that when foreign officers took the oaths, made and
subscribed the declaration, and received the sacrament,
they were legally in the same position as British and entitled to their pay from the beginning. Meeting on April
1 in the presence of Loudoun and Barrington, the Treasury with reluctance agreed ''to regard the necessity of
the service'' by ordering the six months advance. But it
fortified its position by inserting in the minutes the answers of the deputy secretary at war to several questions,

[21] The clothing of the Royal American Regiment differed from the standard pattern, for it was the first regiment in the army to remove the lace
from privates' uniforms, to shorten the coat, and thereby to furnish a more
serviceable uniform for brush warfare. Milne and Terry, *Annals of the
King's Royal Rifle Corps*, appendix.

by which it learned that it was a "constant practice" to begin establishments from Christmas and to give officers' commissions an early date to entitle them to begin their pay.[22] This caution on the part of the Treasury prevented the foreign officers from sailing in March. Once more in this same month and in connection with this regiment the Treasury delayed matters. Though the king's warrant of March 4, countersigned by the secretary at war, for the payment of twenty thousand pounds levy money for the raising of the regiment, had been properly docqueted by the Treasury, Dupplin, the paymaster general, objected to issuing such a large sum to a regiment which would probably not be raised for several months. He asked for a special Treasury warrant. At its meeting of March 11 the Treasury gave its opinion that the deputy paymasters general in America should be authorized to advance money in proportion to the rate of the levies, but it did not countersign the warrant until the end of March.

The list of obstructions in the launching of this regiment, unique in the British army, is not yet ended. Loudoun boldly settled one cause of possible dispute by making over to the four colonels commandant the off-reckonings upon clothing, which were the largest of the traditional perquisites attached to the command of a regiment. Prevost, however, loth to leave Europe and anxious for such small profits as could be had, started another hare by proposing to recruit men in Germany. At the suggestion of Joseph Yorke at the Hague it was decided that these men—limited to four hundred—should be enlisted under the guise of "planters" for the New World, lest Prussian and Danish officers object to the en-

---

[22] Treasury Minutes, March 26, April 1, Treas. 29: 32; Report of the attorney and solicitor general, March 31, Treas. 1: 368. But Calcraft, the regimental agent, acting upon Barrington's order of March 14 (W.O. 4: 51), seems to have advanced subsistence to a few foreign officers (LO 934, 935).

croachment upon their recruiting territory. Prevost offered to assume complete charge provided he were paid in advance. Such a proposal was unusual, for in England when a single field officer raised a regiment he bore the cost himself and was reimbursed when he had finished. When Loudoun was asked to advance part of the necessary sum out of his contingent allowance of £2000, intended to cover his expenses in London, he naturally objected to such a drain upon an account which had no connection with regimental monies. Though he signed the "bargire" with Prevost at the request of Cumberland and Fox, for there was no other way of doing it, he arranged that the £4800 estimated as the cost be paid by the regimental agent out of the recruiting fund. Finally, at the last moment, it occurred to Cumberland and Loudoun that perhaps there might not be any arms for the regiment in America. The services of Sir John Ligonier, lieutenant general of the Ordnance, were invoked; "3741 Long Land Service Musquets of the King's Pattern in store deemed serviceable but not fit for regular regiments" were immediately packed; and so, late in the season, another ship was ordered from the Admiralty to transport them.

When one bears in mind that the creation of this Royal American regiment had the approval of a cabinet council and that every department knew what was happening, one can see in each of the steps in its formation how ill-fitted British administration was to cope with a novelty. The whole conception was a sorry one; if Americans had been unwilling to enlist in the past under British officers, what presumption was there that they would rush to the call of German or Swiss? But once the decision was made, it would have been necessary in no other country for every subordinate step to be accompanied by a fresh examination of the issues and a tardily given executive order. Nevertheless, some praise is due the departments that they could go ahead at all before the final seal of approval was placed on the plan by parliament. If the Treasury seemed unduly cautious and temporizing, it was only because the Treasury, more than any other department, was strictly accountable for its control of funds to the House of Commons. That the opposition in parliament chose to make an issue of the Royal American regiment had as much to do as anything with the halting pace of its formation.

Still answering the question why it should have taken four months to get Loudoun away to America, we now pass to the consideration of what could happen in this British administration when a part of the ministry, without the calling of a cabinet, decided to alter a decision reached earlier by them all. In February those people most interested in American affairs, Cumberland, Fox, Halifax, and Loudoun, came to the conclusion that the decision of January 20 needed revision in three important particulars. In order that Loudoun might have a larger British force in the 1756 campaign and be less dependent upon the vagaries of American recruiting, they determined that the 35th and 42d should be immediately recruited to full strength in England and Scotland, and not in the colonies. Convinced also that a shortage of provisions had been primarily responsible for the failure of Shirley against Niagara and of Johnson against Crown Point, and remembering past experiences in Flanders,[23] they decided to employ a British provision contractor and not depend upon the energy of colonial governors or the ability of provincial contractors. Finally, in accordance with the clear recommendations of Halifax in his report

---

[23] From Cumberland's commissary general in Flanders Loudoun got a long detailed report upon provisioning an army. Lawrence Dundas to Loudoun, Jan. 27, 1756, LO 490.

of January 7, and from conversation with such men as Rutherford and Thomas Pownall, they came to the conclusion that provincial troops should be employed in addition to the regular regiments. Cumberland's rooted objections to such troops had to give way to the hard fact that unless such a plan were followed Loudoun would begin his career in America with a force considerably weaker than the French. These three decisions meant a second revision of the Braddock plan, and implied the further extension of the very point Newcastle opposed, the financial support of the war from England. The ministry therefore was divided upon a fundamental matter of policy at the very moment when it should have been united in pushing along preparations. Upon Loudoun, who had no official standing in the government, fell the chief responsibility for making matters run smoothly.

The consequences of the decision to employ provincial troops were not at once apparent, but the determination to recruit in England and Scotland and to employ a British provision contractor added further complications to the factors already making for delay.

The first change of plan, which, as it developed, became inextricably mixed with the business of shipping stores, led to a pretty squabble between the military and naval departments. Recruiting for foreign service was always precarious. It was the more difficult in February and March because the officers of the ten new regiments added to the army the preceding December were also seeking men. The 42d raised men in the Highlands, a rich recruiting ground as yet unencroached upon by other regiments, with comparative ease. In England the press act helped, as did the pardoning of convicts on condition that they enlisted for life in the 35th.[24] But since the

---

[24] For the rigor of the press law, 29 Geo. II, c. 4, showing how powerfully the invasion menace influenced parliament, see C. N. Clode, *Military Forces of the Crown*, II, 17.

Admiralty could not be asked to provide transports in advance for recruits who might not be raised, the proportion between men and ships had to be carefully balanced. On February 24 the Admiralty, willing to save time by acting without a secretary of state's order provided it had oral assurance such order would eventually be given, instructed the Navy Board to take up transports for sixteen hundred men at Plymouth, including those ordered on January 24. When, three days later, the letter came from Fox, it asked for transports, not for sixteen hundred, but for two thousand men. At this point there began to appear, at aimless intervals, various odd lots of stores to be shipped to America. To the baggage of the 35th and 42d was added on March 25 the two hundred tons of baggage for the Royal American regiment. Acting on Loudoun's memorial of March 23 and the royal warrant of March 26, the Ordnance Board prepared 678 tons of artillery and stores to be shipped with the troops.[25] Tents for the 35th and 42d were ordered on February 19, and for the Royal Americans on March 1. The apothecary general had the medicines for the general hospital ready by February 25. A large selection of Indian presents could not be purchased until the Treasury in April countersigned the warrants for them, and not until May 6 did the Ordnance receive the royal warrant for issuing as a part of those presents seven hundred "India guns", bullets, bar lead, and powder. On April 14 the small cannon and stores for the two brigantines, *Halifax* and *Loudoun*, which were being built on Lake Ontario, were

[25] Basing his request on a knowledge of the ordnance already in America, and influenced by the same considerations of lightness and calibre which had dictated Braddock's selection of ordnance, Loudoun asked for ten light twelve-pounders, ten sixes, ten threes, four eight-inch howitzers, ten brass 5½-inch mortars, and fifteen coehorn mortars. Marlborough slightly reduced the number of pieces to conform to the theoretical proportions allotted to an army of twelve thousand men and sent six sixes and eleven coehorns.

ordered shipped on the transports, and on April 20 Marlborough added four more light sixes weighing 28¾ tons, to Loudoun's train of artillery. Loudoun's own baggage, including several cases of wine for which the Admiralty sent a special ship to the Channel Islands, nearly filled one transport. In proportion as both recruits and stores were assembled at intervals, transports were ordered. On March 25 Fox asked for transports for five hundred men at Glasgow, and a ship of five hundred tons in the Thames. Next day he ordered a storeship; on April 9, five hundred additional tons; on April 13, further transports for two hundred men at Glasgow; and on April 17, for two hundred more men in the Thames. On May 15 he ordered a ship for the four thousand stand of Royal American arms. In accordance with these scattered orders, the Navy Board contracted for five transports on March 1, and for one each on March 26, April 5, April 15, April 19, April 22, and May 15. There was further confusion when some of the transports first ordered to Plymouth had to be detained to embark London recruits and stores in the river. Loudoun discovered on April 15 that the Navy Board had distributed the 678 tons of ordnance stores in an impossible fashion—all the powder on one ship, all the brass sixes on another—and equalization among the transports made alterations and reshipping necessary.

But these things, though they furnished the Navy Board with excuses, did not wholly justify its slowness. Joshua Loring and Archibald Kennedy, newly appointed captains of the brigantines on Lake Ontario, were made transport agents on March 15 and March 29, with special instructions to hasten matters.[26] Of the five transports contracted for on March 1, the *Wilmington* was substi-

[26] The two brigantines were registered in the Royal Navy, and the complement of each fixed at thirty-six men, Ad. 2: 76, p. 294; Ad. 2: 219, p. 546.

tuted for the *Stafford* in the first fleet, the *Pennsylvania*, the *Betty Sally*, and the *Integrity* were ready for stores by March 30, and the *Isabella Maria* by April 5. The five contracted for from March 26 to April 22 all developed trouble. The *Earl of Halifax* had carpenters at work on her bottom on April 27, and lacked her lower shrouds; on May 5 her foremast was condemned, but she was shipping the stores of the 35th; on May 10 she was completing her rigging and taking in Royal American stores; on May 22 she lacked twenty-two beds; and on May 23, having but fourteen men in her crew and no master, she missed stays putting down the river, and grounded. The *Neptune* applied on April 14 for a travelling protection to complete her crew, and on May 17 had two men pressed by the *Macclesfield* armed sloop. The *Mary,* whose master in Kennedy's opinion was not at all anxious for the voyage, was not ready to put down to Gravesend till May 3, and on June 4 ran ashore as she was rounding Dungeness. On March 30 three masters refused to ship powder without a direct order from the Navy Board. It was to be expected that as the month of May wore on and the transports remained in the Thames, mutual recriminations should have passed between the Navy Board and the army officers in charge of recruits. The former, through Kennedy, maintained that the delay was caused by the absence of arms, stores, baggage, and clothing; the latter, that all stores and troops were long ready and waiting for the ships. On May 19 Fox, with the two reports before him, ordered the fleet to sail at once without tarrying for another article. Thereupon the Navy Board commissioners appeared in person to hasten away transports which still lacked their full complement of crew, and rowed from ship to ship "more anxious to get us off to sea than to get us ready."[27]

27 James Robertson (in charge of the troops) to Loudoun, Aug. 18, 1756, LO 1515.

By May 30 the ships were in the Downs. On June 19 they sailed from Spithead. They reached New York the middle of August, much too late for the men and stores they carried to be of great use in the 1756 campaign. This whole incident, notorious enough to get into the public press, is the most convincing illustration of the depths to which an administration without a sole coördinating head could sink.

The second change in the plan of January 20, to employ a British firm of provision contractors, was the greatest increase in the costs of the war yet made, for the complete victualling of both regulars and provincials was contemplated. Here one can see what happened when there was no basic cabinet agreement and a department could exercise its own judgment. But if Newcastle, as first lord of the Treasury, took his time in considering a proposal that depended for its validity upon the board's signature, it was less because he disliked the aggressiveness of Cumberland and Fox than because, as guardian of the public monies, he had a very real fear of accepting the sole responsibility for so costly a decision. The provision contractors within the next two years were to receive nearly a million pounds. Cumberland and Loudoun, on the other hand, knew that the sooner this business was completed the more quickly could the service in America go on, and they paid scant attention to Newcastle's scruples. In their haste to get the contract drawn and signed they chose a provision contractor, Alderman Baker, without first consulting the Treasury. It was a splendid effort to cut red tape; according to the usual method the Treasury would have advertised for bids and chosen the best and lowest. As it was, after a preliminary conversation with Newcastle, Loudoun appeared before the Treasury on February 27 to prove that twenty thousand men should be provisioned in America for a year, while Baker and his associate Christopher Kilby waited outside in readiness to dash in and present estimates and plans the moment they were called for. This manoeuvre did nothing except show Loudoun's urgency. At its next meeting, March 4, the Treasury reduced the figure to twelve thousand men for six months, and intimated its suspicions of the high rate per man per day, sixpence. That rate was the same as in Baker's other contract for Nova Scotia, where everything had to be imported; it should be less, thought the Treasury, for a country where some provisions could be bought on the spot.[28] On March 11 there was a full discussion. Loudoun argued that advertising for bidders might bring in people "not equal in credit and substance to the weight of that service"; Baker and Kilby defended their prices against some anonymous remarks on the cheapness of provisions in Pennsylvania; and finally, with great reluctance and shifting as much of the responsibility to Loudoun as it could, the Treasury ordered a contract prepared for twelve thousand men for a year. At the same time it urged Loudoun not to let the matter rest, but to see whether the price could be reduced, or some of the costs be either met by the colonies or else deducted from the pay of the troops. But even then normal Treasury routine held up the contract. Unlike the Admiralty and Ordnance Boards, which could in emergency issue orders without the attendance of every member, the Treasury conducted no business except in full meeting. It met but four times in February, and five times

28 As news spread that the subject was being discussed, a few bids did reach the Treasury. Israel Pemberton of Pennsylvania was proposed as a contractor who could supply troops entirely with American provisions and not, as Baker and Kilby planned, partly with Irish and English meat and butter. The Earl of Stirling and Andrew Drummond proposed to deliver provisions anywhere in America at ninepence a day, whereas Baker and Kilby were to deliver only at general warehouses designated by the commander in chief. Treas. 1: 365.

in March; impending business had to wait upon those meetings. Loudoun felt it necessary to submit a memorial on March 24 asking that the contract be signed, "all preparations being at a stop till that is done", and not until April 1 could he give Baker and Kilby official orders for putting it into immediate effect. The Irish beef and butter, cause of so much earlier trouble, were now taken over by the contractors; they agreed also to purchase the remaining supplies of Shirley's contractors. The consequences of these negotiations were two-fold: by its delay the Treasury jeopardized the campaign in America in June and July; by its precipitancy, as Newcastle had feared, it offered to opponents of the administration in the House of Commons a loophole for attack the next year. The chief importance of the affair, however, is that it marked another step in the slow process by which the war in America came to be supported from England.[29]

As early as the middle of February, when it became clear to Cumberland and Loudoun that, at the rate things were moving, Loudoun could not hope to arrive in America before the end of June, an effort was made to nullify the disastrous consequences to the campaign of all these administrative delays. They decided to hurry an officer to New York to make preparations there. Daniel Webb, Loudoun's third in command, was chosen;[30] by February 17 a commission was rushed through appointing him commander in chief in America until the arrival either of James Abercromby, the second in command, or

---

[29] In the Hardwicke Papers, Additional MSS. 35,909, f. 223, is a long analysis of the history of this contract, based upon the Treasury minutes in Treas. 29: 32.

[30] Webb, as a major, commanded a squadron of Ligonier's horse at Dettingen and was promoted after Fontenoy. In 1754 he was given the great task of settling in Holland the accounts between England and Holland for the campaigns, 1745 to 1748, and for the years 1749 to 1751. Cumberland Papers.

of Loudoun himself.[31] Loudoun, with Cumberland's advice, drew up the heads of Webb's instructions,[32] and was so sanguine of his immediate departure that on February 27 he persuaded Anson at the Admiralty to order the *Nottingham* to be stored for North America and to be ready within a week. On March 4 the Admiralty ordered the *Nottingham* to be completed in preference to all other ships. But nothing could hurry the clerks of the secretary of state's office. Not until March 13 were Webb's instructions ready for the royal signature. On the same day Fox wrote to the American governors the letter which Webb was to deliver. When Webb reached Portsmouth on March 26 he found two difficulties. Captain Marshall of the *Nottingham* had orders to take on board the commissioned officers of the Royal American Regiment, but not the forty-two non-commissioned officers, and as his ship was small he refused to admit them. He was also burdened with the convoy of "a heavy bottomed old Lady" of a storeship laden with ordnance supplies for Nova Scotia, and therefore had to wait for a favorable wind.[33]

31 It was under the signet and sign manual, C.O. 324: 38, f. 444.

32 The instructions limited Webb's powers to preparing for the campaign. He was to recruit to the full establishment, to fortify Albany strongly, to provide space at Albany for hospitals, barracks and storehouses, with the assistance, if possible, of the New York assembly. He was to keep open the communications to Oswego by assisting Sir William Johnson to build forts in the Onondaga country; he was to store provisions at Albany, Fort Edward, Oswego, and Fort William Henry, to provide by contract boats and carriages, to negotiate with Sir Charles Hardy and other governors in getting rangers enlisted in the provincial troops for 1756, to assist Hardy in building ships on Lake Ontario, and to build travelling carriages for the new field train. W.O. 26: 23. HM 1717, vol. 11.

33 The *Nottingham* herself was ordered to carry these ordnance stores on March 3, and it was not until March 22 that the Admiralty wrote to the secretary of state what had apparently just been told them, that a man of war could not carry stores when she was provisioned for six months. Ad. Minutes, March 6, Ad. 3: 64; Admiralty to Ordnance, March 1, Ad. 2: 219, f. 512; Admiralty to Secretary of State, March 22, S.P. 42: 39.

By this time it was hoped that the transports ordered on January 24 might be got around to Plymouth and proceed with Webb; Marshall was ordered on March 27 to put himself under the command of Captain Holmes of the *Grafton,* the new commander of the fleet on the American station, who was instructed to convoy the transports to America.

Undoubtedly Webb would have waited longer had it not been for the curious affair of the intercepted letters, which threw the ministry into a temporary panic. These letters had been written to the Duc de Mirepoix by some- one in Pennsylvania who signed himself Pierre Fidele.[34] He seemed to have accurate knowledge of military and Indian affairs in the colonies. He told of an instruction from Shirley to Johnson which the ministry knew nothing about—an order to raise a large body of the Six Nations and proceed to Pennsylvania where he should join "a large force actually in readiness" of southern Indians. Pierre Fidele wrote that he himself, in accordance with this plan, had raised ten thousand men. Ministers at once suspected a general Indian uprising under French leader- ship, and when, on March 17, they received a copy of Shirley's instruction, not from the general, but enclosed in Johnson's letter of December 18, they saw a devilish plot hatching.[35] Shirley's part in the whole transaction seemed very suspicious. Fox wrote: "I don't suspect Shirley of Treachery, but I have no doubt of his having great schemes, and that he trusts the execution to Trai- tors, and that he ought not to stay in North America." Cumberland was for sending Shirley home a prisoner. Hardwicke preferred a gentler method. Meeting on

[34] These letters are printed in full in American Historical Association *Re-port,* 1896, I, 660-703.

[35] The instruction is in *Shirley Correspondence,* II, 367. The date of ar- rival of Johnson's letter is in the indexes of the Board of Trade, Ind. 8328.

March 29, the cabinet decided upon Shirley's immediate recall as governor.[36] Fox drafted a short, blunt letter ordering him to England "as soon as you shall receive this Letter from Colonel Webb", on the ground that he would be able to give very useful lights and information to the king on American matters.[37]

It was now imperative that Webb get away at once. The Admiralty orders were again changed. Webb went to Plymouth in the *Nottingham,* thence to Falmouth in the *Gosport,* where he caught the *General Wall* packet on April 13 to New York. The Royal American officers also went by packet. As for the troops, who were ready to sail as soon as the transports arrived, they were put under Abercromby, for whom instructions like Webb's in every particular were signed on April 1. Two days after Webb left Falmouth, Abercromby and the transports sailed from Plymouth with a fair wind. This whole series of causes and events explains and partially justifies the reasons why Webb replaced Shirley, Abercromby replaced Webb, and Loudoun replaced Abercromby, as commander in chief in America in June and July—a procession that appeared ridiculous to colonials and has been described by the most recent narrator of these events, more mildly than by his predecessors, as "a classic

[36] Cabinet minute, Mar. 29, 1756, from the Holland House papers, Ilchester, *Henry Fox, First Lord Holland,* I, 320-2.

[37] Loudoun was given copies of the intercepted letters and urged to discover the identity of Pierre Fidele. He never got any further than learning from Benjamin Franklin that the Allen mentioned in them was a Nova Scotia recruiting officer and that George Croghan seemed a likely person. Once, indeed, he thought that he was on the right track. He learned that a Wall Street merchant, VanHorn, while on a business trip to Philadelphia, had heard a stranger making enquiries in a coffee house there about the decoy packet left, in the name of Pierre Fidele, in the port house at New York. VanHorn described the stranger, a tall, black man, in a red coat, with a sword. Just before he left for Philadelphia, Loudoun got from Captain Kennedy a personal description of George Washington. "A man about 6

example of the absurdities of which the Newcastle ministry was capable.''[38]

Only the most important elements in American preparations have been considered, but they are enough to illustrate the nature of British administration in its unre-
formed days. In January the inner cabinet had decided to
send two regiments to North America, to raise another
regiment in Pennsylvania and adjacent colonies, and to
give to a new commander in chief greater authority than
his predecessors had enjoyed. In February the military
members of the government had proposed to recruit a
thousand more men in England and Scotland for the first
two regiments, and to employ a British provision contractor. With these five major divisions of preparations
the administrative departments of the greatest colonial
power of the eighteenth century concerned themselves.
Handicapped by fear of the French army at Boulogne, by
bitter disagreements in the ministry, and by their own
traditional methods, they were not able to supersede
Shirley on American shores until June 10, or to land reinforcements at New York until June 17, or to permit Loudoun to begin his command until July 23, or to land the
additional recruits and all the stores and paraphernalia
of war until the middle of August. In minor details also
they moved through an elaborate maze of system, a com-

foot high of a black complection black hair which he . . . wore in a Bag,
looks like a Furrener, a Strang Man . . . The colonel at that time wore his
uniform which was blue faced with red and laced.'' When Kennedy met him,
Washington had just returned from visiting Shirley at Boston. Since the
writer of the intercepted letters was someone in the southern colonies whô
commanded a large force of troops and knew more of campaign plans than
the ministry itself, there was enough in all this to raise Loudoun's immediate suspicions. But after he reached Philadelphia, either a single talk with
Washington, or a single conversation with Dinwiddie, was enough to convince him that he had not got the right man. He doesn't mention the matter
again in his diary. HM 1717, vol. 1, January 1, March 26, 1757.

    [38] H. L. Osgood, *American Colonies in the Eighteenth Century*, IV, 382.

plicated arrangement of balances and checks, each designed at one time or another in the past to prevent corruption or to assure an equalizing of powers, but serving in the mass to clog the wheels of routine beyond belief. Under such a government England undertook offensive war in America in 1756.

Loudoun's notebooks show how he shouldered the task of unifying and concentrating the attention of departments on American preparations. His ignorance of administrative channels and his fear of prolonging the delays by applying to the wrong people made him hesitate to interfere in February, but in March and April he overcame such scruples. But though he called upon Anson, Newcastle, and Halifax at various times, and though he was constantly in touch with Barrington, he acted always after consultation with Cumberland. Together, Cumberland and Loudoun drew up memorials to the Treasury and the Ordnance, and settled many details. Loudoun thus became one of the channels by which Cumberland exercised influence in affairs in England. But since his conversations with Cumberland dealt also with problems that might arise in America, Loudoun became in a very special sense Cumberland's appointee as commander in chief in America. His conception of the office, its duties and powers, approached as close to Cumberland's ideas as he could make it. By the very nature of the circumstances which sent him to America, Loudoun was to consider himself primarily responsible to the captain general and not to the secretary of state. His fortunes at the outset intermingled with those of his military superior.

No general in England or on Continental service wielded the power which the commander in chief in America possessed. Slow as the process may have been, in the end every department, with certain definitely named limitations, transferred its authority in America to Loudoun. He issued all warrants for the payment of money; he authorized the issuing of arms and stores from the Ordnance Office in America; he appointed officers to every vacancy except that of colonel; he reviewed court martial findings; he supervised the superintendency of Indian affairs; and he gave orders to the naval officers on the interior lakes. He was therefore the representative for military affairs in America of the king, the Ordnance Board, the War Office, the Treasury, and to some extent, the Admiralty. He was England's military government extended to the colonies.

Nearly absolute in such power as England could give him over the army, Loudoun exercised in relation to the civil governments of North America an ambiguous authority. More than a commander of the army alone, he was considerably less than a civil viceroy. He was empowered to ask the colonies for recruits, money, quarters, and transport, and to request the aid of provincial troops; but he could not compel them to grant his requests. All of these colonies were still jealous of one another, separate and distinct, and five of the most centrally located, with sixty per cent of the total North American population, were by their charters removed from the direct control of the Crown. According to the theory of the revised Braddock plan, upon these colonies still was to fall the chief burden of the war in men, whether as recruits for the regular army or as provincial troops, though the British government was prepared to support the total cost of feeding them and part of the expense of raising them. In his efforts to unite these colonies for military purposes, Loudoun was therefore constrained to exert as far as possible the discretionary powers in his commission. How far he could succeed depended upon his own tact no less than upon the support he received from England, and his career in America is largely the story of his attempt to translate into reality the rather nebulous implications of that commission.

On May 17 Loudoun left London in his chariot, accompanied by his close friend, Major John Young of the Royal Americans. Three days later he boarded the *Nightingale* at Spithead, with Young; Captain McAdam, his aide de camp; Thomas Pownall, his "Secretary Extraordinary"; John Appy, his secretary; Dr. Richard Huck, a surgeon of the general hospital; and seventeen servants, including a "matter de Hottell", a "vallet de Chamber", a cook, a groom, a coachman, a postilion, footmen, helpers, and two women, one of them, Jean Masson, his mistress. He had wound up his personal affairs in London, signing a settlement of his estate with reversion of heirs, and coming to satisfactory arrangements with his lady friends. On May 22 the *Nightingale* left the Lizard in a gale, and for a few days made an average of ten knots. Then calm weather, followed by fog, stretched the voyage into a two months' passage.

Loudoun spent much time on the ship in culling from the notebooks he had kept in London all the memoranda and advices of importance, and copying them into a single small book for convenient reference. In addition he drew up a long series of queries and memoranda relating to the situation in America. An excerpt from the queries he planned to put to Shirley gives the general tenor:

A copy of all contracts made by M G Shirley
 What provisions contracted for by M G Shirley
   Of what parties? species? At what price? Where is the grand magazine? What has been issued to the troops? What to Oswego? What to William Henry? What to Fort Edward? What to other forts? In what proportions to each man? What remains in store?
 What advance given to the contractors? What payments

made to him since? What due him now? In what shape can
the remainder be given over to the Treasury contractor?

Similar notes, as detailed, cover the subjects of boats,
wagons, roads, garrisons, barracks, forage, hospitals, artillery, Nova Scotia, the orders given by Webb and Abercromby, the condition of affairs at Albany, and the latest
intelligence of French movements. Thus did this master
of army paper work, this general of the pen, lay his plans
for operations in a country which had never known a well-
ordered campaign. On July 22 the *Nightingale* lay off
Sandy Hook, and the next morning, at four o'clock, Loudoun landed at New York in the pilot boat. Peter Wraxall
saw him that same morning and was favorably impressed.
"His Countenance is full of Candor, his Eyes Sprightly
& good Humoured, he is short, strong made & seems disposed & fit for Action, he lets himself down with great
ease and affability."[39]

[39] *Sir William Johnson Papers*, II, 515.

CHAPTER III

PROVINCIAL TROOPS

On June 7, while Loudoun was still at sea, Webb landed at New York from the packet. He sent off his letters to Shirley at Albany, planning to follow them by the 12th. But when he heard that Abercromby and the fleet were lying fifty leagues off the coast, he decided to await his superior's arrival, and so accomplished none of the tasks set forth with such detail in his instructions. On the 16th Abercromby anchored with all but two of the transports, and four days later, with Webb, he sailed up the Hudson. On the 25th he assumed command at Albany.

There Abercromby found a curiously involved situation. A provincial army of some seven thousand men occupied the forts to the northward. It represented the combined forces of New England and New York, and its commander, General John Winslow, was acting under commissions granted him by the governors of Massachusetts, Connecticut, and New York. This army did not owe its creation to the instructions in Fox's letter of March 13 to the governors, asking them to raise troops for joint service with regulars, for Webb had not forwarded the copies of that letter until his arrival. Instead, it had been brought together by Shirley's driving zeal. In the previous December, when laying plans for the campaign of 1756, Shirley had undertaken the preparation of two expeditions. One, to be composed of regulars, was to attack Fort Frontenac; the other, a wholly provincial force, was to march against Crown Point. He met some resistance

from the Massachusetts assembly, which, still in debt
from the expenditures of 1755, hesitated to assume again
the burden of maintaining troops. But in the midst of its
deliberations Holderness's letter promising reimbursement for the expenses of the last year arrived, and on the
strength of that promise it decided to accede to Shirley's
request.[1] Other New England governments followed the
lead of Massachusetts. Having the upper hand, the assembly was very careful to make sure that the men it
voted and equipped should remain part of a strictly provincial force. It named the officers, and appointed a committee of war to control and supervise the making the
contracts and expenditures, just as it had done in 1755.
Neither as governor nor as commander in chief was
Shirley permitted to take much part. The committee of
war gave out contracts for supplies, some of them to
members of the committee itself, and others to leading
members of the council and assembly.[2] The assembly
limited the territory within which the army was to serve,
framed an act for its governance, and made Shirley agree
that its commander should be a gentleman from among
themselves. Since Shirley's plans were dependent upon
the pleasure of the assembly, he was forced, when dealing
with it, to sink as far as possible his military office in his
office as governor. He issued Winslow's commission
under the great seal of the province, signed it as governor, and had it countersigned by the secretary of the
province.[3] But remembering that he did exercise au-

[1] General Court to William Bollan, March 10, 1756, Massachusetts Archives, Letters, vol. 55.

[2] Contracts were made, for example, with Andrew Oliver and John Erving
of the council, with John Murray of Rutland, Stephen Hall of Medford,
James Otis of Barnstaple, and Thomas Hubbard, the speaker of the assembly.
Massachusetts Archives, Miscellaneous, Pecuniary Military, vol. 136.

[3] Winslow's commission from Shirley is in Winslow's Journal in the
Massachusetts Historical Society; his commission from Governor Hardy of

thority as a British commander in chief, he tried to leave a loophole of ambiguity. In the final clause of the document, which ran in similar provincial commissions, "yourself to observe and follow, such orders and instructions as you shall from time to time receive from me or the Commander in chief of this province for the time being, or other your superior officer", he omitted the key words "of this province". In his instructions to Winslow, which were secret, he defined more precisely what he had in mind: "as you shall at any time hereafter receive from me or the Commander in Chief for the time being of all His Majesty's forces raised or to be raised in North America."[4] Shirley and Winslow, then, were the only men aware of the construction which could be placed on Winslow's commission. To every one else the provincial army was exactly like all other provincial armies, raised in accordance with the conditions imposed by assemblies, independent, owning obedience to no one except a commander who was himself responsible only to the governments which had commissioned him.

Abercromby was thus confronted with a force obviously ready to fight on the same side with him, but removed by the terms of its raising from his jurisdiction.

A second element enhanced the delicacy of the situation. If Winslow had interpreted his commission to mean that he was subject to Abercromby's orders and had united his command with the four British regiments then in eastern New York, he would have changed the status of his army in two respects. According to the first article of the nineteenth section of the Rules and Articles of

New York, July 17, in the Public Record Office, Treas. 1: 368; from Governor Fitch of Connecticut in the *Collections* of the Connecticut Historical Society, XVII, hereafter cited as *Fitch Papers*, I, 202. Neither Wentworth of New Hampshire nor Hopkins of Rhode Island wrote separate commissions, but ordered their field officers to put themselves under Winslow's command.

4 *Shirley Correspondence*, II, 424.

War, a provincial force serving with regulars ceased to be governed by colonial disciplinary measures, but became subject to the Mutiny Act. This meant to the provincial soldier dread punishments and ruthless death sentences for minor offences, the more terrible because he was ignorant of British army justice and a prey to exaggerated rumor.[5] In the second place, and according to the second article of the same section of the Rules and Articles of War, provincial field officers serving in conjunction with regulars lost all rank as such and were reduced to the status of junior captains. Winslow himself would have been subject to the orders of the youngest captain in the British army. This was the real crux of the matter. Colonels and majors who had marched away in all the pomp of their new-found regimentals were liable to sink to the level of their own company commanders. It is wrong to assume, as has often been done, that the British government deliberately created a situation so galling to provincial pride. In its plans laid in 1754 and in January, 1756, the British ministry had no thought of using provincial troops in large numbers. It expected that only a few scattered companies might be joined to Braddock's forces. Cumberland's attention was called to the possibility of disputes over rank by an altercation between the captains of the South Carolina independent companies in Virginia and the Virginian officers.[6] Since he had faced the same problem earlier in the year when regulars joined East India company troops, he adopted the principle he had applied there: all officers not holding British

----

[5] The clause extending British military law to provincial troops serving with regulars was added to the Mutiny Act of 1754, as paragraph seventy-five. A precedent existed from the preceding year, when parliament extended the Mutiny Act to cover East India company troops serving with regulars.

[6] Fox (then secretary at war) to Captain Demeré, Aug. 25, 1754, C.O. 324: 38, p. 428.

commissions were to rank below regular officers of the same rank. But he feared lest in America assemblies take the opportunity to send their few companies to the field under colonels and majors, and he therefore so phrased his order that while provincial captains and inferior officers took post below regulars of like rank, provincial field officers had no rank whatever.[7] It was not Cumberland's fault if provincial assemblies, raising large bodies of troops on their own initiative, ran foul of orders designed to meet another case.

The stage was set for trouble before Abercromby's arrival. If Shirley's original plans had been followed, and the regulars of the 44th, 48th, 50th and 51st had proceeded against Fort Frontenac in the spring, the only difficulty, as in 1755, would have been one of transportation and supply. The somewhat questionable device Shirley had utilized to get a provincial force into the field would have proved successful. But by May he came to the conclusion that the western expedition was unwise, and advised a council of war to employ the 44th and 48th in conjunction with the provincials against Crown Point. In his last month of office Shirley faced the question: how could he, as a British commander in chief, give orders for union to a provincial army expressly created to be independent of his orders? His efforts to solve it did not get far. Apparently he planned to let matters take their course, and if any crisis arose when Winslow actually engaged the French, to use the emergency as an excuse for

---

[7] Paper delivered to Sir Thomas Robinson by Colonel Napier, Oct. 11, 1754, Additional MSS. 32,737, f. 137. With this draft as a basis the sign manual order regulating rank was framed (*New Jersey Archives*, 1st series, VIII, part 2, 29) and incorporated in the Articles of War. In 1744, when Shirley sent to Nova Scotia four companies of Massachusetts troops to serve with the 40th there, Lieutenant Colonel Mascarene adopted the same arrangement (*Shirley Correspondence*, I, 122-124, 134, 157; *The Northcliffe Collection*, p. 29).

his intervention with the regulars.[8] He may not have realized how delicate matters were, thinking that, as in the past, he could minimize the rigor of the Articles of War. For no trouble had arisen in Braddock's army, where the highest provincial officer present was a captain. Nor had Shirley had difficulty in 1755 with the officers of the New Jersey regiment, for the New Jersey assembly expressly put it under his command, and Shirley, at the distant outpost of Oswego, had so far disregarded the rules about rank as to permit Colonel Schuyler to take post at councils of war before British majors.[9] No regular troops had been present with Johnson in 1755, though Captain Eyre of the 44th served the expedition as engineer. Only in Nova Scotia did trouble arise. Winslow and George Scott, acting as lieutenant colonels of two New England battalions raised by direct order of the secretary of state and paid from England, joined with regulars under Monckton. In the instructions which Lieutenant Governor Lawrence signed for Monckton, he ordered that in case the latter were incapacitated the command should pass to Winslow, at that time a half-pay captain from Shirley's broken regiment of 1748, provided he remained a captain in the British army, and that otherwise it should pass to Scott, a captain in the 40th, "and so on to the eldest officer by commission actually in His Majesty's service." There was considerable friction,

---

[8] *Shirley Correspondence*, II, 460, 508.

[9] *New Hampshire Provincial Papers*, VI, 467. *Review of Military Operations in America* (1757), p. 74. Shirley may have considered himself justified in this breach of the Articles of War by the fact that he had appointed Schuyler to be lieutenant colonel of one of two regular regiments which he thought he had been authorized to raise in addition to his own 50th and the two Nova Scotia battalions. He had planned the Nova Scotia troops on his own initiative, and when official confirmation came, he interpreted it as a fresh order. He did not correct his error until December, 1755, *Shirley Correspondence*, II, 347.

and Scott actually brought Captain Hill of the 45th to a court martial for refusing to obey his orders.[10] But the junction had been made, fairly successfully, and Shirley might easily have disregarded the unique nature of the Nova Scotia battalions and treated it as a precedent. Never having commanded regiments from England in the field, he had no experience with the tempers of such lieutenant colonels as Thomas Gage of the 44th and Ralph Burton of the 48th. He hoped the combination of offices in his own person would decrease friction,[11] and so bequeathed the problem to his successors.

Abercromby soon discovered the dangers in enforcing his authority as new commander in chief. Any junction which changed the basis upon which men were raised, he learned from provincial officers, would automatically release them from their enlistments, and would also make it difficult to levy them in the future. At first he forebore to press the point, expecting Loudoun's arrival early in July, but when three weeks had passed, and Loudoun had not appeared, he saw himself faced with the need of making a decision upon the summer campaign, and chiefly upon the use to be made of the king's troops. Four regular regiments could not remain idle. Though a council of war of regular officers on July 20 urged him not to force the issue with the provincials, and though a temporary commander in chief might well have been forgiven for leaving to his superior the ticklish decision upon which might hang the fate of the campaign, Abercromby set aside the advice of his subordinates. In a formal letter to Winslow he demanded to know whether the provincial officers would permit a union. The provincial field officers

---

[10] A General Court martial at Halifax, Jan. 10, 1757, W.O. 71: 44.

[11] When Burton asked Shirley in May if the provincials would obey the King's officers, Shirley replied that they would obey *him*. Extract from a letter from a general officer in America, G.D. 8: 95.

thereupon held a "grand debate" of their own, ten colonels, eleven lieutenant colonels, and ten majors. They maintained a resolute stand, that if junction meant loss of their rank, a "dissolution of the army" would follow. They also implied that the abandoning of the expedition against Fort Frontenac would prejudice the success of their own expedition by permitting the French to reinforce Crown Point. From this clause, a definite attempt to dictate to a commander in chief the conduct of his campaign, ten provincial officers dissociated themselves.

A wiser man than Abercromby would have been puzzled to know what to do. There he was, at the beginning of a campaign, with three thousand regulars and nine field officers who had no better employment than guarding the posts between Albany and Saratoga and waiting to see whether, if the provincials attacked and were beat back, they might think it wise to summon relief. So little faith had Abercromby in the abilities of the provincials, who lay between him and Canada, that he feared to divide his own force lest he leave New York undefended. Meanwhile Winslow's officers, supremely confident in God and themselves and determined that no regulars should steal the credit they were going to reap, slowly got up their supplies and taught their privates, some of them still arriving in July, such principles of warfare as they knew. One favorite story made the rounds of the camp; in Winslow's boyhood an ancient Indian king, when asked whether Canada would ever surrender, had solemnly placed his hand on the future general's head and prophesied, "No takum Canada till this littel boy takum."

At this point, the last day of July, Loudoun arrived at Albany. He took up at once the challenge to his authority. Assuming as a matter of course that his command included the provincials, he wrote a courteous note to Winslow, who had just reached Fort William Henry for the first time that summer, urging him to return to Albany for a talk; "you shall not find me that unpracticable man you at present seem to apprehend."[12] Winslow himself would have been willing, but his officers, distrusting his ability to stand out against Loudoun, encouraged him to avoid a personal meeting,[13] and he therefore begged to be excused. A peremptory command—"as you choose to have the words in direct terms, though I imagined my former letter was sufficient to answer the purpose, 'tis my orders that you repair immediately to Albany"—then brought him down. The two quickly reached the only agreement possible under the circumstances, for Loudoun too had a string to his bow. He could threaten to withhold a loan to the provincials of additional ordnance and ammunition, without which no attempt on Crown Point stood a chance of success. Winslow finally answered for his officers that they would "act in conjunction with His Majesty's troops and put themselves under the command of your Lordship who is commander in chief, so that the terms and conditions agreed upon and established by the several governments to whom they belong and upon which they were raised be not altered."[14] By this compromise, for the first time in the war, the authority of the commander in chief extended to all men in arms. Plans of the British government had at last, after a fashion, merged with the separate plans of colonial govern-

12 Loudoun to Winslow, July 31, 1756, LO 1377.

13 Major Babcock of Rhode Island to the Committee of War, *Rhode Island Colonial Records*, V, 532. Later that year Loudoun made Babcock a lieutenant in the Royal Americans for his usefulness "to me in breaking the concert of the General and Field officers in the Provincials when they would not submit to be under my command." Note on a list of commissions, 1756, Cumberland Papers.

14 *Journals and Papers of Seth Pomeroy* (1926), pp. 152-3. The New York forces took no part in this dispute, for Governor Hardy in July put them under Abercromby's command.

ments. But the misunderstanding had allowed extremists in the provincial camp a chance to air their views, and it left bitter memories. Loudoun's American career began inauspiciously.

During the next three months the provincials remained at the two upper forts, and the regulars, for the most part, in and about Albany. New England officers could still keep their pride and their independency, for Loudoun, when on the fall of Oswego he forbade Winslow to attempt Crown Point, took on himself the blame for their inaction. They even discovered that harmonious relations might be established with regular officers, that the fears so violently expressed in July were unwarranted.

One thing which somewhat allayed their suspicions was a new regulation concerning their rank. Loudoun himself had been responsible for it, and he brought it to America with him.[15] It made a great concession to provincial general and field officers, a marked contrast with the order of 1754, in giving them rank, if they served with regulars, as eldest captains. Whereas in July, if they had combined, they would have taken orders from some forty officers in the four British regiments, in August they ranked below only the three British generals, four lieutenant colonels, and four majors, all of them professional soldiers of long experience. The "grand debate" of Winslow's officers in July occurred while the order of 1754 was in force. But however sound this new order may have been from a military point of view, the ambitions of provincial officers remained unsatisfied until Pitt's regulation of 1757 gave them all rank immediately below British officers of like

[15] Learning from a conversation with Rutherford in February that the order of 1754 was disliked in America, Loudoun, when in March it was decided to ask governors to raise provincial troops, asked that the order be revised. On May 4 Fox wrote that Cumberland preferred the order of 1754 to remain in force, but that if Loudoun desired an alteration he should speak to the duke personally, LO 1110.

rank. It is worth noting that Pitt's concession, seemingly a most gracious gesture, meant far less than it promised on paper. For at the same time that he gave provincial colonels rank after British, he promoted every lieutenant colonel in the British army serving overseas to be "colonel in America only".[16] After Pitt's order provincial colonels took precedence only over the majors of British regiments, about twenty in all; that was the only real difference it made. The change for which Loudoun was responsible was much more significant as far as its effect in the field was concerned.

Both Loudoun and Winslow went to extremes of courtesy in cultivating the appearances of closest harmony; they tempered their correspondence with mutual expressions of approbation and confidence in one another, and set a high standard of conduct for their subordinates to follow. Loudoun, for example, admitted provincial soldiers to the general hospital at Albany; Winslow asked for, and got, a guard of regulars for a Massachusetts dispatch carrier. When the 48th was joined with such provincials in September as had not gone up to the lake, the united force was put under the command of a single British officer, Ralph Burton, who was cautioned to act gently: "you will command [at Fort Edward], and a man of your temper will ease matters with Lyman." But though such tactics avoided an open breach, and though the officers of the two armies even fraternized on occasion, no one was deceived into believing that sweet accord had been reached. Loudoun held on to the provincials until November because their mere presence served as a safeguard against a suspected French attack, but he resolved in the future to employ such troops upon his own terms only.

[16] *Army Lists*, 1758, 1759. Twenty-one were promoted in 1758, and four more in 1759.

Believing himself to have the authority to arrange with governors for future levies of provincial troops, Loudoun studied Winslow's army with considerable care, how it had been raised, what sort of men composed it, and what use such a force might be to a campaign. He came to certain conclusions about the proper function of provincial troops and in 1757 he tried to give them effect. In 1758 and later years of the war no assembly voted men until a secretary of state's letter appeared; neither Abercromby nor Amherst took the initiative. Loudoun, therefore, was the only commander in chief during the war, who, having weighed the value and shortcomings of provincial troops, could attempt to put his ideas into practice.

It is worth while following Loudoun in his analysis, if we want to reach any conclusions on the vexed question of the part such troops played in the war. He was prejudiced, of course, as were most British officers in the colonies, but with the prejudice of his class and training, and not with the bigotry which is afraid to give honor where it is due. He was a professional soldier, on a professional job, and he looked at Winslow's army with an eye to making it as valuable as possible to his Majesty's service.

No professional soldier could walk through the provincial camp, as did Loudoun and his subordinates, without groaning at the pitiful and unnecessary waste of men on every side. In August there were 843 men sick at Fort Edward, and 600 at Fort William Henry; in June there had been but 253 "invalids". Out of the 5346 men in the army twenty-seven per cent were useless for active service—a proportion low enough compared with casualty returns in the West Indies, but extraordinarily high for the climate of New York. At Fort William Henry they were burying from five to eight a day, and the more they buried, the more "poorly" the rest became. Captain Edmund Wells of Gilead in Hebron recited an experience common to the whole army.

Sept. 12 I am feeling very poorly indeed.

Sept. 17 Counted 92 graves in the burying ground at Ft. Edward in 5 weeks.

Sept. 18 Three more persons buried. I am very ill.

Sept. 19 Too poor to attend divine service. A hundred graves today.

Sept. 21 112 graves. Three of my men deserted.[17]

The reason for such horrors was the appalling lack of any camp sanitation. "The fort stinks enough to cause an infection," wrote Burton of Fort William Henry, "they have all their sick in it. The camp nastier than anything I could conceive, their necessary houses, kitchens, graves and places for slaughtering cattle, all mixed through their encampment."[18] No order to build a hospital was given until August 20, nor was any detail of men assigned to keep the streets and quarters of the camp clean.[19] In very gentle words Loudoun made his suggestions: to open the tents to dry the ground within, to bury all refuse, and to construct a proper slaughter house. "If there are only a few dead, we commonly bury them in front before the colours, but when many, they ought to be removed, as it is a sad sight for the men".[20]

Equally disheartening to a commanding officer who knew the value of a soldier and the difficulty of replacing him was the prevalence of desertion from the provincial army. Their homely punishments—a ride on the wooden horse or drumming out of camp—acted as no deterrent, and courts martial refused to impose more stringent

17 From a manuscript diary in the Connecticut State Library at Hartford.

18 Lieutenant Colonel Ralph Burton to Loudoun, Aug. 5, 1756, LO 1424.

19 This appears from the orderly book of Major Moses Deshon of Colonel Gridley's Massachusetts regiment. It is in the Boston Athenaeum.

20 Loudoun to Winslow, Sept. 4, 1756, LO 1706.

penalties. When in September nearly two hundred men deserted in a body, Winslow asked for permission to hang: "although Hanging among the Americans has never as yet been Practised can't but think a Little is necessary." Loudoun replied in helpless amazement that drumming a deserter out of camp was the least of punishments, that he should be made to enlist for life in the West Indies.[21] Colonial assemblies would not impose severe penalties; Connecticut, for example, pardoned those deserters who returned to service and docked their pay for the vacation.[22] Loudoun believed that when provincials were combined with the British the mere knowledge that they were under the Rules and Articles of War would have its effect, even though an actual execution never took place. He was sensible enough to appreciate the abhorrence in which the ordinary colonial held regular army discipline, and the next year he did his best to mitigate it. In 1757 mixed general courts martial condemned several regulars to death for desertion, but not one provincial. They awarded instead the punishment of the lash, in several cases lessened by the commanding officer. In one case, of a New Yorker who stole an officer's horse to facilitate his escape, a court martial found the death penalty, and left it to Webb, who reviewed the evidence, to pardon the offender. From 1755 to 1758 Shirley alone of all the general officers in America approved a death sentence passed on a provincial soldier.[23] Clearly enough, British martial law in the hands of general offi-

[21] Phineas Lyman of Connecticut, in command at Fort Edward, explained this mass desertion "because some vile fellow suggested if they eat the King's Bread they should become King's Soldiers". Lyman to Loudoun, Oct. 6, 1756, LO 2855.

[22] Connecticut Archives, War, VI, 163.

[23] At Oswego, September 17, 1755, on four New Jersey soldiers, W.O. 71: 128. Ignorant of the common army practice of using the clemency with which commissions invested commanding officers, Shirley leaves the impression that

cers who understood how to use it as threat and not as a basis for penalty only, and appreciated the delicacy of trying provincial soldiers, scarcely justified the fears of Winslow's army.

The most unforgivable thing in the provincial army was its ignorance of the elementary rules of warfare. If provincial officers knew nothing of camp sanitation, they could be excused; John Pringle's classic treatise on army diseases, which was to reform one whole aspect of military life, was then but four years old. If they seemed ignorant of military law, the codes prescribed by their assemblies were to blame. But for officers in charge of men to permit them to fire their guns off carelessly after drill, to wander about casually with unloaded pieces in the woods beyond the fort, where hostile raiding parties continually lurked, to sleep on post without reprimand, to take pot shots at game as they marched along—these things passed Loudoun's comprehension. Few scouting parties went out, and those few liable to needless surprises. Provisions were transported without guard; the ships upon which depended the control of Lake George, the only route by which an enemy could transport cannon, were left undefended. "A Motley Herd, almost every man his own Master and a General", John Watts had called Johnson's army of 1755; and Peter Wraxall had written, "The Officers of the Army with very few Exceptions are utter Strangers to Military Life and most of them in no Respect superior to the Men they are put over, They are like the heads and indeed are the heads of a Mob".[24] Johnson had used the same words in condemning the

he wrote his "Approved" on court martial records without ever scrutinizing the facts therein contained. I have found no instance of Shirley's having changed a sentence, whereas British generals mitigated or pardoned fully as many as they let stand.

[24] Wraxall to Fox, Sept. 27, 1755, Cumberland Papers.

popular choice of officers, who were thereby compelled to support their preëminence ''by unworthy condescensions, and indulgences, subversion of order and of the very existence of the army.''[25]

What these provincial officers needed was knowledge and training. In the future, therefore, Loudoun resolved to ask for provincial troops in easily managed standardized companies of a hundred each, without field officers, so that while avoiding all difficulty over rank, he could supervise the conditions under which men served and could impart to their captains and lieutenants some conception of the business of a soldier.

But far from indulging in any blanket condemnation of provincial troops and their officers, Loudoun tempered his judgment with two important qualifications. It is an easy fashion today to imagine that every colonial was an adept in Indian warfare, or that if they could not all follow a trail with Deerslayer's adeptness at least they knew some tricks of the woods and could take care of themselves. That is a fond delusion. Loudoun would have been only too glad if it had been true, if he could have depended upon colonial woodsmen to provide for his command in America what British troops could not provide —a knowledge of the region and of Indian fighting; the first question he had put to Rutherford in January had been about scouts or rangers. But most of the provincial army came from long settled communities which had never seen an Indian in war-paint; Major Deshon was horrified one day to see Robert Rogers bringing in four scalps. The few men who did know their way in the woods, some of the northern New Yorkers, or western Massachusetts and New Hampshire men, were invaluable, and Loudoun's second point, when he asked assemblies for

[25] Johnson to Lieutenant Governor Phips, Oct. 10, 1755, C.O. 5: 46, p. 841.

troops the next year, was that they furnish, if possible, men like these.

Again, both Loudoun and Abercromby came to the conclusion that Winslow's army did not contain that class of colonials who, though not woodsmen, at least represented the best elements in the community. One provincial army did not necessarily resemble its predecessor; because some stories of the sturdy farmer leaving his plow in the field and springing to his place in the ranks are true ones, there is no reason for supposing that year after year in this war the plow patiently awaited its owner's return. If Abercromby is to be believed, this army of 1756 was made up of the "riff-raff," the "Lowest Dregs of the People, both officers and men", and was a far cry from those "True New England Chips of the Old Block", the men who had taken Louisbourg in '45.[26] The valor of those Louisbourg regiments was grown into a legend; it was in the hope of getting such troops again that Shirley had tried vainly to recreate the conditions and the fervent crusading atmosphere which had brought them out, and that Pitt later threw all questions of cost to the winds and asked for twenty thousand men. Loudoun wanted such men, too, and not the pick-ups who had joined Winslow's army for large bounties and pay. He knew that the "real inhabitants, stout, able men" with lives and properties to defend, were in the militia, and he therefore concluded that if provincial assemblies would actually draft their troops out of the militia and not raise them by enlistment, he would see a better army in the field.

Another point about Winslow's army which provoked Loudoun's impatience was the uncertainty of their numbers. He was never sure how many men there actually were. There were supposed to be 8700; Massachusetts

[26] Extracts from letters of a General Officer in America, August 10, 1756, G.D. 8: 95.

had voted 3500; Connecticut, 2500; New Hampshire and Rhode Island, 500 each; and New York, 1700. They were all to have been at Albany on May 20. But a month later, even after Shirley had authorized impressment from the militia to fill a thousand vacancies, Winslow complained that the Massachusetts contingent still lacked eleven hundred men and was "surprized that we should be the most behind of all". The troops of other colonies were incomplete—Oliver DeLancey found New York companies with but a third of their complement[27]—and Massachusetts refused to fill up its ranks unless other governments filled theirs.[28] On June 5 the army numbered 4170; on June 12, 5201; on June 19, 5971; and on June 26, 6775.[29] A month later the report numbered 6900, but the figure was apparently exaggerated, for Brigadier Dwight of Massachusetts told Loudoun in August that there were only 5000, and other generals put the number as low as 4000. Sir John St. Clair estimated 5870 in July, and with other British officers declared the official reports inaccurate. The next return of August 26 supported their suspicions; it put the total at 5346, of whom 2600 were at Fort William Henry, and 2746 at Fort Edward. This was less than two-thirds of the numbers voted. Loudoun believed that if smaller numbers were voted he might stand a better chance of seeing them all in the field early in the year. The one geographical advantage the British possessed was the early opening of creeks and rivers; it was possible for a British force to appear before Ticonderoga in the spring before the ice had melted in the north. A small and mobile force which would not involve the trans-

---

[27] EM 10,992, the Emmett Collection in the New York Public Library, calendared in *Bulletin*, 1900, p. 447.

[28] Massachusetts Archives, Letters, vol. 55; Military, vol. 75.

[29] These figures are from Winslow's journal in the Massachusetts Historical Society.

portation of too many provisions and supplies—this seemed to Loudoun a primary requisite.

Finally, as Loudoun looked over this sickly, incompetent army, so little redeemed by its few virtues, he shuddered to think of the exorbitant sums it cost. He brought to America, of course, the same scale of labor values as applied in England, and for Massachusetts to pay a private soldier 10¼d. sterling a day as against 8d. for the regular soldier and to repeat annually the large bounties offered for enlisting, seemed sheer waste. Whereas the British soldier's actual pay was only 3d. or 4d., for out of the 8d. allotted by parliament came various stoppages both in England and in America, the provincial got all of his; such charges as in England were met by deductions from the pay both of officers and men were included by the Massachusetts assembly in its estimates for the campaign. This difference in private soldiers' pay, coupled with the illuminating fact that a British officer got more than a provincial, illustrates a divergence between England and the colonies in the ideas of a man's social and economic worth which was the natural result of colonial conditions. The incidental expenses of the provincial army likewise seemed large to Loudoun. The civilian members of the committee of war who had charge of provisioning and supply received more than a colonel; their individual expenses in the field were met in addition. Not only was the allowance of the staple provisions greater for the provincial than for the regular, but he received in addition such luxuries as sugar, ginger, rum, and molasses. His marching allowance on the road was thrice as much as the regular's, and after a single summer's service he received outright his hatchet, blanket, and knapsack. If he carried one of the king's musquets— and Shirley had practically exhausted the ten thousand stand of arms sent him the previous winter in arming the provincials—he expected to take that home with him, too. The contracts for such items were rich plums for those who got them; provincial merchants in New England seldom engaged in any venture as large and profitable as the spending of the comparatively vast sums voted by an assembly of which, often, they were members. Surveying the quality of the troops and the wastefulness of their equipment and supply, British officers decided that the whole affair was "a mere Job, chiefly calculated by Mr. Shirley . . . to put money in the leading men's pockets and thereby keep up a Party in the four Provinces." Shirley's advance out of British contingent funds of a loan of £44,592 12s. 1d. to three New England governments to enable them to carry on their preparations increased the suspicion that Winslow's army was designed quite as much to fatten the purses of Shirley's supporters as to march against Crown Point.[30] Such extravagance, favoring the civilian rather than the army, would have seemed to British officers bad enough if it fell only upon colonial taxpayers; it was far less to be forgiven when parliament, by its vote of £115,000 in January to the northern governments, assumed a share. Loudoun knew no way to stop it except by having smaller numbers of troops, fewer officers, and by assuming himself as much control as possible.

The ideal provincial force, in Loudoun's estimation, would be one so small that its supply would not clog his transport service and so complete that he would know upon what numbers he could depend. It would be made up of responsible men who were fighting for their homes and of woodsmen who could undertake the tasks for which the British army was unfitted. It would be con-

[30] Memorial of the Paymaster General upon the Deputy Paymaster General's Account in North America, Pay Office, Oct. 6, 1756, Treas. 29: 32, p. 408. *Shirley Correspondence*, II, 556.

stantly under the supervision of British field officers who could enforce British standards of camp management and discipline and weld it into an effective fighting unit. Such a provincial army would not exhaust the supply of "loose, idle men" available as recruits for the regular army, nor would it add to the British debt, through parliamentary reimbursement, a sum out of proportion to its military value.

CHAPTER IV

RECRUITING THE REGULAR ARMY

THOSE good Americans of today who refer with pride to their ancestor in the last French and Indian war and go on to pour their scorn upon the British regular should make very sure of the facts in their particular case. They may be praising and condemning one and the same man. For in the first two years of that war, if eight thousand colonials wore the provincial blue, nearly an equal number glittered in the red coat and pipeclay of His Majesty's regular army. Such men did not do less than their share in guarding their homes, or, if they fought through the war, in conquering Canada; if anything, they probably did more. They certainly saw more action than their neighbors who filed out for a five months campaign with large bounties and high pay. What provincial corps, unless perhaps the Virginian, could in its service match the record of the 44th, which ranged from Virginia to Montreal? The 44th came to be almost as much of an American corps as the Virginian; three-fourths of the men in its ranks, by 1756, were neither Irish nor English, but men enlisted in the colonies. The same is true of the 47th, the 48th, the 50th and 51st, and to a less extent of the 40th, the 45th, and the 60th. But it is decidedly not true of the other regiments sent to America in 1756 or in later years of the war. This difference in the composition of British regiments is another mark of the great change in British policy between 1754 and 1757. Let us look into the question of where and how the British army in America found its men, and why its policy changed.

It will be remembered how in 1754 the ministry, casting about for troops and eager to tap the numbers of men of fighting age in the colonies—two hundred thousand is a conservative estimate[1]—eschewed Townshend's idea of British-paid American regiments because they seemed untrustworthy and chose instead Cumberland's proposal to fill up in America the skeleton ranks of British regiments. Briefly, these were the essentials of the plan. The two regiments with Braddock, the 44th and 48th, were to recruit five hundred each to complete them to war strength of a thousand each. Shirley's and Pepperrell's, the 50th and 51st, were to be reraised, a thousand each. The three regiments in Nova Scotia, the 40th, 45th, and 47th, were ordered completed to a like number; in their case that meant thirteen hundred men, for the 47th was on the low footing of the Irish establishment and numbered in November, 1755, only 339. In 1755, therefore, the colonies were expected to provide forty-three hundred men, and in addition regiments hoped to make up their normal losses by death, desertion, and discharge. The next year the creation of the Royal American regiment increased that total to eighty-three hundred. The independent companies, four in New York and three in South Carolina, were also to be kept filled. Including the 35th and 42d, Loudoun in 1756 should have commanded a paper force of 13,696, of whom two-thirds of the privates, besides replacements, were meant to be colonials.

These orders released a flood of recruiting parties upon nearly every town and village from New Hampshire to the Carolinas. Americans had known before the desultory

[1] Dinwiddie in 1740 estimated the number of "fighting men" at 135,000 (Account of the Plantations, April, 1740, C.O. 323: 10). The report of the Board of Trade on the military state of the colonies, 1756, estimates the number in all but three of the continental colonies (W.O. 34: 101, f. 21). That estimate is higher than in the brief report of August, 1755 (*New-York Colonial Documents*, VI, 993).

efforts of the New York independent companies, but never had they seen recruiting as the Old World had long known it, eager subalterns marching their small detachments into town, there wheeling into line, beating the drums, and setting out to accost all likely men between the ages of eighteen and forty. How should a poor lad up from the country, or some indentured apprentice with years in his term left to serve, or some dockyard hanger-on without home or property, resist the temptation to share in such pomp, the persuasive arguments of an old-line sergeant, the flash of gold and silver in his hands, the privilege of drinking a health with him? The recruiting sergeant, at least until the autumn of 1756, was in his element; America was a recruiting paradise. Whereas at home he had to move with utmost circumspection lest he run foul of the stringent and detailed legal restrictions which the Mutiny Act placed upon him, in the colonies he could practise the craft of his trade as practised nowhere else except in the German states. He could make men drunk and lug them off; he could twist any sort of reply into an affirmation and make it good by threats or violence. For the articles in the Mutiny Act which dealt with the relations between civilians and recruiting officers did not at first apply to the colonies; the Mutiny Act covered only the discipline of the regular army and such provincial troops as were joined with regulars. Civilians had no sure legal redress. Here and there a magistrate might entertain a civil action, usually for debt, against the recruit to take him out of army's hands, or for trespass or breach of the peace against the officer. Such civil suits, and the occasional imprisonment of an officer or sergeant were deemed nuisances, and the officer was loud in his complaint, but the general impression is that the absence of legal restrictions worked more in his favor than against him.

Civil suits were especially frequent in Pennsylvania and Maryland over the enlisting of indentured servants. Recruiting officers found it easy to persuade such men; they were "glad to goe into the Army to get rid of their slavery and make the best soldiers we get in America, not being as yet debauched and much hardier than the Natives."[2] Every regiment had parties at work in the two provinces. The masters, of course, who had paid for the transportation of their servants and looked upon them as a kind of property, regarded recruiting officers as thieves. They staged a protest so violent that it threatened to become an insurrection; in Maryland Sharpe could see no way to keep the peace except by using "an act of power", and in Pennsylvania one sergeant was killed by a mob.[3] Braddock had permitted his officers to take servants; Shirley forbade them. But in January, 1756, he revoked his order, considering it more important to fill the regiments than to respect property rights.[4] He recognized the point of law involved, whether the King's right to the service of his subjects was not prior to any obligation they might have incurred, and he hoped the courts would settle it. In Maryland matters were temporarily smoothed over by the attorney general's opinion that masters had a right to lodge actions and that the governor could not discharge a suit begun to recover property. While the question remained unsettled recruiting officers got their men and took their chances; a story circulated that one officer, pretending to yield to the complaints of masters, let his own sergeant be jailed, but "filled his pocket with dollars, and that night the sergeant enlisted in gaol seventy servants."[5]

[2] Memorandum got by Loudoun from Rutherford, February, 1756, LO 795.
[3] *Pennsylvania Archives*, II, 578.
[4] *Maryland Archives*, VI, 218; *Pennsylvania Archives*, II, 417, 587.
[5] Webb to Loudoun, April 10, 1756, LO 1034.

These things go far to explain the somewhat surprising success of recruiting in the first two years of the war. The colonist's traditional dislike for the British army did not seem to keep him from succumbing to a recruiting officer's enthusiasm; Cumberland's hopes were substantially vindicated. Take such regimental returns as are available, remembering that such returns, except for the 50th, are not stuffed muster rolls, but of effective men only.[6] Braddock arrived in Virginia with a thousand men in the 44th and 48th; on June 8, at Wills Creek, they numbered 1454. They returned from the Monongahela with 1082 privates, having lost 372. In the next eleven months they recruited enough to make up their losses and to give them by June, 1756, a total of seventeen hundred; a special recruiting report of August in that year credits them with having raised no less than 1562 men, and the figure agrees closely enough with the general returns. The three Nova Scotia regiments, by October, 1756, had raised their numbers to 2718; the 47th alone, reported Robert Monckton, had enlisted over nine hundred men, and the three together about nineteen hundred. The 50th and 51st were thirteen hundred when they encamped at Oswego in 1755; the hardships of the winter reduced them by a half, but by June, 1756, they had made up their losses and numbered 1260. They recruited some fourteen hundred men in 1755, and five hundred in 1756. The new Royal American regiment had 1050 men in August, 1756, and before the year was over had enlisted about five hundred more. These figures include replacements; the normal losses by death, desertion, and discharge were annually about fifteen per cent for troops in New York, and twice that estimate for troops in the severe climate of Nova Scotia.[7] All together

---

[6] Braddock's and Loudoun's returns are in the Loudoun Papers and the Cumberland Papers, and are fairly complete. There are few for Shirley's administration.

[7] For example, an average force of 3800 men, in the six months from June,

some seventy-five hundred men were enlisted by British regiments in two years, a very creditable showing. The British Isles, up to September, 1756, had furnished but forty-five hundred men for the war in America.[8]

Compare these figures with those of 1757. In that year only twelve hundred men were recruited in the colonies; eleven thousand came from England. These were not only fresh regiments, the 22d, the seven sent by Pitt for the attack on Louisbourg, the two battalions of Highlanders raised expressly for American service;[9] but also thirty-six hundred men, drafts from the army in Great Britain or Ireland, or Highland levies, to be used as recruits for the regiments in America. The 22d and the first twelve hundred drafts were sent by Cumberland's direction;[10] the others by Pitt's. This is the striking change in British policy; from using Americans to recruit British regiments, the ministry came to depend almost wholly upon the British Isles.

1756, to January, 1757, lost 150 by death, 85 by desertion, and 88 by discharge, a total of 323. In the following year, for the same period, an average of 18,500 men lost 1727.

[8] This figure includes the original numbers in the 44th and 48th, and in the three Nova Scotia regiments; also the 35th and 42d, which, including the British recruits, 900 strong, who arrived in August, totalled 1854.

[9] The seven regiments sent by Pitt were a battalion of the 1st or Royals, a thousand men; and the 17th, 27th, 28th, 43d, 46th, and 55th, seven hundred each. They arrived completed to full strength.

The usual British regiment in America contained ten companies of a hundred privates each; a few, ten companies of seventy each. A battalion also had a thousand men, but it had no colonel of its own. Fraser and Montgomery of the two Highland battalions were lieutenant colonels; Loudoun was colonel in chief of the Royal American regiment, and each of its four battalions had a colonel commandant. But the terms regiment and battalion were often used interchangeably.

[10] The cabinet originally designed these twelve hundred drafts for Nova Scotia regiments, but the success of the Nova Scotian recruiting parties in 1756 made it unnecessary to send more than three hundred men there, and these Loudoun found in the remnants of the 50th and 51st, which were broken early in 1757. Minutes, July 20, Oct. 1, 1756, Additional MSS. 32,-997, ff. 5, 52.

The ministry's motive becomes apparent from a study of the returns. Even in 1755 and 1756, when some ten thousand men were enrolled in nine regiments during twenty months, that number was insufficient to keep the ranks complete. In the autumn of 1756 the 44th and 48th lacked 427 men of their complete strength; the three Nova Scotia regiments, 402; and the 50th and 51st, 700. Creditable as the raising of recruits in America may have been, and it more than met Cumberland's expectations of 1755, it was not enough to offset the losses of campaigning, the deaths at the Monongahela and Oswego, the slow drain by sickness, desertion, and discharge.

Nor throughout the remainder of the war was it possible to keep the regiments full.[11] Recruiting in America continued. In 1756 men were offered additional inducements: the promise of two hundred acres of land in New Hampshire, New York, or Nova Scotia. Loudoun lowered the physical standards. Whereas Nova Scotia parties in 1755 looked only for "straight, well-made, broad-shouldered, strong-limbed" men of "healthy complexion", five feet six inches in height at least, later parties were instructed to take any man "free from Ruptures, Convulsions, and Infirmitys, and fit for service", five feet five inches, "except growing lads whom they may take at Five feet four inches." But in January, 1758, twenty-one battalions lacked 1710 of their full strength; in October, twenty-three battalions and ten companies lacked 3280; in 1759 twenty-five battalions and seven companies needed 4492 to complete their ranks; and in March, 1760, the same number, 4750.[12] In October, 1760, Amherst reported that nearly seven thousand men were wanting to

11 Except the Scottish regiments, for which detachments of fresh Highland recruits kept arriving.

12 The figures for the latter years of the war are from a comprehensive account of the forces in W.O. 17: 1489.

complete, and new establishments for all the regiments in America were signed cutting down their paper strength by one-fourth. By special instructions from England, Amherst in 1762 tried to raise 4300 men to fill up these regiments, but in spite of some aid from colonial assemblies could collect only 670 recruits.[13] That belated revival of the Braddock plan, by ministers who were Pitt's rivals, stood less chance of success than the original.

The experience of one regiment, the Royal American, the last to have any considerable number of colonials in its ranks, emphasizes this change in recruiting. Its successes in the summer of 1756, when its foreign and British officers, having landed fresh from the packet, were given a monopoly in Pennsylvania, had faded away by the winter. Though Loudoun appealed to southern governors for assistance, by January the regiment could muster only eighteen hundred. That figure included Prevost's first detachment of "planters", two hundred and fifty absentees from his second detachment who had been taken prisoner in their passage, and some supernumeraries of the 42d, who remained with their countrymen for service but were paid from Royal American funds.[14] When the 50th and 51st were broken, the 60th got their sergeants, corporals, drums, sixty-two men either in jail, sick, or newly recruited, and 141 deserters. The lion's share of the drafts from Ireland which arrived with O'Farrell's (the

13 Quotas and Numbers raised for Regular Service, Nov. 1, 1762, W.O. 34: 74, f. 170. An appendix to J. C. Webster's edition of *The Journal of Jeffery Amherst*, p. 331, puts the total raised at 788.

14 Prevost's first 170 German recruits gave the names of more than thirty states or cities as their birthplaces, from Hamburg to the "Tirol", from "Elsas" and Worms to Bohemia, Poland, and Austria (LO 1607). They sailed from Hamburg the 4th of June, properly insured, complied with the Navigation Acts by getting clearances from the customs officers in the Orkney Islands, with Cumberland's assistance, and arrived in New York the 27th of August. The English and Scottish officers of the regiment thought them a poor lot. John Young wrote to Loudoun of "12 strange little lads they call

22d) in December went to swell its ranks, but by April it could muster only 2878 out of its four thousand men. With the second detachment of drafts, in the autumn of 1757, it became as nearly complete as it ever was, thirty-nine hundred. But by January, 1759, it had shrunk again to thirty-two hundred. Thus the splendid scheme that was to bring Pennsylvania Germans thronging to enlist under men who spoke their own tongue ended in ignominious failure. This regiment, destined to become one of the most famous in the army, began its career with a weird collection, a sprinkling of Germans from the Continent, one-fourth colonials, and the majority the "refuse of the army in Ireland".

How shall we account for these altered conditions of American recruiting which compelled the ministry to surrender one of the most cherished tenets of the Braddock plan and instead to support the war with regiments and drafts from the British Isles? It is not enough to ascribe the change to Pitt. For if the Braddock plan had worked, Pitt would certainly have used it; and even in February, 1756, we have seen that Cumberland took the first steps in altering it by recruiting the 35th and 42d in Great Britain. Nor is it enough to say that some several thousand men were raised in 1755 and 1756 when Shirley, well-known in the colonies, was commander in chief, and that recruiting stopped when Loudoun assumed the command. There is doubtless some unascertainable measure of truth in the implication. But nearly as many men, some eighteen hundred, joined the colors during Braddock's eight months as enlisted during Shirley's ten, and in Loudoun's

---

miners and 10 boys for drums, pray is he to be allowed for such upon the footing of recruits?" This group also included a handful of German protestants, who, first enlisted in the French service, were captured on the high seas, and readily transferred their allegiance to the British.

The Royal American was originally numbered the 62d, but after February, 1757, when the 50th and 51st were broken, it became the 60th.

first half-year the 47th made its phenomenal gains and the Royal Americans garnered their rich harvest. We must look for other causes than one based on personalities alone.

British officers came to agree that one circumstance above all others ruined the chances of recruiting. Year after year they watched recruiting parties struggling to gather in a few score men, while every March and April provincial officers sent out their summons and their promises to amass between ten and twenty thousand. "The vast reward of twelve pounds levie money great pay and full cloaths for eight months service only in the Jersey Provincials has entierly put a stop to recruiting in this province which I think must every way hurt the service", wrote John Stanwix of the Royal Americans.[15] Four months after his arrival Loudoun was writing home that three of his officers had tried for two months in New England without getting one man, because the militia men who were drafted into the provincial army that year had offered ten pounds to anyone who would take their places. In 1760 Amherst could put the same point succinctly, "Men can't be recruited here, owing to the vast bounty money given by provincials." He was probably right. Those men upon whom both the provincial and the regular army in large measure depended, men without ties of home, property, or occupation, the floating elements in a population of over a million, would naturally prefer enlistment in the provincial forces, where they could spend in the winter what they had earned during the campaign, to the arduous service of British regiments. There were no long vacations in the regular army.

For such large provincial levies and such high bounties colonial assemblies were responsible. It is worth while,

[15] Stanwix to Loudoun, April 20, 1757, LO 3407.

therefore, to enquire into their attitude towards regular recruiting. In 1754 the British government had been sanguine enough to hope that they would defray all costs of collecting men; governors had been asked to have three thousand men in readiness for immediate enlistment into four regiments, while the common fund, made up of contributions from each colony, was to be used by the commander in chief for recruiting purposes. It was an illjudged expectation. The governors of Virginia and Maryland assembled 432 men for Braddock to incorporate into the 44th and 48th; Connecticut and Rhode Island raised four hundred for Shirley's.[16] These were all; the rest of the men raised in 1755 came through the slow work of recruiting parties. The common fund did not materialize, for though various colonies voted sums under the name of such a fund, they used it for their own needs, and little of it reached the commander in chief's hands.[17] In the autumn of 1756, when Loudoun urged southern governors to furnish recruits for the Royal Americans, Dinwiddie sent a hundred and twenty and Sharpe a hundred and fifty.[18] These were the last men to

[16] *Maryland Archives*, VI, 157, 165, 186, 189, 192, 208, 211; *Pennsylvania Archives*, II, 401, 412; *Rhode Island Colonial Records*, V, 409, 412; *Colonial Records of Connecticut*, X, 330-331.

[17] *Colonial Records of Connecticut*, X, 331; *Statutes of South Carolina*, IV, 17; *North Carolina Colonial Records*, V, 229 seq.; *Journal of the House of Burgesses of Virginia*, 1754, 226; *Maryland Archives*, VI, 88, 163, 170. Robert Orme, Braddock's aide de camp, is authority for the statement that the only money raised by the provinces which ever passed through Braddock's hands was four thousand pounds, in colonial currency, from the governor of South Carolina, Winthrop Sargent, *History of Braddock's Expedition*, p. 325. Maryland voted Loudoun three thousand pounds, but sent it in the form of eight thousand bushels of wheat, which, when sold, netted only £1,799. Loudoun used it as contingencies. HM 1717, vol. 2, Oct. 4, 1757.

[18] Hening, *Statutes at Large of Virginia*, VII, 61; *Journal of the House of Burgesses*, 1756, 402, 404, 410; 1757, 413; *Dinwiddie Papers*, II, 554, 583, 586; *Maryland Archives*, VI, 489, 491, 497, 524. Virginia voted £8000; Maryland, £3000. The Virginian recruits came from the lowest class of the

be raised for British regiments at colonial expense until
Amherst's intensive recruiting campaign of 1762. Colonial assemblies obviously would not lend their active support to regular army schemes. Nor were they willing to
sit passively by and watch recruiting parties carry away
their young men. We must not accept too readily as
reasons for their attitude the arguments which the Massachusetts assembly sent to its agent in England to use
in opposing the creation of American regiments. Those
arguments disclose too unexpected a concern for Great
Britain's interests. Every young man enlisted in the
British army, so they ran, meant a family lost to the
province, for land was so plentiful that anyone, even
without a farthing, could marry; the population therefore ceased to multiply rapidly, and consequently fewer
British manufactures found a sale. Moreover, Americans
made bad soldiers, for if confined to garrisons or to any
service "they soon grow troublesome and uneasy by reflecting upon their Folly in bringing themselves into a
State of Subjection, when they might have continued free
and independent."[19] There was an earmark of truth in
both these arguments. John Cosnan of the 45th reëchoed
the first by discovering that the "general backwardness"
to the King's service, "encouraged by all sorts of
people", was because "they seem to consider every man,
we enlist, as a real loss to the province, though at the
same time not one in Ten are Natives."[20] And most British officers would have subscribed to the second, for they
always expected to find traces of a "levelling spirit" in

community. Dinwiddie thought them "the most dastardly and inactive mortals he ever met with", while Loudoun wrote, "Of the 120 recruits that
came from Virginia, we have taken 115, though very bad". HM 1717, vol. 3,
Feb. 24, 1757.

[19] Massachusetts General Court to William Bollan, Sept. 26, 1755, *Shirley
Correspondence*, II, 287.

[20] John Cosnan to Colonel Forbes, Jan. 9, 1758, Boston, LO 5377.

their American levies, without going to the extremes of
Governor Lawrence, who thought Americans "unfitt for
the Business of Soldiers, nor are they likely ever to become troops that may be depended upon."[21] But the real
considerations which moved colonial assemblies no agent
would dare to use: not a pride in their population figures,
nor anxiety for the best interests of the British army, but
fear lest their own frontiers remain undefended while
the regulars fought on distant campaigns; ambitions of
their leading men for military glory in the field and commercial profits from provincial contracts; and perhaps
most of all a determined resolve to control as far as they
could the military affairs of their own province. Such
objectives might be gained through the use of provincial
troops, but never if the regular army took complete
charge.

Recruiting began to fall off in the colonies at the same
time that the "Act for the better recruiting His Majesty's Forces on the Continent of North America" began
to receive publicity.[22] The coincidence is close enough to
suggest a connection. The heads of that act had been
drawn up in London by Cumberland, Barrington, and
Loudoun the preceding March. They meant it to serve
two purposes: to protect recruiting officers everywhere
against hot-tempered colonial magistrates, and to settle
the legal point involved in the indentured servant question. To gain the first, the act extended to the colonies
nine sections of the Mutiny Act which defined the legal
procedure of a recruiting party.[23] Henceforth the officer

[21] Lawrence to Loudoun, Oct. 19, 1756, LO 2039. Against such bigoted
statements should be placed Loudoun's opinion that the 44th and 48th were
his best corps.

[22] 29 George II, c. 35. The full title was "Act for the better recruiting
His Majesty's Forces on the Continent of North America and for the better
Regulation of the Army, and preventing Desertion therein".

[23] The first two sections of the act concern indentured servants; the third

in charge had a beating order, often printed, and signed by the commanding officer, formally authorizing him to enlist volunteers and requiring the assistance of all civil officers. When he reached the chief town of a district, he presented this public order to its magistrate before he turned his sergeants and drummers into the streets. Though the acceptance of a recruit was immediately clinched by the payment of part or all of the bounty money, the enlistment was not legal until, in not more than four days or less than twenty-four hours, the recruit made formal attestation before a justice of the peace or other magistrate, "declaring upon the Holy Evangels of Almighty God that he is a Protestant and Hath Duly Inlisted himself a Soldier . . . and has heard the Second and Sixth Articles of War [on mutiny and desertion] and taken the Oath of Fidelity." If the recruit refused to declare, returned his bounty money and paid a fine of twenty shillings, he was to have his liberty. In the second place, the Act permitted indentured servants to be enlisted, any law, custom, or usage to the contrary notwithstanding, and provided that masters should be recompensed for the loss of servants in proportion to the original purchase money. That meant, said Loudoun, that officers were to pay no more for a servant than enough to recompense the master for the remainder of the time he had still to serve, "computing each year equal in the time of his service." "Suppose he was bought for five years, and Ten Pounds paid for him, and that he has served four years of his time, the Justice has no power to determine the price, to be paid by the Recruiting Officer, to be any more than forty Shillings."[24] Though the

---

to the eleventh, inclusive, are, respectively, sections lxvi, lxvii, lx, li, lii, liii, liv, lxxi, and lxxi of the Mutiny Act of 1756, all somewhat abridged. Section twelve is the conclusion.

[24] Loudoun to Colonel Stanwix, Sept. 23, 1756, LO 1885.

act received royal assent in May, and took effect from March 25, it was not known at all in the colonies until Loudoun brought it out with him, and was not widely spread until printed copies arrived for distribution towards the end of the year.[25] Even as late as August, 1757, Pownall thought it wise to send copies to justices of the peace, for he "verily believed half their Errors were from Ignorance."

By thus putting recruiting in the colonies on a legal basis, the act afforded colonial magistrates a handle for stopping the laxity of recruiting parties. Though the evidence is by no means complete, it seems to show that such legal protection decreased the numbers of men enlisted. Lieutenant McAulay of a New York independent company, for instance, presented a long list of complaints against justices who "used Illegal and unfair means to deprive your memorialist of recruits", Joseph Kissam of Jamaica in Long Island even going so far, after the "most abusive and Scurrilous Language", as to collect a "numerous mobb of people" and to rescue a recruit with "uncommon violence."[26] When John Scudder of New Jersey refused to be influenced by the arguments of the attesting justice, and "shewed a great desire to be a soldier", his father procured his discharge on the ground that the twenty-four hours allowed by parliament had not elapsed before his attestation.[27] Various complaints were laid before Loudoun at Philadelphia in 1757: that at York recruiting parties had "listed by force first the son and then the father and lett them both off for money"; that

---

[25] Loudoun to Dobbs, Sept. 22, 1756, LO 1879. See the discussion in Mc-Cormac, *White Servitude in Maryland*, Johns Hopkins University Studies, XXII.

[26] Memorial of Lieutenant Archibald McAulay, LO 4357.

[27] Affidavits of Ensign William Skinner and Sergeant John Hutchinson of the 35th, LO 3310, 3311.

two officers "got a man to . . . buy some papper [*sic*] and then insisted he was enlisted by the money they gave him to pay for it and took a pistole from him to lett him off."[28] Since Loudoun had to enforce the act, he published a notice in the Pennsylvania *Gazette* promising redress to all who applied either to the commanding officer at Philadelphia or to himself at New York.[29] The act specified that no volunteer was liable to a criminal process unless for some criminal matter or for a real debt of the value of ten pounds. In Massachusetts justices seized upon this clause, and entertained actions for false debts to obtain the discharge of recruits.[30] Jeremiah Gridley summed up the situation for Massachusetts: "Recruiting is an unfavoured Cause, unless for the Royal American Regiment, and even there if any native of the province inlists, the inlistment is critically examined, every imaginary flaw is made a real one, and the Desertion of such a person is encouraged. This is the popular temper, and the magistrates, always in some shape or other dependent upon the people, are in my opinion too complaisant to it."[31] Such illustrations, drawn from four provinces, suggests that all colonial magistrates knew how to shape to their own purposes the provisions of the Mutiny Act.

We are on surer ground, however, with regard to indentured servants. The act decreased the numbers of servants enlisted simply because, in order to conserve recruiting funds, Loudoun forbade the enlistment of any man to whose master a justice allowed more than three pounds. But the dissatisfaction of masters was by no

<hr />

[28] HM 1717, vol. 3, March 26, 1757.

[29] *Pennsylvania Gazette*, §1475, March 31, 1757.

[30] "There's no alternative, but if a person will swear to any act if it exceeds £10 sterling, true or false, no enquiry is made into it, and the man is lost". Sam Mackay of the 40th to Colonel Forbes, Feb. 6, 1758, LO 5549.

[31] Gridley to Loudoun, June 6, 1757, Brookline, LO 3797.

means allayed. As Benjamin Franklin pointed out, in a letter meant for Cumberland's eyes, the last year or two of a servant's time was worth far more than the early years before he had learned his trade, yet the army took only that servant whose time was about to expire. Moreover, Franklin went on to say, the taking of a few servants from a complex business with different branches left the rest useless. "Taking the Compositors from a Printing House (my own Case) the Servants who are Pressmen, tho' left behind, not knowing how to compose, must remain idle." Finally the master who took back an enlisted servant when the officer refused to pay the proportional sum allotted had himself to pay back the enlisting money, which the servant had usually spent in drink. "Then there being no Provision to prevent the Servant's Inlisting again, he may repeat the Frolick as often as he pleases."[32] Nor was it clear whether colonial assemblies or the British army were to recompense masters for servants enlisted between March 25 and the time when the act became known in the colonies. Maryland definitely refused to create a fund, but the Pennsylvania assembly advertised for masters to bring in accounts and fully intended, Loudoun thought, to pay them.[33] The assembly, however, saw in the indentured servant question a means of approaching parliament, and only after considerable difficulty did Loudoun, insisting that he and not parliament was in charge of recruiting, manage to see a copy of the accounts. Had they been complete and properly drawn, it would have been his duty to have settled them, for the act applied even where its terms were unknown. But he found the names of men enlisted before March,

[32] Benjamin Franklin to Sir Everard Fawkener, July 27, 1756, Cumberland Papers. Fawkener was the postmaster general, and Cumberland's secretary.

[33] *Pennsylvania Gazette*, §1456, Nov. 18, 1756.

1756, upon them, and uncertainty about the justice of many of the claims.[34] He therefore washed his hands of the whole affair, and Franklin, who knew the list to be incomplete and expected little from Loudoun, departed to obtain redress in London.[35] The number of names on the list, 616, suggests that in 1755 and 1756 perhaps from a seventh to a fifth of all American recruits were Pennsylvania servants; this is a conjecture, but serves to show how fertile had been the field which the act, and Loudoun's application of it, curtailed.

The need of conserving recruiting funds points to another reason for the decrease in the numbers of volunteers. The process by which recruiting was financed was both costly and complicated. There was no general or central fund which the commander in chief could draw upon; instead, each regiment had its own separate accounts and funds. One might have plenty of money to spare while another was virtually bankrupt. The British army still bore traces of the days when it consisted of independent units, each the property of its colonel. Regiments had two sums available for recruiting. The first, enjoyed only on rare occasions, was the amount granted by parliament for a specific augmentation or devoted to that purpose from a general grant. Levy money for the augmentations to war strength of the 44th, the 48th, and the three Nova Scotia regiments came out of the million pounds voted in 1755 for land and sea defense. Levy money for the Royal American regiment, twenty thousand pounds, was voted directly in 1756, and that for the augmentations of the 35th and 42d came from the million voted in 1756. Parliament defrayed the expense of raising the Highland battalions in 1757, of the additional companies for Scottish regiments, and of a subsequent

34 HM 1717, vol. 3, March 26, April 25, 1757. The list is in LO 3415.
35 *Franklin's Works* (Sparks edition), VII, 141.

addition to the 22d.[36] But such grants came only once during a war. Regiments were expected to pay for their replacements out of their regimental funds. Each one was accredited annually at the Pay Office with a sum representing the complete pay and only the pay of every officer and enlisted man on the establishment. For a typical regiment of 1145—including commissioned and non-commissioned officers—this sum amounted to £20,175 7s. 6d. Of this there was retained in England the full pay of all commissioned officers, and a sum stopped from the pay of the others to cover clothing costs and customary charges, a total of £9590 7s. 6d. The remainder, £10,585, called "subsistence", was transmitted to the deputy paymaster general in America for the use of the regiment. Out of that amount came the pay of the troops. If the regiment were incomplete, the pay of the difference between actual strength and the strength on the establishment would remain in the deputy paymaster general's hands. That variable sum constituted the "non-effective" fund, from which the expenses of recruiting were paid. As with every sum the paymaster issued, a warrant from the commander in chief was required before regimental officers could touch their own "non-effective" funds, and Loudoun therefore could exercise a general supervision.[37] Since the cost of levying a single man was estimated at five pounds, two hundred and fifty days would have to

36 27 *House of Commons Journal* 385, 657, 736, 749, 751.

37 Braddock was prohibited by his instructions from drawing upon the "non-effective" funds, since recruiting expenses were to come out of the common fund established by the colonies. Though Loudoun's instructions contained the same restrictive clause, he understood that he might practically disregard it until it was formally changed, as it was in December, 1756 (Pitt to Loudoun, Dec. 22, 1756, LO 2383). The clause was designed to prevent the corruption that might ensue from two separate sums for a single expense; Loudoun tried to reduce fraud by allowing no recruiting accounts to be passed without an itemized list of monies actually expended.

elapse after a regiment lost a man before his accumulated subsistence, at five pence a day, would permit his replacement.[38]

This five pounds served three purposes. In the first place, the recruiting officer himself received a reward for every volunteer, fixed by a general order of November, 1757, at £3 10s. a man, £2 for indentured servants, with the additional inducement, so scarce were recruits, of another pound for every man after the first fifteen. This was "levy money". In the second place, the recruit himself received out of the officer's £3 10s. his "listing money". A variable sum, but usually fixed at a "pistole and a dollar" (a guinea), it was to be expended partly in beer but mostly in providing necessaries. In the third place, the sum was meant to pay the cost of transportation for the party and recruits, including horse hire and ferriage, part of the cost of provisions, and the subsistence of recruits till they joined the regiment. The officer in charge of a party got a preliminary warrant before he left; if he intended to recruit ten men, he drew fifty pounds. When he returned, he made out his itemized list of expenses and settled with the paymaster. If he ran over the fifty pounds, he bore the additional expense out of his own pocket, or, if he had been selected by the regiment to recruit for all companies in it, all the officers bore the loss. Since America was a land of distances, some officers were ruined by the recruiting service. It cost a great deal to keep recruits attached to a party and to provision them for the time that elapsed before they could be safely sent to the regiment. In the early stages of the war officers often returned before they had finished their jobs. Shirley helped to relieve the situation by al-

---

[38] Company stoppages of one penny a day, deducted from the sixpence subsistence of effective men, were also charged upon the "non-effective" men.

lowing fourpence a day for provisions for each member
of the party and each recruit, to be paid out of contingencies, and not out of non-effective funds. Loudoun continued the practice. But such a departure from usual
custom was insufficient relief. Fourpence a day might be
specified in the Mutiny Act as the cost of a soldier's food,
but no tavern keeper in the colonies would accept so little.
Lieutenant MacKinnon paid £2 6s. for a week's board for
his small party over and above the fourpences; a more
usual charge in New England was six shillings sterling
a week. At that rate it would not take long to use up the
allowance of five pounds a man, and to deplete the regiment's funds.

To provide a further safeguard for the recruiting
funds the commanding officers of all regiments in
America officially petitioned Loudoun to allow them, as
in Flanders during the previous war,[39] forty contingent
men for a regiment of a thousand, and thirty for a regiment of seven hundred. This would have been an extension of a practice already allowed by custom and by
warrant, by which each captain was given the pay of two
men, called "contingent" or "warrant" men, to form a
permanent nucleus for the non-effective fund. Loudoun
himself, since his arrival in America, had urged a step
which would add a pound a day to a regiment's recruiting funds, and after July, 1757, he actually granted warrants for subsistence with these additional men included.
But neither Pitt nor Cumberland would sanction the
change, and the army in America, which needed the relief, remained financially upon an inadequate footing.[40]

[39] *Report of Committees of the House of Commons* (1746), II, Misc., pp.
128, 129.

[40] Barrington to Holderness, May 12, 1757, LO 3607. *Pitt Correspondence,*
I, 20. The only wealthy regiment in Loudoun's army was the 60th, which got
£20,000 levy money from parliament, began to draw pay from December,

British officials were obviously afraid that the privilege might be abused, for the non-effective fund, after the deduction of a sum large enough to recruit to the full establishment of five pounds a man, was divided annually among the captains of the regiments. This was called "clearances", perhaps the fattest of the traditional perquisites attached to a commission. The general effect of this effort to extend to America the complex financial red-tape of the British army can be summarized in a sentence: whenever the cost of recruiting threatened to exceed five pounds a man, it was to the regiment's advantage not to recruit.

Throughout this discussion has been discernible the latent hostility of the average American towards the British army. It was an old heritage, made up of bitter memories of the companies which came with Andros, the loss of transports on the Quebec expedition of 1711—Loudoun found one man still nursing this forty-five-year-old grudge—the treatment of the American regiment on the Cartagena expedition, the broken promises of 1746. The failure of British arms in the early years of the war, especially the loss of Fort William Henry in 1757, seemed to colonials to justify their convictions that British soldiers were incapable, and every story of army methods which leaked out exaggerated the evils and suppressed the truth. Echoes of that popular feeling against Braddock's and Loudoun's troops still sound faintly through the years and embody themselves in our text-books. At times it found vent against recruiting parties, the only British soldiers whom the majority of colonials ever had a chance to see. In Wilmington, for example, accord-

1755, had by the end of its first year only some 1800 men on its rolls, and paid for the drafts which filled it the standard rate of £5 a man. Under Amherst, it may be noted, regiments enjoyed the benefit of these additional contingent men.

ing to Lieutenant Cruikshank, rioters offered his party
"impudent and unparalleled insults", cursed and
wounded his men, damned Loudoun and all the army.[41]
No reason was given, but to judge from other similar
cases there must have been some suspicious action of
Cruikshank's men which kindled the smouldering hostility into flame. For recruiting parties, even after the
passage of the act regulating enlistments, seem often to
have employed the methods used so freely in 1755. Corbin
Lee, a Maryland overseer, complained of an officer who
entered his plantation at night, soaked the servants in
drink, and carried them off.[42] Pownall wished officers
would avoid imprudences: "To see a Drunken man
lugged through the streets on a souldiers back guarded
by others whether it was or not to carry him before a
Justice to swear must certainly give a strange impression
of the method of enlisting." James Avery of New Jersey,
a lad of sixteen, made affidavit that he was forcibly carried before the recruiting captain because a sergeant had
"put a dollar on his hand which he threw on the floor, and
threatened [him] with gaol if he did not enlist or get two
men."

A similar incident, occurring in New London in December, 1757, illustrates so well both provincial feeling and
recruiting methods that it merits a fuller description. As
the story unfolded to Loudoun, it seemed an obstruction
to the service on the part of a private colony flagrant
enough to deserve the severest treatment. He first learned
of the affair from Lieutenant Robert MacKinnon of the
Royals, a recruiting officer, who wrote that the sheriff of
New London, acting under a warrant from Daniel Coit,
a justice of the peace, had assembled a group of sailors

[41] Cruikshank to Loudoun, Dec. 14, 1757, LO 5012.

[42] Corbin Lee to Sharpe, April 30, 1757, LO 3506. *Maryland Archives*, VI,
555.

from a letter of marque ship in the harbor, armed with cutlasses, and had rescued a recruit. The language of the warrant was forcible: "Whereas I am instantly informed that a number of men now in the town of New London with red coats (called soldiers) have by strong hand taken a market man belonging to Stonington, named Woodward . . . these are in His Majesty's name to command you forthwith to repair to the said house, taking with you a sufficient assistance and take the said Woodward, and all other persons who shall any ways molest or hinder you in taking him . . . and bring him and them before myself." Coit accompanied the sheriff, struck one of the soldiers, and according to MacKinnon, violently refused to examine into the validity of the enlistment. Loudoun at once complained to Governor Fitch, and suggested that Coit's name be struck from the list of justices. Fitch in reply pleaded his inability to remove an official appointed by the assembly, and himself complained of the insolent manner in which another recruiting officer, a captain of the 17th, had appeared with his whole party to demand billets and had refused to present credentials. Thereupon Loudoun sent to Norwalk, Fitch's home, one of his most trusted officers, Major James Robertson. He had instructions to settle the Coit affair justly, to move forward if necessary a body of troops, and to explain to Fitch that the captain of the 17th had not drawn up in a "mutinous manner" but had simply "formed his party", that an officer could not divulge recruiting instructions but only beating orders, and that any officer found in the wrong would be punished. Since Norwalk was but a short distance from New York, Robertson seems to have made a holiday of the trip, for he took along to Fitch's residence the wife of one of Loudoun's aides, Mrs. McAdam. Fitch found them playing cards in the house and told them it was against law; "we all declared our ignorance

and Sorrow and threw away the Cards." After this brush
Robertson's efforts to move the governor were unavail-
ing; "all my assiduity and a tedious course of Civilitys
could draw no returns from this mulish magistrate."
Finally the truth came out. MacKinnon had not been
present at the actual enlisting, but had got his knowledge
at second hand from his party. Witnesses of the enlisting
made affidavit that Woodward, going about his daily job,
had sold a turkey to the owner of the house where the
soldiers were lounging. The owner had not the exact
change. A soldier offered to pay, gave Woodward a dollar and a half crown. Then, with a fine appreciation of
the essentials of a valid enlistment, he insisted that
Woodward was "a King's soldier, for he had got the
King's money", and carried him off by force. The final
act in this drama was a plea from Fitch that MacKinnon,
from whom the truth had obviously been concealed, be
not punished. This whole story is a superb illustration
of the chasm between the colonial and the army points of
view.[43]

Much of the trouble occurred when recruiting parties
tried to take up deserters. That was their second task,
and they got twenty shillings for every man restored to
his regiment. But any American, who, having found life
in the British army not to his taste, deserted and returned to his home, could depend upon the assistance of
his neighbors. Lieutenant Vaughan of the 45th described
how a provincial company rescued a deserter from his
party, and beat his "sergeant and corporal in a sevear
manner".[44] Captain Charteris of the Royal Americans
had a deserter rescued from his party near the court-
house in Boston and carried off in triumph. Impelled by

[43] LO 5058, 5121, 5325, 5332, 5348, 5356, 5359.

[44] Thomas Vaughan, Method of sending Home Invalids from Nova Scotia,
LO 5178.

"the too frequent practise of rescuing and harboring Deserters in this Province", he got a warrant from a justice, surrounded Caleb Dana's house, forced an entrance, and got the wrong man. Dana swore the peace against him and his party, and would have had them all imprisoned if Jeremiah Gridley had not discovered a flaw in the indictment.[45] In New York deserters who joined the crew of a privateer could make use of the cutlasses of their mates. On three occasions in 1757 soldiers and sailors clashed in the streets of the city, and once, in a pitched battle, blood was shed.[46] The highest excitement was reached in New Hampshire. At Brintwood "the people in a tumultuous and riotous manner assembled, and seemed to have in view, not only to rescue the prisoner which they effected, but to murder the recruiting party . . . the cry was blood for blood, to irritate the people to take revenge for a deserter inlisted there who was shot at Oswego." Denied aid by the civil magistrate, who probably could not furnish protection, the party escaped, and for four miles was pursued by the mob, armed with axes.[47] That incident brought recruiting in New Hampshire to an end.

[45] "All the gentlemen of the place," wrote Charteris to Loudoun (June 11, 1757, Boston, LO 3816), "do not assist, but as the Jury consist generally of men whose greatest Merit is a Rigid adherence to The Old Charter Privileges, everything that has the Appearance of infringing them is an Unfavour'd Cause . . . as I have just reason to believe that the lower Class of Men here will Swear to the greatest Untruths rather than the Military shall escape."

[46] Loudoun told Lieutenant Governor DeLancey that if magistrates persisted in condoning the carrying away by privateers of troops sent from England for the defense of the colonies it was his "Duty to putt the best stop to it I am able, for that I can not answer setting stil with my legs a cross and see the army I am putt at the Head of Destroyed . . . in utter Violation of the Laws and to the imminent Danger of Losing these Provinces." HM 1717, vol. 2, Oct. 2, 1757.

[47] *New Hampshire Provincial Papers*, VI, 640, 641.

Most of these fracases between civilians and recruiting parties occurred either in the middle colonies, where the indentured servant question raised the economic issue, or in New England, where traditional hostility to the red-coat was strongest. In the south there was little recruiting; in South Carolina the fear of negro uprising practically prevented it altogether. But in every New England colony except Rhode Island there was unpleasantness, and in Rhode Island no recruiting party ever remained long, because privateers lured away all available men by the promise of rich booty. Doubtless the treatment given to those colonials who had enlisted in Shirley's and Pepperrell's regiments did a good deal to aggravate suspicion. For when those two regiments, which had more New Englanders than any other corps, were broken, their men were drafted into other regular regiments of the line. The 1st or Royals got most of those captured at Oswego, and it had no connection whatever with the colonies. Its officers described these unfortunates as "right New England men", "the most irregular sett of people" they ever met; and the stories of making good soldiers out of them by draining the town of whip-cord did not ring agreeably in the ears of friends and family about New England firesides.

One can see from this account of recruiting in the colonies how fatuous was the hope that the war could be fought through by Americans serving in British regiments. But at the same time it does not do to condemn that policy out of hand. To judge from the reports both of provincial and regular officers, there were men in the colonies who were willing to serve in any army. The popular distrust of the redcoat did not affect them very much; they were an idle and propertyless group, willing to sell themselves to the highest bidder. Both Loudoun and Cumberland wanted the British army to be able to

solicit that class of men without competition from provincial troops, into whose ranks Loudoun hoped a better
class of colonials would go, the stalwarts who had taken
Louisbourg. If provincial troops could be limited in numbers and confined to such men, recruiting parties would
stand some chance of success. That was a sound policy,
and a cheap one, and deserved a longer trial than it had.

CHAPTER V

SHIRLEY AND OSWEGO

In August, 1756, a bitter dispute broke out between Loudoun and Shirley, who was still in his government. It was a misfortune for Loudoun at the beginning of his American career, for it arrayed against him the governor's powerful supporters whom he might otherwise have made his friends. But no conscientious soldier could have avoided some sort of inquiry into Shirley's conduct of affairs. Shirley had affronted the British military code in too many ways; he had left the command in too great confusion; he had afforded too many grounds for suspecting his honesty.

Since the chief interest of this dispute is not the limits of personal invective it reached, that side of it can be briefly dismissed. Loudoun arrived at New York prepared to reflect towards Shirley the ministry's own cool and suspicious attitude; Shirley was under a cloud for his interference with Johnson's Indians and for the unexplained affair of the intercepted letters. Loudoun was acting correctly, though he doubtless failed to conceal the professional soldier's distrust of a layman's competence in military affairs. He expected Shirley to answer his questions, put necessary information at his disposal, and retire gracefully from the scene, in keeping with the requirements of military etiquette and in obedience to the direct orders from England. The report of their first conversation discloses no ill will; Shirley answered questions about the terms on which the provincials were raised, about batteauxmen, and about the lack of adequate shelter for provisions at Oswego.[1] Loudoun's early letters to Shirley were deliberately courteous. If Shirley, who had had three months to put his affairs in order,[2] had followed his avowed intention of returning to England as soon as he had "consulted" with Loudoun, the later accusations of both men would never have reached the stage of venomous retort. But Shirley did not retire gracefully. He remained for two months longer and took as active a share as he could in the army's business. He wrote to Loudoun twenty distinct letters, nine of them in the first week after Loudoun's arrival,[3] and other letters to subordinate officers in the regular army. Though he may have had the highest intentions, he played the role of a busybody. The indignation aroused by his failure to act as a superseded commander should, with a studied disinterestedness, slowly turned into a suspicion that he was laying foundations to reëstablish himself in his former posts. As Loudoun attributed to Shirley the responsibility for the trouble he met with the provincial army, so he became inclined to impute to Shirley, a convenient scapegoat, the blame for the inadequacy of transport facilities, for the lack of a dependable means of getting intelligence of enemy movements, for the insufficiency of fortifications and storehouses—for everything, in short, that went wrong. The conviction grew that the unmilitary condition of affairs was not due to Shirley's inexperience, but to his deliberate mismanagement for the sake of gain. Such a conviction was encouraged by the De-

---

[1] HM 1717, vol. 9, July 24, 1756. There are no notes of the previous day's conversation.

[2] Shirley learned unofficially of his recall as early as April, Shirley to Morris, April 18, *Shirley Correspondence*, II, 428. Both Webb and Abercromby urged him to remain until he had talked with Loudoun.

[3] The *Shirley Correspondence* contains seven of the twenty; the others can be found in the Loudoun Papers.

Lancey-Johnson faction in New York, which had been snubbed when Shirley sided with its political enemy, the Livingston-Morris clique. In September Loudoun came to the conclusion that the fall of Oswego was the inevitable result of fraud instigated by Shirley, and when he continued to receive calmly explanatory letters from a man whom he had come to regard as an archvillain, his patience was exhausted, and he bluntly ordered Shirley home. In the exchange of recriminatory letters, Shirley, who had nothing more to lose and much to gain, preserved an air of maligned righteousness which contrasted sharply with the public prosecutor's attitude of his successor, and in the opinions of those who see in him one of the earliest and staunchest protagonists of the British Empire he emerged with something like a martyr's crown.

The real interest is to watch Shirley, inexperienced and unfamiliar with an army routine so complicated with detail that men grown grey in the service could scarcely comprehend it, trying to carry on too big a task without sufficient support from England. As commander in chief, Shirley was still acting under the unrevised Braddock plan and depending upon colonial resources. But the six major criticisms brought against him, which cover a good deal of army business, point more often to defects in the man himself than to defects in the plan imposed upon him. Shirley was impatient of detail, upon which success ultimately had to depend. A visionary and idealist, he was fond of planning to move masses of troops here and there, of contriving feints against the enemy, and of talking glibly about the control of inland waterways. To others he left the business of finding wagons, assembling supplies, inspecting equipment, and calculating costs. The British army in America in 1755 and 1756 needed no theoretical strategists on the grand scale; before the war could be won, an organization of supply and transport had to be perfected, and troops trained to meet the requirements of wilderness fighting. It is the measure of Shirley's failure as a commander that he made but scanty progress towards that end.

Shirley's carelessness in essential matters is shown by his relations with his contractors. The two contractors, Peter vanBrugh Livingston and Lewis Morris, Junior, were members of a New York political faction. With the former was associated William Alexander, Shirley's private secretary; with the latter, John Erving, a member of the Massachusetts council and Shirley's son-in-law. Of these four only Livingston could bring to the service both experience and leisure. With them Shirley made a general contract sweeping in its requirements. They agreed to furnish provisions for the army; to transport them to Albany; to provide all materials for "building, fitting, rigging, and arming" three ships for Lake Ontario; to assemble carpenters, sawyers, and artificers to build them; to purchase all necessary equipment for the naval force; to provide working tools for the army; to build at Schenectady five hundred batteaux "of the strongest kind with oak bottoms" and four hundred whaleboats; and to repair and fit for service all small boats used the previous year.[4] By thus transferring the responsibility to private individuals, to whom he paid a five per cent commission, Shirley freed himself from much detail. Some of these tasks, and some of the responsibility, belonged to the army, to aides de camp, quartermasters, or special officers. As it was, the contractors, unable to supervise everything themselves, made supplementary contracts with other firms who charged their commission also of five per cent or more; when these minor accounts were in-

[4] Orders and Instructions to Peter vanBrugh Livingston and Lewis Morris, Junior, Merchants, January 14, 1756, LO 760.

cluded in the general bill, Livingston and Morris added
their regular five per cent. Thus for a number of items
which Shirley's officers should have supervised themselves he paid a commission of ten per cent or more, and
the general contractors collected a tidy profit by acting as
banker of the army's money, which would have been as
safe in the deputy paymaster general's hands. For example, ninety per cent of the entire expense of Shirley's
Niagara expedition of 1755 was paid by warrants drawn
in favor of the contractors.[5] The carpenters who worked
at Oswego from September, 1755, to August, 1756, were
provided by Richards and Coddington of Rhode Island,
who took a commission of £123 on a total cost of £3800.
These carpenters worked under the direction of officers
of the army or navy, but they were paid by the commissary of stores, Francis Lewis, for the account of the contractors. Though a staff officer, he took a five per cent
commission for paying them, and the contractors of
course took theirs.[6] The cost of shipping goods to Oswego
in the boats which belonged to the Crown and were
guarded by army detachments was charged in contractors' accounts, though the regular method was to pay
directly by warrant. When Shirley on one occasion him-

[5] An Accompt of Monies paid by Abraham Mortier . . . Pursuant to
General Shirley's Warrants for the Contingent and Extraordinary Service
of His Majesty's Troops, LO 6716. Including the warrants to William Johnston, the deputy paymaster general at Albany, Shirley spent in all £224,080
10s. 7½d. sterling. Of this about £35,000 was used on the Niagara expedition.

[6] A General Abstract of Moneys paid by order and for the account of
William Alexander, Esq., and Company for His Majesty's Service on the
Niagara Expedition and other Contingent Charges of the Garrison at Os-
wego, signed Francis Lewis, LO 1483. Lewis handled a total sum of £4928
12s. 7d. currency. An Account of William Alexander and Company with
Francis Lewis, Oswego, May 1, 1756 [C.O. 5: 46, f. 487] contains the item:
"To my Commission on £3183 10s moneys paid the Working Parties and
other Expences of the Expedition at Five percent, £159 3s 6d."

self paid a bill for shipwright's services, out of his private account, Erving repaid the sum to him, and incorporated it in the general accounts of the contractors, with the five per cent added.[7] The bills which Livingston and Morris submitted contained an itemized list only, without vouchers showing that the services had been performed, and Shirley drew his warrants in their favor without attaching the itemized accounts that army practice demanded. Their total profits from June 12, 1755, to Loudoun's arrival, when the contract was completely broken, were £8558 13s. 10d.[8]

Nor were the contractors as efficient in the trust reposed in them as they were greedy to dip into the inexhaustible resources of the British exchequer. In collecting provisions, their chief task, they did not always get either the best or the cheapest. On September 22, 1755, for example, they paid 75s. a barrel for pork to Matthew Ernst, Livingston's brother, and 70s. to Thomas Ludlow, not a relation to any of them. They paid £243 for renting storehouses in Albany, a sum too great to have hired all the storehouses in a town where the rent of the best was not above £45. They charged freight from New York to Albany on some 250 sheep purchased at Albany.[9] Commissary Robert Leake of the regular army, an earnest

[7] Account of Charles Apthorp & Son with Governor Shirley, LO 2697. Apthorp was agent to the London money contractors, Thomlinson and Hanbury, but neither as governor nor as commander in chief, would Shirley have any public dealings with him, who dealt in the Crown's money only with the deputy paymasters general. This was a private account. The memorial of Livingston and Morris of Nov. 1, 1756, contains these same items for shipwright's services and sloop hire.

[8] Report of Oliver DeLancey on the contractors' account, Feb. 6, 1758, LO 6925.

[9] Though these comments are taken from the report of Oliver DeLancey, who, as an agent of the London contractors, Baker and Kilby, was not unbiased, I have checked them as far as possible against the accounts of Livingston and Morris [LO 573] and found them accurate.

and painstaking bookkeeper, complained that Shirley's contractors had agreed with John Hunter of Virginia for nine hundred barrels of pork, without marks or invoice, "in all probability bad Carolina pork, as there is no good pork near the seacoast in Virginia."[10] DeLancey made a similar complaint late in June when he was checking over the provisions in stock preparatory to buying them for the new London contractors or discarding them. A return of provisions at that time shows that Livingston and Morris had laid in an eccentric supply; there were pork and bread for four months, peas and butter for a few days, and a thousand barrels of rum. Such carelessness Shirley should have made it his business to correct.

In their own justification Livingston and Morris stated that they had supplied everything they had stipulated, with the exception of twelve hundred live cattle not due until September. The part of the contract which related to dry provision came to an end in July, but not until August 23 did Loudoun discontinue the clause relating to fresh meat, and then only on the ground that it was so loosely phrased he could not be sure the army would be supplied, nor at what price.[11] On his arrival Loudoun had ordered all outstanding accounts laid before him, and those which were properly certified, with attached vouchers, he paid. But as the passing weeks brought to light more and more evidence that fraud might be present, he determined not to implicate his own records, but to leave all of Shirley's accounts to be settled by Shirley himself and his agents in London. It was a justifiable move—

[10] Memorial of Robert Leake, July 30, 1756, LO 1275. The Rhode Island committee of war had a similar experience, *Rhode Island Colonial Records*, VI, 5, 6.

[11] Loudoun to Livingston, Aug. 23, 1756, LO 1561. The contract with Baker and Kilby permitted Loudoun to make his own arrangements for supplying fresh meat, and to substitute it when he wished for salted pork and beef.

Shirley had himself left unsettled the accounts of Braddock's wagoners—but it bore heavily on those people whom Shirley's carelessness involved. The contractors presented their final bill in December for £14,298 9s. 10d., audited by three New York merchants under Governor Hardy's warrant of July 8. Though the auditing was doubtless carefully done, it did not answer Loudoun's objection that no vouchers were attached to show that the services had been performed. Outstanding among these unpaid claims were those of the contractors' batteauxmen and carpenters at Oswego, many of whom were ruined. Pathetic memorials from them, and from the wives of those captured at Oswego, kept appearing. Pownall relieved a few needy cases from his own pocket when he became governor of Massachusetts. Loudoun's refusal to pay this particular account increased the antagonism for the regular army. It made the raising of batteauxmen difficult in later years of the war, but it was January, 1763, before Amherst, on instruction from London, settled a part of this long overdue bill.[12] Correspondence about the carpenters' accounts continued until 1769.[13]

Shirley would doubtless have paid the two chief accounts—of £14,000 for provisions and £12,000 for Bradstreet's batteauxmen—before he relinquished his com-

[12] Abstract of monies paid . . . to liquidate the debts to Stevenson, Visger and Van Eps for waggonage, batteauxmen, etc., in 1755-1756, Jan. 1763, W.O. 34: 58, f. 270. Account of money paid by Colonel Robertson in 1761 to fifty-seven artificers taken at Oswego, W.O. 34: 74, f. 70. In 1761 Amherst was ordered by the Treasury to re-examine Shirley's provision accounts in America, the lack of vouchers making it impossible in London, S. Martin to Amherst, June 13, 1761, W.O. 34: 72, f. 170.

[13] C. E. Carter, ed., *Correspondence of Thomas Gage*, I, 234. Loudoun paid but one bill, for diplomatic reasons, to James Otis: ''But as the Colonel semes realy to have payed it and is a very leading man in the assembly with whom I have business I have promised to pay him'', HM 1717, vol. 3, Feb. 3. 1757. Boston.

mand, if there had been any money in the military chest.[14] But his many warrants had drained it; the two deputy paymasters general could furnish at the end of June but £16,972 5s. for both contingent and regimental charges.[15] This situation constituted a second major criticism against Shirley. At the beginning of a summer's campaign, when a cautious commander would have assured himself of ample funds to meet emergencies, he hampered himself and his successors.[16] The most objectionable of his many warrants, from the point of view of the Pay Office, were those drawn in March to three New England governments, £44,592 12s. 1d., as a loan to enable them to carry on preparations for their Crown Point expedition.[17] For such an expenditure, which came under no service of the regular army, Shirley had no authority. He tried later to answer this general criticism by stating first that since he had made all necessary preparations, the British generals had no need of money; and second, that the term "military chest" was a misnomer, for the deputy paymasters general sold bills to obtain funds, and if they failed to sell them in June, that it was certainly not his fault. As with many of Shirley's statements, this defense was based on half-truths. Later we shall see the effect of the scarcity of money at Oswego; preparations were not completed there. It was true that the agents for

[14] Bradstreet's two thousand batteauxmen were hired directly by him and were not connected with those hired by the contractors. Loudoun settled Bradstreet's bills in the autumn of 1756. Declared Accounts of John Bradstreet, A.O. 1: 1339: 335.

[15] A Statement of Cash in the Deputy Paymaster General's Hands, LO 1164.

[16] Loudoun, for example, ordered Mortier always to keep £10,000 in reserve, and Amherst, when in July, 1759, he was faced with a shortage of cash, took the unprecedented step of borrowing £150,000 from the government of New York. Declared Accounts of Abraham Mortier, P.M.G. 14: 1.

[17] Memorial of the Paymaster General upon the Deputy Paymaster's General's Account in North America, Oct. 6, 1756, Treas. 1: 367.

Thomlinson and Hanbury got most of the army's money by selling bills, but bills could not always be sold on a moment's notice. After Loudoun's arrival, when funds were still short, the agents were forced to pay the high exchange rate of eighty-five per cent in order to raise within a week a sum of five or six thousand pounds; and they succeeded only because the packet was about to sail. The most lenient view to take of this affair is that Shirley neglected sensible precautions; the harshest, and the view Loudoun took, was that Shirley, knowing he was to be superseded, drew warrants right and left to cover up his misfeasances.

Shirley had better success in meeting the third of the accusations against him, the mismanagement of the regimental funds of the 50th and 51st. He was able, in time, to demonstrate that Newcastle's policy of rigid economy in American expenses had forced him to employ irregular channels. To these two alone of all the regiments raised or augmented in North America in 1755 and 1756 was a special parliamentary grant of levy money denied. Suspicious of American colonels since the first establishment of these regiments in the last war,[18] the ministry persuaded itself that their recruiting expenses would be adequately defrayed either by the common fund from the colonies, or by a considerable accretion in the non-effective fund, for it expected no men to be raised for six months. Therefore, though it discussed the affair in September, 1754, though a royal warrant of October 7 appointed a temporary agent for the regiments, though on November 4 Fox ordered Lieutenant Colonels Ellison and

---

[18] The first establishment of Shirley's and Pepperrell's began Sept. 24, 1745, and three months advance subsistence was ordered to raise them. In 1750 Shirley demanded levy money for 1103 men at £7 12s. 1d. a man, and was paid £6691 13s. 4d.; Pepperrell asked levy money for 832 men at £7 11s. 3d. each, and got £5733 7s. Additional MSS. 33,046, f. 293.

Mercer to proceed to America to begin recruiting, the regiments did not go on the establishment until December 24.[19] But Shirley with commendable zeal began to raise men in 1754, mustered 863 in February, 1755, and 1019 in April.[20] If that figure is true, it is clear that the only sum voted the regiment by parliament to that date, £3528, was nearly consumed in pay. There was nothing to meet the costs of recruiting. These costs, some £7700 (1114 levies at an average of five guineas each with contingent expenses added), were defrayed, not by Shirley, a poor man, but largely by his son-in-law, Judge Hutchinson, who kept separate accounts from those of the regiment. When Shirley became commander in chief, he tried very naturally to recompense Hutchinson and others by utilizing the general contingencies. He committed that most heinous of crimes in army paper work, the allocation of general contingent funds to regimental expenses. From January to June, 1756, he drew six warrants totalling £7700 in favor of private individuals, two to Apthorp, two to Erving, one to Robert Temple, a son-in-law, and one, the largest of all, to his aide de camp, Lieutenant George Bartman of the 50th. Two of these warrants specified the sum "to be for Sundrys supplied the Ni-

---

[19] W.O. 26: 22, p. 338; 27 *House of Commons Journal* 317.

[20] Pepperrell had raised only 522 by October 24, most of them in New York and Pennsylvania. He complained that Shirley's monopoly of New England gave him greater success, and also that Shirley had rewarded by commissions in the two New England battalions raising for Nova Scotia anyone who was of service to him in raising the 50th (Usher Parsons, *Life of Sir William Pepperrell*, p. 275). Loudoun got from Governor Lawrence the story that "when General Shirley raised the 2000 men for Nova Scotia he gave the commissions to the officers according to the men they could raise and that of those he took 2 thirds to his own regiment which was raising at the same time. And Captain Rous informs me that even when the men for Nova Scotia were on the Key embarking the sargents of the 50th regiment came and pickt out the handsomest fellows and caryed them off before the officers faces". HM 1717, vol. 1, Jan. 29, 1757.

agara Expedition''; two ''on account of Raising the non-Commission Officers and Soldiers of His Majesty's (50th) Regiment''; two without any specified account.[21] In at least two cases, and probably in all, Shirley received the money after these middlemen had drawn it from the deputy paymaster general, and gave them a receipt. Erving's receipt had the highly suspicious clause: ''I do hereby certifie that the Warrant is applyed to my use and that the said Erving is no way accountable for the money, it only being drawn in his name for the sake of form.'' What form could that possibly be, thought Loudoun, when this receipt found its way into his hands, unless that Shirley, embezzling himself, had been forced by Erving to sign this acquittal? For Shirley's story of the raising of his regiment did not come out all at once, but in driblets which exaggerated the hints of fraud. The full explanation was not given until long after Shirley arrived in London.

Mixed up with this recruiting confusion were other strange financial practices. Where, for instance, had the subsistence of the 50th regiment gone? Captain More, its paymaster, asserted that all but £2500 of the total sum issued by parliament, £16,995 4s. 8d., for its support, had been devoted to pay and company expenses. But he offered in evidence the muster rolls, which were obviously false, for they put the regiment's strength in February, 1756, at 959 men, when it was actually half that number; and on June 24 at 908, when a return at Oswego credited it with but 633.[22] The paymaster received subsistence according to these incorrect rolls, for Shirley disregarded

[21] Account of the Expence of Raising His Majesty's 50th Regiment and contingent expenses from their time in barracks till they marched for Niagara, Cumberland Papers.

[22] The regiment had no field day until the summer of 1756, when James Pitcher, the muster master, made the trip to Oswego.

the clause in his instructions to pay only for effective men. Yet the men themselves, from October 24, 1755, until the next June, got not a shilling of their pay. In June those at Oswego were paid in full, but not those serving in detachments along the Mohawk. One can accept the paymaster's explanation that the transportation of cash during the winter was hazardous without understanding any more clearly who had pocketed the pay of the non-effectives. The 51st regiment got into similar difficulties. Because Major Charles Craven, its paymaster, diverted to the recruiting service the subsistence for the first four months of 1756, he had insufficient funds to pay his men in June, when the 50th received theirs. Loudoun discovered this fact when he asked Craven to pay the detachment of the 50th along the Mohawk from August to December, 1756; Craven instead advanced £1252, their back pay from the preceding October. The 50th had nothing with which to repay the loan, and Craven was left without money for his own regiment. Loudoun tried to attach Shirley's private balance in Apthorp's hands, but the attorney general of Massachusetts refused to aid. In the summer of 1757 an incipient mutiny of the men drafted from the 51st into the 1st (Royals) for their back pay since 1755 compelled Loudoun to issue them £753, which he charged to the still unsettled accounts of the 50th.

It is clear from this brief account of the financial history of these two regiments that where there was so much confusion, so many deliberate efforts to screen irregularities, there were justifiable grounds for suspecting embezzlement. For his jugglery with recruiting accounts, chief cause of the entanglements, Shirley deserves exoneration; the ministry had set him an impossible task in raising a regiment without funds. For the chaos in the distribution of subsistence Shirley's inexperience and impatience with detail were to blame. Not understanding army finance himself, he permitted every officer entrusted with money to dispose of it according to his own methods of bookkeeping. The account book submitted by Craven in his defense was a slovenly affair, with payments to men in driblets, payments for clothing and recruits mixed together with no attempt at classification.[23] Only one officer in the two regiments was dismissed the service.[24] Craven cleared himself at last in 1764, but as he had missed all chances for promotion his career was ruined.[25] Loudoun thought that much of the subsistence had been paid to the officers in the form of "slap-gelt" (victualling and billeting allowance), a practice he did not countenance,[26] and the evidence of the falsified muster rolls leads to the conclusion that some of the officers, at least, profited under Shirley's careless management.

The condition of the regimental accounts, the numerous

[23] Craven's account book of the 51st, to Aug. 24, 1756, LO 473.

[24] Lieutenant Nathaniel Williams of the 51st, on Craven's accusation, for disobeying Craven's orders, for behaving in a scandalous manner unbecoming the character of an officer and a gentleman by selling rum, and for not transmitting regular accounts. A General Court martial at New York, Dec. 13, 1756, W.O. 71: 129.

[25] *Pitt Correspondence*, I, 172-175.

[26] Shirley himself drew for his own use all the extra sums that could be squeezed from old army customs. During the winter of 1755-56, though he spent most of it as governor at Boston, he signed warrants for his own "fireing", for "slap-gelt", £545 9s. 1d., for forage for his horses, £617 10s., and for his expenses in travelling, as governor, from Boston to Alexandria and back, £225 (from a note of payments made to General Shirley by William Johnston, and received by Loudoun June 12, 1759, LO 6714). This journey was made in the spring of 1755, when Braddock was commander in chief; by no conceivable interpretation ought the Crown to have borne the expense. While in the field Shirley lived luxuriously, paying a butler sixty guineas for a campaign, and including in his larder such dainties as hams, tongues, pickles, anchovies, capers, olives, raisins, figs, currants, prunes, ketchup, Indian sweetmeats, limes and lemons, and firkins of eggs packed in salt (Livingston Rutherfurd, *Family Records and Events*, pp. 65, 66). Loudoun never attained such heights of epicurean bliss, though his pork and flour were of a special fineness and fresh fowls and fish were plentiful, his tea was exorbitantly dear and his wine bill tremendous.

reports of the undisciplined and untrustworthy character of the two regiments, and the capture of the majority of them at Oswego, led in January, 1757, to the decision that they be broken. The survivors among the prisoners taken at Oswego, 944 rank and file, were slowly exchanged in England and drafted into British regiments there, most of them into the Royals. The three hundred men on detachment along the Mohawk went into the Nova Scotia regiments, or into the 60th. Some of the officers went on half-pay, thereby losing rank in the army; Loudoun favored others in his promotion lists by assigning them posts the day after they were officially broken in America, March 7. Thus ended ingloriously an enterprise, which, had it succeeded, might have knit more closely together British soldiers and provincials. Judged by military standards the regiments were unfit to belong to an army composed of separate units, each one responsible for its own efficiency. But breaking them was an affront to New England, where, as Shirley pointed out, they were esteemed as "New England Corps",[27] and the drafting into British regiments of men who had enlisted into American ones was ethically a breach of faith. The memory of the 50th and 51st was added to the other counts which colonials had against the regular army.

A fourth criticism, important only because Loudoun thought his own rights infringed upon, concerned Shirley's conduct between June 12, the day he received his letter of demission from Webb,[28] and June 26, when he formally surrendered the command to Abercromby. Was he commander in chief during the interval? According to the custom of the army his signatures and warrants were still valid, but he was expected to give only the orders necessary for forwarding the service, and to touch

[27] Shirley to Pitt, Jan. 7, 1757, G.D. 8: 56.
[28] Shirley to Loudoun, Sept. 12, 1756, W.O. 1: 4, f. 399.

nothing which could wait for his successor. If Shirley
knew of this custom, he ignored it. He tried to clear up
his accounts by issuing warrants, the largest to William
Alexander for £5385 14s. 4d., and he signed several commissions. Among these were the four caused by the promotion in England of Captain Eyre of the 44th, news of
which Webb carried with him.[29] Loudoun, saying that
Shirley had no more right to sign these commissions than
his footman, superseded them all. For though sometimes,
as a gracious gesture, a departing commander in chief
was permitted to fill vacancies which had occurred during
his term of office and even to antedate and sign commissions, Shirley had forfeited such consideration by incur-
ring the suspicion of the War Office. The previous year he
had signed fifteen commissions without authority. Webb
brought the list out with him for investigation. Three of
them were in the two regiments which Shirley thought he
had a right to raise in 1755. The others were for special
staff officers on the Niagara Expedition, such as lieutenant of the train, commissary of provisions, judge advocate, adjutant general, surgeon to the hospital, master
apothecary, engineer to the expedition, secretary to the
Niagara expedition (the ubiquitous William Alexander),
and secretary to the command (William Alexander).
Shirley defended himself by pleading necessity, or ignorance—"the irregularity was occasioned by not having
a right understanding of the proper manner of appointing them."[30] Poor Shirley! He would adopt anything
which his friends said was army custom. The trick was an
old one, and Shirley a gullible victim.

Another of the accusations brought against Shirley was

[29] Shirley dated these four commissions January 8, the day after Eyre's
commission, LO 2542. *Army Lists,* 1757, 1758.

[30] Observations on the List of Commissions Granted by Major General
Shirley Ordered to be examined into by the Secretary at War, LO 2565.

more serious. The Crown could bear a loss of money and the army could recover from mismanagement, but the loss of Oswego threatened the success of the war by driving the Six Nations further into the arms of the French and by stopping British efforts to cut French communications between Canada and the south. Shirley must bear some of the responsibility for the accumulation of disasters which led to the fall of Oswego.

The scheme formulated by Braddock's council of war at Alexandria for the defense of Oswego was theoretically as sound as the exposed position of the post and the vulnerability of its lines of communications made possible: that is, to construct ships of war strong enough to gain the mastery of the lake and so to prevent transportation of enemy artillery; and to build forts capable of withstanding any small-arms attack from a force marching overland. Shirley undertook the execution of these tasks, and in accordance with the suggestions of Commodore Keppel, who drew specifications, supplied rigging and stores, and appointed naval commanders, he sent Bradstreet to Oswego in May, 1755, to begin the construction of two schooners of seventy tons each, a schooner boat of twenty tons, and a row galley.[31] Shirley himself reached Oswego in August, having spent nearly three months in leading the 50th and 51st over the hazardous route from Albany. Since he considered the old trading house, Fort George, so trifling that it could not be repaired, he threw about it a hornwork with one half-bastion and a ravelin. He also laid out two new forts: one, new Fort Oswego, a square with bastions, on the west side of the river on a height seventy feet above the lake and some five hundred yards behind the old fort; the other, Fort Ontario, a four-pointed star, timbered and palisaded, on the fifty foot

[31] Bradstreet to Robinson, May 30, 1755, C.O. 5: 46, f. 773.

bluff on the east bank. The new forts were commanded by nearby heights, but the contours seemed to permit of no better sites. Alexander and Bradstreet, neither a trained engineer, drew the plans.[32] Shirley returned to New York convinced that the Lake Ontario region ought to be the chief theatre of operations in 1756. He planned an expedition of six thousand men against Fort Frontenac.[33] In preparation he contracted with Livingston and Morris for the building and equipping of three new ships, two brigs and a sloop; he put in Bradstreet's hands the entire batteaux service from Albany to the lake; and he ordered Patrick Mackellar, the engineer en second, to survey the fortifications at Oswego and make advisable additions.[34] But during the next three months, which he spent at Boston, he gradually came to see the impossibility of assembling six thousand men, and so lost heart in the Ontario venture. It was May 25 before he proposed to a council of war the abandonment of the scheme and the employment of the 44th and 48th against Crown Point. Having relinquished offensive plans in the west, he made no new provisions for Oswego's defense. Some supplies and recruits went forward with Bradstreet, and the communications he further protected by ordering Mackellar to lay out, and Craven to build, new forts at the carrying place at the head of the Mohawk. Evidently persuaded, to judge from his statements, that the place was adequately guarded, that the forts he had planned were finished, and that the ships were well on their way to completion, he took no other steps.

[32] George Demler, who later asserted that he served the expedition as engineer, objected to these plans (LO 1185). But Loudoun had a low opinion of Demler's technical capacities, HM 1717, vol. 3, May 16, 1757.

[33] *New Hampshire Provincial Papers*, VI, 463-467. This force would include the 44th, 48th, 50th, 51st, and probably the two new regiments he thought himself authorized to raise.

[34] Ordnance Board Minutes, March 26, 1756, W.O. 47: 47, p. 324.

The map opposite, with the above cartouche, is a reproduction, by permission, of the essential portions of Mackellar's original drawing,
twenty-five by twenty-five and a half inches, in the
Royal Library at Windsor Castle.

Such optimism was unsupported by the facts. Mackellar, reaching Oswego on May 16, found little there to approve. New Fort Oswego was not half finished, the ditch being sunk on two sides only, and the other two enclosed by a palisade. The men quartered there ran great risk of being cut off, and they were withdrawn on June 13. The blockhouse in Fort George mounted but three cannon, on the curving wall fronting the river; they were the only guns in the entire work facing in that direction, but they could not be fired for fear of bringing down the wall, already cracked in three places. The hornwork protected only the west and south sides, leaving the north side next the lake exposed; both wings were enfiladed from end to end. Mackellar deemed the ravelin of no use whatever, for its gorge was so close to the curtain and raised so high that it obstructed two-thirds of the fire from the flanks. On these two wings seven cannon were mounted, six of them on the west side. Directly south of the blockhouse was a continuation of the hornwork made of fascines and earth, mounting eight cannon which could not shoot except through the town, itself unprotected in any way on south and west. When on June 16 a large party of Indians cut off the batteaux guard and the cannon were fired, the platforms beneath the guns gave way. The powder magazine, which Bradstreet had built, was sunk four feet in the ground, covered with sod permitting moisture to penetrate, and not secure from enemy fire. Fort Ontario, though built of good timber, was improperly placed, for, at a distance of four hundred and fifty yards, it could not protect the harbor, nor, at a distance of a hundred yards and fifty feet above the level of the water, the lake's edge. It was commanded by a small height eighty or a hundred yards to the east, while fourteen hundred yards beyond rose a hill fifty feet above the top level of the pickets. Badly shaped, the effectiveness of its fire was diminished by the barracks built against the stockade, and there were no loopholes for small-arm fire. A gallery above the buildings did, however, provide "a tolerable defence against small arms".[35] None of the new ships were finished. At the time, therefore, when Shirley was reporting to his May council of war that Oswego's defenses were adequate, they were in fact but little advanced beyond the stage at which he had left them the preceding autumn.

The reason is not far to seek. From September until the spring the garrison lived on three-quarter or half rations. Before Shirley left provisions were low.[36] On August 30 a riot broke out among three hundred armed soldiers, who demanded full provision allowance and their pay, which threatened to become a general mutiny, and was with difficulty quelled.[37] During the winter daily rations dwindled to two ounces of pork and eight of bread.[38] Mercer, the commandant, was on the point of abandoning the fort in March, having but six days' provisions left, when a few laden batteaux arrived to save the situation. By that time the men were so weak that the strongest guard they could mount was sixteen or eighteen, and half of those supported themselves with sticks. The relief lifted the ones who had fallen to their feet, and assisted them to their cold tents, bark huts, or colder barracks, for one barrack, at least, constructed of green wood, let in the

[35] Mackellar to Montrésor, May 25, 1756, in A Journal of Transactions at Oswego from the 16th of May to the 14th of August, 1756, by Patrick Mackellar, Cumberland Papers.

[36] John Shirley to Governor Morris, *Pennsylvania Archives*, II, 404, 406, 424, 427.

[37] Court martial at Oswego, Sept. 1, 1755, W.O. 71: 128. The court was sympathetic, gave light sentences to six ringleaders, and acquitted two others.

[38] William A. Whitehead, *Contributions to East Jersey History*, p. 114.

drifting snow through great seams.[39] There were neither beds nor bedding. Captain Vickers had fifty men in his company when Shirley left; by the spring thirty-nine were dead. Each of the eight companies of the 50th lost thirty men. The 51st, stationed in Fort Ontario, suffered less. In the end of April the garrison learned of ten bat- teaux-loads of provisions lying at the falls, twelve miles distant, but they were too weak to muster a guard to bring them in. Carpenters who arrived in February could not work for want of a guard, could not be adequately fed, and were themselves often compelled to assume guard duty.

Such ghastly suffering was heightened for the troops by the knowledge that under lock and key in the store- houses within the fort lay blankets, clothing, beef, bread, sugar, rum, and wine. Money could buy them; Demler bought blankets at fifteen shillings each, and Colonel Schuyler paid ten and one-half pence a pound for beef and flour. Wine cost twelve to twenty shilling a gallon. Dr. Stakes of New Jersey paid eighteen shillings a day, pro- vincial currency, for his "diet, soup, and a bed". Vickers loaned money to his men, and several died in his debt. But the army as a whole, for reasons already explained, had no money. Shirley tried to remedy the situation by having a number of slips of paper printed, to be signed by Craven as paymaster and Mercer as commandant, to pass as currency in the garrison of Oswego only. Mercer, evi- dently afraid to complicate further the financial entangle- ments, suppressed the slips as soon as they arrived. These supplies, though under the charge of Francis Lewis, the

[39] From the report of Captain John Vickers of the 50th, whom the winter totally incapacitated for future service. He went on half-pay when the 50th was broken. (Jan. 5, 1757, LO 2636). Vickers gave the information orally to Loudoun, who took it down "as he said it." Vickers signed it. The original paper is in the Cumberland Papers.

commissary, were the property, not of the Crown, but of private merchants, among them a favored firm consisting of Morse, E. Best, William Kelly, and John Gill. George Jackson, their representative at Oswego, received the goods they sent up, turned them over to Francis Lewis to sell, and remitted to his employers bills for the value of goods sold, signed by Lewis, and drawn on Alexander and Livingston.[40] Lewis used the actual cash obtained in such transactions for paying both army accounts and contractors' accounts.[41] It seems clear enough that William Alexander profited in his private capacity as a merchant by using his official powers as a member of Shirley's staff to assign trading privileges. In another case Robert Livingston advised a certain Charles De Witt to follow the army as a trader, to see Alexander about it, and to offer him one-third interest.[42] These goods went up to Oswego at a time when there was no contract for batteauxmen and justices could with difficulty impress them. Some goods, reported both Demler and William Williams of the 51st, went in the Crown's batteaux. "Whether 67 batteau loads be enough, or too much for a commissary and sutler for such a number of officers and men I leave to better Judges but that such number were employed upon the government's charge, as also a number that were loaded with trunks and bales that went to Oswego with the General [Shirley] and were as Mr. Alexander told me presents for the Indians is what I am sure of."[43] Thus pri-

[40] John Gill to George Jackson, Aug. 12, 1756, LO 1476. William Kelly to George Jackson, Aug. 12, 1756, LO 1477. These letters were on the way to Oswego when the fort surrendered, and thus fell into Loudoun's hands.

[41] Account of William Alexander & Company with Francis Lewis, Oswego, May 1, 1756, C.O. 5: 46, f. 487.

[42] EM 2588, Calendar of the Emmett Collection, New York Public Library *Bulletin*, 1900, p. 165.

[43] Report of William Williams, in answer to Loudoun's questions, Sept. 10, 1756, LO 1763. Colonel John Henry Lydius, who said that Shirley ap-

vate trading ambitions contended with and took precedence over government needs.

While Shirley may not have known of this condition of affairs, for he seemed to have learned of the famine at Oswego as late as March, he looked in general with favor upon Indian trading posts combined with garrisons as a sure means of retaining Indian friendship, and recommended the extension to Oswego of some such system as Massachusetts practised.[44] He probably gave his sanction to Alexander's proposals, and left the whole business, as usual, in Alexander's hands. Upon this man, the *soi-disant* Earl of Stirling, whom Shirley implicitly trusted, falls much of the responsibility for the wretched condition of Oswego. Shirley was easy to hoodwink.

It is harder to excuse Shirley for neglecting to safeguard and improve the means of communication between Schenectady and Oswego. Various reasons were given for the failure of stores to reach Oswego in the autumn of 1755: they were not collected at Schenectady until the creeks were too low for water transport; the Germans at the Flatts, entrusted with the transportation across the carrying place, "a most selfish, ignorant, unsocial and intolerable set of mortals",[45] proved unreliable; or—and this was Shirley's excuse—the governor of New York refused to impress batteauxmen. But Shirley made no effort to improve the transportation until 1756, when he instructed John Bradstreet, a captain of the 51st, to raise and take command of forty companies of fifty batteauxmen each, and formed a working party under

pointed him as colonel of Indians on the Niagara expedition, maintained that the Indian goods bought with Crown funds for distribution at Oswego were never used for that purpose, and that he did not know whether they ever arrived at Oswego, Sept. 21, 1756, G.D. 8: 95.

[44] *Shirley Correspondence*, II, 373-377.

[45] Journal of the Siege of Oswego, *Military History of Great Britain, 1756-1757* (London, 1757).

James Fairservice to clear the creeks. Even then he did
nothing about land transport, relying as before upon the
wagons of nearby farmers. In selecting Bradstreet, Shirley, seldom a good judge of men, made perhaps the wisest
appointment of his career. A splendid leader of irregu-
lars, Bradstreet had lived among the woodsmen of Nova
Scotia and had learned regular army discipline from long
service in the 40th. His work alone, of all that Shirley
authorized, won the unqualified praise of Shirley's successors.

While conditions at Oswego improved in the spring
and summer, the fortifications in August were but little
stronger than before. Utterly demoralized by the hardships of the winter and persuaded that Shirley had forgotten them, the garrison suffered constantly from the
attacks of hostile raiding parties. It is not hard to visual-
ize that small garrison, isolated nearly three hundred
miles from civilization, its communications insecure,
spending the summer under a ceaseless scrutiny from the
surrounding forests. The day after Mackellar's arrival
Indians attacked a party guarding Bradstreet's batteaux
above the rift in the river and killed two men, one of them
Lieutenant Blair of the 51st. A week later, at eleven at
night, they fell upon an encampment of batteauxmen
forty yards from the town, killed four, scalped a drunken
soldier sleeping away from his post—who afterwards
recovered—and pursued the rest into the very street of
the town. The next week two men were killed at work in
the woods about Fort Ontario. On June 16 a hundred and
fifty Indians cut off the batteaux guard of fourteen men,
and captured and killed all but two. The next day five
whaleboats scouting along the shore twenty miles to the
eastward were fired upon, and on June 25, under similar
circumstances, the Indians captured one whaleboat, taking its crew of eleven men, and forced the other crews

to flee to the shelter of the accompanying schooner and
scuttle their craft. Two days later the French fleet took
one of the schooners, thereby making the completion of
new ships more imperative.[46] On July 3 Bradstreet, who
had arrived two days before with six hundred batteaux
loads of provisions, rigging, and guns for the new ships,
was attacked on his return journey by a mixed party of
French regulars, Canadians, and Indians. He succeeded
in beating them off. From the 8th of July on, persistent
reports came in from scouts and Indians that the enemy
was gathering in force for a final attack. Thus the French
tactics, which had begun with the capture of Fort Bull
at the carrying place in March, successfully contributed
to the demoralization of the garrison and hindered work
on both fortifications and ships.

Other factors prevented work on the forts. When Mackellar on May 17 asked for a working party, a council of
war decided that the completion of the ships was more
important. Men could not be spared for both services,
especially since no party could work without a strong
guard. No laborers were employed on the forts until June
17, when twenty men repaired the platforms which had
given way in the firing on the 16th; during the rest of the
month an average force of sixty men a day built an advance outpost to prevent further raids on the town. When
the small schooner was lost, and the enemy showed its
superiority on the lake, a council of war decided to begin
work on the forts, in accordance with the instructions received by Mackellar from Montrésor and Shirley in answer to his letter of May 25. For the first two days of July

[46] This narrative is related in detail by W. L. Grant, ''The Capture of
Oswego by Montcalm in 1756: A Study in Naval Power; with an appendix
of Letters from Captain Housman Broadley,'' *Transactions* of the Royal
Society of Canada (1914), series III, vol. viii, p. 193. See also F. H. Sever-
ance, *An Old Frontier of France*, II, 160-179.

fifty men constructed fascines and erected a battery at the north end of the hornwork fronting the lake, for in Mackellar's opinion Fort George had the only walls fit for mounting cannon. On the 3d and 4th work was stopped for James Pitcher, commissary of the musters, who arrived with Bradstreet, to muster the regiments. On the 3d also, the brig and the sloop were launched, but they were not ready for use until the 29th.

On the 5th the double consequence of Shirley's recall and the want of money was felt. In his first letter Mackellar had represented to Shirley his need for cash, for soldiers who performed laborer's work customarily got additional pay and would not work without it. Shirley's reply of June 10 authorized Mackellar to draw upon the traders' money in Lewis's hands, and in June working parties were so paid. But when Shirley was superseded, William Alexander sent off posthaste a letter to Lewis disclaiming further responsibility for bills for soldiers' labor. Neither he nor Shirley offered suggestions; they washed their hands completely of Oswego. Lewis, therefore, told a council of war on July 5 that he could not continue payment, and as a result all work on the forts was stopped. The temper of the troops showed too plainly that forced labor would only increase the desertion already prevalent. When on July 22 Ensign Grant, returning from a scouting expedition, reported a body of the enemy encamped in force up the lake and when a captured Indian revealed the news that Montcalm was expected at Fort Frontenac, the officers persuaded the men to work on trust. From July 23 to August 13 an average of two hundred and twenty men a day sunk ditches about Forts Ontario and George, made platforms, cut loopholes, and repaired the parapets. This was the only work done on the forts themselves since they were built, and its inadequacy is seen from Mackellar's estimate of June that to proceed upon necessary repairs would require four hundred men a day for three months.[47]

The effect of the unskilful designing and faulty location of the forts was seen during the siege. The French, with a vastly superior force, invested Fort Ontario on August 11. "The Garrison was pent up in a Pickitted Fort, with a Ditch begun but not Compleated, & too weak to admitt of a Sortie, & but one Entrance to the Fort, the Picketts of this Fort which were fourteen feet high, were below the Level of a little hill to Eastw^d about eighty Yards, on which their Battery was raised, so that we could not bring one Gun to bear upon the Enemy."[48] It was evacuated on August 13. The enemy then erected a battery on the edge of the bluff in front of the fort, and on the morning of the 14th began to play upon Fort George. That fort replied with six guns and four mortars, of which three, on the hornwork to the west of the blockhouse, were reversed on their platforms. The parapet designed to protect them was in their rear, and the feet of the men serving them were in plain view of the enemy. Other guns were erected on hastily-raised platforms of pork barrels. At the same time the French crossed the river above the rift and surrounded the fort on south and west. In a council of war Mackellar declared it untenable; the chamade was beat, and the articles of surrender signed.

As for the ships, at no time during the summer could they give the British command of the lake. The new brig and sloop could only be fitted for service by stripping one of the old schooners, for there was available for them

[47] All data about fortifications is taken from Mackellar's journal in the Cumberland Papers.

[48] An Account of the Strength of the Garrison, & State of the Works at Oswego at the Time of its being invested . . . [signed by twelve officers of the garrison], Cumberland Papers.

in July neither rigging, twine, sails, nor guns. The materials prepared in London the preceding spring for these ships were on the high seas in July, as were the officers designed to command them. The new snow, ordered by Shirley to replace one of the brigs, was launched on July 22, but was useless without men, rigging, or guns. While Captain Housman Broadley of the Royal Navy, the commander on the lake, may not have had enough fresh water experience to make the best use of his fleet, he never had the opportunity to meet the French on an even footing. He could put to sea in July with only three vessels.[49]

Some of the responsibility for the misfortunes and disasters which led to Oswego's surrender belongs to the commander in chief. Shirley laid out badly-planned forts, left the garrison with a shortage of provisions, placed the contracts for workmen and equipment in the hands of an inefficient firm, and failed to keep himself informed of the progress of events. His difficulties were of course very great. Upon the Indians he could not rely to defend the communications, and for that he blamed Johnson; nor were there wagons enough, in a sparsely populated country, for land transport. Great Britain gave him no aid in furnishing ordnance supplies and naval equipment which the colonies could produce either slowly or not at all. Skilled navigators or seamen on the lakes could not be found. The construction of a stone fort capable of resisting a long siege was out of the question; the general orders from England prohibited such heavy expense. Shirley worked alone under great handicaps, and suffered from the British policy of conducting the war with colonial resources. But such difficulties do not excuse him from having failed to do everything that he could within the limits prescribed.

[49] Broadley to Shirley, July 15, 1756, C.O. 5: 47, p. 135.

The most obscure point in the whole Oswego affair, and the one most discreditable to Shirley, concerns the amount of information which Shirley passed on to his successors. When Abercromby arrived at Albany on June 25 Shirley had received Mackellar's first report, and had presumably talked with Bradstreet. He knew the condition of the garrison when he left it the preceding autumn; he had heard from Mercer and the officers along the Mohawk of its sufferings during the winter. He should have been aware that the statements made to his council of war on May 25 were either untrue or unduly optimistic. Yet in the two long letters which he wrote to Abercromby summarizing the situation there is no suggestion that Oswego was in a critical condition.[50] He described the dangers of the communications and what he had done to lessen them, mentioned his dealings with the Indians, enclosed copies of councils of war of the previous September and of May 25, summarized his orders to Mackellar, and suggested that things were in such great forwardness that an expedition could be undertaken against Fort Frontenac. He was not sure of the strength of the 50th or 51st, though on April 24, 1755, the former had contained 940 men; he knew that their arms were bad and that their clothing was worn out, and he supposed that they were not as well disciplined as they might be. While most of these statements, by themselves, were true enough, they were but a small part of the whole truth, and the proposal to resurrect the offensive against Fort Frontenac, which Shirley had himself abandoned in May, left an erroneous impression. There was nothing about the want of money at Oswego, nor about Mackel-

[50] The letter of June 27 is in *Shirley Correspondence*, II, 468; that of June 28 in LO 1258. Abercromby summarized the two in his letter to Loudoun of June 30 (LO 1263), which expressed no anxiety for Oswego.

lar's report, except "I have asked him for his opinion regarding the building of a more respectable fort upon the point where Ontario stands."

But there is not sufficient evidence to accuse Shirley of deliberately concealing information in the hope that his own mismanagement would not appear until his successors had been long enough in command to assume the blame. That would seem to be a rational deduction from the facts, and to bear out the startling accusation brought by Governor Hardy against Shirley the preceding November. "I have had many Conversations with Mr. Shirley [wrote Hardy], whom I left at Albany, and I must take leave to say I never met his Equal to transact Business with. Let me entreat your Lordship not wholly to give Ear to his Representations, and however hard the Task is to reflect on any Gentleman, the honour & respect I have for your Lordship oblige me to inform you that *I fear he is no better than an artfull Deceiver* ready to advance any thing in his Representations of Things as Facts, when he is perhaps *more a Stranger to the Facts he asserts than those he lays them before.*"[51] But if one remembers that Shirley disliked detail; that he might well have discounted Mackellar's observations as coming from an engineer who applied European standards of fortification to an outlying American post; that Bradstreet, whom he trusted, compared the Oswego of May, 1756, with the Oswego of May, 1755, and was optimistic; and that Alexander, his repository of information and his right-hand man, had personal reasons for assuring the general that all was well—then Shirley emerges as the honest, well-meaning, and gullible person that he was.

Abercromby would seem to have learned of Oswego's condition only after Bradstreet arrived at Albany on

---

[51] Hardy to Halifax, November 27, 1755, Cumberland Papers.

July 10, bringing the news of the attack he had beaten off and letters from Mercer, Mackellar, Broadley, and Elias Marsh, who was in charge of the carpenters. He ordered Gage to hold the 44th in readiness to march, and Bradstreet and Sir John St. Clair to prepare necessary supplies. It was then found that Shirley's contractors had in store at Schenectady only seven barrels of pork and eight of bread, none of which was edible,[52] and that to transport from Albany to Schenectady enough of the London contractors' provisions to serve the regiment, for which an order was given,[53] required wagons which were not to be had. The provincial army was at the same time carrying provisions to Fort William Henry, and on July 4 Winslow estimated that they needed 455 wagons above their 121 oxteams for the purpose.[54] The farmers at Schenectady had only a hundred and forty wagons, and even when these were pressed into service, as they were on Hardy's warrant, they could not be used in two places at once. Abercromby complained that the "people who had waggons were so malicious that they cut tacklings and sent the Horses into the Woods."[55] By the 28th only a half of the provisions needed for the 44th for one month

[52] Stores left at Schenectady when Shirley was superseded, received from Oliver DeLancey, March 1, 1757, LO 6560. The return also included 445 barrels of rum, 13 skipple of peas, 48½ tierces of rice, 28 barrels of salt, and 1 firkin of butter.

[53] Particular quantity of provisions got from the contractors to compleat the provisions to go with Major General Webb in July, 1756 [signed] Robert Leake, Com'ry, LO 1182. Shirley's account of this transaction, based upon hearsay evidence of rumors circulating in Albany, was that Webb refused to take Livingston and Morris's provisions and that Baker and Kilby had not enough in stock. Affidavit of John Murray, Sept. 4, 1756, C.O. 5: 46, f. 677.

[54] Kimball, ed., *Correspondence of the Colonial Governors of Rhode Island*, II, 222.

[55] General James Abercromby to James Abercromby (the agent), May 23, 1758, LO 5833.

had been got to Schenectady,[56] and as late as August 10 Webb wrote that supplies there were still short.

But this is not the whole story, for neither Abercromby nor Loudoun acted as if they feared an attack on Oswego. Abercromby's council of war of July 20 considered the information which Bradstreet brought, decided to send a regiment to put the works into a condition of defense, to build a road from the Flatts to the lake, and to construct as large a ship as the harbor would hold. Loudoun's orders to Webb to advance with the 44th suggested a leisurely progress: Webb was to review troops along the way, examine the condition of forts up the Mohawk, order storehouses to be erected, and leave Major Eyre to build a fort at Oswego Falls.[57] Arriving at Oswego, Webb was to build a respectable fort, and stiffen the discipline of the 50th and 51st. He carried orders to Mercer to build as large a brigantine as the port would allow, and a "small vessell somewhat in the nature of a Quarter Galley", and to send in his demands for the naval stores needed. These are not the kind of orders an anxious commander gives. Both the British generals deserve blame for not reading into the technical reports of the officers at Oswego more than was actually stated, and for not making inquiries from such men as Vickers, who returned with Bradstreet, as to the real condition of affairs. But it is also true that they did not begin to distrust Shirley until August 10—none of the documents quoted in the criticisms of his conduct were in their hands in July— and that they had no specific reasons for thinking his report on Oswego incomplete.[58]

---

[56] A Return of Provisions at Schenectady, July 17-28, [signed] Cornelius Cuyler, Assistant Commissary, LO 1217. It included 47 tierces of bread, 71 barrels of flour, and 103 barrels of pork.

[57] Loudoun to Webb, August 4, 1756, LO 1414.

[58] Late in the night of August 17, when Webb and the 44th had reached

From this account of Shirley's administration as commander in chief, it is clear that the evidence upon which Cumberland and the Treasury based their recommendations for his court martial was not the prejudiced tales of his political enemies in Massachusetts and New York, but rather the impartial and more damning indictment to be found in ledgers, returns, and accounts. He was careless in financial matters; he was too trusting of his subordinates; he was ignorant of army routine, and therefore an excellent example of the evils that flow from civilian control in the field. But he was no deliberate criminal, and it was four years before British officials could reach the conclusion that a bungler is not necessarily a thief. Eager as the War Office was to bring him before a court martial, it could not prove that he had broken any of the Articles of War, nor advance any evidence beyond Loudoun's accusations and enclosures, themselves unauthenticated by oath, that would meet the rigid requirements of court martial procedure. Pitt was lukewarm, and after Cumberland's resignation in the

German Flatts, he got news of the attack on Oswego. The next day a soldier of the 50th brought word of its surrender, and the possibility that the French might utilize the captured batteaux to proceed up Wood Creek. Webb, on his own initiative and without orders from Loudoun, sent orders to Major Craven, commanding at the Great Carrying Place between the Mohawk and Wood Creek, to obstruct the passage of the latter by felling trees into it. These orders merited, and received, stringent disapproval from Loudoun, who nevertheless so far believed in the report of the French advance that he ordered Winslow at Fort William Henry not to attempt the projected attack against Ticonderoga. When Webb reached the Carrying Place on August 20, saw the half-finished forts which Craven was building and the undisciplined state of Craven's troops, and heard exaggerated, conflicting rumors of enemy movements, he could not keep a balanced judgment. Again without orders from Loudoun, he destroyed Craven's forts, on August 31, and the next day retreated down the Mohawk. The correspondence between Loudoun, Webb, and Craven is in LO 1502, 1508, 1509, 1517, 1521, 1646, 1692. There is a good map of the forts in Hurlburt, *Historic Highways*, VII, and in *New York Documentary History*, IV, 524.

autumn of 1757 the whole matter was dropped, except for the passing of accounts.[59]

Shirley left to his successors the heritage of his mismanagement. As far as the construction of an adequate service of transportation, supply, and intelligence was concerned, Loudoun had to begin at the bottom, without foundations.

[59] W.O. 1: 4. Barrington to Cumberland, June 3; Cumberland to Barrington, June 13, 1757, Cumberland Papers.

CHAPTER VI

THE TEMPER OF COLONIAL ASSEMBLIES

By the end of August Loudoun was settled in a house in New York, rented from Mrs. Frances Moore, widow of Colonel John Moore who had been a wealthy merchant and a member of the council. Conveniently situated in Whitehall, a stone's throw from Fort George, it was to be his headquarters until the next year, when DeLancey, whose asthma thrived less in the country, invited him into the governor's mansion in the fort itself. In it he set up the retinue of servants brought from England; in its stables his grooms and his nineteen horses with their housings of green velvet and of black and gold, his travelling coach, his chariot, his street coach. Every evening, except when his hospitality was repaid elsewhere, there dined with him at the long table, heavily weighted with silver, his own intimate "family" made up of his aides de camp Captain James Cunningham and Lieutenant Gilbert McAdam, his secretary John Appy, Thomas Pownall, and such members of the general staff as Sir John St. Clair, Webb and his aide Captain Roger Morris. Doctor Richard Huck, the gay and learned wit who had been surgeon in Loudoun's Scottish regiment in the '45, was often there, as were John Young of the Royal Americans, Loudoun's special protégé, and James Robertson, later governor of New York, upon whose good sense Loudoun came more and more to rely. Governor Sir Charles Hardy and the DeLanceys were regular guests. They drank much wine—nineteen dozen bottles of claret, thirty-one dozen of Madeira, a dozen of Burgundy, four bottles of port and eight of Rhenish in a single week at Christmas of 1757—and their conversation abounded in the application of such military terms as scaling ladders, approaches, stolen marches, to the attempted conquest of colonial beauties. Of these the loveliest was charming Polly Philipse, heiress to Philipse Manor, in whose "Dependent Company" no British officer with a spark of manhood in him failed at one time or another to enlist. Even Loudoun "muster'd occasionally".

But for the most part he kept too busy for many amusements, and as his stay in America lengthened, he devoted more and more time to his work. He burdened himself with endless detail, customarily writing out all letters in longhand before giving them to Appy and the staff of clerks to copy. No one who had cause to see the commander in chief was denied entrance; Loudoun prided himself that his door stood open from morning till night. He tried to apply to the army the paternalism of a Scots laird for his tenants, of a colonel for the regiment he loved. Young officers who blundered received from him wise and acceptable advice, delivered in characteristically outspoken fashion. It was his way of getting work done and until he himself, in the autumn of 1757, bent under the strain of worries and disappointments, he succeeded in inspiring the corps of officers nearest to him with his own industry, good nature, and loyalty.

In such fashion the British staff, then as now, extended to strange shores the life it knew at home. That merry, self-contained society was out of key with the colonials with whom it was supposed to work. When Loudoun left New York to travel to other provinces, the contrast between his "family" and the curious crowds which thronged the governor's house in Norwalk to see him, or the stilted ceremony which the students in Philadelphia put on in his honor, emphasized his conviction that provincials were a decidedly inferior lot. Their customs were odd, though he might for policy's sake honor them by an occasional conformity. Their manners were apt to be uncouth, though in dealing with such provincials as Nathaniel Meserve, the New Hampshire ship carpenter, who earnestly gave their best to the British service, Loudoun did not let their rude ways mar the genial expression of that affability for which he was famous. Their very produce fell below British standards. Of American fish, for instance, Loudoun had a low opinion.

The Cod all over this country even what I saw in the winter which is the season for them are a lean soft fish no way comparable to those we have in Europe. The trout caught in Lake George are very good, the small scate are good and some of their flounders and I think none of their other fish except Lobsters, crabs and clams are tolerable. The large scate, particularly that they call Ray with a longhorn on his tail, bad; the sammon that I have seen at New York, bad; the bass, both sea and fresh water, bad; their oisters unshaply being made long and irregular shape very soft and bad . . . The fish they value most is a sheepes head which comes in June. He is a thick stout fish and his teeth and lips resemble a sheepes mouth but all his mouth within is sett with broad headed teeth flatt at top, and you find the fore teeth of the old ones often very much wore and broke. They say he lives on shell fish such as clams and oisters and with those teeth that he crackes them. I think him but a very Indifferent fish.[1]

Such statements illustrate the unequivocal quality of Loudoun's mind; there were but two sides to any question, the right one and the wrong one. The provincials were of the wrong sort, but he had to make use of them. What he had learned of them in England, and what he

[1] HM 1717, vol. 4, June 29, 1757. This was written after a week at sea, and Loudoun was a bad sailor: ''my head is always muddy and not able to write one sentence to an end and get throw a letter only by Perseverance.'' Loudoun to Cumberland, June 22, 1757, Cumberland Papers.

had seen with his own eyes in the summer of 1756, convinced him that they were people whom one might cajole and flatter, but to whom, in the end, one gave commands.

With such notions in his mind Loudoun on three occasions in the autumn of 1756 crossed swords with colonial opinion in its most independent and virulent form, the elective assembly. He knew something of the troubles he would have; the fate of the common fund in the Braddock plan and the support Winslow's officers had got from their governments were enough to show him that assemblies needed careful treatment. But it is doubtful whether he, or any newly-arrived British official, appreciated the solid strength of their position. He thought their opposition the result of mere local prejudices and petty vanities and expected it to disappear before the extraordinary authorities with which his commission vested him. He failed to realize that each of these popularly-chosen groups was in its own way as immovable, as potent, as parliament, and was already hide-bound by a set of precedents of its own making which yielded to no authority. They were all dedicated to the continuance of a struggle in which they had already registered far more gains than losses, the advancement of their powers at the expense of the Crown. When Loudoun loomed on their horizons, they were by tradition and temperament forced to regard him, the Crown's supreme military representative, as much of a foe to their constitutional advancement as any governor had ever been, and they employed the same tactics which had won them success before. In this battle of Loudoun and the assemblies, quite as much of a contest for him as the war with the French and by far the more significant aspect of his American career, there is much to be said on both sides. Loudoun's position is apparent: a soldier must always consider victory by the most direct route as the paramount objective in war. The assemblies thought the war important, but less so than the maintenance of their liberties; they had a double objective, and they were undeniably right when they suspected that military union under a commander in chief, if completely attained, spelled a curtailment of their powers. Thus there were two issues, the war and constitutional liberty; and three protagonists, each against the other two, Loudoun, the assemblies, and the French.

Let us run through, colony by colony, the answers of the assemblies to Loudoun's two requests, one of August 20, the other of September 30, for additional provincial troops. We shall see how intermixed were the causes of their procrastination: here they were jealous of one another, there fearful of the menace in Loudoun's supreme command, there hampered simply by the lack of an effective machinery for putting troops promptly into the field. We shall see how their tactics differed, yet all contributed to the same end, and for us, as for Loudoun, his experiences in these two months will constitute an introduction to his efforts to bend all assemblies to a single purpose in the next year's campaign.

The fall of Oswego furnished Loudoun with his first occasion for summoning aid. On August 20, when he first learned the news, the British position, though not as precarious as he believed—for the French were as fearful of him as he of them—was perhaps as dangerous as at any period of the war. He had arrived expecting to command some seventeen thousand men. He had, for reasons already explained, considerably less than half that number, distributed over two hundred miles of territory in northern New York. The 44th occupied the unfinished forts at the Oneida carrying place; along the hundred and thirty-seven miles of the winding Mohawk were small detachments of the 50th, 51st, the New Jersey regiment, four North Carolina provincial companies, and the four

New York independent companies. At Albany the nine hundred men of the 35th and 42d secured the magazines, storehouses, and communications. The 48th held the posts up the seventy miles of the Hudson to Fort Edward, where lay half the provincial army. Fourteen miles to the north, at the end of Lake George, was the other half. The raw recruits of the 35th, convicts and conscripted men, and of the 42d, fresh from the Highlands, were still on the high seas, and the thousand new men of the Royal Americans, not a month in the service and distributed among four battalions, had not yet joined him. He had no intelligence on which to depend, either from sporadic scouting parties of provincials, from the two companies of rangers, or from the Indians. He had no knowledge of the country, and could find no one who had; he was without transport facilities. Opposed to him was an enemy reported to have had at Oswego four thousand men, well-trained and supported by Indians, and capable of moving against him, either from west or north, with the batteaux captured there. Under these circumstances he deemed immediate reinforcement a necessity. His letter of August 20 to the four New England governments, New York, and New Jersey, asked for men, and for the wagons which New York alone could not supply.

The assembly of Rhode Island, a private colony, happened to be in session when Loudoun's letter arrived, discussing the sinking of bills of credit, and upon it fell the initiative. It at once took the usual measures it employed whenever, out of a clear sky, such requests appeared. It voted to send suitable men to Massachusetts and Connecticut to discover what those governments were doing "upon this extraordinary event", and it appointed the committee of war, the field officers of every regiment of militia in the colony, and the deputies of each town as a massive committee of inquiry to find "where provisions, arms, blankets, war-like and other stores of all sorts can be had for five hundred men." Having thus set in motion the wheels that might some day grind out the reinforcement Loudoun wanted at once, it adjourned.[2] Two weeks later it came together again. Unhappily neither Massachusetts nor Connecticut had replied.[3] The five hundred men had, therefore, to be forgotten, but as a gesture of its willingness the assembly voted to raise a company of sixty men. It named the officers, with the usual provision that if any should refuse to serve the committee of war might appoint others. If sixty volunteers should not appear by September 25, the committee of war might take necessary measures. Then, with the satisfaction that comes from duty well done, it appointed a committee to congratulate Loudoun upon his safe arrival in America, to lay before him the colony's exposed and defenseless position, and to plead his assistance.

Governor Belcher of the royal province of New Jersey, where council and assembly had long been at odds with each other, next dealt with Loudoun's letter. On August 27 he laid it before his council; did they not think so important a question demanded the immediate calling of the assembly? The council knew well the assembly's reluctance to assume fresh burdens and the shortness of its temper when called together unnecessarily. Therefore, it decided in the negative on the ground that Loudoun's information of Oswego's surrender was perhaps inaccurate, and that the assembly had already, at its last meeting, considered most of the matters in Loudoun's letter. Nearly a month later—there then being no doubt that Oswego was lost—Belcher laid the letter before them

---

[2] *Rhode Island Colonial Records*, V, 510.

[3] Governor Hopkins to Loudoun, Oct. 23, 1756, LO 2072. *Correspondence of the Colonial Governors of Rhode Island*, II, 233.

again, stressed the "uncommon and extraordinary Situation of Affairs", and asked whether the general safety and "in Particular that of this Province" did not warrant calling the assembly. The council agreed; the assembly was summoned for October 12.[4]

Governor Wentworth of New Hampshire, another royal colony, laid Loudoun's letter before his council on August 30. The council appreciated the force of the emergency and advised the governor to enlist or impress from the militia two companies of fifty men each, but also suggested that he postpone the levying until the assembly had met and defrayed the costs. On September 2 Wentworth addressed the assembly, and pointed out to them that if they failed to comply with Loudoun's request "we shall soon become Provinces and Subjects of the French King, Subjected to a Government whose civil Polity is Tyranny, and to a religion, teaching superstition and the worship of wood and stone, instead of that pure and uncorrupted adoration due only to the Supreme Being." To this stately argument the assembly yielded, and though aware that New Hampshire already had more than its proportion of men in service, agreed to the raising of a hundred more, and instructed the committee of war for the Crown Point expedition to supervise their equipping and transportation to Albany. The raising of them it left to the governor. This action may appear to have been unusually prompt; only a week had passed since Loudoun's letter reached Portsmouth, and here were men about to cross the mountains to his relief. But we must not be deceived. As the council had passed on the responsibility to the assembly, so the assembly, with canniness born of long experience, passed it on to the governor. In New Hampshire the fines assessed by the

---

[4] *New Jersey Archives*, 1st series, XVII, 57, 61, 62.

militia law when an impressed man refused to serve were
so low that it was no financial drain for any officer or
private to pay them and escape. Whole companies in turn
paid the fine; by the end of the month the hundred men
were not yet collected.[5]

Massachusetts was a semi-royal colony with a charter
which, among other things, forbade militia to march outside its bounds without express order of its general court.
Governor Shirley was anxious to redeem his reputation
with Loudoun, and he had, moreover, a special knowledge of the military situation. In the early part of August
he had prevailed upon the assembly to press six hundred
men from the militia to complete the Massachusetts
troops in Winslow's army, and now, on August 30, he
laid Loudoun's letter before it. Emphatically he dwelt
upon the dangers that would follow the loss of Oswego.
Two days later an express messenger whom he had sent
to Albany returned with confirmation of Oswego's surrender, and on September 2 he again insisted upon a vote
of men. Five days later the assembly agreed upon a
masterly compromise. It empowered Shirley to lodge
orders with Colonel Williams of Hatfield and Colonel
Worthington of Springfield to draft three hundred and
fifty men each out of their militia regiments, and Colonel
Chandler of Worcester and the chief officer of the regiment of Colonel Ruggles of Hardwick to draft a hundred
and fifty each out of the western parts of their respective
regiments, these thousand men to be held in readiness to
march the moment they received news from Loudoun or
Winslow that the enemy were actually advancing to attack the upper forts. But since the French were less than
thirty-five miles from Fort William Henry and these
militia at least a hundred and fifty, the aid they could

[5] *New Hampshire Provincial Papers*, VI, 536, 538, 539.

furnish seemed of dubious value. Shirley expostulated
in vain. He alone of New England governors heeded Loudoun's request for wagons or oxteams and issued at once
his warrants for impressing them. The subsequent history of the six hundred men impressed in August, whom
the assembly made an excuse for not voting more gen-
erously in September, was not a wholly convincing
testimony of the colony's promptness. On October 1 two
hundred and eighty of that group had joined the army,
seventy-six were ready to leave Albany, twenty-five were
sick on the road, seven had deserted, and two hundred
and four had not yet reached Albany.[6]

The solution reached in Massachusetts was doubly important, for it affected debates elsewhere. Shirley wrote
on the 13th of September to the governors of the four
colonies adjoining his, told them what Massachusetts had
done, and urged them all to do everything they could.
Thus, as usual, Massachusetts acted as leader of New
England.

In Connecticut, another private colony, Governor Fitch
had summoned the assembly before Shirley wrote. It met
the 6th, not knowing quite what to do. It therefore sought
to gain time by asking Loudoun his purpose in wanting
reinforcements: did he mean to attack Crown Point, or
simply to "sustain the Army where it is"? And what
answers had he got from other governments? Loudoun
thought the request "a fair one" and replied in a thousand words that the danger of August 20 had somewhat
abated, that he scarcely could think it wise to divulge
campaign plans to assemblymen with wives and friends,
and that he hoped to gain the assembly's confidence in
the same manner as he held the confidence of the king.[7]

[6] A Return of the Recruits sent to joyn the Provincial Troops at Lake
George [signed], Benjamin Goldthwait, LO 2810.

[7] *Fitch Papers*, I, 256-259.

His letter reached the assembly the same day that it learned from Shirley of Massachusetts' action. Without more ado, having learned what it wanted, it proceeded to improve upon that device. It resolved that when Governor Fitch and the committee of war were informed that the enemy were approaching the provincial army they should detach a thousand men from the militia, appoint officers, and send them forward.[8] For all practical purposes this vote was wasted effort.

New York alone, where the danger lay, furnished Loudoun promptly with aid. Acting on the governor's and not the assembly's authority, Sir William Johnson, commander of militia in the county of Albany, got together a thousand men by August 24.[9] Loudoun kept them in service until the first week in September, longer than Hardy thought advisable, for militia grumbled if continued in camp without action.

In answer to his first request for aid, therefore, Loudoun got the services of a thousand men for ten days, and that through no action of an assembly. Loudoun thought Shirley's influence in Massachusetts the chief cause of New England indifference; if he were gone, his faction would be supplanted by high-principled men devoted to the Crown's interest. But no single individual caused the ponderosity of New England military arrangements, any more than a single individual could animate them into life. Shirley did his best, but could not break down the habitual routine of years, combined with the eternal tendency of assemblies to resist every exhibition of royal authority. His departure did not affect the situation. The response of assemblies to Loudoun's second request for

[8] *Colonial Records of Connecticut*, X, 545. The *Fitch Papers* contain the draft of a proposed bill to raise men which did not pass the assembly.

[9] *New-York Colonial Documents*, VII, 124; *Sir William Johnson Papers*, II, 548, 549.

aid in the autumn of 1756 was but a replica of their response to his first.

As far as any assembly knew, the second request came from an actual crisis. Throughout September such intelligence as Loudoun and Winslow managed to get pointed towards a French attack on the northern forts; Loudoun concentrated the majority of the provincials at Fort William Henry, joined the 48th with the remainder at Fort Edward, and used the recruits of the 35th, 42d, and Royal Americans as a reserve at Albany. On September 27 Winslow, who lived this month in constant trepidation, mistook a returning scouting party of his own for the enemy. He sent off a series of brief, frantic notes to Loudoun at Albany: the enemy were approaching in boats, Montcalm had sixty-five hundred men and many nine-pounders, the wind had rendered their own boats useless, the enemy were close enough to the garrison to answer its shouts.[10] Loudoun wrote in haste to the four New England governments to exercise the utmost expedition in whatever they intended to do, since on Winslow's information the French were attacking with their entire force.

Thus arose the emergency which Massachusetts and Connecticut had made provision to meet. From the former province Lieutenant Governor Phips—Shirley had by this time sailed for England—replied on October 13 that he could not march militia outside the province without an act of the general court, that he had no information about public affairs, for Shirley had told him nothing and as lieutenant governor he had had no seat at the council.[11] Six days later he learned to his "mortifica-

---

[10] Massachusetts Historical Society *Collections*, 1st series, VI, 38; Winslow to Loudoun, Sept. 27 (two letters) LO 1906, 1707; Sept. 29, LO 1920.
[11] Phips to Loudoun, Oct. 13, LO 2019.

tion'' that the thousand men prepared for such a crisis had been obliged to return home because by some oversight no field officers had been appointed for them, nor could any suitable persons be prevailed upon to take command. By October 22 they were at last ready to march. But the assembly, learning that the dread scourge of colonial America, the smallpox, had broken out at Albany, insisted that Phips ask Loudoun to discharge them, since only one man out of every hundred had had that disease. Phips's letter crossed Loudoun's of the 24th, ordering the march of all troops stopped, as it was too late to make use of them.

In Connecticut the committee of war thought that Loudoun's ''apprehensions of the motions of the enemy seem . . . not so fully to comport with the vote of the assembly'', but was willing to have the matter discussed. Meeting on October 14, the assembly took steps for ''expeditious and effectual aid . . . to sustain and assist our troops.'' It voted that eight hundred men be drafted out of the militia regiments according to a proportion included in the bill; it named the officers, who were to provide their men with weapons and powder; and it ordered eighteen shillings bounty money paid to everyone who enlisted within twenty-four hours.[12] The smallpox, which it knew Loudoun would keep away from the army, held no terrors; that was bravely brushed aside. By November 1 the militia colonels began to receive word from their subordinates that the required numbers of men ''of the company of the parrish of Goshen in Lebanon'', or ''belonging to the company in the first Society in Hebron'', were impressed and were being supplied with arms and ammunition. Some officers had difficulty; Captain Daniel Cone of the South Military company in the Society in

---

[12] *Colonial Records of Connecticut*, X, 554-557.

East Haddam wrote to Colonel Trumble of the 12th regiment that he had got his three able-bodied men and had pressed one firelock, but that one of the men declared he would not go if he could help it and Cone would have to press another.[13] By this time Loudoun had written to stop all preparations.

Rhode Island actually got men on the march by the end of October. Meeting on October 14 the assembly increased to four hundred the sixty men voted in September but not yet gone. They were to be raised in this fashion: on October 21 the governor was to call together all the companies of foot and horse in the colony and draft the four hundred; all the males between the ages of sixteen and sixty were to be included in the lists of the companies, except the governor, deputy governor, assistants, members of the house of deputies, justices of superior and inferior courts, sheriffs, town council men, town clerks, justices of the peace, commissioned officers, ministers of the gospel, and all those who had sustained the offices of governor, deputy governor, assistants, and justices of the superior courts, together with all those who had made or should make oath or affirmation that it is against their conscience to bear arms. If this manoeuvre failed, the companies were to meet in every town, in the presence of the town council, and vote whether the officers should impress or choose by lot the numbers needed to complete their respective proportions. The field officers, or in their absence the town council, could discharge any person really unfit for duty, or anyone who "hath any other reasonable excuse". Impressed privates who failed to appear or deserted were to be fined a hundred pounds, old tenor, and officers who neglected to call together their companies a thousand pounds. Officers were ordered to purchase or

[13] Cone to Trumble, Nov. 1, 1756, from manuscripts in the Connecticut Historical Society at Hartford.

impress blankets; the committee of war was to furnish bounty money, kettles, powder, ball, and to provide material and cloth for tents. The assembly then resolved itself into grand committee and selected the officers.[14] All this elaborate procedure—the only one which had ever been used—followed the receipt of information that the entire forces of Canada were within striking distance of the provincial army. Nine days later the assembly met to stop the march of the four hundred; for news of the smallpox at Albany had reached Rhode Island.[15] By then Loudoun had replied to Hopkins' letter of October 23, the first notice he had received of the assembly's vote, and had stopped the march. He begged Hopkins to return a hearty thanks to the assembly, "as I do sincerely to you."

Governor Wentworth, who had corroborative evidence from a provincial officer at Charlestown of the supposed French attack,[16] met his assembly the 12th of October and recommended an increase in the hundred men voted in September and a stiffening of the fines for refusal to serve. A joint committee report from assembly and council flatly denied aid at the moment on the ground that the season was too far advanced for any good to come of it, but professed willingness to alter the militia law "when there may be occasion therefor."[17] Wentworth then tried to raise the hundred already voted. He waited a reasonable time for voluntary enlistments, and one volunteer appeared. He then ordered an impress and appointed a rendezvous. Thirteen men came; the others had paid

---

[14] *Rhode Island Colonial Records*, V, 534-542.

[15] There was a basis for this smallpox scare. The Albany magistrates proposed that a sentry be stationed before every infected house and no one except doctors and nurses be allowed to enter, Webb to Loudoun, Oct. 13, 1756, LO 2020. But Loudoun wrote Hopkins that the disease was confined to seven families and had not got among the troops, Nov. 5, LO 2160.

[16] Captain Parker to Colonel Williams, Oct. 3, 1756, LO 1965.

[17] *New Hampshire Provincial Papers*, VI, 538-541.

their fines, four pounds provincial currency apiece. He repeated the procedure "sundry times to get the complement", and when finally it was secured, proposed to send it by transport to Albany, for the men could not be trusted to march overland. "Until there is some Further powers in the King's Governors, a due obedience to His Majesty's Commands in affording succours to your Lordship . . . cannot be depended on." On October 22 Loudoun turned back the hard-won hundred men.

Though New Jersey was not among the colonies from whom Loudoun asked aid on September 30, Belcher called the assembly on October 12 to propose that it fill up the ranks of the New Jersey regiment, half of which was prisoner in Canada. The assembly sat two days, adjourned to November 11, met again on December 17 to consider a letter from Captain John Parker at Schenectady to the effect that his men, paid only to October 6, were deserting. It voted to pay them until March, and adjourned.

The New York assembly, in marked contrast to the others, voted to maintain a regiment of eight hundred and three men, not for the emergency of September, but for the winter. It appropriated £8950 for their pay till March 31, and £2400 to clothe them with warm waistcoats and buckskin breeches. But such action was to be expected; the war with Canada was, as it had always been, primarily New York's war.

As the bare outline of these legislative manoeuvres is unfolded, it may seem evidence adequate enough both to destroy one still commonly-held assumption, that the colonies threw themselves heart and soul into this war with the French, and to support another, that any union of them under British direction was as much an impossibility then as later. But Loudoun, who watched them with considerable shrewdness, did not think them either re-

luctant to fight or incapable of working together. Every
one of them, after all, had voted men to help him this
autumn, even though their hopes for a glorious victory
against Crown Point had been broken and though his request for troops at that late season of the year was, as
they said, an uncommon and extraordinary thing. He did
not despair of better responses in the future. For he saw
that the causes of their tactics, in part at least, were based
upon misapprehensions: they were suspicious of him because they distrusted his motives, and they were suspicious of one another because they were separate little
groups, each always plotted against by its neighbors,
valiantly holding out for such measure of local independence as it possessed. If he posed always as a friend anxious to save them money and trouble, and if he held so just
a balance between them that the burden fell equally on all,
Loudoun thought he might correct their errors of understanding. The tone of his letters to them was remarkably
gentle, even when, by setting their interpretation of the
state of affairs in New York above his, they most flagrantly affronted his professional instincts and his supreme command.

Loudoun's third contact with assemblies this autumn
showed him how pitifully exaggerated was their deep-
rooted fear of his motives. The incident arose over the
provincial army's provision supply. The assemblies had
arranged to feed their troops before Fox's letter of
March 13 arrived to promise that the British government
would assume that charge. Loudoun preferred not to mix
his provision accounts with provincial ones, and, concluding that a supply of food originally designed to feed
eighty-seven hundred men was sufficient for the five thousand that remained, intended to leave for settlement in
England the whole matter of recompense and adjustment.
But early in September Winslow reported that while the

Massachusetts stock was more than ample to meet the needs of her troops, the stores of the other colonies were low; at Fort Edward only ten days' provisions remained. He asked Loudoun to supply the deficiencies. Loudoun thereupon offered to purchase from the commissioners of the five colonies present with the army all provisions still in store, and thereafter to supply the provincial army at the king's expense. Oliver DeLancey, for New York, and Rufus Hopkins, for Rhode Island, immediately and gratefully accepted the proposal,[18] and the New Hampshire council instructed its commissioners to accept also. But in Connecticut the assembly was more cautious. The proposal seemed expedient and aboveboard, but some diabolical contrivance to lose them money, or to bring their forces under the king's command, might lurk within it. Not trusting its agent at Albany, it appointed Hezekiah Huntington and Jabez Hamlin a committee of two to repair to Albany and deal with Loudoun.[19] The two had explicit instructions to prevent any change in the independent status of the troops. Thus the assembly betrayed the same underlying fear of deception prevalent in the provincial camp itself, when men deserted in a body because, as Lyman said, "some vile fellow suggested that if they eat the King's bread they become King's soldiers." Loudoun calmed their fears, and on September 26 the two emissaries accepted his offer.

Massachusetts had less to gain than the others from Loudoun's proposal. The council declined immediate compliance with it for three reasons: since an act of the entire legislature had raised and provisioned the troops, only by the same power should the act be modified; since the Massachusetts troops were supplied, there was no need

---

[18] DeLancey to Loudoun, Sept. 12, LO 1777; *Rhode Island Colonial Records*, V, 565.

[19] *Colonial Records of Connecticut*, X, 545-546.

for haste and the question could await the assembly's consideration; and finally, a comparison of Loudoun's proposal with other parts of his letter left room to suppose that the victualling of provincial troops in the same manner as regulars might be construed as putting them under the sole power of the king's general. Therefore, because of the privileges granted to Massachusetts by the royal charter, the council felt it had no right to decide.[20] When the assembly met it repudiated such excessive caution, received Loudoun's offer (so wrote Secretary Josiah Willard) "as an instance of your Lordship's great Regard and Concern for His Majesty's Service and the Interest of His Colonies," and accepted it amid compliments and proffers of harmonious aid. But by then it was the middle of October, and Loudoun had been forced to add to the supplies of the other colonies at Fort William Henry, though the Massachusetts stock would have fed the whole of the rapidly diminishing army there. He attributed the cause of this particular evasiveness to a deliberate attempt on the part of Shirley's friends to annoy him.

Beyond the ignorance of these assemblies, their traditional hostility to the Crown and to one another, and their antiquated methods of raising troops, Loudoun thought he saw yet another cause of opposition. It was elusive, and he could not define it exactly because it was new to him. The trouble, he wrote to Halifax, was that royal governors had been forced to give up the powers of the Crown to assemblies in return for their salaries; that since assemblies had thus become important, all ambitious people struggled to get into them; that in order to get votes in their own neighborhoods, each one had forfeited that power of leadership which a magistrate ought to enforce and had allowed men to follow the dictates of their own wills, without control. "From whence there is no Law

[20] Extract from the council records, Sept. 21, 1756, LO 1868.

prevailing at present here, that I have met with, but the
Rule every man pleases to lay down to himself.''[21] Loudoun was being initiated into the bugaboo of the nobility
of his day. His is no bad definition of practical democ-
racy, that the only law is that which public opinion is
willing to follow. He instinctively distrusted it, and the
remedy he proposed was intervention from England, the
creation of a fund independent of the provinces, ''to pay
the governors, and new model the governments.'' Such
action must not be put off, for ''if you delay until a peace,
you will not have force to exert any British Act of Parliament here.''[22] As for the war itself, he came early to the
conclusion that it would have to be fought and won from
England; ''the King must trust in this country to himself,
and those he sends . . . for this Country will not run
when he calls.''[23] Here, then, was the path which a commander in chief should follow: to make such use of provincial governments as he could without giving them their
head; to turn the British army in America into a self-
sufficing unit, independent of provincial aid; to combat
the further extension of assembly power in military affairs; and to insist, in his letters to England, upon full
support for such a program.

[21] Loudoun to Halifax, Dec. 26, 1756, LO 2416.
[22] Loudoun to Cumberland, Nov. 23, 1756, LO 2262.
[23] Loudoun to Hardy, Sept. 16, 1756, LO 1820.

CHAPTER VII

QUARTERING

THE contest in the colonies over the quartering of regular troops, which in time was to reach there as violent a stage as in England under the Stuarts and to lead to a clause in the Declaration of Independence, began with Loudoun. Only once did it ever approach the popular conception of quartering, redcoats forcing their way into private houses and driving the owner and his family to the thin comforts of the attic; it was really a legal contest, whether civil magistrates were to quarter troops by virtue of the acts of the colonial assemblies, or by virtue of the royal prerogative as vested in the commander in chief. Save in this one matter alone, the whole history of the British army in America is an attempt to extend the military procedure which had grown up in England; but whereas the British government admitted that in England the right of quarter was a legal question, it took no steps during Loudoun's administration to define its legal basis in the colonies. Loudoun was left with no better buckler than that vaguest of terms, the prerogative, against the time-honored English arguments that no man shall be quartered upon except by law. If parliament had dealt with the question before the assemblies took it up, it would probably never have become a popular war-cry and ensuing bitterness would not have arisen.

Troops on the march and during winter need warm shelter for their health's sake and to be kept together for discipline's sake. Let us see what solution to this problem had been reached in Great Britain and in the colonies

before Loudoun's time. In England and Wales troops
were stationed in permanent camps, and when they took
to the road, along a route determined by a civil official, the
secretary at war, they found shelter according to the rigid
specifications of the Mutiny Act in the inns and public
houses with which the country abounded. That act forbade quartering on private subjects against their will, but
enjoined the constables of towns designated in a marching order to place troops in public houses, and permitted
the proprietor to choose between supplying officers and
men with victuals and beer—at a maximum cost of one
shilling for the former and fourpence for the latter—and
furnishing them gratis with candles, vinegar, salt, five
pints a day of small beer or cider, utensils, and firing. At
the end of their stay the proprietor's legal charges were
paid by the paymaster out of the troops' subsistence, and
his additional expenses were considered to partake of the
nature of an additional tax. If some military emergency
required the presence of troops in a region for more than
a temporary period, as in the case of the Hessians and
Hanoverians quartered in southern England during the
invasion scare of 1756, parliament often reimbursed public-house keepers for their abnormal expenditures.[1] In
Scotland, where the only public houses were single rooms
incapable of housing troops, a solution was found far less
protective of civilian rights than in England. The Mutiny
Act provided that both officers and privates should receive lodging, coals, and candles in private houses in Scotland, but throughout the eighteenth century it was uncertain whether these provisions applied in time of peace, or
only in time of war, and whether to permanent or only to
transient quarters.[2]

[1] Treas. 1: 367, Mar. 27, 1756; 27 *House of Commons Journal* 917.

[2] The Act of Union continued the laws in force in Scotland regarding
quartering, with the addition that no officer should pay for permanent billets

In none of the three extensions of the Mutiny Act, or parts of it, to the colonies—that of 1723 relating to the discipline of British soldiers abroad, of 1754 applying to provincial troops serving in conjunction with regulars, and of 1756 providing a legal basis for recruiting—were the sections concerning quartering included. Nor, prior to 1756, did any minister in England ever give careful consideration to the problem of quartering permanent troops in the colonies.[3] Except in Nova Scotia, Rattan, or Georgia, where the Crown as a matter of course built barracks or forts for troops stationed there, the question was left to local governments. In the West Indies, Jamaica, Antigua, and Barbados, the assembly paid for quarters for British regiments;[4] in 1746 the Virginia House of Burgesses appropriated £600 to shelter soldiers temporarily thrown upon the mercy of the province in their voyage to Cape Breton;[5] during the entire career of the four companies in New York the assembly provided barracks, firewood, and candles for them.

In 1754, when plans for Braddock's expedition were being drawn, the ministry apparently had in mind some

except in the suburbs of Edinburgh. Those laws were indefinite. The Scottish parliament in 1695, 1696, and 1698 provided that officers should pay for permanent quarters, but that privates should have them gratis. The Claim of Right in Scotland, 1689, however, forbade quartering in private houses in time of peace without the consent of parliament. In 1708 the Lord Advocate of Scotland interpreted this discrepancy to mean that men might be quartered in time of war upon such private houses as were "fortalices and castles . . . reputed to be strengths built for the security of the Kingdom" (*House of Lords Manuscripts*, New Series, VIII, 186). But in 1787 the Lord Advocate, Ilay Campbell, seemed to sanction quartering on all private houses at all times, and raised only the question of permanent or transient quarters (W.O. 1: 1034, Miscellanies, p. 251).

[3] In all the plans drawn for St. Clair's expedition of 1746, for example, I have found no mention of quartering.

[4] *Calendar State Papers, Colonial, 1704-1705*, §§151, 399, 603, 754, 902, 1323; *1705*, §§ 1421, 1459; *1706-1707*, §§ 613, 838, 973, 1132, 1146.

[5] *Journal House of Burgesses*, 1745, p. 164.

such solution of the quartering question as assemblies
had reached in the past: that is, reimbursement out of
colonial treasuries of those persons upon whom the actual
charges fell. The secretary of state ordered governors to
quarter such troops as the commander in chief desired,
but failed to specify what kind of quarters they should be,
or by whom payment was to be made, or how much, if
any, was to be paid. In America, as in Scotland, the only
public houses were small single rooms, grog shops, incapable of housing many soldiers, few in number and
owned by poor men. Were troops to be crowded permanently into such places? Were they to have the incidentals of quartering, such as firing, candles, utensils,
and small beer, to which they were accustomed and for
which the financial practices of the army made no allowance? Since provisions were furnished the troops in
America at the expense of the Crown, was it fair to the
provision contractors to allow householders to victual
men, as they could do in England, at the fourpence a day
specified by the Mutiny Act? Or, since diet was dearer in
America than in England, was it fair to colonial innkeepers to allot them only fourpence? Could men on the
march be furnished with free beer in one colony and not
in another? These, and many similar questions, the ministry left unanswered.

As a result, various solutions were reached in the colonies in 1755, when there were few regular troops to be
provided for. The Virginia and Maryland assemblies
appropriated funds to pay public-house keepers for the
short time troops were lodged with them on the march
to and from Wills Creek, where barracks had been built
out of the funds in Dinwiddie's hands. In Massachusetts
the general court built barracks on Castle Island for the
50th and 51st, but Shirley drew on the Crown's money
to provide beds, bolsters, firewood, and barrack uten-

sils.[6] Shirley also ordered barracks built at Albany, the cost to be borne by the New York assembly if they would assume it, and if not, by the Crown.[7] The blockhouses at the corners of the stockade were thereupon converted into barracks. As for officers, Shirley followed the continental practice of paying them "slap-gelt" for quarters; in May, 1756, his warrant for "slap-gelt" amounted to as much as £1953 4s. Shirley thus avoided raising the quartering issue by the simple expedient of scattering the Crown's money with a lavish hand; if he had had twenty thousand men to care for instead of four thousand, distributed in six or seven colonies instead of two, he would have run up enormous bills.

The Pennsylvania assembly, in 1755, faced with the necessity of quartering the 44th, the 48th, and the two independent companies of New York on their march from Virginia to New York, found a different solution still, and raised for the first time the legal point. Instead of appropriating money it extended to the province those sections of the Mutiny Act which dealt with quarters in England, and so laid the burden upon public-house keepers. A preamble explained the reasons: it was an undoubted right of subjects not to have soldiers quartered on them against their will; no officer civil or military should presume to transgress this right; any subject could refuse, legally, to quarter.[8] By the time this act reached the Privy Council for consideration, in the summer of 1756, the ministry, while uncertain as to the best way to deal with quartering in the colonies, was at least

[6] *Acts and Resolves of Massachusetts Bay*, XV, 293. Account of the Expense of raising the 50th regiment, Cumberland Papers.

[7] *Shirley Correspondence*, II, 305, 306, 334. *Review of Military Operations* (1757), p. 89. Barracks were also built at Schenectady; they were on the further side of the Mill-kill from the point where the King's road from Albany entered the main street of the town.

[8] *Statutes at Large of Pennsylvania*, V, 194.

agreed that local assemblies should not be allowed to raise the question of legal privilege. The act was therefore disallowed on the general ground that it would cramp the service, and the attorney general, in recommending its disallowance, pointed out that the propositions which had applied to England in the seventeenth century, in time of peace, when no standing army could exist without the consent of parliament, could scarcely be expected to apply to Pennsylvania in time of war for "troops raised for their Protection by the Authority" of parliament.[9]

This statement of the attorney general may serve to show how unformed were the notions in the ministers' minds at the time of Loudoun's appointment. For it was an ambiguous statement; it attempted to deduce three reasons why the parliamentary encroachments upon the prerogative of the Crown in England, which the Crown's ministers at times could wish had been less thorough, did not extend to those prerogatives in the colonies. If the distinction between a state of war and a state of peace was to be the fundamental point of difference, then distinctions between the status of civilians in England and in the colonies, or between the authority of a colonial assembly and of parliament, lost some of their force. In any case such a statement did nothing to solve Loudoun's practical problems. Nor was the definition which Cumberland gave, in answer to his direct question, of much more use: "Quarters," said Cumberland, "must be taken in the plantations as they are in Britain in time of war."[10] Did this mean that men were to be quartered upon public houses as the Mutiny Act specified for England, or upon private houses as in Scotland? To what lengths might an army go in England itself during actual

9 *Acts Privy Council, Colonial*, 1745-1766, §314.
10 HM 1717, vol. 6, p. 10.

invasion? There was no precise answer to that latter question, for it had never arisen since the Mutiny Act was first framed. Neither the invasion of 1715 nor that of 1745 were sufficient for the proclaiming of martial law, the suspending of the Mutiny Act, and the setting aside the liberties of the individual. And if one remembers how rigorous was the adherence of parliament to private rights as defined by statute, it is doubtful whether any invasion would have justified their suspension throughout the whole of England. Yet Cumberland would seem to have settled that constitutional point which had never arisen in England by the simple dogma of the professional soldier: in time of war, everything is justifiable. Loudoun's instructions threw no light on the problem; they simply required him to aid and assist governors in obeying his instructions for quartering troops.

Loudoun had to sift all these ambiguities into a practical plan. He interpreted them to mean, therefore, that he was allowed to take quarters, both for officers and men, either in public or private houses, whenever he deemed it necessary for the good of the service, and that such quarters should include the incidentals specified in the Mutiny Act for England, candles, vinegar, salt, small beer, utensils, and firing. To troops in passage he gave a marching order, couched in the same terms as in England, directing magistrates of towns designated therein to quarter the troops. The governors remained responsible, as in the past, and if they chose to have assemblies reimburse inhabitants, or construct barracks, Loudoun at first considered it no business of his as long as he got quarters where he wanted, and with the incidentals included. If they were denied, or were insufficient, he considered the immediate health of his men sufficient excuse for taking the matter out of the hands of civilian officials and employing the threat of forced quarter.

Legally Loudoun stood on insecure ground. The orders to governors could scarcely be interpreted to cover the extension of such precise British routine to the colonies. If he maintained, as he did in justifying himself with colonials, that the articles on quartering in the Mutiny Act extended to America—notwithstanding the fact that he agreed that its other articles did not—he had no basis for applying the Scottish practice in regard to private houses and the English one in regard to incidentals. His marching orders, unlike those in England, were not signed by a civil minister and therefore had no real significance. Loudoun recognized at once the fallibility of his position, and throughout his career kept urging the need of parliamentary action. At first he recommended the extension of the articles for quartering in England, and later, when he understood American conditions better, those for Scotland. In December, 1756, Pitt promised that a clause would be inserted in the Mutiny Act for the purpose,[11] but in February he seemed to consider that means ineffectual—as indeed it was—and was planning "how far a Provision of that Sort may be framed by a Separate Act of Parliament."[12] Pownall was probably responsible for changing Pitt's opinion. For Pownall proposed that by act of parliament any extraordinary expense incurred by a single colonial innkeeper in quartering and providing for troops should either be met by a general tax among all the innkeepers in the province, or be defrayed from some other provincial fund.[13] This

[11] Pitt to Loudoun, Dec. 22, 1756, LO 2383.

[12] Pitt to Loudoun, Feb. 4, 1757, LO 2765. A statement in a letter of Newcastle's to Pitt (*Correspondence of the Earl of Chatham* (1836), I, 238) leaves the impression that Pitt had not discussed the question with his chief colleague. "My Lord Loudoun, I find, mentions an act of parliament to be passed here. I don't well understand what he means by it."

[13] Mr. Pownall's Scheme for Quartering Troops in America, W.O. 1: 972, no. 349. A copy is in G.D. 8: 97.

raised the question of taxation of the colonies by parliament in an indirect way, and either for that reason, or because he was having political troubles of his own in the spring of 1757, or because parliament was an uncertain quantity, Pitt laid the question altogether aside, and did not attempt to resurrect it during the rest of the war. The commander in chief was left to fight his own way.

Thus the issue was clearly drawn. On the side of the colonists were the precedents of past assemblies and the cogent reasoning of the Bill of Rights: freedom from arbitrary quartering was a fundamental liberty of Englishmen, applicable to them everywhere, and when parliament omitted to preserve such rights abroad, the assemblies became the custodians. On Loudoun's side were very uncertain legal arguments, but very practical ones in the necessity of finding shelter for his troops, of treating all the colonies uniformly, and of saving the Crown unwarranted expense.

The clashes between the commander in chief and the assemblies were neither as many nor as long drawn out as contemporary rumor indicated, or subsequent history has implied, but they were severe enough to widen further the breach between the regular army and the colonies. The severest of all implicated no particular assembly, but was an affair between the army and the town officials of Albany. As the center of military operations and the home of Dutch traders who in Shirley's time carried on a profitable trade with the French, Albany alone saw quarters actually taken by force. The three hundred and twenty-nine families in the town could in 1756 shelter with ease a hundred and forty-six officers and fourteen hundred and forty-three men—so ran the room to room survey of the town—and in necessity could quarter a hundred and ninety officers and two thousand and eighty-two men. The public houses could hold only fifty.[14] When in the summer of 1756 Loudoun attempted to quarter the 35th and 42d on the inhabitants, the mayor seized the opportunity for heroics; they would rather die than submit. Loudoun replied that he could not be expected to prevent that, and quartered troops by his own quartermasters. He refrained from billeting officers until a "Canadian trader threw an officer's baggage into the streets, and barricaded the door, and I sent a file of men, and put the officer into Possession; my resolution is, if I find any more of this work, whenever I find a leading man, shut out any of the people, to take the whole house for an hospital, or a storehouse, and let him shift for himself."[15] To mitigate the fear such proceedings caused, Loudoun paid for his own quarters, at the princely rate of five pounds a week,[16] supplied the troops with beds and firing at the Crown's expense, and began the construction of the barracks, at the cost of the Crown, which Webb had arrived too late to undertake. The inhabitants replaced their trade with the French with a more lucrative one with the army, and no further trouble arose until the autumn of 1757, when Loudoun's greatly enlarged army went into winter quarters. Contemplating a winter attack upon Ticonderoga, he put eight battalions into the county of Albany. One battalion went into the small settlements along the Hudson—Kinderhook, Claverack, and Livingston Manor; another along the river from Luneburg to Albany; two along the Mohawk; one at Fort

---

[14] This seventeen page folio report gives the names of owners, size of families, number of fireplaces, and number of officers and men that each house could accommodate, LO 3515.

[15] Loudoun to Cumberland, Aug. 29, 1756, Cumberland Papers; Loudoun to Halifax, Dec. 26, 1756, LO 2416.

[16] H. Dreessen, householder, to the Earl of Loudoun, £14 5s. 10d. for lodging from July 29 to August 18, and £2 11s. 9d. "for my negroes attendance", LO 3774.

Edward; and three in the town of Albany. To prepare
for so many soldiers, the barracks at Albany were enlarged, at the Crown's expense. The new ones, completed
in November, were an impressive group, with main buildings and four wings, stone cellars, twelve staircases, a
network of chimneys, glassed windows, sanded approaches. They were furnished with double bedsteads,
each to contain four men, with tables and benches.[17] The
new general hospital boasted a main building surmounted
with a cupola, two wings, a balcony, and a garden; it
could house comfortably three hundred men. But the
troops arrived before the buildings were finished, and
Loudoun had to quarter them on the town. He seized as
an excuse the action of the town sheriff in releasing from
jail on a writ of habeas corpus a man who had been committed by one of Loudoun's quartermasters for obstruct-
ing the service. "To prevent every littel lawyer in the
country prosecuting my officers", he asked shelter, with
beds, firing, and candles, for thirteen hundred men. He
demanded the use of the Dutch church as a magazine, and
ordered the pews removed. He asked the sheriff for the
use of part of the town jail.[18] These measures, more
stringent than before, produced the first petition from
the mayor and council which they had made against
quartering; but they complained, not of quartering in
general, but of the unaccustomed charges for fuel and
bedding.[19] When by the end of November the barracks

[17] State of the works at Albany from the 10th of May to the 26th of October, 1757, LO 6108.

[18] "He seemed to think he had no business with me but I must acquaint
him that it is his duty to attend me from the time I enter his districk till I
go out of it and . . . if he neglected to execute this order I would for the
future execute all his offices myself." HM 1717, vol. 2, Albany, Nov. 2,
1757.

[19] Minutes of the Common Council of Albany, *Collections on the History
of Albany*, I, 110.

were finished and Loudoun resumed payments for fuel, this flurry of actual oppression, to show the inhabitants the lengths to which a commander in chief might go if he were a less merciful man, came to an end. From the country about Albany complaint came only from John Herkimer, a justice of the peace, for whose two stone houses on the Mohawk, fortified and strategically located, he was paid twenty-five pounds a year rental.[20] In the later years of the war, when British garrisons began to occupy forts hitherto French, there were never more troops at Albany than the barracks could accommodate. At Albany, therefore, a frontier town in the war area, with a non-English population commercially drawn to the French, Loudoun during twenty months took forceful measures to quarter troops on two brief occasions only, and on the other hand used the Crown's money to provide fuel and bedding and to build and furnish barracks. Such retraction from the severe standards he had set himself he preferred to have regarded as an act of clemency, and by no means an extenuation of his rights.

The first conflict in which an assembly took any part occurred in New York city. The New York assembly, warned by Loudoun's letter to Hardy that he expected to lodge a battalion of the Royal Americans in the city during the winter, began in September with the discussion of a bill to legalize quartering. The assembly passed it on October 9; it remained in the hands of the council until November 26. By that time the troops had arrived. As Loudoun invoked at Albany the offices of the mayor and sheriff in dealing with civilians, so at New York he left it to the mayor and town council to provide for the battalion. They encountered his determined resolve not to lessen his rights. "I do expect to get through, for the

20 Declared Account of Abraham Mortier, P.M.G. 14: 1.

People in this Country, tho' they are very obstinate, will generally submit when they see you are determined."[21] "From the rule that in time of war troops are quartered on the inhabitants, not even the people of the first fashion in England are exempted. The necessity has always justified the proceeding in every disinterested man's mind, for I do not know any instance of its ever having been complained of, though I have seen it often practiced."[22] To the mayor's objections Loudoun threatened to march in three or four battalions and take quarters by force. The town council submitted and agreed to pay the cost of beds and firing.[23] "As to the small beer, I have established my right to it, but said I should not insist much on it, at present." Oliver DeLancey, the contractors' agent and a friend of the army, expected a dispensation in his favor; Loudoun instead sent him additional officers to shelter. The governor's assent to the bill was finally given on December 1; it provided for the quartering of soldiers in public houses, and if they were insufficient, in private houses, the magistrates to settle the rates to be paid by the colony.[24] Most of the first battalion of the 62d, which was not complete, found quarters in the blockhouses fitted for them, and beds, candles, and firing were provided by the assembly. In late December O'Far-

21 Loudoun to Fox, Nov. 22, 1756, LO 2263.

22 Loudoun to Hardy, Nov. 21, 1756, LO 2250. Hardy needed some blunt speaking, though he must have known that whatever truth there was in Loudoun's statement referred to Scotland rather than to England. He deserves some of the blame for these quartering troubles in New York city, for in his speech to the general assembly of September 24 he recommended the passing of an act for quartering in no such definite terms as Loudoun's letter warranted, nor did he put pressure on the council to hurry along the bill. *Journal of the Votes and Proceedings of the General Assembly of the Colony of New-York*, II, 498, 504.

23 *Minutes of the Common Council of the City of New York*, VI, 74.

24 *Laws of the Colony of New York*, IV, 123; *Journal of the General Assembly*, II, 521; *New-York Colonial Documents*, VII, 204.

rell's regiment arrived with additional companies of drafts, and Loudoun agreed to the dispersal of these forces in Long Island and nearby towns. Hardy could write the Board of Trade in February that since by the act of the assembly some color and authority was given the magistrates, "it is with pleasure I can acquaint your Lordships that little or no difficultys have arisen in quartering the Forces."[25] The difficulty in New York city had been due rather to Hardy's inaction than to assembly resistance.

In 1757 the New York town council solved the quartering problem by building additional barracks. A two-story building, with twenty rooms, was hastily erected upon "some common lands belonging to the corporation, to the southward of freshwater between the new Gaol house and the house of Calemuts." The assembly agreed to defray the cost, £3500.[26] The mayor fitted a house near the barracks for the use of officers. These new barracks accommodated seven hundred and two men; the fourteen rooms in the old barracks in the fort, two hundred and sixteen; and the six blockhouses, eighteen each.

It was in Pennsylvania that the quartering question was first made the occasion for a trial of strength between the commander in chief and an elective assembly. Loudoun made his request for quarters for the second battalion of the Royal Americans on September 22; a month later the assembly met to discuss it. The public-house keepers, when asked how many men they could lodge, exaggerated the number, under the mistaken im-

[25] *New-York Colonial Documents*, VII, 217. The scarcity of fuel furnished the chief difficulty, for the men who customarily supplied it were in the New York regiment, which was maintained during the winter, or with the army, Hardy to Loudoun, Nov. 9, 1756, LO 2185.

[26] *Minutes of the Common Council of the City of New York*, VI, 111; *New-York Colonial Documents*, VII, 342. This figure included cost of firing and candles.

pression that they were to be well paid for their lodgers, and thereupon the assembly passed the same kind of act as in 1755, though without the obnoxious preamble. It extended the Mutiny Act sections on quartering paragraph by paragraph, and even included the provision for the cashiering of officers who did not conform. Two days after the act passed, December 8, the troops arrived, Henry Bouquet at the head of the column. As Governor Denny had foreseen, the public houses were incapable of accommodating the five hundred men in the battalion. In addition, and it was the first time the subject had been mentioned, Bouquet asked for a hospital to check the spread of smallpox which had broken out; his surgeon assured him that "as their quarters are so dispersed & the conveniences for their attendance so bad, unless a proper hospital is soon provided for them, I could almost venture to affirm that every house in this place will be an hospital in a fortnight." A survey of the town showed a hundred and twenty-four men without shelter. At Bouquet's solicitation Denny granted him a warrant to the sheriff to quarter in private houses, but the sheriff laid it before the assembly instead of executing it, and the assembly, seeing in it a blunt contradiction of the act just passed, adjourned without providing anything more. They appointed commissioners to recount the beds in the public houses. During the adjournment Denny got a letter from Loudoun threatening, as in New York, to march instantly as many troops as were necessary to take quarters, "and find Quarter for the whole they make necessary." The threat had effect. The commissioners, of whom Franklin was one, promised to turn over the new provincial hospital, just completed and unoccupied, and within three weeks to meet all of Bouquet's wishes. The town corporation found it convenient to pay officers instead of billeting them on private houses, at the weekly rate of eighteen shillings, provincial currency, for the colonel and six shillings for subalterns. The dispute was thus settled, though again with a threat of force. To Denny, himself an army officer, "this obstinate persisting in an open neglect of Humanity was the highest Instance I have ever met with of the Depravity of human nature."[27]

In the next year Pennsylvania built barracks, as New York had done. The selection of the site and the construction of the buildings became a matter of dispute between governor and assembly. The latter finally took matters into its own hands and completed the work without accepting the suggestions either of Lieutenant Colonel Haldimand, "a good judge of barracks", or of Lieutenant Meyer, a Royal American engineer, whom Loudoun sent to Philadelphia for consultation with the contractors.

Similar friction between a commanding officer and an assembly occurred in South Carolina in 1757. Loudoun sent Bouquet with five companies of Royal Americans to Charlestown in June, 1757, and Pitt, at the express request of the assembly, sent in September direct to the colony Montgomery's fresh-raised battalion of Highlanders. Bouquet's troops encamped without the town from the 15th of June to the 25th of August, for fear of spreading the smallpox they had brought with them, and when they were driven in by the rains found shelter in the old brick barracks, in need of repair and devoid of necessaries. Montgomery's arrived September 3, a thousand strong with a hundred and thirteen supernumeraries, and only thirteen men on the sick list. Though Bouquet had

---

[27] *Pennsylvania Colonial Records*, VII, 271-381; *Pennsylvania Archives*, III, 82, 85, 110-112. The act of December 8 (*Statutes at Large of Pennsylvania*, V, 269) was referred to the Privy Council on May 12, and in accordance with the terms of the charter, became law by lapse.

asked quarters for them on August 29, they could find no
coverage except in a damp, half-finished church without
straw for beds and without blankets. By the end of September five hundred were sick, and sixty dead. Some of
the townspeople, out of sheer compassion, took about two
hundred voluntarily into their homes. The assembly
finally voted to build new barracks, but adjourned without providing beds or blankets. Bouquet deeply resented
"this ill usage in a good town", and came to the conclusion that though the Carolinians, frugal as they were,
gave blankets to their slaves, an expense they would
forego if possible, "they . . . are apt to believe that
anything is well enough for officers and soldiers." A few
houses meanwhile were fitted as barracks, and when the
assembly met again in December it voted one blanket for
every two men, and two cords of wood a week for every
hundred. On Bouquet's objection it increased this allowance, but made no provision for a hospital, guard-room,
or billets for officers. Bouquet's own troops remained in
the lodgings they had taken in town, and his intimation
that perhaps the Crown would assume the charges, which
he withdrew after receiving instructions from Loudoun
to insist upon the fullest right of quartering, formed another source of dispute. In February, 1758, matters were
but little better than they had been several months before, and the next month the troops were withdrawn.

Loudoun himself could take no active hand in the South
Carolina fracas, for the delivery of messages needed a
month by sea, and three by land. But two letters which
he wrote to Bouquet show how much the threats he made
about quartering were bluff. In a public letter he wrote:
"If barracks are not ready, do you demand quarters in
town, and if they are so blind as to refuse you quarters
. . . they drive me to the disagreeable necessity of giving you the following order, which is, to quarter the

King's troops by your own Authority, for I dare not take it on me . . . to allow the rich province of South Carolina to be given up, nor the Troops sent for its defence to die for want of quarters." But a private accompanying letter was softer: "You will receive along with this a Letter which I thought it was right to write, in the present situation of things . . . but at the same time, I would have you act very Tenderly in it, and must beg that on all occasions, you will take care as far as possible, to keep up that good correspondence between you and Governor Lyttelton, and from the nature of the people of this Country, I do not doubt things will be brought about without any necessity of coming to violence, which must be avoided on all occasions if possible."[28]

Loudoun's opinion that the "people of this Country" would take to the free supporting of regular soldiers in their towns or homes "when they see you are determined" seemed to be justified by the fact that these four were the only serious disputes he had over the quartering of large bodies of men for long periods of time. Elsewhere, though there was much discontent and bitterness, no resistance was offered. In Maryland, in 1756, Sharpe quartered seven companies of the 3d battalion of the Royal Americans in Cecil and Kent counties, where the towns were small and poor. The inhabitants furnished necessaries in the belief that the assembly, as in the past, would recompense them. In 1757, after local disputes between council and assembly had abruptly halted Maryland's active coöperation in the war, Loudoun let the recalcitrant assemblymen feel the weight of the king's

[28] Bouquet's dispute over quarters is narrated, somewhat sketchily, in Douglas Brymner's calendar of the thirty volumes of Bouquet papers in the British Museum, transcribed for the Canadian Archives (*Canadian Archives*, 1889). The Loudoun Papers contain the letters between Loudoun, Bouquet, Montgomery, Lyttelton, and excerpts from the votes of the assembly. LO 3871, 4649, 4682, 4689, 4929, 4937, 4989, 4994, 5098, 5099, 5521, 5677, 5763.

hand, and quartered five companies in Annapolis.[29] The town had but a hundred families, and the previous year Sharpe had estimated that at best it could accommodate but a hundred men. Nevertheless the companies remained until March. The New Jersey assembly, after Belcher had corrected his first impression that the army would pay the costs, reimbursed those on whom the expense fell; "an unusual thing," wrote Loudoun, "but no affair of mine."[30] One assemblyman, John Wetherill, less cautious than his perhaps similarly minded colleagues, openly declared that "he will put an end to the crown being able to quarter one man in America."[31] Connecticut, in 1757, gave Fraser's battalion of Highlanders comfortable quarters and no trouble. Stamford, Milford, Stratford, Fairfield, and Norwalk accommodated thirteen hundred men from November 20, 1757, to March 30, 1758. Though uneasy at the expense, and wishful that the troops might be more equitably distributed throughout the colony, the selectmen of these towns realised that "compactness was necessary for the good of the troops" and that some towns would have to suffer. They provided house-room, bedding, firewood, candles, cider, guard-houses and hospitals, submitted their account to the assembly when the battalion left, and were recompensed to the extent of £2358 12s. 11d.[32] Even in Massachusetts, where Shirley had equipped barracks with Crown funds, the assembly acceded, though dubiously, to Loudoun's demands. They sent a committee to interview him, primed with the same

29 Loudoun to Stanwix, Nov. 3, 1757, LO 4743. See p. 221 below for the constitutional points involved in the Maryland situation.

30 *New Jersey Archives*, 1st series, XVII, 67, 68; Loudoun to Belcher, Dec. 16, 1756, LO 2357 and April 7, 1757, LO 3307.

31 HM 1717, vol. 3, May 6, 1757.

32 Loudoun to Fitch, Oct. 19, 1757, LO 4670. Connecticut Archives, War, VII, 298-313. Abercromby subsequently repaid the colony their charges for a hospital, cider, candles, and nurses, W.O. 34: 76.

seventeenth century arguments which Pennsylvanians had used in 1755. The committee questioned the legality of Loudoun's extension of the quartering sections of the Articles of War to the colonies, asked whether the army did not customarily pay for quarters. Loudoun could find no satisfactory answer to the first. Nevertheless the assembly finally voted a sum to pay for equipment, and in 1757 it increased the size of the barracks, and provided them with beds, kettles, bowls, spoons, half a cord of wood a week for each fireplace, lamps, and oil.[33]

Who was the victor up to this time in the quartering dispute, "the eternal struggle in America", as Bouquet called it, is questionable. Loudoun undoubtedly thought that he was, for in every case he had got his way. The colonies might assume "to themselves, what they call Rights and Priviledges, Totally unknown in the Mother Country", but he had circumvented them, he thought, by the diplomatic procedure of actually insisting upon less than he explained was his rightful due, by seeming to lay all his cards, which were not many, upon the table, and by holding always in the background the threat of force. But the colonies, less gullible than he imagined, had in reality taken matters into their own hands. Only in Albany was Loudoun's interpretation of the right of quartering accepted under pressure. Elsewhere it had become less of a right because consequent upon an act of a colonial assembly. If an assembly should omit to pass an annual act, and thereby divest quartering of the only legality it had, civilians could presumably bring suit against officers for trespass or against magistrates for damages. Assemblies had effectually constituted themselves the custodians of an Englishman's liberty.

Loudoun seems scarcely to have realised the slow un-

[33] *Acts and Resolves of Massachusetts Bay*, Resolves, XVI, 67.

dermining of the decision which after two years he thought he was still enforcing as Cumberland had authorized. It took an assault by an assembly upon a cherished stronghold of army routine, never before questioned, to convince him. In Massachusetts, in the late autumn of 1757, justices of the peace, reflecting the growing hostility of their constituents towards the regular army, refused to issue warrants to Nova Scotia recruiting officers for the quartering of their small parties in public houses. The officers appealed to Pownall. When he attempted to reason with assemblymen, he met the plain answer that no subject, whether an innkeeper or a private person, could have troops quartered on him except by law. With such sentiments Pownall was in complete sympathy, and after he had satisfied himself that neither in the statute books of England nor in those of Massachusetts was there an act to cover the case, he yielded and recommended the passage of an act. Meanwhile he quartered the parties in the barracks on Castle Island. But splendid as barracks may have been for permanent troops, they were useless for recruiting parties which had to live in the midst of a town, and the officers preferred to pay the high prices demanded by innkeepers until their commander in chief should have settled the matter.

It seems never to have occurred to Loudoun that the old legal arguments against quartering could be applied to recruiting parties. They were transients, could easily be put up at inns, and the whole success of their work depended upon the ease with which they could move among the civil population. In the army's business they occupied a different category from that of regiments provided with winter quartering. So he expostulated at once, and in so doing revealed the weakness of his legal position. "The provincial law . . . can neither deprive the King and Mother Country of the right they have in this in time of Peace, or govern the Rules and custom of War which are established and justified by the necessity of it." No act of assembly was needed; the magistrates had simply to do their duty in following the Mutiny Act, which applied wherever the king had troops. If in forty-eight hours—this was the last card in Loudoun's hand—the question still remained open, he would order into Boston the three battalions from New York and Connecticut, and if more were needed, he had two in the Jerseys. He took Pownall to task for pleading with his assembly to pass an act for the sake of policy; such tactics were Shirley's, see where they had got him, you must insist upon it as right. Pownall replied that there was no instance of any governor ever having carried the king's instructions into effect when the people disputed them; since he was without that power to enforce which Loudoun possessed, he was unwilling to hazard the king's dignity. At this stage, December 1, the assembly passed the act, authorizing selectmen to quarter recruiting parties in public houses, with the incidentals and small beer included. Loudoun deemed it a direct affront. "I see this has put all further negotiations out of Doors and put me under the disagreeable necessity of settling it myself, to prevent the fatal consequences of the measures they have entered into, and in which they are entirely volunteers." "This last act of your assembly attempts to take away the king's undoubted prerogative and the rights of the mother country and the act of parliament. I am liable to have all the troops in North America thrown into the streets, for they will hear the news before I can write. Every man must see the indispensible necessity the proceedings of your assembly have laid me under of quelling this ruinous mischief on the spot." Three weeks later his temper had cooled, and he tried to retire gracefully. "As to the dispute the gentlemen seem willing to enter into, of the necessity of a provincial law to enforce a British act of parliament, I shall not enter into it at all." To which the assembly, with complete justification, replied, "The authority of all acts of parliament which concern the colonies and extend to them are ever acknowledged in all the courts of law."[34] Thereafter recruiting parties received prompt service in Massachusetts. Rhode Island followed suit at once, passing a similar act, and the next year Connecticut adopted the same solution.[35]

In every colony, therefore, in which British troops were located—with the exception of Albany itself—assemblies assumed the legal responsibility for sheltering them, and made their presence conditional upon a series of local enactments. If it was not the solution which Cumberland had authorized Loudoun to follow, it was nevertheless a very practical one under the unusual circumstances in America. But the home government, though it left the question untouched for the rest of the war, never surrendered the basic assumption in all of Loudoun's arguments, that this question of quartering, as with all questions involving British troops, belonged to Great Britain. In 1765 it belatedly passed a Mutiny Act for North America, in which assemblies were required to bear the expense of providing and furnishing quarters.[36] The government thus tried to legalize and make uniform the very method which had grown up in opposi-

---

[34] The extensive correspondence between Pownall and Loudoun, the representations of the assembly, and the letters of recruiting officers, are in the Loudoun Papers. Pownall's brief explanation can be found in *Pitt Correspondence*, I, 128.

[35] *Rhode Island Colonial Records*, VI, 120; *Colonial Records of Connecticut*, XI, 175.

[36] 5 George III, c. 33.

tion to Loudoun's far more rigorous demands. Such a measure might have succeeded in 1756, but in 1765 it challenged the position which colonial assemblies had held for ten years without opposition from England.

Loudoun's difficulties, of course, were the result of the failure of the home government to support him. He had to try to carry out Cumberland's verbal instructions for which he had no constitutional authority. But it is difficult to see what other course he could have taken compatible with the health of the troops and the financial regulations of the army. The Treasury would never have sanctioned payment for quarters, nor the construction of great concentration camps in various parts of the country. Soldiers could not have been kept during the winter in the forts or in their tents. They had to be sent to milder climates, or moved about in preparation for the coming campaign. If Loudoun had accepted at once the position which the assemblies took, and had attempted to negotiate with them individually, he would have met inevitable delays and jealousies. Such delays were not critical when they concerned such a matter as the raising of provincial troops; but they might, as with Montgomery's battalion in South Carolina, seriously impair a regiment's strength. Loudoun could see no way out except by maintaining the principle that he should have quarters when and where he wanted them, and so laid himself, and the prerogative for which he stood, open to direct rebuff.

CHAPTER VIII

MILITARY UNION OF THE COLONIES–I

In common with many men on both sides of the Atlantic, Loudoun believed that the war in America could be won only "by striking at the root", Quebec. His plan of operations for 1757 staked everything on an expedition against that citadel by sea, with a supporting fleet to block the St. Lawrence. It was a hazardous venture, but no more so than any mixed land and sea expedition in an age of sail, where victory was determined as much by the "luckie chance" as by the fitness of men and ships. He planned to take with him to the north the bulk of his small regular army, the 22d, 42d, 44th, 48th, and two battalions of the 60th, a total of 5506 men. He would leave behind in New York province, to carry on a purely defensive campaign, the 35th, a battalion of the 60th, and the four independent companies, which, with six thousand provincial troops from New England, New York, and New Jersey, would make a total of 7744. In the south another battalion of the 60th would join such provincials as could be raised. This plan was Loudoun's own. Though he communicated its main lines to the ministry in September, 1756, the political upheaval which brought Pitt to be secretary of state was accompanied with so much confusion in England that he received no detailed official confirmation until late the next spring. Compelled to undertake preparations on his own responsibility, he planned to meet at Boston commissioners from the four New England colonies, duly authorized to agree to the number of troops each should raise, and then to hold a council of war at Philadelphia of southern governors for the settlement of campaign details in their territory. With New York and New Jersey he would deal separately.

This was the first time in the history of the colonies that a British commander in chief, endowed with suitable powers and acting on his own initiative, had undertaken to direct the military resources of eleven colonies as a unit in a general plan of operations.

Loudoun's experiences the previous summer determined the details of his carefully devised scheme. In his opinion the provincial army of 1756 had been created less for military purposes than for filling the pockets of New England contractors and for giving staid civilians a chance to gratify their exhibitionist tendencies as generals and field officers in an independent command. He meant to put an end to such profit making, and to create as serviceable a body of troops as possible. He therefore asked for only four thousand men from New England, but insisted that all of them take the field so that he might know upon whom he could count and that the pay of absentees might not become the perquisites of officers. These troops were to be raised expressly to serve with regulars; they should be formed in standard companies of a hundred each, four officers to a company, and only one field officer to a colony. Loudoun was ready to agree that provincial officers should compose courts martial upon their own men in all but the grossest cases, and that the regular recruiting provision allowance should be paid by the Crown to all provincials until they reached Albany. Since the ministry the previous year had authorized payment by the Crown of all charges for victualling, transport, ammunition, artillery, and hospitals, the only expenses remaining for the colonies were those of raising, paying, arming, and clothing their troops. Loudoun expected this great saving of money, together with the decreased cost which would follow conformance to his own proposals, to compensate assemblies as a whole for the loss by certain individuals of their private profits. But aware that if he dealt with assemblies directly he might unleash those same tendencies to delay and compromise which he had already sadly experienced, he resolved to keep his counsels secret until he could meet at Boston with a few properly qualified commissioners. With those men, removed from the influence of their assemblies, he hoped to be able to deal quickly and rationally.

If Loudoun had been able to keep his lips sealed, his plans might have succeeded. But he made the blunder of divulging his secrets to a popularly elected governor, Fitch of Connecticut. The incident occurred at Norwalk. Loudoun's letter of December 22 had asked governors to have commissioners appointed, but Fitch, thinking it absurd to call the assembly when he could himself deal with Loudoun on the latter's journey north, had disregarded the letter. Stopping at Norwalk, Loudoun, in most affable vein, soon wrung from the governor an admission that he could not guarantee his assembly's coöperation. He then went on to his conventional point that without a uniform procedure jealousy might arise and the common cause suffer, and he begged Fitch to summon the assembly. When that promise had been given, Loudoun, though on the understanding that the information would go no further, revealed the number of men he intended to ask from New England. He should have kept that figure back at all costs, for the news found its way to the assembly. The commissioners it appointed had secret instructions to agree to no larger a proportion of the four thousand men than twelve hundred and fifty.[1] This was

[1] *Colonial Records of Connecticut*, X, 593-594, 594n.; HM 1717, vol. 3, Jan. 11, 1757.

Connecticut's share according to the Albany quotas of 1754, which admittedly weighed less heavily on her than on her neighbors.

When Loudoun reached Boston on January 20,[2] he found only the Rhode Island commissioners fully authorized to speak for their assemblies. Theodore Atkinson, the secretary of New Hampshire, was present simply as an observer to learn Loudoun's proposals and communicate them to Portsmouth. The Massachusetts general court, though in session, had not yet appointed commissioners. The Rhode Islanders felt imposed upon, and therefore the more ready to fall in with Atkinson's suggestions that they make an alliance against the "insinuations of the Greater Provinces", refuse to agree to any quota division, and insist the proportion be left to each separate assembly.[3] The old story of intercolonial polemics, evasions, and delays was about to begin.

The meeting finally opened on January 29, Hutchinson heading the Massachusetts delegation, and Fitch the Connecticut. Loudoun read an address written for the most part by Hutchinson himself, who determined to a nicety the balance between phraseology that, while still appealing to the commander in chief, would not prejudice the commissioners. He asked for his four thousand men, according to proportions which they should determine. In answer to a written question over the signature of Fitch, he refused to set limits beyond which he would not march the troops but promised not to send them where they, or the commissioners, would not want to go.[4] The commis-

---

[2] Loudoun's diary during this ten days winter journey, and the return, February 10 to 20, gives a suggestive picture of colonial travel. He used his own heavy coach, making five or six miles an hour over the stony or icy roads.

[3] *Rhode Island Colonial Records*, VI, 28; *New Hampshire Provincial Papers*, VI, 556.

[4] *New Hampshire Provincial Papers*, VI, 556-558; *Fitch Papers*, I, 280, 284-285.

sioners then withdrew to discuss the quotas. It was the same wearisome business as in the past; the numbers of men voted the preceding year seemed to make the Albany quotas obsolete, and the whole tale of comparative populations, previous grants, pleas of poverty, and local frontier exigencies appeared on the table. But nevertheless an agreement would have been reached if the Connecticut commissioners, publicly instructed to agree to any figure, but secretly limited to the Albany quota, had not produced their orders. They caused a deadlock, for none of the others would agree to so low a figure for Connecticut. On February 4 all came to Loudoun separately, each group complaining of the others. "I showed them that the effect of their not agreeing among themselves must have the effect of my dealing with them separately, which was not my plan, for I chose to sement their union and not to divide them. That it was better any colony should furnish the number disputed about than that the French should know there was the least difficulty." In the end he had to name the quotas himself, but as the commissioners had no power to bind their assemblies when acting separately, and could not agree together on Loudoun's figures, they could only promise to place the proportions before their masters.[5]

[5] A table of the quotas proposed at Boston.

	Albany quotas	Massachusetts proposals	Connecticut proposals	Rhode Island proposals	Loudoun's proposals
Massachusetts	1750	1750	1870	2000	1800
Connecticut	1250	1450	1330	1333	1400
Rhode Island	500	450	400	334	450
New Hampshire	500	350	400	333	350

Governor Hopkins of Rhode Island was apparently responsible for augmenting his colony's proportion; his zeal and "constant Endeavours to raise and furnish our proper Quotas of Men on all Occasions, have been charged on Me as Crimes", he wrote Loudoun (April 26, 1757, LO 3482), and lost him the spring election.

All four assemblies, in the end, voted troops according to Loudoun's proportions. But they failed to comply with some of his other recommendations designed to save them expense and himself trouble. Rhode Island alone appointed no field officers. Connecticut sent a lieutenant colonel and a major besides Colonel Lyman; New Hampshire appropriated funds for two field officers and Massachusetts for a lieutenant colonel and two majors. Massachusetts voted a new blue coat lapelled with red and a hat to each soldier, and refused to follow Loudoun's advice that the cost be deducted from the soldiers' pay.[6] Massachusetts also increased the Crown's provision allowance by two shillings and fourpence sterling a week. "The charge of these forces", wrote Hutchinson, who kept Loudoun informed of all developments at Boston, "will exceed that of any in His Majesty's dominions", and he suspected that since the funds appropriated consisted of taxes to be levied within the next two years on people already well taxed for that period the burden of the expense was meant to rest in the end, not on the colony, but on the Crown.

None of the New England troops were ready by March 25, the date of rendezvous. In Rhode Island the spring elections, "the popular Alterations incident to our Constitution", prevented. The two hundred New Hampshire men, assigned to garrison Number Four on the upper Connecticut river until the arrival of a Connecticut detachment, failed to put in an appearance, and left the tiny fort defenseless against an Indian attack in April which cost seven lives.[7] Wentworth put the blame on the committee of war, negligent in providing supplies. When in Massachusetts Lieutenant Governor Phips died early in

[6] Hutchinson to Loudoun, March 7, 1757, LO 2983. Rhode Island actually made such a deduction, *Rhode Island Colonial Records*, VI, 24.

[7] *Pitt Correspondence*, I, 50, 51.

April, the government devolved on the council of twenty-eight members, of whom a majority was required by the charter for even as simple a business as the signing of an ensign's commission. Fortunately most of the preparations were already completed through the energy of Colonel Fry, "a sensible man"; by the middle of May the seventeen companies of Massachusetts troops were at Albany.

One of the charges which the colonies were expected to support, that of arming their troops, was left to the Crown. The Massachusetts assembly, while admitting that its troops might find muskets useful, thought it a foolish extravagance to vote money for guns which could not be bought in the province, and suggested that Loudoun permit again the use of the two thousand stand of king's arms issued by Shirley in 1756. A week later it was found that Winslow's soldiers had returned only three hundred of these to the king's ordnance office at Boston; the rest were either still in their possession or had been sold. Loudoun agreed to supply guns from his own scanty store, provided the colony indented for them and included in the indenture the two thousand issued in 1756. He put the price for embezzled arms at two pounds each, three shillings higher than the price at the Tower in London. Connecticut could collect, out of the two thousand stand issued to her troops the previous spring, barely enough to arm her fourteen hundred men. The Rhode Islanders arrived at Albany without any arms at all, thereby leaving it bluntly to the commanding officer to determine the degree of their usefulness.[8]

8 Account of Arms delivered to Provincials . . . belonging to the Ordnance Office, Boston, LO 1376; Phips to General Court, Feb. 18, 1757, LO 2857; Gridley to McAdam, Feb. 26, LO 2929; Loudoun to Phips, Feb. 27, LO 2930; Loudoun to Hutchinson, Feb. 27, LO 2931; *Colonial Records of Connecticut*, X, 598; *Fitch Papers*, I, 293; *Rhode Island Colonial Records*, VI, 70.

Loudoun's first effort to set up practical machinery for a union of the New England colonies can scarcely be called a success. He had wanted to meet men legally authorized to sign agreements; two assemblies instead had refused to trust their agents and one had acceded with reluctance. But his venture must not be judged too harshly. As an initial attempt it was distinctly promising and if he had played his hand more cannily at Norwalk he might have gone further still. He did gain one object, of no small importance, in creating a dependent provincial army, better organized than in previous years, and a month earlier in the field. Colonial union had to be a plant of slow growth. If Loudoun or any other equally fair-minded commander could have met commissioners again after a year of success, he might have been able to mitigate further their suspicions of himself and of one another.

As far as the making of plans was concerned, Loudoun's parley with the governors of the southern provinces met with far greater success. On March 14, at Philadelphia, he conferred with Denny of Pennsylvania, Sharpe of Maryland, Dinwiddie of Virginia, and Dobbs of North Carolina.[9] All were intelligent men and all represented the prerogative, either directly or through a lord proprietor. Each one submitted his own suggestions as to quota proportions and a statement of his colony's particular needs. Loudoun studied the material, discussed it with the governors separately and as a group, called in such expert opinion as that of Washington, who here met Loudoun for the first time, and finally drafted his own

9 The original date set for the meeting, February 17, had to be altered because of the delays at Boston, the need of getting off dispatches to England, and Loudoun's conference with Abercromby on the military preparations for the spring. Abercromby was delayed by the weather in coming down from Albany to New York.

schemes. Of the three sets of quotas from Dinwiddie, Dobbs, and Sharpe, he followed most closely the last. The Albany quotas, as at Boston, were disregarded.[10] To the thirty-eight hundred provincials Loudoun proposed to add twelve hundred regulars. The governors agreed to ask their assemblies for the numbers suggested, and Dobbs, Dinwiddie, and Denny consented that, if possible, a proportion of each of their forces should be sent to South Carolina, where Lyttelton feared a French and Indian invasion from Louisiana.[11] The rest of the North Carolina troops were to garrison frontier forts; the Marylanders were to be in Forts Cumberland and Frederick; the Pennsylvanians distributed among their many small frontier posts; and the Virginians at Forts Loudoun, Cumberland, the Cherokee fort, the small forts between, or ranging on the frontier. Bouquet would command in South Carolina and Colonel Stanwix of the 1st battalion of the 60th in Pennsylvania. Under the latter Dagworthy of Maryland would command at Fort Cumberland. The Crown would provision the troops sent to South Carolina, but not those on the frontiers. After some discussion with Washington the distribution of the Virginia troops was slightly altered.

[10] A table of quotas proposed. The Albany quotas are estimated on a basis of 3800 men from the five provinces.

	Dinwiddie's	Sharpe's	Dobb's	Albany quotas	Loudoun's
Pennsylvania	1000	1400	1000	912	1400
Maryland	500	600	500	608	500
Virginia	800	1000	1000	1064	1000
North Carolina	400		200	608	400
South Carolina				608	500

[11] The forces in South Carolina were to be five hundred South Carolinians, the three independent companies of South Carolina, two hundred North Carolinians, four hundred Virginians, two hundred Pennsylvanians, and five companies of the 1st battalion of the 60th, a total of two thousand men. HM 1717, vol. 3, March 19, 1757.

All this was settled in four days, a bright contrast to the meeting at Boston. A true council of war, of the type projected in Loudoun's instructions, it blocked out rapidly and unanimously the main lines of defense, and even arranged such minute details as the stationing of thirty North Carolina troops at Topsail Inlet.

But its plans were on paper only. Each governor, returning home, had to fight his own battle with his assembly, and the results in the end were less gratifying than in the north. Virginia and North Carolina very nearly fulfilled the promises of their governors. The former colony, though so tardily as to raise Loudoun's fears lest no troops be voted, resolved in June to increase the number of men in service to fifteen hundred, appropriated eighty thousand pounds in payment of arrears, and agreed to send, not four hundred, but two hundred men to South Carolina.[12] In July, however, Washington had but seven hundred men under his command. The North Carolina assembly expressed its willingness to send two hundred men, the number specified at Philadelphia, to South Carolina, but before they were ready to leave the Highlanders unexpectedly arrived at Charlestown, and Lyttelton wrote that he wanted no more troops, as he was having difficulty in quartering those already there.[13] South Carolina kept up two companies until July, then disbanded them and voted a regiment of seven hundred, which was never completely raised.

In the two proprietary colonies the assemblies seized the opportunity to use the immediate needs of the war as an additional leverage in their constitutional struggles,

[12] *Dinwiddie Papers*, II, 642. Two companies of Virginians accompanied Bouquet in June. He later sent a hundred of them to Georgia, where Governor Ellis highly praised their conduct, Nov. 28, 1757, LO 4911.

[13] *Dinwiddie Papers*, II, 666; *North Carolina Colonial Records*, V, 761-762.

with the proprietary council in Maryland and with the governor in Pennsylvania. Neither colony, therefore, executed the obligations their governors had assumed. The Maryland House of Delegates adopted original tactics to render its aid ineffectual. Though it voted men as Sharpe asked, it took the position that Fort Cumberland was not within the limits of Maryland and that therefore no garrison of Maryland troops, under the command of a Marylander, should be maintained there when the province itself was suffering from Indian raids. It forbade Dagworthy to keep the post to which Loudoun and the governors had assigned him, under penalty of forfeiting his pay, but agreed that Maryland companies might garrison the fort provided they were changed, according to a rather elaborate schedule, every month. Sharpe would have accepted this cumbersome disposition, but Stanwix, interpreting it as a challenge to the commander in chief's authority, bluntly ordered Dagworthy to keep his post. The assembly stopped the supply of provisions at the fort; Stanwix fed the troops from the king's stores. In October the assembly took the definite step of severing relations with the British army. It refused to permit the Maryland troops to serve under British officers and to pay them longer if they remained at their station. Loudoun thereupon promised to take them into the pay of the Crown, and planned himself to visit Annapolis and settle what he regarded as the most dangerous precedent, and the boldest attack on the prerogative, of any he had experienced in the colonies.[14]

[14] *Maryland Archives*, VI, 543, 549, 550, 551, 555; IX, 1, 16-17, 21-22, 23, 31, 91; Stanwix to Dagworthy, May 12, 1757, LO 3611; Loudoun to Cumberland, June 22, 1757, LO 3869; J. W. Black, *Maryland's Attitude in the Struggle for Canada*, Johns Hopkins University *Studies*, July, 1892, pp. 63-64. The original proposal to take the troops into the pay of the Crown came from Loudoun and not from Forbes, Loudoun to Sharpe, Jan. 2, 1758, LO 5317. Sharpe accepted the offer in his letter of Jan. 22, 1758, LO 5439.

In Pennsylvania the withdrawal from active politics of the old Quaker group did not lessen the assembly's attempts to limit the governor's powers. It superintended the expenditure of all sums it appropriated, withheld the governor's salary and the customary present for the voyage from England, nominated to all offices created by it, sat on its own adjournment or adjourned contrary to the governor's express order, kept its minutes secret, and excluded the governor from any share in the control of Indian trade.[15] When Loudoun arrived at Philadelphia, he found that since the beginning of the session in November the assembly had been refusing to appropriate any sums for military needs unless the governor should waive his positive instructions from the proprietor, Thomas Penn, and should agree to the taxation of proprietary as well as non-proprietary lands.[16] Since Penn had agreed to Cumberland's nomination of Denny as governor in 1756 to avoid a possible loss of his charter, and since Denny had been made a lieutenant colonel in the army to increase his effectiveness in aiding the commander in chief, it was natural that he should turn to

Forbes agreed to take the men as rangers after the spring assembly failed to vote their support, Forbes to Sharpe, May 2, 1758, LO 5826. Loudoun's recall, Forbes's independent command in Pennsylvania, and his death, prevented payment to the Marylanders until 1761. They petitioned in November, 1759, for their pay from October, 1757 to April, 1759, a sum of £5677; Loudoun, Abercromby, and Stanwix reported favorably and the Treasury authorized payment. W.O. 34: 72, ff. 136, 146.

15 A memorandum on the government of Pennsylvania, received by Loudoun from Denny, March 14, 1757, LO 3047. ''In short the powers of Government are almost all taken out of the Hands of the Governors and lodged in the Assembly and as to what little remains scarce a Bill comes to the Governor without an Attempt to lessen them.''

16 W. T. Root, The Relations of Pennsylvania with the British Government, 1696-1765, traces this ancient quarrel. But according to a letter written later by Penn to Cumberland, July 18, 1757, he objected as proprietor, not to the taxation of his estates, but to an unfair distribution of the tax. Cumberland Papers.

Loudoun to solve his problem. He had Loudoun meet a committee of the assembly. Franklin, the spokesman, presented a discourse which began with the founding of the colony, defined the right of the assembly to grant money bills as a natural right antecedent to all law, touched upon the vexed question of the appointment of judges, bewailed the weight of taxation resting on the colony, mentioned the question of indentured servants, and ended with a description of the sufferings of merchants whose vessels had been seized by enemy privateers.[17] Striving to understand the points at issue, Loudoun called in the other governors, and on their recommendation urged Denny to waive his instructions and to sign the bill. Denny held off until news came of a threatened attack on a quarter of the frontier where the soldiers, in arrears of pay, were at the end of their short enlistment periods and were going home. Then he signed.[18] Loudoun commented upon other bills before the assembly, the embargo bill, the Indian trade bill, and the militia bill, criticising in them all assembly encroachment upon the governor's executive powers. It should be the governor, he said, and not a committee of the assembly, who signed warrants to the treasurer for the pay of troops; the governor should manage local Indian affairs. He went so far as to propose an unworkable scheme for the settlement of the dispute, in which the assembly's account of its grievances and the governor's answer should be submitted for arbitration to the attorney and solicitor general or to the Board of Trade.[19] The issues were too deep for such a solution.

[17] Franklin's Autobiography, *Franklin's Works* (Spark's ed.), I, 216, and the Report of the Committee of Aggrievances of the Assembly of Pennsylvania, February 22, 1757, *ibid.*, III, 98-104.

[18] *Pennsylvania Archives*, III, 118; Joseph Shippen to his father, Fort Augusta, March 4, 1757, *Pennsylvania Magazine*, XXXVI, 413.

[19] March 13, 1757, LO 3032.

When Denny signed the appropriation bill, six months'
arrears of pay could be given the troops on the frontier.
But more trouble was to come. The assembly refused to
allow levy money for recruiting afresh to be paid until
the three and six months enlistment periods had expired.
So there came a day for each soldier of the Augusta regiment when he could choose between signing up again and
hazarding again the loss of pay, and returning at once to
his home. In most cases he declared himself already satisfied with his military experiences. By June 1 the three
regiments in service could muster only a thousand and
nine men, instead of fourteen hundred. Weiser's and
Armstrong's were nearly complete; the Augusta regiment numbered but seventy-one out of four hundred and
twenty-four rank and file.[20] Stanwix could not spare the
two hundred men for South Carolina, and had to reinforce the Augusta regiment by drafting three companies
from Weiser's, on the frontier between the Delaware and
the Susquehanna.

The campaign in the south this year was meant to be
purely defensive. It is hard to see what more Loudoun
could have done, with his knowledge that victory in the
St. Lawrence would put an end to Indian raids along the
southern mountains. He had no regulars to station along
the frontier; the best he could do was to plan an organized
and intelligent defense. No colony in the south could join
those in the north in asserting that Loudoun's plans neglected local frontiers, but Virginia and North Carolina
were the only ones to carry through their share in those
plans.

On his return journey from Philadelphia Loudoun
stopped in New Jersey, and discovered that there too a

[20] List of the Provincial Troops of Pennsylvania as paid last muster,
April 20 to June 1, 1757, signed Commissary Young, LO 3769; Denny to
Loudoun, April 27, 1757, LO 3485; Nov. 10, 1757, LO 4793.

local dispute between governor and assembly, this time over the paper money question, was made an excuse by the latter for not complying with his request for men. The assembly was willing to keep up the New Jersey regiment to five hundred men, but pleaded that the great scarcity of money in the province kept them from voting the thousand men Loudoun asked. At Belcher's insistence Loudoun met the assembly in person. He pointed out that the high bounties offered for recruits, twelve pounds a man, were enough to support a thousand men for the campaign if they were drafted from the militia. But the assembly resolutely maintained its plea of poverty, and alone of all the colonies in North America failed to vote the proportion of men asked for in 1757.[21] The New York assembly promptly voted the thousand men Loudoun asked; they were raised and at Albany before the end of April.

On May 1, after these tedious negotiations with colonial assemblies had been finished, Pitt's circular letter of February 4 to the governors arrived. In it Pitt asked governors to summon their assemblies, and to urge them, with the utmost expedition, to raise the same number of troops as in 1756. Since it was obviously impossible, so late in the season, for governors to comply—troops voted in May could not have reached Albany before August—Loudoun compromised by asking them to substitute for the difference between the numbers already voted and the numbers requested by Pitt the assurance that their militia would be held in readiness to march on the first warning of invasion. Thus he hoped to obey instructions and at the same time to strengthen, if necessary, the forces in New York. The replies again reflected the temper of the

---

[21] *New Jersey Archives*, 1st series, XVII, 93; *Pitt Correspondence*, I, 41-44, a letter where Loudoun advocated a general parliamentary tax as the only sure method for carrying on the war. According to the Albany quotas New Jersey's proportion was considerably less than a thousand.

assemblies. Rhode Island, on the ground that its quota was already exceeded, voted that only a hundred and fifty of the militia—this being the difference between the numbers of 1756 and 1757—should hold themselves in readiness. The New Hampshire assembly agreed that captains of militia should be given special orders, but made no provision for granting stores and supplies. Wentworth was certain that "they will prevent my marching any more of the Militia than is now upon actual Service." Connecticut made no effort to reform its antiquated militia laws, but simply passed on, as did New York, Loudoun's orders to the colonels. The Massachusetts council did likewise, but at the same time informed Loudoun that no militia could march outside the province without an express vote of the assembly. New Jersey passed a new militia act and authorized Belcher to call out a thousand men in an emergency. Pennsylvania had no militia act, for the governor refused to sign a bill that permitted the election of officers and deprived him of military power, and to Loudoun's specific request for five hundred men the assembly returned only a fervent vindication of its position. Sharpe issued a proclamation requiring militia officers to exercise their men frequently, but explained that Maryland's defective militia laws did not invest officers "with a sufficient power to compel the Men to obey all such Orders as they may think proper to issue." The House of Burgesses augmented the Virginia regiment, which it should have done before, but Dinwiddie thought the militia laws remained defective in forbidding him to march troops outside the colony. Dobbs and Lyttelton both put their militia directly under Bouquet's command. In general the responses of the colonies to this request paralleled those to Loudoun's earlier one.[22]

[22] *Rhode Island Colonial Records*, VI, 39, 51-52; *New Hampshire Provincial Papers*, VI, 594-598; Wentworth to Loudoun, May 20, 1757, LO 3683;

In one sense this military union of the colonies which Loudoun tried to inaugurate can be called a success. For the first time in colonial history, a commander in chief directed the posting of men along a fifteen hundred mile frontier from New Hampshire to Georgia, and provincial officers corresponded with regulars, who in turn kept their superior informed. The armed forces of the continent were thus brought to a unity of command. But if we mean by a military union that local governments delegate to some central group a share of their powers, which was the kind of union Loudoun wanted, then of course this experiment of his failed. In the north he had had to deal with separate assemblies instead of qualified commissioners; in the south governors had promised what they could not perform. He neither got the number of men he had set as a minimum, nor equipped as he asked, nor at the time he specified. The reasons for the failure were strangely intermixed: in some colonies the particular local political dispute in which at the moment they happened to be engaged; in others a traditional jealousy of their neighbors; in others a positive recognition of the fact that Loudoun represented, in another form, the same royal prerogative that they had contended with since their formation, and a dislike, born out of individual selfishness as much as out of a collective effort for complete self-government, to the interference in their military affairs of British control.

Colonial Records of Connecticut, XI, 8; *New Jersey Archives,* 1st series, XVII, 104-110; *Pennsylvania Archives,* III, 150; *Pennsylvania Colonial Records,* VII, 525, 562-563, 573-578; Lyttelton to Colonels of Militia, Sept. 10, 1757, LO 4445; *North Carolina Colonial Records,* V, 763; *Maryland Archives,* IX, 3; *Dinwiddie Papers,* II, 628.

CHAPTER IX

THE CAMPAIGN OF 1757

THE accession to power in December, 1756, of William Pitt and his Leicester House adherents changed the character of the American war. Newcastle and Fox went out of office, and Cumberland, who held his post of captain general by commission, was effectually prevented from playing a dominant part in the determination of American policy by his exclusion from important meetings of the inner cabinet. Pitt's ministry, though it included Devonshire, Granville, Holderness, and Halifax[1] as well as his immediate followers, maintained from December to April a precarious position against the covert opposition of Newcastle, whose patronage in both houses of parliament continued his influence, and of Cumberland, who still retained the favor of the king. It could not therefore completely effect its purpose. But as a ministry it constituted a more efficient body than its predecessors, for since its very existence depended upon the personal ability of its leader, Pitt was enabled to exercise over it, especially in December and January, an authority both in policy and administration that was singularly unrestrained.

Pitt belongs to that small group of eighteenth century statesmen who, accepting the repeated opinions of merchants, came to believe that England's wealth, and therefore her greatness, was tied up with her colonies. Most

---

[1] Halifax, though without a ministerial post, sat in inner cabinet meetings on American questions, and tried to make a permanent seat there the price of his political support.

ministers would have subscribed to the general dictum
that the colonies were too precious a possession to be lost,
but never with the same passionate intensity with which
Pitt subscribed to it. For Pitt, as Halifax, had steeped
himself in the documents; he had taken exceptional pains
to get information; he had not been content with a perfunctory faith in the merchants' credo but had asked
them for reasoned proof.[2] James Abercromby, the Virginia agent who had puzzled for years over colonial problems and had seen his ideas shelved, now at last had an
audience. Pitt studied his report on the colonial military
situation, replied graciously, and was given access to some
of Abercromby's American correspondence.[3] By such
means Pitt, even more than Halifax before him, strengthened his conviction that the expulsion of the French from
America was an objective calling for the unrestricted expenditure of British resources. The arguments he used
to gain his point were strangely diversified. With Newcastle and Hardwicke, who judged that the chief value of
any conquest in the New World would be diplomatic, bargaining pieces for the restoration of Minorca and the
return of Flanders and Germany to the *status quo,* he
maintained that the war in America, far from being a
sideshow, was the real arena "where England and Europe are to be fought for."[4] But with the king he paraded

[2] The report of London merchants on the value of the Virginia and Maryland trade, January 6, 1757, was in answer to Pitt's specific request. G.D.
8: 95.

[3] Some Remarks on the Encroachments made by France, on our Colonies
in North America, James Abercromby to Pitt, November, 1756, G.D. 8: 95.
In the Chatham Papers are various letters to James Abercromby from General James Abercromby and from Lieutenant James Abercrombie, the general's aide de camp. Abercromby's (the agent) most impressive work on the
colonies is a comprehensive and thoughtful general survey. One copy is in
the Huntington Library; another among the Shelburne Papers in the William L. Clements Library.

[4] Pitt to Newcastle, December 27, 1757, Additional MSS. 32,876, f. 455.

the new conception of an enlarged British dominion
which lay close to his heart. And in time the king too,
notwithstanding Newcastle's misgivings, came to see that
when the English had taken Canada, driven out the
French, and kept up troops in Germany as well, "then
we shall be a great nation."[5] It is not the least of Pitt's
achievements that he won George II's consent to the en-
largement of his empire.

Arrogant in temperament, Pitt considered no man except himself fit for the execution of so great an enterprise. Under Cumberland's tutelage Loudoun had gone
to the colonies with power to control all military matters
and with considerable authority over civilian governments. Whenever American affairs were discussed in
cabinet meetings, details of the disposition of troops and
a latitude in following orders were left to the commander
in chief.[6] Cumberland expressed complete confidence that
in time Loudoun would reduce the military chaos in
America to order. He agreed with Loudoun's whole plan
of operations for 1757 and promised his support.[7] From
Pitt such confidence was impossible. Pitt believed the
American situation so hopelessly embroiled that none of

[5] Newcastle to Hardwicke, August 26, 1758, Additional MSS. 35,417, f.
268.

[6] Minutes, October 16, 1756, Additional MSS. 32,997, f. 52. The cabinet
agreed that the drafts sent in the autumn of 1756 should go to Nova Scotia
unless Loudoun thought that he should keep them and that Nova Scotia was
secured without them.

[7] Cumberland to Loudoun, October 22, December 2, December 23, 1756,
Cumberland Papers. In a "most private letter", to be burned when read,
Cumberland unofficially informed Loudoun that the king would spare him
six thousand fresh men. "I will send you my Thoughts more fully with a
Plan of mine for your operations, which you shall be left at Liberty, either to
adopt, in part, or not at all, as you shall find it proper, from your better information." This letter was not burned; it was too important, being the
only justification which Loudoun had for proceeding with his plans. See
Charteris, *William Augustus Duke of Cumberland and the Seven Years' War*,
p. 205.

the arrangements of his predecessors could save it, for the sources of his information were either men who, having experienced ministerial indifference before, purposely exaggerated any description they wrote for home consumption, or men like Thomas Pownall and later Governor Hardy, who were politicians enough to agree with the arbiter of their personal destinies.[8] He determined therefore to abrogate Loudoun's unique authority as far as he could. He corresponded directly with governors on military matters and he substituted his own plans for the operations of 1757. Loudoun, like the commanders in chief who succeeded him, became simply the executor of Pitt's will.

Since Pitt's avowal that he was the only person who could save England was justified in the end by victory, there is not perhaps readily apparent the incongruity of a civilian minister dictating the details of a military campaign three thousand miles distant in a country of which he knew nothing at first hand. In the American Revolution this same plan, re-adopted, was to end in the disaster it deserved. But even in 1757 and 1758 Pitt's virtual assumption of the chief command had serious consequences. There are some grounds for believing that he hindered, quite as much as he contributed to, the prosecution of the war. What those grounds are an examination of the details of the campaign of 1757 will partly disclose.

In the first place, Pitt's original plans for 1757, purely as a problem in comparative strategy, were less embracing than Loudoun's. His alteration of Loudoun's objective for the main expedition threw out of balance the latter's plans for the defense of New York. Loudoun had intended that his attack on Quebec, as early in the spring as possible, would compel Montcalm to retain his forces

---

[8] Pownall went to England to present Loudoun's side of the Shirley dispute, won Pitt's favor, and returned as governor of Massachusetts.

in Canada for its defense and would prevent him from raiding the northern frontier. By ordering the main attack against Louisbourg first and then later in the summer against Quebec, Pitt destroyed the equipoise of Loudoun's strategy and left Montcalm to his own devices. This decision would seem to have been Pitt's own, for his cabinet, though naming the number of troops to go from England and Ireland, took no resolves upon their destination.[9] His letter to Loudoun of February 4 left the general some discretion and latitude "to decide on the Time and Manner of Carrying these Attempts into Execution", but none as to the objectives.[10] Shortly after these orders were written, a rapprochement between Fox and Devonshire rendered Pitt's tenure of office less secure, and he was compelled to relax the rigidity of his instructions by the strenuous protests from Loudoun's powerful friends. Cumberland, sitting for the first time that year in a cabinet, was able to assure for his appointee some latitude in orders.[11] Pitt's second letter on the campaign, March 17, repeated verbatim the opinion of the cabinet: "By my Letter of the 4th past, your Lordship is directed to begin with an Attack upon Louisburgh, and to proceed, in the next Place, to Quebeck; The King still thinks those Two Places the great Objects of Offensive Operations for the Ensuing Campaign in America, and judges the Taking of Louisburgh to be the more practicable Enterprize: His Majesty, nevertheless, is pleased to leave it to your Lordship to use your Discretion, with regard to which of the Two abovementioned Attempts, you shall judge it most advisable first to proceed.'"[12]

9 Minutes of a cabinet council, January 26, 1757, G.D. 8: 95.

10 Pitt to Loudoun, February 4, 1757, Received May 1, LO 2766.

11 Minutes, March 13, 1757, G.D. 8: 95.

12 Pitt to Loudoun, March 17, 1757, received July 9, LO 3076.

In the second place, and of far more practical importance, since the weather rendered the original plans of
both Pitt and Loudoun abortive, Pitt furnished his commander in chief with such scanty information that he
was badly handicapped in making his preparations in
America. Pitt wrote that the train of artillery for the
expedition included a "number of brass 24-pounders and
13-inch mortars, which your Lordship represents as absolutely necessary," but neither he nor the Ordnance
Board sent an itemized list. Knowing nothing of the other
calibers, Loudoun could only decide to take from New
York some of his own brass twelves and sixes, which he
could ill afford to spare from the service there. As it was
the fleet brought out a train deficient only in 13-inch
mortars.[13] A similar shortsightedness on Pitt's part
caused unnecessary confusion in the provision supply.
Pitt ordered Loudoun, both in December and in February, to collect at Halifax sufficient provisions for both
his own forces and those from England. With considerable effort Loudoun and Governor Lawrence of Nova
Scotia assembled stores for twelve thousand men for
six months. But at the same time William Baker, the contractor, was engaged in sending from England a supply
for both forces.[14] As a result there was a superfluity of
provisions and Loudoun carried back with him a large
quantity that was later proved to have been spoiled by
the weather and the reshipments.

Pitt likewise kept Loudoun in ignorance of the officers
coming out with the expedition and so compelled him to

13 Pitt to Loudoun, February 19, 1757, LO 2859. Loudoun took from New
York 4 brass twelves, 10 brass sixes, 4 threes, and 4 8-inch howitzers. There
arrived from England 18 heavy brass 24-pounders, 12 heavy brass 12-
pounders, 4 light brass 6-pounders, 4 royal howitzers, 2 13-inch mortars,
2 10-inch, 4 8-inch, and 30 cohorns (4⅖-inch).

14 *Pitt Correspondence*, I, 3; William Baker to his agent Thomas Saul at
Halifax, Feb. 21, 1757, LO 2875.

distribute his own general and field officers, scarcely enough for a single service, among several. He felt obliged to take Abercromby to Halifax, lest, by his death, the command of the major expedition should pass to a colonel and it was belated relief to find, when he reached Halifax, that two major generals, Peregrine Hopson and Lord Charles Hay, had been added to his staff. For the command in New York the only available officer was General Webb, whose illness in the spring of 1757 was making him timid, melancholic, and "diffident".[15] Nor could he easily find another officer to support Webb. Out of his nine regiments he could muster, in 1757, but three colonels, Stanwix, James Prevost, and Dusseaux; the others were in England. Of these three he assigned the first to Pennsylvania; the last was ill, and Prevost unfit for command. He had few lieutenant colonels. Bouquet, the only man who could be spared, commanded in South Carolina. Gage and Burton, of the 44th and 48th, which Loudoun considered his best corps,[16] he refused to detach from their regiments, and Rollo of the 22d had just arrived in New York, and was unproved. He finally left with Webb, Monro of the 35th and Young of the 60th, both capable, but without sufficient authority to presume to advise the

[15] "Hardy says Webb spent much time with him while I was away and says he could neither read nor write a page without its making his head turn round so that he did not know what he was doing." HM 1717, vol. 3, March 30, 1757. Webb suffered from the palsy, which "to another man would have been of very little Consequence; but all his People have died of that disease, and he is still low and down, and I cannot get his spirits up." Loudoun to Cumberland, Jan. 5, 1757, Cumberland Papers.

[16] "Lt. Col. Gage is a good officer and keeps up Discipline strictly. The Regiment is in Rags, but looks like Soldiers. Lt. Col. Burton I did not know before; but he is a diligent sensible man and I think will be of great use here. Both these Regiments have some men in them, that with all the Severity they are able to use they are not able to cure of Theft and Drunkenness. But I must do them the justice to say, they have no Bowels on them." Loudoun to Cumberland, Oct. 2, 1756, Cumberland Papers.

general. If he had known that young Lord Howe, perhaps the ablest officer in the army, was coming over to
assume command of Jeffrey's vacant battalion in the
60th, he would have felt far less anxious about the New
York command.

The actual decision as to the number of regular forces
to be stationed in New York was Loudoun's, but it was
based upon a consensus in both England and America.
Pitt ordered as many regiments to Nova Scotia as could
possibly be spared; Cumberland thought two battalions
sufficient for the New York frontier.[17] Hardy, Abercromby, and Webb agreed on the same number, if they
were supported by the fifty-five hundred provincials, and
in emergency the militia, and if the British retained the
superiority of the lake, the only route by which cannon
could be transported.[18] With some seventy-five hundred
men, a fleet of three sloops, five bayboats, four gondolas,
and twelve whaleboats,[19] and a reserve of militia, a capable commander should have held the frontier.

In general, the late arrival of campaign plans, for
which the political situation in England was partly re-

[17] Cumberland to Loudoun, Dec. 15, 1756, LO 2065.

[18] A distribution of troops for the 1757 campaign, Cumberland Papers.
Webb had the 35th, 859; the 3d battalion of the 60th, 727; the sick and re-
covery men of the 42d, 44th, 48th, the 2d and 4th battalions of the 60th, 241;
the four New York companies, 243; the detachment of Royal Artillery, 36;
rangers, 200; carpenters, 48; New Hampshire provincials, 250; Massachusetts, 1800; Rhode Island, 450; Connecticut, 1400; New York, 1000; and
New Jersey, 500; a total of 7744, excluding regular commissioned and non-
commissioned officers. Of this total number, 500 Connecticut provincials were
assigned to the defense of Number Four.

[19] Whiting's return of Nov. 19, 1756 (LO 2242) listed 4 sloops, 5 bayboats, 4 gondolas, 12 whaleboats, and 209 batteaux. Rigaud's March attack
on Fort William Henry (described in Parkman's *Montcalm and Wolfe*, I,
448-451) was successful in burning an unfinished sloop on the stocks, nearly
all the batteaux, and in damaging, though not destroying, two sloops in the
water, Eyre to Loudoun, Mar. 26, 1757, LO 3179. Loudoun suggested that

sponsible, and Pitt's secretiveness about essential details, compelled Loudoun to provide for the defense of New York from meagre materials.

The campaign itself began with commendable activity both in England and America. Pitt's ministry, which "made it a condition, sine quâ non, to be refused nothing",[20] was so forward in getting the transports chartered and fitted that they were on their way from the Thames to Spithead before the War Office had the camp necessaries for the Irish regiments ready.[21] By February 17 the fleet, under Vice-admiral Holburne, sailed from Spithead and anchored in St. Helen's, awaiting only the cessation of the westerly winds to proceed to Cork and embark the Irish regiments.[22] In America Loudoun—acting upon the only information in his possession, Cumberland's unofficial letter of December 23—purchased a supply of "junk" for the artillery from New England contractors,[23] collected provisions, and with Hardy,[24] and the assistance of the indefatigable Bradstreet and the transport agent appointed by the Admiralty, assembled in New York harbor before the end of April some thirty

Webb have built in addition "20 large boats, to carry 30 men each . . . and 4 quarter galleys, according to Montresor's plan, to carry ordnance at their prow," Webb's queries and Loudoun's answers, April 26, 1757, LO 3473.

20 Argyll to Loudoun, February, 1757, LO 2946.

21 J. Cleveland to Barrington, Feb. 8, 1757, W.O. 1: 857.

22 Admiralty to Francis Holburne, Feb. 25, Ad. 2: 1331, p. 168.

23 The New Englanders, so Loudoun was informed, "are of opinion any metal will do for cannon balls and . . . if I do not care they will make them of mettel so brittle that if you lett one ball fall on another they will break like glass . . . their ore in New England is very bad and all the good iron they work is made with ore brought from Philadelphia." HM 1717, vol. 3, Feb. 3, 1757.

24 Sir Charles Hardy was appointed Rear-admiral of the Blue, and ordered to Halifax under Holburne's command, Feb. 4, 1757, Ad. 2: 1331, p. 160.

transports, fitted with berths and watercasks.[25] As soon as the provincial troops reached Albany to take over from the 42d, 44th, and 48th the northern forts, these three regiments sailed to New York, and were ready to embark by May 14. To re-capture the sailors from the transports, who had deserted to join the crews of privateers just arrived with rich prizes, Loudoun, on the advice of the governor and lieutenant governor, surrounded the town with the regiments and impressed enough men for his purpose.[26] On May 21 the six regiments assigned to Halifax embarked; on the 23d the pilots took them down to the Hook.

But already the success of the campaign was threatened. Persistent up-channel winds kept Holburne at St. Helen's until April 16. On April 25 he embarked the regiments at Cork, and on May 8 sailed for Nova Scotia. He anchored at Halifax on July 9, after beating about outside for two days in a heavy fog. Meanwhile three French squadrons—Revest's from Toulon, Beaufremont's from Martinique, and de la Motte's from Brest—had escaped Pitt's cruising fleets and sailed for Louisbourg, twenty-two ships of the line in all, a larger and heavier force than Holburne's.[27] They arrived there before the end of June. If Pitt had remained in office, he would have sent

[25] Bradstreet to Loudoun, Mar. 11, LO 3022; to Abercromby, Mar. 28, LO 3196. Shackerley, the agent, signed the charter-parties, and payment was made from England, T. 29: 32, p. 471; T. 27: 27, p. 294.

[26] The town constables, assisting with the press on land, tried to screen sailors, who in some cases were so confident of escaping that they boldly looked out the windows of houses which the constables had declared empty, and so fell an easy prey to the navy crews who scrambled in after them, HM 1717, vol. 3, May 20, 1757.

[27] Journal kept by the Chevalier Barbier de Lescoet, second captain on the *Formidable* from April to November, 1757; Anonymous journal of the Cruise of the Squadron of M. Du Bois de la Motte in 1757, written by one of the Officers of *L'Inflexible*, *Report on Canadian Archives*, 1905, I.

Holburne immediate reinforcement as soon as he learned of the French movements. But his political enemies succeeded in driving him out in April without being able themselves to form a stable ministry, and during that critical period in the late spring, when Cumberland's interests were centered on his German campaign, Holderness had American affairs in charge. A cabinet of April 28, learning that four French ships had sailed northwest from Gibraltar,[28] did decide to increase Holburne's fifteen ships to eighteen, but that was insufficient reinforcement. When Pitt returned to office in July, having made his arrangements with Newcastle and purchased Fox's support by giving him the Pay Office, Holburne was sent the information of the French movements accessible in London, and strengthened with a suitable reinforcement.[29] News of Beaufremont's fleet passing off the New York coasts was brought to Loudoun as he was about to sail, and in spite of the risk to his transports, under convoy of the *Sutherland,* 50 guns, and two frigates, he and Hardy sailed, and reached Halifax on June 30.[30] An unconnected group of circumstances had thus united to delay the junction of the two British forces in Nova Scotia, and to give the French—their ships riding in safety behind the narrow rocky entrance to Louisbourg harbor, and their four thousand men ensconced behind the stone bastions of one of the sturdiest fortresses in America—a strategical superiority.

Three harrowing weeks of indecision for the two commanders followed, combined with persistent fogs and un-

[28] Granville, Devonshire, Bedford, Winchelsea, Holderness, April 28, Cumberland Papers.

[29] Pitt to Holburne, July 7, 1757, LO 3907, received by Loudoun, Oct. 15. Pitt sent as reinforcement the *Somerset,* 70 guns, the *Devonshire,* 70, the *Prince Frederick,* 64, and the *Eagle,* 60.

[30] See Sir Julian Corbett, *England in the Seven Years' War,* I, 166-178.

favorable winds. The exact strength of the French was
unknown to the British, for Loudoun's knowledge of
Revest and Beaufremont was vague and uncertain, as
was Holburne's of de la Motte who had preceded him
west. Both Hardy and Holburne sent out sloops and
frigates to ascertain the truth, but fogs prevented them
from examining Louisbourg harbor, and they returned,
on July 13 and 20, with second hand and inconclusive information.[31] For four hours on July 13 the wind came
fair; for the rest of July it remained adverse.[32] To lessen
the tension of the troops, as well as to restore them to
health—Holburne landed a thousand sick on July 9—and
to teach them the rudiments of siege tactics, Loudoun
ordered lines of fortifications blocked out and sham
battles fought under the eyes of critical engineers.[33] Ri-
valry between officers of the army and navy contributed
to the general atmosphere of nervous strain, for if the
former pointed out British advantages in numbers, the
latter replied that fogs invariably veiled the coasts in
August and that Louisbourg harbor could not be forced
with eight ships of the line in it. For the two commanding
officers the memory of Byng's execution three months
before was an unpleasant warning; Byng had been con-

[31] Report of the schooner *Resolution*, LO 3937; ĦM 1717, vol. 4, July 18,
1757.

[32] Holburne to Holderness, Aug. 4, 1757, Cumberland Papers.

[33] General Orders, July 3, 24, 1757, LO 3576. Loudoun has been severely
criticized for using troops to "plant cabbages"—even Osgood's brief account, *American Colonies in the Eighteenth Century*, IV, 395, mentions it.
As a matter of fact, the general orders for July 21 show that only 200 men
were employed in making a garden, and that 20 "Gardners from the Line"
were all that spent any time on it. Pitt ordered Loudoun to supply fresh
vegetables from New England, but the late season there prevented, *Pitt
Correspondence*, I, 54. A. G. Bradley's readable book, *The Fight with France
for North America*, p. 182, points out the wisdom of taking every precaution
to avoid scurvy; fresh vegetables supplemented the spruce beer with which
the troops had been supplied since July 4.

demned by a court martial for failing "to do his Utmost"
in the action off Minorca in 1756. In this overwrought sus-
pense a council of war, first suggested by Holburne at his
arrival, met to consider the only question that a professional group could consider, "Was it advisable to proceed
against Louisbourg at the late season of the year?" The
Quebec attack was beyond consideration. The council was
composed of four major generals and four officers from
the fleet. During nine days it received all available information and examined twenty witnesses.

Councils of war were in bad odor in the eighteenth century. They cast doubts upon the capabilities of a commander without shifting his responsibility. This one
managed to clothe itself in such ridicule, partly because
of the conduct of one of its members, Major General Lord
Charles Hay, that Loudoun was ashamed to send its
minutes home. Though Hay was a man of winning personal charm, boundless egotism, and undisputed bravery,
in the stress of action, or impending action, a streak of
insanity, never far below the surface, assumed control of
his mind, and lent a tragic somberness to the qualities
that won him high rank in the army.[34] Having prejudged
his colleagues to be cowards, Hay spent the long hours at
the council of war sitting informally in the window, at
times dozing off, gazing wistfully out over the harbor, or
gesticulating and grimacing in an obvious loss of self-
restraint. To every witness, soldiers acquainted with
Louisbourg fortifications, sailors intimate with the coasts,
he put but one question: could Louisbourg be attacked
with any prospects of success? Such a query left to inferior officers the answering of the question before the
council. Some forebore to reply; a few, such as Bradstreet, advised the attack, but the majority agreed in

[34] For his cool bravado in leading a cheer for the French guards at
Fontenoy, see Skrine, *Fontenoy*, p. 172.

answering Hay that the harbor could not be forced against an enemy fleet and that a siege would last until the treacherous weather of the autumn set in.[35] With Hay in a censorious mood, the rest of the council, fearful that the discussion of their uncertainties in his presence would supply him with information damaging to their reputations, met secretly and unofficially without him, and decided on a unanimous front. At this point it occurred to Hopson to re-read Pitt's instructions, and he came to the conclusion, which Loudoun also adopted, that they did not allow the settlement of such a question as that before the council. Unless Loudoun attacked either Louisbourg or Quebec, he laid himself open to the charge of flat disobedience.[36] On the last day of July, therefore, he put a new question: Which of the two places will you advise me to proceed to, in order to form an attack? The council unanimously advised Louisbourg.

Within two days the sixteen regiments embarked, and waited only for a change in wind, still "foul" since July

[35] The original forty-six page draft of the council of war, July 23-31, signed by Loudoun, Holburne, Abercromby, Hardy, Hopson, Hay, Charles Holmes and Fowkes, is in LO 3982; a copy, with copies of all documents laid before it, in W.O. 34: 101, no. 181. On July 30, Hay, as general of the day, gave vent before the soldiers and townspeople to his personal opinions: "This affair was what happened in the Mediterranean, that Byng has suffered, and that he hoped to God some people would suffer for their behaviour here before six months were at an end." For such remarks, and for his refusal to obey Loudoun's orders to accompany the troops to New York instead of returning to England, Loudoun put him in arrest. He subsequently demanded a trial to clear his reputation; the court martial, Feb. 12 to Mar. 6, 1760, was a farce, and when one of its members, Lieutenant General Onslow, died before the court had come to a decision, the king refused to grant a warrant for a retrial. Hay himself died May 1. The court martial is in W.O. 71: 24, pp. 4-68.

[36] "But as the King may have given orders for such assistance as may make us equal to the Task altho he has not yet acquainted me with it I do not see how I can be disperced from obeying the orders which his ministers communicate to me so peremptory." HM 1717, vol. 4, July 31, 1757.

13. No sensible man thought the enforced choice of the council a wise one; the captains of the fleet told Loudoun it was a "mad work" to proceed so late in the year. On August 4 the wind came fair, but before the sails were unfurled, Holburne hurriedly came on shore with new and exact information of the strength of the French fleet,[37] and gave it as his opinion that there was no probability of success. Loudoun then made the final decision, to abandon the campaign, and to return to New York. Holburne himself, in obedience to Pitt's new orders, later took the fleet to look into Louisbourg harbor, and convinced himself anew that Loudoun's final choice was wise. Hardy was equally positive; a landing attempted in the heavy fog would have ended with the ruin of the army. A month later Holburne's fleet was broken in a hurricane; half the ships were dismasted, one was lost. Hardy took three cripples on to England, and some, too shattered to trust to the seas, remained at Halifax. "Thus, sir, ends our Famous expedition to America in the year 1757."[38]

In the final analysis the failure of the expedition was due neither to the late arrival at Albany of the provincial troops, which kept the regular regiments in service there until May; nor to Pitt's tardy dispatch of his orders for the campaign, which left Loudoun in ignorance until May 1; nor to the political situation in England, which removed Pitt from office at a critical time; nor to the council of war at Halifax, which consumed nine days; nor even to the escape of the three French squadrons from British intercepting fleets. Any or all of these circum-

[37] The *Gosport*, stationed at Newfoundland, captured a French Schooner which had sailed from Louisbourg July 6, LO 4069. She gave the names and armament of the French fleet, information which was sent on to Halifax in the schooner *Surprize*.

[38] Holburne to Loudoun, Aug. 25, LO 4311; Nov. 10, LO 4801; Hardy to Loudoun, Sept. 28, 1757, LO 4541.

stances might have become disastrous, but they never took full effect because overshadowed by the one outstanding factor—the persistently unfavorable weather which kept the main fleet from arriving in America before July, and then confined it helpless in Halifax harbor. Certainly no blame for the failure of the expedition can be assigned to the commander in chief. His decision to sail northward from New York in the face of a superior French fleet showed considerable daring; while his resolve to disobey the explicit orders of a ministry who might try to justify themselves by making him the victim, as in the case of Byng, was even heroic.

The delayed arrival of the fleet was also indirectly responsible for the second British reverse of 1757, Montcalm's capture of Fort William Henry in August. If Loudoun could have invested Quebec in July, according to his original plan and the discretionary orders given by Pitt in March, the New York forts would have remained unmolested. The enforced inaction of the bulk of the British army at Halifax gave Montcalm an opportunity he was quick to seize, and to fulfill with a sure adroitness. But his exploit was nevertheless in the nature of a raid, undertaken with only ten days supply of provisions and a mob of Indians who would not endure a long campaign, and if the British commander in New York had followed out the suggestions which Loudoun left him, or taken advantage of his own sources of strength, it would probably have failed. But Webb, the only general officer whom Loudoun could possibly leave in command, exhibited throughout the entire summer the timid self-depreciation of a sick man.

In the first place, Webb, whom Loudoun had given complete freedom to act "as Circumstances and your own Prudence directs you", took no steps to form an offensive against Ticonderoga early in the summer, when it was weak, as Loudoun had suggested. He assumed command in April, but it was the 23d of June before he left Albany for Fort Edward, and July 25 before he visited Fort William Henry.[39] Nor did he take all precautions for defense, though Loudoun wrote him on June 20 that Montcalm would probably feel free to move against him.[40] The critical point in defensive preparations was the naval control of the lake, but Webb built none of the large boats advised by Loudoun, and the two sailing galleys on which his carpenters worked were still unfinished on August 3, when Montcalm drew his first parallels. Even more disastrous was Webb's carelessness with the twenty-seven boats on the lake. Though without authorization, Captain Parker of the New Jersey provincials was not prevented from taking the lot on a scouting expedition on July 23; he was ambushed, two hundred and fifty of his three hundred men were captured, and twenty-four of the boats lost.[41] That piece of stupidity gave the French unmolested passage for their artillery.

Again, Webb distributed his forces improperly. He insisted that early in August he could put but 2100 men into Fort William Henry, and had left at Fort Edward but 1600. Yet on paper he had nearly 7500 men, and according to his own returns of troops he could have collected at Fort Edward between 3500 and 4000. The provincials were reasonably complete—4591 out of 5000

[39] James Montrésor's Report to the Ordnance Board of the Transactions of the Campaign, June 1 to Oct. 1, 1757, W.O. 55: 283. This is a much fuller account than the one in Montrésor's own papers, printed in New York Historical Society *Collections*, 1881.

[40] Loudoun to Webb, June 20, 1757, Cumberland Papers.

[41] Webb to Loudoun, Aug. 1, LO 4020. Webb maintained that Monro, commanding at Fort William Henry, gave Parker orders, Webb to Barrington, Aug. 17, 1757, W.O. 1: 1, ff. 545. He also excused his failure to finish the galleys by the fact that there were only twelve ship-wrights among the forty-eight artificers under his command.

voted—early in the summer.[42] On July 30 there were
3432 at Fort Edward, and only 800 of these—the Massachusetts troops under Fry—went to Fort William Henry
in the belated reinforcement of August 2.[43] To these 2600
provincials remaining at Fort Edward, only 350 of them
sick, Webb could have added 1400 regulars.[44] Though
these figures are based upon insufficient returns, when
they are compared with the figures of the autumn, and
due allowance made for deaths and for desertion,[45] which

[42] First return of provincials, July 15, 1757, LO 4004 (1).

	officers	men	total voted
Massachusetts	157	1554	1800
Connecticut	85	756	1400*
New York	23	873	1000
New Jersey	45(?)	440	500
New Hampshire	35	226	350
Rhode Island	45	354	450
	388	4203	5500

* Of the Connecticut troops at Number Four, not included in the return,
487 were present out of 500, LO 4574.

[43] Second return of provincial troops, July 30, 1757, LO 4004 (2) Massachusetts, 1552; Connecticut, 735; New York, 801; Rhode Island, 344. The
total, including 277 officers, was 3709. The New Hampshire and New Jersey
troops were at Fort William Henry.

[44] 880 of Webb's 2300 regulars were at Fort William Henry. 6 companies
of the 35th, 540; a detachment of the 60th, 100; New York independent
companies, 100; and 140 rangers. Monro's return received Nov. 1. The list
in *New York Colonial Documents*, X, 621, includes officers.

[45] LO 4004 (3, 4, 5).

	Aug. 30	Sept. 30	Nov. 7
Massachusetts	529	507	504
Connecticut	703	695	678
New York	745	692	685
Rhode Island	319	295	288
	2296	2189	2155

These figures do not include officers. 800 Massachusetts troops, and the New
Jersey and the New Hampshire regiments were in the capitulation of Fort
William Henry, and not included in these lists.

was very great after the surrender of the fort, they still lead to the conclusion that if Webb could muster at the two forts but 3700 men on August 3, he must have left 2500 men elsewhere in New York, either at Albany, the posts up the Hudson, or along the Mohawk. Such a division of forces was unnecessary and inexcusable.

More important still, Webb failed to write to the colonies for the militia that were presumably ready for emergencies until it was too late for them to arrive in time. He had ample information of Montcalm's preparations. On July 3 two deserters told him that Montcalm was daily expected at Ticonderoga, with four battalions of regulars, five hundred Indians, the Canadian troops, and forty pieces of artillery. On July 10 the Indians brought in a French prisoner with news of preparations and of the construction of boats. For the rest of the month every British scouting party that went out encountered strong enemy ambushes, and on the 23d a group of French and Indians attacked the carpenters' guard at Fort Edward. Two days later after the command of the lake was lost, Webb went up to Fort William Henry to examine and strengthen its defenses and on the 28th learned from a scouting party that the enemy were encamped along the shore of the lake on their way to the fort. On the 29th he returned to Fort Edward, and on the 30th wrote his first letters to the governors asking for the militia.[46] It was too late; by no conceivable burst of speed could they have reached Fort Edward within a week. Pownall reached Boston on August 3,[47] received Webb's first letter on August 6, assumed the responsibility of giving orders to march the militia out of the province,

[46] Montrésor's Report, W.O. 55: 283; Webb to Loudoun, Aug. 1, 1757, LO 4020.

[47] He had come out from England in Holburne's fleet.

and saw them on the road by the 8th.[48] Fitch received the letter on the 5th; a fourth of the militia were ready by the 9th and 10th; some reached Fort Edward on the 14th.[49] DeLancey heard the news on August 4; he hurried to Albany, and learned to his satisfaction that Sir William Johnson had got two thousand men to Fort Edward by the 6th.[50] On the 9th, the day that Monro surrendered, there were thirty-three hundred militia encamped there.

All things considered, the rusty and cumbersome militia system of the northern colonies worked quickly enough in this emergency to justify Pownall's contention that it deserved praise. If Webb had sent out his appeal on July 24, when he learned of Parker's defeat, he might have had seven to ten thousand men at Fort Edward by August 6. As it was, he turned back the majority on the 13th, before they reached him; those who were at Fort Edward he kept without excuse, and so antagonized men whose crops were waiting in the fields. There were, of course, grounds for criticism of the militia. The Rhode Islanders never arrived, for the assembly, realizing that the hundred and fifty men they had authorized in May were ignominiously few, met on August 10 and called out a sixth part of the whole instead.[51] The New Hampshire men, two hundred foot and two hundred horse, did not reach Fort Edward, and when Wentworth later tried to post some of them at Number

[48] Pownall transmitted three sets of orders to militia colonels: 1) to march immediately; 2) to march beyond the borders; 3) to march wherever the enemy was. Pownall to Loudoun, August 13, 1757, LO 4213.

[49] Fitch to Loudoun, September 7, 1757, LO 4412. Reports from militia captains to their colonels, Connecticut Historical Society.

[50] *Sir William Johnson Papers*, II, 730; DeLancey to Loudoun, August 10, LO 4192. Montrésor's Report.

[51] *Rhode Island Colonial Records*, VI, 81. See *ante*, p. 226.

Four to relieve Whiting's Connecticut troops, they deserted.[52] Israel Williams thought the Massachusetts militia dispirited, but Pepperrell wrote that "they went off on a sudden with great Freedom in great numbers."[53] DeLancey found militia loitering on the road, and deserting in groups. British officers reported that as many turned back home as came forward, and Sir John St. Clair, who accompanied some of the Massachusetts militia in an unofficial capacity, suspected they would make his presence an excuse for returning. James Montrésor at Fort Edward thought a desire to desert or run away the only reason why the militia refused to occupy a small unfortified hill seven hundred yards north of the fort on the road to the lake. They relieved their spirits by cursing Webb, and some went so far as to advocate hanging him as he deserved; when they returned home under a cloud not of their own devising, having lost money and time themselves, and having cost their provinces a thousand pounds a day, they aroused the resentment of the whole countryside, first against Webb, and then, by an easy transition, against Loudoun and the British army.

Finally, Webb destroyed the morale of the Fort William Henry garrison by abandoning them to their own resources. When he visited the fort on July 25, orders were given to prepare it for attack: the regulars of the 35th and a thousand provincials, for whom there was no room in the fort, were moved from their previous dangerous situation near the woods to Johnson's old camp of 1755; outworks by the fort were demolished, the funnels of the powder magazine were filled with sand bags, the east bastion was heightened, and additional embrasures

---

[52] Wentworth to Loudoun, LO 4315; Whiting to Webb, September 1, LO 4375.

[53] Williams to Pownall, August 11, 1757, LO 4197; Pepperrell to Captain Christie (commanding at Albany), August 13, LO 4211.

were cut for musket fire. But though Monro compelled
Webb to admit that Fort William Henry was more likely
to be attacked than Fort Edward, he could not persuade
the general to spare more than a thousand men.[54] Monro
later accused Webb of withholding from him at the time
the information, received on the evening of the 28th, that
the enemy were on their way down the lake, and com-
municating it by letter from Fort Edward.[55] During the
siege itself, which lasted six days, Monro could have en-
dured the havoc wrought by Montcalm's artillery,[56] or
the behavior of the provincials,[57] if only reinforcements,
or a promise of aid, had come from Webb. But he received
but two letters during the course of the siege, one on the
evening of August 3, promising assistance, and one on
the 6th, delivered to him by Montcalm's aide de camp
under a flag of truce, advising surrender.[58] It was the

[54] Queries made by Lieutenant Colonel Monro to Major General Webb,
July 28, 1757, LO 3994.

[55] HM 1717, vol. 2, October 31, 1757. Monro died early in November, having spent the last two months of his life nursing such a fury against Webb
that it undoubtedly hastened the apoplexy which caused his death.

[56] The timbers of the east bastion and of the northwest curtain were
driven three or four feet into the parapet. Of Monro's own twenty-four guns,
six had burst by the third day, one with such violence that thirteen men were
killed or wounded; ''one of which was a provincial Officer that never was
heard of but part of his Coat was found.'' A ten-inch shell burst one of the
ammunition boxes and killed sixteen. Remarks upon the effect of Artillery
fire on Fort William Henry, by Lieutenant Thomas Collins of the Royal
Artillery, September 3, 1757, LO 4394.

[57] The provincials in the fort, Monro told Loudoun, instead of firing over
the parapet, lay down and fired into the air. The Massachusetts men in the
fortified enclosure declared on the last day that they were worn out, and
would stay no longer, preferring to be knocked on the head by the enemy
than remain to perish behind the breastworks. Monro's remarks on the siege,
LO 4479.

[58] Bartman to Monro, August 3, 1757, one-half after four, LO 4032; August 4, 1757, twelve o'clock, LO 4050. ''The General has order'd me to acquaint you he does not think it prudent as you know his Strength at this
place to attempt a Junction or to assist you till reinforc'd by the Militia of

growing conviction that Webb had left them to their fate which sapped the spirits of the men, and not their losses, for only a hundred and thirty had been killed or wounded. On the morning of the 9th, the representation of the Massachusetts provincials caused the calling of a council of war in the camp, which advised Monro to surrender, since "there was not the Least Expectation either of Relief or Succour from General Webb; without which it was impossible to Continue the defense of the Fort and Camp longer."[59] Monro thereupon signed the capitulation.[60]

This campaign ruined Webb's reputation, already damaged by his precipitous and unauthorized destruction of the Mohawk forts in 1756. An ill man, disheartened by the difficulties of carrying on the war in America and distrustful of the value of provincial aid, he considered himself doomed when he saw Loudoun taking the bulk of the regular army, the choicest artillery, half of the rangers, most of the engineers, to Halifax, and leaving him alone without field officers. Lord Howe, who came over with Holburne, arrived at Fort Edward to take command of

the Colonies . . . in case he should be so unfortunate from the delays of the Militia not to have it in his power to give you timely Assistance, you might be able to make the best Terms were left in your power."

[59] It was signed by Lieutenant Colonel Young, four captains and two lieutenants of the regulars, Colonels Fry, Parker, and Goffe of the provincials, Major Gilman of New Hampshire, Captain Salstonstall of Massachusetts, and Captain Ogden of the rangers, LO 4158.

[60] The Loudoun papers add little to well-known accounts of the "massacre" by the French Indians which followed. Monro himself saw no murders, but was informed by his officers that two men were killed in the camp and twenty towards Fort Edward, HM 1717, vol. 2, November 1, 1757. Montrésor was startled by the appearance at Fort Edward of half-naked terrified fugitives, but others who came in later under the guard of French regulars did not think the affair "quite so horrid." The French undoubtedly prevented a general massacre by carrying back to Quebec no less than four hundred and thirty-four men, including eight to ten wounded, the majority of them provincials; Captain Faesh returned in December with one hundred and forty-four of these men, HM 1717, vol. 2, December 2, 1757.

his battalion on August 6, too late to be of service. But, to repeat an earlier remark, Loudoun had no other officers to leave in New York, and no means of knowing whether the major expedition would be adequately supplied with the necessary accessories to an offensive campaign.

The disasters of 1757 had a different effect upon the secretary of state and his American commander. Pitt, who did not at first know all the circumstances, judged that Loudoun's inactivity was a political manoeuvre to discredit him and restore Cumberland's influence.[61] It strengthened his resolve, not to decrease supervision from England, but to increase it; not to allow generals in America more latitude, but to find men who would obey his orders. On the other hand, Loudoun felt that Pitt's decision to control from England the conduct of the war placed the commander in chief in a dilemma from which there was no escape. The sending to South Carolina of Montgomery's battalion, on the application of Charles Pinckney and other South Carolinians,[62] seemed to Loudoun an infringement upon his right to distribute troops according to military needs. More humiliating still were Pitt's orders on the objectives of the campaign, for Loudoun blamed them for making a burlesque of his council of war. He wrote his opinions to Pitt in a critical letter which subsequently played a part in his recall. "The Country may be undone [he said] by a punctual Obedience to the most prudent Orders at the time they were given, or the Person that has the honor to command, must depart from them with a Halter about his Neck . . . if

61 "Mr. Pitt is highly offended, and suspects that the Fleet, and army from England, carried *Hints* to his Lordship, which made Him alter, His first Intention, and that Lord Loudoun, when he went from New York, was a different Man from Lord Loudoun at Halifax, after the arrival of Holbourne from England," Newcastle to Hardwicke, September 3, 1757, Additional MSS. 35,417, f. 40.

62 Representation of Charles Pinckney, December 6, 1756, G.D. 8: 95.

the person in Command, is not thought proper to be entrusted with the Power of taking such measures as the Change of the Situation of things make necessary, he is certainly most improper of His Office, and it is absolutely necessary for the King's Service, that a better should be sent in His Place, in whom it may be fitt to place such a Confidence."[63] Since he had not been supported in his plan for 1757, he determined to send no plan of his own for the operations of 1758, but only information on which a plan could be based; and to beg that orders be posted early.

Loudoun, however, does not emerge from this campaign with reputation unblemished. No commander who permits circumstances to cover him with ridicule, as in the strange story of the council of war, is entirely praiseworthy. He should have seen to it that the bastions of Fort William Henry were encased in stone, for Montrésor repeated Mackellar's statement on Oswego that they could not stand twenty-four hours against cannon. He should have definitely assured the control of Lake George, for the British had resources to build an effective fleet. But in concentrating attention upon his relations with the colonies, Loudoun left to subordinates the supervision of such details. He suffered from the paucity and incompetence of his staff. Abercromby and Amherst, in 1758, had such brigadiers as Wolfe, Howe, and Forbes; Loudoun had only Abercromby and Webb. The affair at Halifax discredited him with the army, and the loss of Fort William Henry hardened the antipathies of the colonies.

[63] Loudoun to Pitt, August 16, 1757, LO 4239.

CHAPTER X

MILITARY UNION OF THE COLONIES–II

In the appraisal of the extent to which Loudoun succeeded in drawing together the military resources of the colonies, his relations with the superintendents of Indian affairs and with the governors, who were the principal British officials connected with the war, assume an importance equal to his relations with the assemblies. By accepting his superior authority and lending their support to his aims, such officials gave a powerful cohesive force to the idea of unity; by setting their ambitions above his management of the war, or by concurring in and yielding to the local, separate aims of assemblies, they damaged it irreparably.

Indian affairs, when Loudoun arrived in America, were still conceived of as divided into two parts, political and commercial. Control of the former was assigned to Sir William Johnson, as colonel of the Six Nations and Sole Agent and Superintendent of their affairs, under the direction of the commander in chief; it was his task to restore the Iroquois to their ancient allegiance, broken in 1753, and not firmly cemented since by either the Albany conference or British efforts. Commercial relations, on the other hand, remained under the control of the various agencies who had exploited the Indian trade in the past, such as the governors and committees of assembly. Deprived legally of the political management they had once enjoyed, they still continued their land-grabbing schemes and their extortionate victimizing of the race they considered to be distinctly inferior to their own, and they still tried to negotiate treaties and wage war, if necessary, in pursuit of their aims. To the commander in chief was assigned the duty of aiding the superintendent in confining such agencies to their proper sphere.

In New York, during Loudoun's career, Johnson's supreme management was not contested, but in Pennsylvania the westward movement, which continued irrespective of the war, raised complications that neither of them could settle. The crux of the difficulty there was the constitutional and agrarian contest between the proprietary interests, represented by the governor, and private interests, represented by the assembly. Both desired to settle and exploit the new tracts of lands in western Pennsylvania purchased by the Pennsylvania commissioners to the Albany conference from the Iroquois, who considered themselves overlords of the region. New Jersey and Connecticut likewise had interests and claims in the same region, while the Delawares and Shawnees, who had been attached to British interests, looked upon themselves as the rightful owners of the territory and were affronted that the sale had been made without their full consent. In 1755 they attacked the upper Susquehanna frontier. Johnson undertook to make peace and finally accomplished it in July, 1756, but his efforts were considerably hampered by the hostile attitude of the governors of New Jersey and Pennsylvania. Belcher actually declared war in June, 1756, and a month later ended it, after Abercromby, at Johnson's request, had intervened. After Johnson's treaty, settlement of the frontier continued. The Pennsylvania assembly undertook to negotiate with the Delawares by virtue of a former treaty if the governor should refuse that task, and the latter, fearful of damaging proprietary interests, yielded to their pressure. Loudoun expressly forbade him to interfere in Johnson's sole management of such matters: "I do not at all enter into the Merits of this Affair, because these have been consider'd by his Majesty and what I now direct is by His Majesty's Order thereupon."[1] But the letter had little effect; in December Denny again negotiated treaties. In 1757 a great conference at Easton, approved by the Board of Trade as a means to settle conflicting claims, was attended by the governor and his agents, by George Croghan, representing Johnson and the Crown, and unofficially by private members of the assembly. No decision was reached, but Croghan and Denny worked together until December, 1757, in some harmony, and might have reached a stable basis of agreement if private individuals had not intervened by sending belts of invitation to the Senecas and Cayougas, and by carrying on trade at Wyoming. Once more Denny felt obliged to interfere, and Loudoun's second remonstrance, which pointed out the need of unity between Johnson and the governors in a matter so closely connected with the conduct of the war, had no more effect than his first.[2] Johnson believed the remedy, for the time being, to be the renunciation by Pennsylvania of at least that part of the lands which lay to the west of the Alleghenies, for which payment had not been made, but while Denny alone might have been persuaded to such a course, the assembly would not allow the sacrifice.[3]

Loudoun's second duty in connection with Indian affairs in the north was the discovery of some formula whereby he and Johnson could work in unison. Johnson

---

[1] Loudoun to Denny, September 22, 1756, LO 1876.

[2] Loudoun to Denny, January 21, 1758, LO 5433.

[3] This paragraph is based upon available printed material: *New York Colonial Documents*, VII, 117-120; *New York Documentary History*, II, 728-762, 770-780; *Sir William Johnson Papers*, II, 555-558, 716, 769-771; *New Jersey Archives*, 1st series, XVII, 29, 50-51; *Pennsylvania Colonial Records*, VII, passim.

justifiably considered his own methods the sole channel
through which the six nations could be re-attached to
British interests, and, as his experience with Shirley
showed, he distrusted any interference from a commander in chief who might regard the Iroquois as vas-
sals bound to take the field when ordered, and not as
independent allies whose services only patient diplomacy
could win.[4] But he was dependent upon the commander
in chief for his expenses. Though Loudoun recognized
the value of Indian allies both as combatants and for
procuring intelligence, and though he permitted Johnson
to draw considerable sums, he hesitated to sink any large
proportion of his contingent funds in an enterprise from
which he was receiving such scant military aid. He was
convinced that Shirley's subsidizing of Indians by giving
them money in lieu of presents had increased Indian expenses unwarrantably, and that, if governors and assemblies could be kept from competing with Johnson, the
sums he allotted would be sufficient. With that opinion
Halifax was inclined to agree.[5] But while there were
these marked differences of opinion between Loudoun
and Johnson, both realized that they could not afford to
disagree. They settled together the broad outlines of
Indian policy, and Johnson was given a free hand in
working out details. Loudoun offered suggestions from
time to time, but he never gave orders, or drew up, as
Shirley had done, a set of rigid instructions. In only one
instance did he seem to interfere in Johnson's management by dealing directly with the Stockbridge Indians,
"domiciliated Indians living with the whites", whom he

---

[4] *New York Colonial Documents*, VII, 14.

[5] Loudoun to Halifax, December 26, 1756, LO 2416. Halifax to Loudoun,
March 11, 1757, LO 3018. "I entirely agree in opinion with you, that till the
Governors of His Majesty's Provinces shall be put upon a more respectable
and independent Footing, it is in vain to expect that these Abuses [in regard
to Indian affairs] will be wholly remedied."

had formed into a ranging company paid by the Crown. He thought it necessary to keep them away from the Iroquois, lest they too be persuaded to withdraw active military aid. "Therefore, as You know I am Order'd to look into, and direct You in Indian Affairs, dont let it enter into Your mind, that by this, I mean to interfere in the Management of Indian Affairs, by taking it into my own hands, or by turning it into any other Channel than thro' You, for it is farthest from my thought; for in the first place, there is no Man in America, I wish to have the Management of them but yourself, and as to me I am very far from wishing to encrease my business, for I have more in my other departments to do, than is fitt for any one Man to Execute, as business ought to be done."[6]

In his general attitude towards the Indians, Loudoun shared the typical Old World opinion of his time that they were noble savages, endued with the heroic virtues of the ancients. When some soldiers of the 44th murdered in cold blood a renegade Indian, Jerry, in retaliation for his massacre of their comrades at the Monongahela a year before, Loudoun demanded that they be sought out and punished. "For I have never yet seen Men of any Country or any Rank but who know what Justice is and Revere it; and the surest bond of Friendship is to shew we will do Justice to them, and that we expect it from them."[7] Though his subordinates urged him to drop the enquiry, as no one in the regiment would testify, and though Johnson, having pacified the Indians, hinted that further probing of the affair would raise their insolence, Loudoun stuck doggedly to his opinion, and nearly a year later raised it again in somewhat similar circumstances. "I likewise disapproved of this plan I saw now established

6 *Sir William Johnson Papers*, II, 760, 765.

7 Loudoun to Johnson, August 8, 1756, LO 1442; *Sir William Johnson Papers*, II, 529, 533, 720.

all over the coloneys of never putting a white man to
death for killing an Indean as I saw you could never expect to establish either friendship or confidence in the
Indeans whilst that was the case.'"⁸

With the southern Indians Loudoun had far less concern than with the northern. They were too remote from
the main field of the war. But nominally his relations with
Edmund Atkin, commissioned in the spring of 1756 as
superintendent in the south, were the same as with Johnson. Fox and Halifax were very dubious about the
wisdom of choosing Atkin; they knew little of his abilities
except his own estimate of them, set forth in a volumi-
nous report of 1754 upon southern Indian affairs. In
London, when soliciting in person for the office, he appeared more anxious to have increased its allotted salary,
£600 a year, than to discuss proposals for regaining the
alliance of southern tribes.⁹ Fox, therefore, privately instructed Loudoun to dispense with Atkin's services if he
saw fit, and to employ whomsoever he chose.¹⁰ After Atkin finally reached America, late in 1756, neither Johnson
nor Loudoun found cause to disagree with Fox's opinion
of him. They settled, in Johnson's favor, a clash of juris-
dictions between the two superintendents, for each had
been given authority over certain minor tribes allied with
the principal nations both in the north and the south.
Atkin was then unwilling to assume his duties until Loudoun paid his salary and gave him unlimited credit for
Indian presents. He followed Loudoun from Albany to
New York, and from New York to Boston and back. Loudoun finally paid him to mid-summer, 1757, but refused
to allow him further funds until he demonstrated his

⁸ HM 1717, vol. 3, April 29, 1757; *New York Colonial Documents*, VII,
248, 249, 250.
⁹ Observations touching Atkin's appointment, LO 559.
¹⁰ Fox to Loudoun, May 12, 1756, LO 1142.

ability to dispose wisely of the presents already entrusted to him.[11] After Atkin left for the south, fourteen months after the date of his commission, he corresponded, not with the commander in chief, but with the Board of Trade and various governors, continually seeking to augment his income. In time Loudoun lost all trace of and all confidence in him and in the spring of 1758, when he wanted five hundred Cherokees to accompany an expedition against Fort Duquesne, he made use of the discretion Fox had allowed him to appoint William Byrd as the special agent for that purpose.[12] But while Atkin's character may have merited such distrust, it is true that he had a larger and more expensive task than Johnson. Johnson could call the Iroquois to his own castle; Atkin had to range from Georgia to Maryland, and interview five great nations unconnected by a confederation. Johnson had only the governor of Pennsylvania to dispute his authority; Atkin dealt with six governors. But to Loudoun, burdened with many duties, the north was the more important area. As he tended to minimize the usefulness of offensive campaigns in the south, corresponded comparatively little with southern governors, and concentrated on his major objective, the conquest of Canada, so he tended to neglect Indian affairs in Atkin's department.

While it is scarcely true to say that Loudoun's authority over the superintendents of Indian affairs was merely a nominal one, as it later became under Amherst, the force of circumstances was clearly towards such a compromise. Loudoun had too much else to do to acquaint himself thoroughly with the shifting sands of Indian

---

[11] By four warrants, dated March 7, 12, 27, 1757, Atkin received £669 9d., Declared Accounts of A. Mortier, P.M.G. 14: 1. Volwiler, in *Croghan and the Westward Movement* (1926), presents Atkin's side of this dispute.

[12] Loudoun to Lyttelton, Feb. 13, 1758, LO 5576.

opinion, and it was the part of wisdom to leave all decisions to the expert in Indian affairs. His chief responsibility came to be the interposition of his authority between the Indian superintendent and the civil officials.

The relations between the commander in chief and the governors, on the other hand, were far more important; they fall conveniently into two divisions. The first concerns those aids to the service which the governors could furnish in their executive capacity, without recourse to an assembly: as when they sat with the commander in chief in a council of war, or issued warrants for the requisition of horses and carriages for express messengers and baggage, or gave orders for quartering troops and recruiting parties. The second involved those aids which, requiring financial outlay or raising a question of right, elicited the action or intervention of an assembly, as in the raising, equipping, and paying of provincial troops. In such cases the governors acted as connecting links between the commander in chief and the assemblies.

The authority which the commander in chief invoked in asking the governors for both kinds of aid rested upon a questionable legal basis. By their commissions royal governors, and according to the terms of charters, the governors of proprietary colonies, acted as commanders in chief of all military affairs within their respective provinces. Legally the governor of Massachusetts was commander in chief of the Rhode Island militia, and the governor of New York of the Connecticut militia, but in practice the two corporate colonies controlled their own troops. Loudoun's commission under the great seal was meant to be an abrogation of the military powers of governors, and the union in one office of thirteen hitherto distinct commands. The devolution clause in that commission, by which, in the event of Loudoun's death, the chief command passed to subordinates in the army, and

never to a governor, Loudoun interpreted as meaning
that governors were deprived of all voice in general military affairs unless their opinion or aid was requested by
a commanding officer. But since the military clauses in
the governors' commissions were not actually revoked,[13]
the way was left open for a clash upon the constitutional
question involved, and it was Loudoun's task, while insisting upon the fullest interpretation of his authority, to
placate the governors for their loss of power.

In general, it may be said at once that the high character of the particular group of governors in office in
1756 and 1757 made possible their acquiescence in Loudoun's authority. No abler set of men, more devoted to
British interests, can be found in any other period of
colonial history than Wentworth of New Hampshire,
Pownall of Massachusetts, Hopkins of Rhode Island,
Fitch of Connecticut, Hardy and DeLancey of New York,
Sharpe of Maryland, Dinwiddie of Virginia, and Dobbs
and Lyttelton of the Carolinas. Denny, an army officer,
was appointed to bring Pennsylvania into the war. Only
two governors, Belcher of New Jersey, and, for a time,
Phips of Massachusetts, were weak; old and infirm, they
both died in 1757, leaving their governments in temporary confusion. Loudoun treated them all with the utmost tact and courtesy at his command. His private correspondence with them was frank, unreserved, and replete
with the graceful compliments of the age; in his public
letters, designed to be laid before council or assembly,
the tone of friendliness gave way to a sterner formality.
He met personally every governor in America except
Wentworth, Lyttelton, and Reynolds and Ellis of Georgia,
and by his amiability won the good will of such different
men as Hopkins and Sharpe. With Pownall, who was for
a time a member of his official "family", he reached a

13 See *ante*, p. 53.

stage of affectionate intimacy, while Hardy and De-Lancey often dined at his table.

These personal factors had much to do with grouping together all the governors but one—Pownall, who will be discussed later—in support of the commander in chief's conduct of the war. Realizing that his scrupulous sense of justice and his obvious desire to promote harmony would keep Loudoun from infringing upon any civilian business of theirs unconnected with the war, they showed themselves willing to incur the added criticism from the populace which obedience to his requests brought, and to put themselves to considerable personal trouble, as when the southern governors travelled to Philadelphia for the only council of war to which he summoned them. In no instance did they refuse to grant warrants or give orders for the impressment of horses or the requisition of quarters, unless, as in quartering, the assembly raised a constitutional point. Hardy and DeLancey in New York were especially coöperative, and the former probably accorded Loudoun more assistance than any other civil magistrate in the colonies. Loudoun consulted him upon a variety of topics, including campaign plans and the allotment of provincial quotas. Hardy gave standing orders to the New York militia to consider themselves under Loudoun's direct command, and he closed his eyes to the steps of doubtful legality which Loudoun took at times at Albany in commandeering timber, wagons, and necessaries. He supplied cooking utensils to the 35th and the 42d when they arrived in June, 1756, without camp necessaries; and in the spring of 1757 he bore the principal share of planning and fitting the transports for the summer campaign. In other colonies where the army was less in evidence, not so much was asked of the governors. Only in New Jersey did Loudoun find grounds for objection in regard to minor aids to the service: ''Horses [he wrote

Belcher] are not to be had for payment, nor Warrants had from the Justices for pressing them, when the Service Requires it, and . . . there are Instances where the Justices have given Orders for pressing horses, that the Country have Rose in a Riotous manner and taken their Horses from the Officers, and Expresses tho' on the most urging publick business, which I will endeavour to put an End to by every method that the Law directs and Custom authorizes.'"[14] Since the main routes south passed through Bordentown or Burlington, demands for horses in New Jersey were constant, and Belcher was too infirm to push matters aggressively. He laid Loudoun's letter before the assembly, which did not improve the situation.[15]

Though a few governors at times challenged Loudoun's claim to the sole command of troops, they submitted readily to his explanation. Denny, both as lieutenant colonel and as governor, expected at his arrival to assume the command of the recruits raised in Pennsylvania for the Royal American regiment, but soon recognized the fact that his army rank was meant to increase his dignity and influence in his government, and not to give him authority over regulars.[16] In 1757 he accepted without demur Stanwix's command in his province of both regulars and provincials. Hardy raised a similar issue both with regard to the New York independent companies, which the governor had always commanded in the past, and to the New York provincial regiment, which was kept up during the winter of 1757-1758, and which Hardy, upon the solicitations of the inhabitants of the Kingston-Goshen frontier, wished to order to their relief. In his reply Loudoun surveyed briefly the historical

14 Loudoun to Belcher, April 7, 1757, LO 3307.
15 *New Jersey Archives*, 1st series, XVII, 110.
16 Rutherford to Loudoun, August 23, 1756, LO 1549.

development of the colonies, from the various chartered
governments of the seventeenth century, through the appointment of royal governors, to the time when French
encroachments caused the dispatch of a commander in
chief, at first with a simple military commission, and
then with a commission under the great seal, by which
the king totally divested the civil power of all command
over troops in America. No governor, he added, ought to
give paroles or receive reports, since they were ensigns
of command. As for military honors, the king prescribed
for the commander in chief three ruffles of the drum,
rested arms, and officers to salute; for governors in their
provinces two ruffles, and rested arms; for governors out
of their province one ruffle, and rested arms.[17] Hardy
yielded to this argument, and put the New York regiment
under Loudoun's command. Loudoun at once sent it to
the frontier. As for the independent companies, he carefully avoided stationing them in Fort George under
Hardy's nose, but kept them in northern New York in the
summer, and in the winter quartered them in New Jersey
or Pennsylvania. Lawrence in Nova Scotia likewise had
to be convinced that his command of troops in Loudoun's
absence arose, not from his commission as lieutenant
governor, but from his army rank as eldest lieutenant
colonel. If a colonel appeared, Lawrence would have to
give way. "This surprised him a good deal but on my
showing him that by their commissions all governors
had the same powers, that they were superceded by
the King's commission to me under the Great Seal in
which commission the command was carried down to
the next in rank and so on to prevent interfering between the command of the troops and the governor, he

17 Loudoun to Hardy, November 21, 1756, LO 2250; Regulation of
Honors, LO 743. The first Regulation of Honors, 1729, prescribed for governors not general officers one ruffle only, and rested arms, W.O. 26: 17, p. 280.

was convinced."[18] To prevent possible friction between Lawrence and Lieutenant Colonel Wilmot, Loudoun signed for the former an order giving him command at Fort Cumberland, "not to be produced except he found occasion for it."

Hardy also raised the question of the jurisdiction of New York harbor in connection with Loudoun's detention of packets, and argued that he had authority there, if not over troops, and that if Loudoun wanted a packet held, he ought apply to the governor, and not send a file of soldiers to take charge of the ship.[19]

But while such instances show that the governors did not submit without argument to a detraction of their military powers, the evidence in general emphasizes their compliance with it. The best single example of their willingness to coöperate in matters that did not require the consent of an assembly appeared in the celerity with which they acceded to Loudoun's request of March 2, 1757, that they lay an embargo upon all ships in port. Hardy originally suggested the measure to ensure an ample supply of transports for the summer expedition, and hoped also that it might prevent intelligence from reaching the French. By the middle of March every governor, from New Hampshire to Maryland, wrote that the embargo was laid, and Fairfax, acting in place of Dinwiddie who was in Philadelphia, replied by the end of the month.[20] In general the embargo was well kept, in spite of

18 HM 1717, vol. 4, August 13, 1757.

19 Hardy to Loudoun, November 25, 1756, LO 2278. Loudoun kept packets in 1756 and 1757; in the latter year he detained the *Harriott* packet from May 1 to October 20, that he might make sure of a ship to send dispatches. He justified himself on the ground that packets were primarily for public business, and not for merchants' letters, Loudoun to Postmasters general at London, October 20, 1757, LO 4673.

20 Hardy replied formally on March 2. Belcher wrote March 3 to ask what form was used. Denny's answer came on the 5th, with a list of ships in

the fact that everywhere merchants exerted great pressure on governors, especially in Philadelphia, where breadstuffs already in the holds were in danger of perishing;[21] in Massachusetts, where the fishermen were preparing their spring excursion to the north; and in Virginia, where the tobacco was loaded for England. To prevent ships clearing from Philadelphia, Loudoun asked Hardy to send there a privateer, manned with a detachment of the 22d, and under the command of the naval officers appointed in England to service on Lake Ontario.[22] Bradstreet and Hutchinson declared that fishermen left Boston harbor without opposition; and that the embargo was not kept at all in New Hampshire. But these were the only serious breaches until Dinwiddie, on May 8, excusing himself by the refusal of the House of Burgesses to vote supplies unless the embargo were lifted, officially permitted all ships to depart.[23] Loudoun, deeply annoyed that his own government of Virginia was the first to break through his orders, thought that Dinwiddie, who was engaged in private trade, was trying to line his

port. Phips wrote on the 9th that the embargo was laid until April 10 and would be extended longer if necessary. It was so extended five times [Massachusetts Historical Society *Collections* (1922), volume 75, 49-50]. Hopkins received the letter on the 7th, and boasted that on the 8th the embargo was in force. Wentworth wrote on the 11th that since Massachusetts had complied, he would at once follow suit. Fitch wrote on the 14th that the embargo was laid on all vessels over forty tons. Sharpe gave his orders to the officers of the customs on March 9; and Fairfax's letter was dated the 30th. LO 2960, 2962, 2973, 2997, 3007, 3014, 3051, 3217. *Maryland Archives*, XXXI, 184.

[21] Loudoun permitted ships laden with provisions for navy contractors to leave Philadelphia, but scrupled to permit ships to depart for the West Indies, where the inhabitants supplied the enemy, or to Newfoundland, except under convoy of ships of war, or to South Carolina, where there were no men of war to prevent foodstuffs reaching enemy hands. *Pennsylvania Colonial Records*, VII, 482; *Pennsylvania Archives*, II, 141.

[22] HM 1717, vol. 3, April 8, 9, May 13, 1757.

[23] *Dinwiddie Papers*, II, 618.

own pocket before he resigned.[24] Sharpe followed Dinwiddie's lead early in June, lest Maryland tobacco suffer
in competition with Virginian.[25] In May Loudoun permitted all ships actually loaded in March to sail, and
ordered the embargo to be completely lifted seven days
after his departure for Halifax.[26] Contemporary histo-
rians denounced this embargo in bitter terms, probably
because it was better enforced than those which governors had laid in the past, acting on their own initiative
or under the orders of the Board of Trade; or those
which commanders in chief in later years, acting under
Pitt's orders, asked to have laid.[27]

The conclusion to which this survey leads is that when
a governor opposed only his private desires to the commander in chief, the latter could bring enough pressure
to bear to maintain his authority and win support. But
when a governor's wishes coincided with the opinion of
an assembly, as in the case of Dinwiddie and the embargo,
or when an assembly interposed its own ambitions and
compelled the governor to accede, as in the case of Denny
and Indian affairs, the commander in chief gave way.
When the governors acted as intermediaries between the

[24] Information from William Byrd in regard to earlier embargoes laid
from England was the source of this suspicion, HM 1717, vol. 2, November
14, 16, 1757.

[25] *Maryland Archives*, XXXI, 219.

[26] *Pennsylvania Colonial Records*, VII, 495, 560.

[27] In a letter of May 2, which Sharpe received June 12 (*Maryland Archives*, XXXI, 220), Fitch July 19 (*Fitch Papers*, I, 304), and Loudoun
August 4, Holderness ordered this embargo lifted to relieve a crop shortage
in England and Ireland. Pitt subsequently denied that this letter forbade
commanders in chief to lay embargoes, and ordered governors to follow any
directions Amherst might give in that regard (*Pitt Correspondence*, I, 355).
This embargo must not be confused with those laid by orders from England
to prevent colonial trade with the French (Beer, *British Colonial Policy,
1754-1765*, chs. VI, VII), though it served incidentally to limit that trade
somewhat, and to assure an ample supply of provisions for army contractors.

commander in chief and the assemblies in soliciting provincial troops, the degree of interest which they displayed had influence, not only in getting the men raised,
but in getting them equipped and officered as Loudoun
wished. The best example of the evils that resulted when
a governor was as antagonistic to a commander in chief's
methods as was his assembly, occurred at the very end
of Loudoun's career, December, 1757, to the following
March. In its various features the tripartite relation-
ships between Pownall, the Massachusetts assembly, and
the commander in chief, which, as they developed, came
to include the whole of New England, were the real
climax, not only of Loudoun's personal tenure, but of the
idea of military union involved in his appointment.

Pownall, as other governors before him, had preten-
sions to the command of troops. But in him such preten-
sions were more deeply and stubbornly rooted, partly
because his personal vanity and ambition were greater,
and partly because he based them upon a principle. They
were the natural corollary to his oft-expressed fear, later
repeated in the *Administration of the Colonies,* that the
office of commander in chief encroached further upon the
rights of civil government than the spirit of English law
ought to sanction. In 1756, as secretary-extraordinary to
the commander in chief, living and dining daily with him,
Pownall objected to Loudoun's impressment of wagons
at Albany as a "terrific infringement on the liberty of
the subject", notwithstanding the justification of Hardy's
warrants, and insisted also that the command of troops
in New York city belonged to the governor of New York.
"I beat him out of that [wrote Loudoun], but his next
point was whether in case the governor should call out
the Militia to defend any part of the country whilst I
was at a Distance with the Army, if I would take the
command of them. I showed him by the King's Commis-

sion I was to have the Command of every man in arms, but then he could not imagine I was so fond of command as to be riding all over the Country to command Militia, but that wherever I was I must command all men in arms.''[28] Later that year Pownall went to England to inform the ministry of American affairs and to present Loudoun's side of the dispute with Shirley. In spite of his sentiments upon the office of governor, ''I had rather be nobody & nothing at my own Disposal & in my own way, than a Pompous Titled nothing where I can neither be of use to those I am to govern nor an adequate servant to those who employ me: which is the real case of an American Governor,'' he accepted the governorship of Massachusetts Bay, with which his name had often been coupled. He came out with Holburne's fleet, went on to Boston in the *Nightingale* with Lord Howe, and assumed his duties there in August, 1757. He was then in a position to test his opinions, in which perhaps Pitt, with whom he had long conversations, encouraged him, that a secretary of state's letter asking governors to aid a commander in chief ''cannot supersede a command, cannot revoke a trust, created not only by a commission, but by a charter of government.''[29] Loudoun thought such notions arose from his ''superficial reading of law at school with-

28 Loudoun to Cumberland, October 17, 1757, Cumberland Papers. This answer scarcely fitted the facts, for on the rare occasions during Loudoun's tenure of office when militia took the field, they served under his or the commanding officer's command because either a governor or an assembly had so ordered them. Doubtless a dispute might have arisen, but any emergency which justified the summoning of these reserve troops, except possibly in the south, was serious enough to claim the attention of a British general whose authority over other troops at the critical point was uncontroverted. The question whether an inferior commanding officer acting under Loudoun's orders enjoyed the same authority in regard to the governor as the commander in chief himself, was not raised during Loudoun's career.

29 Pownall's speech in parliament, May 8, 1770, *Parliamentary History*, XVI, 990.

out any practice", but he still considered Pownall "the greatest Man I have yet met, and from whom I foresee more trouble to whoever commands in this Country than from all the People on the Continent." But at the same time that Pownall saw the powers of a governor infringed by a commander in chief, he saw them abridged by the assembly. In 1757 he wrote an elaborate analysis of the government of Massachusetts Bay to prove that it had already become independent of orders from England in "the Legislature, the Treasury, the Chancery, the Ordinary, the Powers of Admiralty", and had so far limited the governor's military powers that he had nothing left to do except sign his name.[30] Now Pownall's method of dealing with assembly-men was not so much to give them orders in the name of the king as to placate them by seeming to agree with their point of view: "In a free Government [he said] where there is a public Legislature, and People act by their representatives, a governor must endeavour to *lead* those people for he cannot *drive* them and he must lead them step by step as he can *gett footing.*"[31] He tended to side with the provincial faction in the assembly rather than with the prerogative group, and those members who objected to Loudoun's management of the war found in him a ready listener. But when he discovered that such men feared lest his close associations with Loudoun might lead him to sanction the "military government" which they fancied Loudoun was trying to erect, he was forced boldly and openly to disavow any sympathy with Loudoun in order to gain their support. Thus his private ambition, his temperament, his legal training, his political difficulties in Massachusetts, and perhaps his relations with Pitt, all encouraged Pow-

[30] State of the Government of Massachusetts Bay as it stood in the Year 1757. C.O. 325: 2.

[31] Pownall to Loudoun, December 15, 1757, LO 5014.

nall to oppose the man to whom he was personally attached.[32]

Pownall's objective was some form of military command, either over whatever regulars were in his province, or over an independent provincial army, formed as in 1755 and 1756, in the raising of which his adherents in the assembly would gain financial profit and military glory. He first asked, without avail, to have the command of troops quartered at Castle Island, and it was to avoid friction with him that Loudoun assigned no regiment to that post during the winter. He then began to write to England his own opinions on the strategy of the war. To Napier he explained "That without two Fleets and two Armies we cou'd do Nothing," and "I don't see how to form two such armies, unless one a provincial one, and an effectual one is impossible to perform till they are put on a different establishment within themselves, stand better with the regulars, and after all twill be but a poor shift unless some body with quite new & enterprizing notions

---

[32] Two quotations may show the degree of intimacy between Pownall and Loudoun.

"My Lord, believe me my attachment to you is not that of Interest. 'Tis that of a Zeal of the Cause you are engaged in. 'Tis that of a thoroughly weighed Esteem for your Public Character and a love for your amiable private one, and all this rooted in my mind by a Gratitude for the Civilities & Friendship I have received from you." Pownall to Loudoun, November 18, 1756, LO 2236.

When Pownall, in the midst of the quartering dispute of December, 1757, threatened to resign, Loudoun wrote:

"Pardon me, my Friend, to say, that you have taken a very few Troubles too much to Heart. If you continue in any publick employment depend on it that you will have a great many, that will be much more difficult, than what you have met with yet; and I speak from experience, I have lived a great while, and been in many different stages in life, in all of which I have met with disagreeable things at times, and I believe you think I am not entirely without them at present, and yet I go on; they may ruffle me for a moment, but I never allow them to vex me." Loudoun to Pownall, private, December 26, 1757, LO 5105.

has the Lead of them."[33] To Pitt he pointed out in several letters the great importance of constructing a fort on the Penobscot, about which Loudoun, in keeping with his usual practice of concentrating on main objectives and avoiding sideshows, had done nothing.[34] At a meeting of governors at Hartford in February, 1758, called by Loudoun to discuss with him the quotas for the 1758 campaign, Pownall's point of view clearly appeared. When Loudoun mentioned his plan of attacking Louisbourg by a combined force of New Englanders and regulars, Pownall wanted to go as second in command, and upon Loudoun's explaining again the separation of civil and military powers, intimated that Pitt did not accede to such views. Anyone with common sense, he argued, could act as second. "I thought it best not to meddel with that, as it was my present business to get him to assist in the service, and said a very sensible gentleman in that situation would find himself puzzled how to proceed." He next interpreted the prohibition laid upon governors to draw monies themselves from the paymaster[35] as authority that they should draw whatever sums they desired for military purposes from the commander in chief, and asked Loudoun for a thousand pounds to build a fort on the Penobscot. Loudoun evaded the suggestion, and finally "put him in good humour by promising that he should have the supplying of necessaries for the Louisbourg expedition, as thereby he would oblige certain people in Boston who would be of use."[36]

[33] Pownall to General Napier (Cumberland's aide). September 4, 1757, LO 4400.

[34] *Pitt Correspondence,* I, 164-166.

[35] On June 17, 1755, the Lords Justices ordered that Braddock's bills on the paymaster general should be answered, but that no other person was to draw bills or issue warrants for military expenses, S.P. 45: 6. Robinson thereupon communicated this order to the governors, June 19, 1755, Connecticut Historical Society *Collections,* I, 263.

[36] HM 1717, vol. 5, Hartford, February 23, 24, 1757.

Pownall's pronounced sympathy with the popular faction made him, in a sense, the rallying-point for the general discontent of New England assemblies with Loudoun's management. In the opinion of assemblies Loudoun definitely subordinated them to a dependent part in the war, limited the field of operations of their committees of war, denied them rank equivalent to British field officers and so lessened their dignity, curtailed their individual profits, and exercised a power, as no governor could, which in the final sense depended upon force of arms. When Pownall permitted such mixed constitutional, economic, and personal motives to gain control in Massachusetts, the recognized leader among the New England colonies, he encouraged similar motives elsewhere.

The discontent expressed itself in two forms. In the first place, there originated in New England a scheme which, had it been successful, would have destroyed Loudoun's efforts towards military union by substituting the old form of independent union, a meeting of provincial commissioners to discuss problems of defense without reference to the commander in chief.[37] Fitch hoped these commissioners could alter the quotas, for neither Loudoun's nor the Albany ones were satisfactory to all colonies, and perhaps take measures towards applying offensively the combined New England forces. Governor Greene of Rhode Island flatly refused to consider the project, deeming it a flagrant affront to the commander in chief. DeLancey likewise violently discountenanced a plan that proposed to apply provincial troops to the private purposes of each government, and thought its whole object was to put power into the governor's hands. Went-

[37] The actual invitation came from the House of Representatives of Massachusetts, *Fitch Papers*, I, 317, 321; *Rhode Island Colonial Records*, VI, 115. But Hutchinson, who was well informed, later told Loudoun that the scheme originated in Connecticut, from a dissatisfaction of provincial officers to serve under regulars, HM 1717, vol. 5, February 24, 1758.

worth was non-committal, but permitted the assembly to appoint a commissioner who did not, in the end, attend the meeting. But Pownall seems to have thrown himself into the scheme with enthusiasm: "you may depend upon it," wrote Gridley, who belonged to the prerogative faction in the Massachusetts assembly, "that a great man said we are to depend for our defense upon our own forces and not upon the regulars, and that the design of an union is founded upon the Spirit of this Saying."[38] To the five commissioners, headed by Hutchinson, whom the assembly appointed, he gave a general authority without limitations. Fitch included in the commission of the Connecticut representatives the phrase "to meet and confer . . . upon the respective quotas and measures for duly applying the combined forces especially of the militia . . . on any sudden and extraordinary emergency as also touching such further matters as by the Earl of Loudoun may be suggested or during their conference may be judged proper and expedient . . ." When the commissioners finally met, Hutchinson had sufficient influence to prevent their taking any overt steps. Most of the articles to which they agreed dealt with militia, and the only objections which Loudoun had were in regard to a stipulation that five hundred men ought to be detached for the defense of Number Four, that the Penobscot ought to be secured, and that the troops engaged on that expedition ought to form a part of the general quota for the 1758 campaign.[39] From Pownall's point of view the meeting was a failure.

In the second place, Pownall's attitude encouraged the Massachusetts assembly to oppose Loudoun in regard to quartering, and more important, in regard to the voting

[38] J. Gridley to Kilby, January 28, 1758, LO 5485.
[39] *Fitch Papers*, I, 322-327; HM 1717, vol. 2, February 20, 1758.

of provincial troops. In the autumn of 1757, Loudoun proposed to the six northern colonies to dismiss the provincial troops then in service provided each colony raise and equip its proportion of ten hundred and eighty rangers to do duty throughout the winter.[40] New York and New Jersey, which had kept up men before during a winter, at once agreed. Connecticut, though Fitch objected to the quota, voted the three companies.[41] Rhode Island at first reduced Loudoun's proportion by twenty, but hastily increased the number, not to ninety, but to two hundred and fifty, when in reply he made a pointed allusion to Rhode Island's clandestine trade with the French.[42] New Hampshire voted the fifty rangers in January, but did not increase the fines for dereliction of duty, and Wentworth was unable to impress the men from the troops in service.[43] In Massachusetts, with Pownall playing a passive part, the assembly refused to authorize the raising of rangers at all, on the ground that Massachusetts' quota should be determined with reference to her local frontier expenses, which other colonies escaped.

[40] *Rhode Island Colonial Records*, X, 161. The quotas were those Loudoun had determined the preceding February: New Hampshire, fifty; Massachusetts, three hundred and sixty; Rhode Island, ninety; Connecticut, two hundred and eighty; New York, two hundred; and New Jersey, one hundred. HM 1717, vol. 4, September 7, 1757.

[41] *Colonial Records of Connecticut*, XI, 61.

[42] ''I have informed myself of the abilities of your province, of the losses they sustain by the war, and of the profits they have made during it; and the means by which those profits were made; and I know that I have done you no injustice in the number I then fixed for you to furnish; and I am ready to prove it to the King, our master.'' Loudoun to Greene, October 8, 1757, *Rhode Island Colonial Records*, VI, 89-90; 106-110. Loudoun refused the two hundred and fifty men.

[43] Wentworth wrote that there were two parties in his assembly: one in favor of waiting to see what Massachusetts would do, the other opposed to making any grant at all. Wentworth to Loudoun, December 23, 1757, LO 5076; January 11, 1758, LO 5394; *New Hampshire Provincial Papers*, VI, 608-613.

Loudoun disbanded all the Massachusetts troops except the three hundred and sixty he was asking, advanced them two months pay, and threatened to use, if necessary, an "Act of Power" to keep them in service, and to prevent Massachusetts' failure to provide for them from prejudicing the unanimity of provincial action. But when their term of service was over, early in March, he permitted them to return home unmolested.[44]

Having successfully stood out against Loudoun on the question of rangers, the Massachusetts assembly came to the very point of refusing to vote any troops for the 1758 campaign. Loudoun had met a council of governors at Hartford to determine the quotas for 1758: they proportioned the seven thousand men he wanted according to the old Albany figures.[45] He then set out for Boston to confront the assembly, and to make full use of the political influence of his own friends, chief among whom were Hutchinson and Gridley. On March 9 a committee of the assembly presented him with queries concerning the length of service, payment and equipment, officers, and destination of the troops in 1758. Innocent though these queries seemed, Pownall assured Loudoun that the house

[44] Thackeray, *Life of Pitt*, II, 425; *Pitt Correspondence*, I, 165, 187-8; Gridley to Kilby, January 18, 1758, LO 5419; Loudoun to Pownall, January 9, 1758, LO 5372.

[45] The governors were called to Hartford as to a council of war, for if the independent meeting of provincial commissioners, which met the previous week at Boston, had presumed to determine quotas and station troops, Loudoun intended to oppose its decisions with the greater authority of the governors. Pownall resented the fact that nothing but quotas was discussed, insisted that the meeting was a real council of war, and refused to stay in the room with the representatives from Rhode Island, who attended in place of Greene. The proportions settled were: Massachusetts, 2128; Connecticut, 1520; New York, 1216; New Jersey, 912; and New Hampshire and Rhode Island, 608 each. The total, 6992, was the nearest figure to 7000 divisible by the Albany ratios, and the governors refused to add one man more to each colony's proportion lest that slight deviation offer grounds for objection. HM 1717, vol. 5, Hartford, February 23, 24, 1757.

would not vote the men unless he answered "in such a manner as to ease the Minds not only of the House but of the Body of the People they represent." Loudoun drew up the obvious answers; Pownall deleted two passages referring to the king's orders and the secretary of state's letter of the previous year.[46] On the morning of the 10th, the day that these answers were to be discussed in the assembly, Pitt's letters of December 30, 1757, arrived, bringing the news of Loudoun's recall, urging the colonies to put as many troops into the field as they could, and promising reimbursement from England for their expenses. On the afternoon of the 10th, the house voted seven thousand men, unanimously.

Thus dramatically Pitt's revolutionary changes in the management of the war took effect. By official fiat from England the opposition of colonial assemblies to the prerogative as represented by the commander in chief was condoned. Henceforth they were free to spend money as liberally and extravagantly as they pleased, in the assurance that specie payments from England would increase in direct ratio to the amounts they spent.

Other implications of this change of policy belong properly to a concluding chapter. What is pertinent here concerns the extent to which the attitude of Pownall encouraged the Massachusetts assembly to oppose the commander in chief on the most important single point with which they were called upon to deal. The evidence seems to establish that, whether deliberately and with a full

---

[46] One of these passages read: "and likewise on the Orders the King Our Master may think proper to transmit from Time to Time, during that Period, who I dare say has no Doubt, that His faithful Subjects of the Massachusetts Bay will enable Him to defend and secure His dominions, and the Lives and properties of His subjects in North America"; the other: "I must refer your Excellencies to the Secretary of State's Circular Letter of February 4, 1757, in which you will find, the Destination of the Troops are left to me, which I will conduct according to the Instructions I have or may receive."

knowledge of where his tactics were leading or not, he did
so encourage them, by his avowed sympathy with civil,
popular government, by his choice of factions, and by his
well-known personal repugnance to a diminution of his
powers.[47] If the military union of the colonies as visualized by Cumberland could have continued its growth, the
remedy for such a situation as developed in Massachusetts was obvious: the replacement of Pownall with someone who was neither a great man nor a great theorist, but
an honest, hard-headed supporter of the prerogative.
Loudoun himself realised the immense advantage to his
own influence that would follow the immediate and clear-
cut recall of any governor who failed to support him; he
asked that Dinwiddie's resignation be refused, and that
he be recalled instead for breaking the embargo. One such
indication that the commander in chief was politically
supported from England would have been sufficient. For
in all the royal colonies except Massachusetts his authority was accepted; in some the governor even solicited
his aid against an assembly; while in the corporate colonies a fear of losing their charters compelled their support. Penn's coöperation was likewise ensured, while in
Maryland Governor Sharpe generalized for all the colonies from his own convictions: "you must know that His
Lordship began to be regarded among us as a Vice Roy
and to have great Influence in all the Colonies which I am
apt to think his Successors will never have."[48]

[47] Hutchinson has a carefully-phrased summary of this situation. "Mr.
Pownall at first recommended himself to the esteem of Mr. Hutchinson by
very obliging behaviour, and afterwards at Boston by the like; but the art
which he used to undermine Mr. Shirley had lessened that esteem. He soon
saw the like arts using to distress Ld. Loudoun, from whom he expected the
command of the provincial forces; and Mr. Hutchinson suspected he should
meet with much trouble, unless he joined with him in every measure." *Diary
and Letters of Thomas Hutchinson* (1884), p. 60.

[48] Sharpe to William Sharpe, August 27, 1758, *Maryland Archives*, IX,
254.

CHAPTER XI

THE ADMINISTRATION OF THE ARMY

THE regular army which Loudoun commanded was not a unified force. It reflected that same division of function and authority which, in the London departments and in the colonies, complicated the business of the commander in chief. But at the same time it was more centralized than any civil group in the old British administrative system, and exaggerations of its clumsiness deserve correction. Loudoun's task was to coördinate the various branches of army business, to provide as unified a direction as its disjointed form permitted. Though he was no genius, he had qualities of patient precision in detail and of conscientious persistence peculiarly suited to the requirements of his office at an early stage of the war. In organizing the British army in America Loudoun performed his ablest work, and his ability as a soldier ought to be measured, not by the failure of his one expedition, for which he was not to blame, but by his careful conditioning of the instrument which attained victory in the hands of his successors.

The problems which faced Loudoun arose, in general, either from provincial indifference, hostility, or insufficiency, or from the labyrinth of traditional British military regulations, or from both. It is clear that the problem of finding adequate transportation into the interior, of procuring suitable men to act as scouts and rangers or of collecting local workmen and artisans, depended upon the attitude or the abilities of the colonies. It is perhaps less clear that the provisioning and the financing of the army depended also in some respects upon the colonies. An analysis of certain aspects of military finance with particular reference to the situation in America will clarify other problems.

Financial disbursements for the war, as was to be expected under a constitutional government, were fairly well controlled at the source. No money was spent by any one in America which did not at some time pass the scrutiny of parliamentary inspection. Parliament voted money for the American war under two heads: first, the sums necessary for the regiments on the establishment, from lists prepared by the secretary at war—sums that included the pay of officers and men, the cost of clothing, the charges of recruiting, the usual perquisites or allowances to various individuals, and the charges of general and hospital staffs; second, the sums voted as extraordinaries, from which were paid the provision contractors and all unusual charges for which the regular establishment was insufficient. The ordnance estimates, both the establishment and the extraordinaries, were voted in a separate list.[1]

Clode points out that the control which parliament exercised over expenditures at home through the departmental machinery was lacking over expenditures abroad, where the whole financial edifice rested on the shoulders of the commander in chief.[2] It was his responsibility, and his alone, to see that funds were wisely spent. No money

---

[1] Estimate of charge of His Majesty's forces in the plantations for 1756, 27 *Commons Journal* 317; Account of Charges for the Service of 1756 and how disposed, 27 *Commons Journal* 749; An Acc't of monies issued in part of one million to His Majesty to enable His Majesty to take all measures necessary, 27 *Commons Journal* 751; An account of extraordinary services in 1756 not provided for by parliament, 27 *Commons Journal* 818; Exceedings for which no allowance was made by parliament, 1757, 28 *Commons Journal* 19.

[2] Clode, *Military Forces of the Crown*, I, 128.

was paid by either of the deputy paymasters general except by warrant of the commander in chief, or by those authorized to issue them, as Bouquet in South Carolina, Webb at Fort Edward, Abercromby at Albany, or Hopson in Nova Scotia. Loudoun understood the dangers attached to such responsibility, and knew that if his accounts were not well-ordered enough to pass the scrutiny of the Treasury Board or the Audit Office, he could be called to answer for discrepancies, perhaps be the defendant in a process against him, and perhaps lose position or preferment in the army. Indirect therefore as was the control over expenditure abroad, it remained effective. Loudoun took scrupulous care in his financial measures, and his subordinates soon learned that every account they submitted as a basis for his warrant needed to be perfect in its precision. The same true Scots economy which he employed in his private business dealings he brought to the administration of the army, and at times he gives the impression of placing his anxiety to save the Crown's money above the best needs of the service. But it will be remembered that the ministry which appointed him, unlike Pitt's ministry, was reluctant to have enormous sums spent on the American war.

Loudoun never economized to the detriment of the troops themselves. It was little enough that the private soldier received for his service. Of the sums voted by parliament for his pay, £12 3s. 4d. a year, one-quarter was stopped in England to meet the cost of his clothing, the maintenance of Chelsea hospital, and the perquisites to the agent, the secretary at war, and the paymaster general.[3] The other three-quarters went to America in the form of specie forwarded from England by the money

---

[3] The gross annual stoppages, or off-reckonings, from an infantry private amounted to £3 10d. From this was deducted poundage, a shilling on the pound of his total pay; hospital, one day's full pay; and agency, twopence

contractors, Thomlinson and Hanbury,[4] or procured in
the colonies by the sale of bills of exchange. There the
contractors' agents, Hunter in Virginia and Apthorp in
Boston, turned it over to the deputy paymasters general,
one of whom, Abraham Mortier, had a permanent office
in New York, while the other, William Johnston, though
usually at Albany, took his station wherever the commander in chief desired. Upon a warrant from the commander in chief, these deputy paymasters general paid
in cash to the paymasters of the regiments the subsistence
for all non-commissioned officers and private men actually upon the rolls of the regiment.[5] That sum amounted

on the pound, a total of 14s. 10d. Poundage and hospital were regarded as a
lump sum, from which was paid first the allowance to the paymaster general,
the secretary at war, the commissary general, and the various fees; the
remainder went to Chelsea hospital. The agency was kept separate. The remainder, £2 6s., known as the net off-reckonings, was assigned by the colonel to the regimental clothier, after the Board of General Officers had approved the clothier's patterns. Whatever sums remained after the costs of
clothing and minor accoutrements (such as colors, sergeant's sashes, swords,
waist belts, pouches with shoulder belts, and slings) had been met, were the
colonel's profits. The cost of a complete new private's clothing, exclusive of
accoutrements, was £2 6s. 8d. [Galfridus Mann's charge for the Royal American Regiment, LO 1108; for the 30th regiment it was 1s. 3d. more]; the
second year it was eight to ten shillings less. In 1756 the complete clothing
of the non-commissioned officers and privates of the newly raised Royal
American regiment cost £11,611 7s. 3d.; the net off-reckonings for the year
were £11,947 4s. 8d. The balance would not defray the cost of accoutrements. Loudoun's profits on the clothing of the 30th regiment of seven hundred men, the colonelcy of which he had long held, averaged in 1756 and
1757 less than £300.

   4 In 1756 a new contract with John Thomlinson, John Hanbury, George
Colebrooke, and Arnold Nesbit, replaced the old contract of 1754. In 1758
Osgood Hanbury joined the firm.

   5 The numbers of men for whom subsistence was drawn were taken from
the regular monthly returns, and must not be confused with the official semi-
annual mustering of the regiments by the muster master general, who represented the Commissary general of musters in London, though an officer on
Loudoun's staff. The muster master general made his circuits during the
year, and whenever he came to the headquarters of any regiment or company,
he gave timely notice to the commanding officer to have the regiment drawn

to 3s. 6d., sterling, or 6s. New York currency, a week for every private. Following army custom, the regimental paymaster stopped from the pay of each man three-half-pence, New York currency, weekly, for the surgeon and himself, and following a general order of October, 1756, stopped two shillings tenpence halfpenny weekly for the purchase of camp equipment and necessaries. The remainder, three shillings New York currency weekly, he paid to the troops.[6] At times the soldier was deprived even of this amount. If he were sick, and went to the general hospital, he contributed fivepence sterling a day to its support. If fresh provisions were scarce, and spruce beer ordered to prevent scurvy, the soldier paid for it, with the costs of its transportation and brewing added.[7] The single pair of shoes furnished him annually by his colonel out of the off-reckonings did not last the year, and

up ready to be mustered, with the rolls closed and certified. At the time and place appointed, he called over the name of each commissioned and non-commissioned officer, and each private, ''viewing each separately as he passes by, that he has the proper Cloathing & Accoutrements of the Corps to which he belongs, & his Fire-arm clean and well fixed, with his Sword & other respective Arms in good Order.'' He sent then to the Commissary general in London four copies of the rolls, one being of parchment, with the surgeon's attestations for men too sick to attend. (Instructions for the deputy commissary of musters in North America, LO 1644). The muster master general's office thus provided an additional check upon false payments of money. The regular times of mustering, Christmas and mid-summer, were changed by Loudoun to April 24 and October 25, just before and after regiments took the field for a campaign.

6 General Orders, Fort Edward, Oct. 23, 1756, LO 1538. In 1721 the sign-manual warrant drawn up by the general officers of the army specified that 6d. sterling only should be stopped weekly for ''Shoes, Stockings, Gayters, Medecines, Shaving, Mending of Arms, and loss by Exchange in remittance of their Pay.'' W.O. 26, 16, p. 145.

7 At Halifax, the soldier was stopped 1½d. daily for about a half gallon of spruce beer a day. A gallon of molasses, costing about 2s. 2½d. would make about 25 gallons of beer, with 8d. for the brewing, and 1s. for transportation added. In 1759 ''sowercrout'' was used as an anti-scorbutic [W.O. 34: 58, f. 36]. It was less effective, for it lacked essential vitamins.

for the second pair, costing 3s. 6d. to 3s. 8d., his pay was stopped. If his colonel judged that American winters required warmer clothes, such as "flannel waistcoats" or watch-coats, the private bore the charges. But at that, the private soldier in Loudoun's army received more money to spend on drink than any other soldier in the British service, except in Gibraltar and a few island garrisons. For the crown paid all the charges of his provisioning, sixpence sterling a day; elsewhere, and in America after 1760, he himself contributed either fourpence or twopence halfpenny daily towards his own victuals.[8] Such a policy, inaugurated in 1754 when the colonies were expected to provide food, called down the scorn of men like Wolfe, who thought the crown would waste money and the soldiers ruin themselves by drink.[9] Though Loudoun was allowed the discretion of reverting to the usual method of stopping for provisions if he saw fit, he preferred to leave to the private soldier whatever encouragement the possession of gold and silver offered.

At times the private soldier, if he permitted his pay to accumulate in the regimental paymaster's hands, received gold. Out of the simple fact that some men got gold and some got silver there arose one of the most perplexing monetary problems of Loudoun's career. The value of the Spanish and Portuguese gold coins in circulation in America—pistoles, half-Johannes, and moidore pieces were the most common, though German carolines and French guineas were not unknown—differed in the various colonies. In Pennsylvania, for example, a pistole of four pennyweight eight grains had the same value as a pistole of four pennyweight six grains; while in New York the heavier coin brought a shilling more. The same

---

[8] Jenkinson to Amherst, May 11, 1760, W.O. 34: 72, f. 195.

[9] Wolfe to Sackville, May 24, 1758, Historical Manuscripts Commission *Reports*, Stopford-Sackville MSS., II, 257.

was true of the heavy and light doubloon; eight grains difference in weight made four shillings difference in New York, and none in Pennsylvania.[10] Of more importance was the disproportion between gold and silver. Computed in terms of English prices, every gold coin in the colonies was worth less than its accepted value in silver, which varied from colony to colony. The half-Johannes brought eight Spanish dollars in England, seven and seven-eighths dollars in New York, and seven and two-thirds dollars in Pennsylvania. The moidore was rated at six dollars in England, five and three-fourths dollars in New York, five and four-fifths dollars in Pennsylvania. When computed in sterling at four shillings and eightpence a dollar, the half-Johannes was worth nearly a shilling less in Pennsylvania than in New York; whereas the moidore was worth nearly a shilling more. These ratios themselves fluctuated according to the demand. The confusion that arose when the Pay Office in America attempted to pay men according to a standard rate was from this discrepancy in the value of gold to silver, and not from the varying provincial currency rates alone. If the British army, with men scattered throughout the colonies, had to face only the fact that a Spanish dollar was rated at eight shillings currency in New York, seven and sixpence in Pennsylvania, and five and ninepence in Virginia, it could have pronounced a standard rate of exchange.

In attempting to settle the problem by ordering the proportion at which the army should pay and receive specie the Treasury equated as nearly as possible the value of coins in various provinces, but in so doing increased the disproportion between gold and silver in any

[10] The custom of valuing a coin as a heavy pistole or doubloon when it tipped the scales ever so slightly, led in New York to the practice of ''plugging gold,'' in which the merchant plugged a light coin with a pennyworth of gold, and passed it as a heavy coin, *Pitt Correspondence*, I, 49-50.

one province. It ordered specie in Pennsylvania to be valued by weight, gold at £4 7¼d. an ounce, silver at 5s. 4½d. an ounce: at which reckoning a half-Johannes was worth in sterling £1 17s. 1½d.; a moidore, £1 7s. 11½d.; a dollar, 4s. 8d. In New York it ordered the army to pay and receive the half-Johannes at £1 17s. 4d., the moidore at £1 8s., and the dollar at 4s. 8d. When the deputy pay-masters general attempted to apply these rates in paying troops, they found that the local proportions between gold and silver decreased the real or purchasing value of the gold. If they paid two men £1 17s. 4d. each, but gave the first a half-Johannes, and the second eight dollars (its equivalent at 4s. 8d. to the dollar), the first would receive in New York currency 63 shillings, and the second 64. If one man got a moidore at £1 8s., and another the equiva-lent value of six dollars, the first would get in New York currency only 46 shillings, while the second's silver was worth 48 shillings. In New York gold was worth, com-pared with English ratios, at an average five and three-fourths per cent less than silver, in Pennsylvania three per cent. For this reason William Johnston persuaded Abercromby, on his arrival in 1756, to issue an order for paying the dollar at 4s. 8d., "and all other Coins and Species of Money in Proportion making the Dollar the Standard by which all other Coins are to be registered." Johnston then disregarded the Treasury orders fixing the value of gold coins, and substituted their value in New York, while continuing to pay dollars at 4s. 8d. This alteration later cost him his position. Loudoun revoked Abercromby's order, but soon found it necessary to re-issue it, with the proviso that payment should be made to troops in milled dollars only, and in a series of letters and memorials presented the situation to the Treasury. In February, 1757, the Treasury decided that all troops must be paid on the same footing, that whatever gold there was in America should be rated by the dollar at 4s. 8d., but that all future payments should be made, if possible, in silver. Thus they hoped to assure a standard, full pay to the soldier, and to avoid the loss to the public which would result from yielding to "the imperfect regulations of any particular colony."[11]

This decision to pay only in silver raised another problem. Silver was scarce in the colonies. In England a shilling was worth less than its market price as bullion, and coined silver was clandestinely melted into ingots for export. The contractors could not possibly assemble enough milled dollars to meet the demand, and in the shipment which arrived in August, 1757, one hundred and twenty chests of two thousand ounces of silver each, the greater part consisted of small unmilled pieces, sixteenths, eighths, and quarter parts of dollars. Now in the colonies unmilled money was rated at from nine to fourteen dollars less per thousand ounces than milled money, because no colonial merchant could handle an unmilled piece without well-founded suspicions that it had been clipped. If the troops were paid in rials (an eighth of a dollar) at the standard rate of 4s. 8d. to the dollar, a milled rial, worth seven pence sterling, would pass in New York for seven pence halfpenny, while an unmilled rial, worth also seven pence sterling, would pass for only sixpence. This difference, more than twenty per cent, was far greater than the discrepancies between gold and silver. Loudoun therefore asked the contractors' agent to write Hanbury to send no more small specie. The only adequate

---

[11] Memorial and state of the exchange, Cumberland Papers; Treasury minutes, February 15, 1755; March 11, 1756; August 11, 1756; December 16, 1756; February 25, 1757, T. 29: 32; Memorial of William Johnston to Loudoun, T. 1: 365; Thomlinson and Hanbury to Loudoun, August 1756, LO 1659; Loudoun to Newcastle, December 26, 1756, LO 2409; Loudoun to Dupplin, LO 2412.

solution to the monetary problem would have been the erection by act of parliament of a colonial bank, with branches in the various colonies, enforcing a standard rate. Loudoun's own working solution was to pay the troops as frequently as possible in provincial currency rates, and to let the loss arising from the difference in value between gold and silver fall upon the Treasury.[12]

Additional loss fell upon the Treasury whenever the contractors let the supply of specie in their agents' hands in America sink so low that colonial merchants, the purchasers of bills of exchange, could set their own exchange rates on such bills. The par of exchange, quoted either at the number of dollars in £100 sterling, based upon an arbitrary selection from the fluctuating prices of silver in London, or in the provincial currency equivalent to £100 sterling, was set by the various assemblies. Since bills of exchange were a merchandise fluctuating both according to demand and to the price of silver in London, the current rate might rise considerably above par, and in all the colonies except Massachusetts usually did. When in 1756 Apthorp had to sell bills hurriedly to meet the drain on the military chest that Shirley's warrants had caused, he lost nearly fifteen per cent—a loss that fell on the British public, for Thomlinson and Hanbury acted only as middlemen, taking a two per cent commission on all money they furnished. But while shipments of specie for the army decreased this demand for money, they did not concern the payment of officers. With officers' subsistence neither the contractors nor the commander in

12 In Nova Scotia before 1757 the dollar was rated at five shillings in the money contract between the Treasury and William Baker. To avoid the trouble that would ensue if Nova Scotian troops were paid at five shillings and others at four and eight, the Treasury altered the Nova Scotia rate. Thomas Saul (agent for William Baker) to Hopson, September 19, 1757, LO 4496; Percey Furye to Saul, July 28, 1757, LO 3801.

chief had anything to do. The Pay Office transmitted officers' pay to the various regimental agents in London, and
regimental paymasters in America sold bills on the
agents for the amounts due. They were therefore at the
mercy of merchants, who sometimes refused to buy bills
at all, and always bought at a profit.

In the payment of certain customary perquisites to
officers, Loudoun followed the same scheme as in paying
the troops, calculating the amounts in New York currency
at a proportion of 12 to 7 sterling. The most important
of these were bas (bass, later bat) money, for providing
servants to look after officers' horses; baggage money, to
cover the costs of transporting baggage; and forage
money, so many rations of forage at sixpence a ration,
to feed the horses during the winter months when they
could not be put to grass.[13] On St. Clair's representation
that officers could not possibly bear the expenses themselves in a land of great distances, and that these allowances were cheaper than using the king's wagons for
officers' baggage, Loudoun agreed to issue a baggage allowance that varied with the rank of the officer and forage
rations for a hundred days. The total cost for a regiment
of one thousand was £432 10d. sterling. The staff and
hospital also participated in this allowance. Loudoun's
own share, a hundred rations a day for a hundred days
for a hundred horses, amounted to £912 10d. sterling, "in
New York Curr'y at 4/8 the dollar £1564.8 which was
payed into John Campbells hands my servants for my
use."[14]

---

[13] Forage money should not be confused with "grass money", which was
a regimental stoppage from the pay of Dragoons, to pay for corn, farriers,
riding masters, grass, and everything, in fact, not covered by the clothing
regulations. W.O. 26: 16, p. 145.

[14] Regulation of Baggage and Forage Money for His Majesty's Forces
now serving in North America, Loudoun Papers; St. Clair to Loudoun, January 5, 1757, LO 2643. "Ordered the forage, bass and baggage according to

Of the money that passed through the hands of the deputy paymasters general in the course of a year, the greater part went for extraordinary or contingent expenses, and not for the subsistence of the regular troops. In 1755, for £50,000 subsistence, Braddock and Shirley spent £119,000 on extraordinaries; in 1756, for some £60,000 subsistence, Shirley and Loudoun spent £210,000 on extras, excluding the £44,592 loaned by Shirley to the New England colonies; in 1757, payments for subsistence were £120,000, those for extraordinaries, £159,000. By 1759 subsistence ran to £180,000 a year, while extraordinaries had mounted to £600,000.[15] These figures show the increasing cost of the war, and also the various amounts which commanders in chief spent on extraordinaries. Whereas of the warrants which Braddock drew, some seventy-one per cent were for extraordinaries, of Shirley's, seventy-eight per cent, of Amherst's, seventy-

HRH orders in Flanders Bass and baggage the first year is for each compy £24. 10 which is £10 for the compy's horse to the Capt £7 and to each subaltern £3.10. The second year they have only £15 which is to the capt £7 and to subaltern £3.10 which makes per company of 100 men £18.15 which is for a battalion of 1000 £187.10. Forage money in Flanders was given for 200 days for the winter and forrage was delivered all the summer. Shirley paid the troops last year forrage money from the day they landed to the 30th of April 1756 at 6d. a ration. I have ordered them 100 days forrage money and have taken this date from its being possible for them to carry their own baggage which was to be caryed by the King." HM 1717, vol. 3, March 7, 1757.

15 These figures are from the declared accounts of the money contractors, A.O. 17: 592: 190. Thomlinson and Hanbury received £473,191 7s. 4d. from 1754 to 1756; their successors, £3,563,642 6s. 4½d. from 1756 to the end of the war. It may be emphasized again that these figures do not include the pay of officers, either regimental or staff, or the stoppages made in England, or the cost of provisions, or the ordnance charges. The estimated expense of the army in North America for 1760 was £1,344,309 12s. 6½d. (Additional MSS. 33,047, f. 371). Of this sum approximately forty per cent went for extraordinaries, nineteen per cent for subsistence, seventeen per cent for officers' pay and stoppages, fifteen per cent for provisions, one per cent for staff and hospital, and eight per cent for ordnance.

seven, but sixty-six per cent of Loudoun's were for that purpose. They were for a variety of charges: to Thomas Hancock, for example, for gunpowder, and for expenses and express boats; to Alexander Colden, the deputy postmaster at New York, for the expense of a regular post between New York and Albany; to Henry Van-Schaack for his service in dispatching the mails at Albany; to John Shepherd for his ranging company; to Captain Gabriel Christie, acting assistant deputy quartermaster general at Albany, for the hiring of wagons; to James Otis for whale-boats; to John Bradstreet for entrenching tools; to Sir William Johnson for the Indian service. For all such warrants Loudoun required an itemized account, with receipts, where necessary, duly attached, and these accounts were affixed to the duplicate of the warrant which he retained. In some cases there was included a five per cent commission, but wherever it was possible for an army officer to arrange the purchase or hire, or wherever a provincial merchant could be dealt with directly, Loudoun chose the cheaper course. Bradstreet estimated that the army saved from fifteen to twenty-five per cent in the cost of such articles as rum by buying them directly, and not through a contractor who would buy from his own friends at their top prices and charge his commission on the gross sum.[16]

With the payment of the provision contractors Loudoun had no direct concern. Baker and Kilby (or Baker, Kilby, and Baker) either collected provisions in England and Ireland and transported them to America, or contracted with provincial merchants. Their charges appear in the lists of extraordinaries voted by parliament. They were paid at intervals by warrants from the Treasury drawn on the paymaster of the forces, on the basis of

[16] Declared accounts of Abraham Mortier, P.M.G. 14: 1; Bradstreet to Abercromby, March 28, 1757, LO 3196.

certificates signed by the commander in chief or those
authorized by him, setting forth that the contractors had
delivered to the troops so many rations, as attested by
Robert Leake, the commissary of stores in North America.
In 1756 and 1757 they delivered nearly five million rations at sixpence a ration, a total of £123,409 11s. 10d. In
1758 their bills amounted to £215,150 10s. 6d., an increase
partly caused by the numbers of provincials in service
that year.[17]

A considerable part of the pork, beef, peas, and butter
with which the contractors supplied the army came from
England and Ireland instead of from the provision colonies. Of about three million rations of beef and pork
stocked in America before March, 1757, over 2,700,000
came from the British Isles; of four and a half million
rations of butter, 4,200,000 was of British produce. The
colonies furnished bread, flour, rice, and the fresh meat
which was issued twice a week, if possible, during the
winter. The contractors found that if they purchased
salted beef and pork in America colonial merchants
would increase the price, and would then salt and bulk
beef instead of selling it fresh. Such a procedure depleted
the supply of later years, for they killed two- and three-
year olds for the purpose, and bulked meat which would
not last the six months specified in the Treasury contract
as the advance period for which provisions were to be
stored. There were some fears that the exportation of
flour to England and the smuggling trade with the French
West Indies would cause a shortage in that article as
well.[18]

---

[17] Declared accounts of Baker, Kilby, and Baker, A.O. 1: 191: 598. A
ration was 1/7 of the weekly allowance of four pounds of pork or seven of
beef, seven pounds of bread or flour, three pints of peas, six ounces of butter,
and half a pound of rice.

[18] A State of the Evidence relating to the Provision Contract, Additional
MSS. 35,909, f. 241; HM 1717, vol. 2, December 3, 1757.

But during Loudoun's term of office the army was always amply supplied with provisions. The method of distribution was direct: the contractors at their own expense collected provisions in such general storehouses as the commander in chief designated, either on the sea-coast or in the interior; they were there inspected by the commissary of stores and his assistants, and issued by the contractors' agents, on the basis of signed returns, to the officers and the quartermasters of the regiments; the latter distributed them to the troops, who prepared them for use in the utensils bought by stoppages from their pay. Officers were allowed to draw rations in proportion to their rank; the commander in chief drew eighteen; major generals, thirteen; colonels, six; captains, three; subalterns, two; and so on through the hospital and engineer staffs. In 1756 Loudoun, intent as usual on saving money, forbade officers to sell back to the contractors what they and their servants did not consume, but in 1757 he was prevailed upon by Abercromby and Webb to allow officers some advantages in a service that weighed so heavily upon them, and thereafter officers could turn unconsumed rations into actual money, usually at fourpence each.[19] This was a customary army perquisite.

In certain other cases the contractors, who normally received sixpence a ration, were permitted to pay men fourpence sterling a day, the charge of a ration in England, instead of issuing them provisions, the charge to be entered on their books as fourpence, and the crown to benefit from the saved twopence. When men were crowded into winter quarters, and could not prepare their own food without causing great inconvenience to the other inhabitants of a house, it was obviously easier for the owners to turn themselves into innkeepers and feed their

[19] General Orders, September 22, 1756, LO 1538. HM 1717, vol. 2, November 26, 1757.

enforced guests. The inhabitants of Newark petitioned to be allowed to feed the sick men quartered on them at the rate of 5s. 6d. New York currency a week, and on Kilby's agreeing to pay that sum if the surgeons testified that the men got proper food, Loudoun permitted it. Other regiments in winter quarters preferred to receive the fourpences instead of rations, even though the inhabitants could not feed the men at that price, but since the contractors had collected a quantity of provisions for which they were responsible for six months only, Loudoun ordered all troops to receive and prepare the customary rations.[20]

The provisions were for the most part good, and few complaints reached Loudoun's ears. Though occasionally provisions were condemned, in every case the contractors had a valid excuse. In 1757, for example, a quantity of peas was condemned, and instead of ordering them destroyed, Loudoun permitted the contractors to dispose of them if they could, and so reimburse themselves to some extent. A month later the bad peas re-appeared, mixed with good, in an issue to provincial troops, and Kilby discovered that the local inhabitants to whom he had sold them as horse fodder had not been able to resist the temptation to make an easy profit. Some bread was condemned at the same time, the fault of a New York baker who deliberately used sour flour. Loudoun had him committed to the provost marshal (an officer on the general staff) and lodged in the provost's room in the New York jail. Such an altogether illegal procedure Loudoun justified by the principle that a power was seated in a commanding officer during war for the preservation of the troops, and that if the man had been confined in a civilian prison, he would have been permitted to escape. In the fall of

[20] Kilby to Loudoun, September 8, 1757, LO 4426. HM 1717, vol. 2, December 3, 1757.

1757 Leake, who merited his post by an unusually suspicious nature, lodged a series of complaints against the contractors, but Kilby adduced evidence to prove that though there were bound to be occasional instances of improper bulking or of spoiled goods, a large part of the provisions Leake had condemned were sweet and fit.[21]

At the price which the contractors received, the provisions deserved to be both ample and good. During the unsettled political situation in the spring of 1757, Charles Townshend, independently and purely as a political manoeuvre, launched in the House of Commons an attack upon the previous administration of Fox and Newcastle by questioning the wisdom of so expensive a contract as Baker and Kilby's. He was supplied with figures by Shirley and Alexander, both of whom appeared before the bar of the house; the former "tired the house in an hour by making a speech in answer to every question"; while the latter, asserting that he could furnish provisions twenty per cent cheaper than Baker and Kilby, was shown to have omitted the costs of transport. But in defending himself Baker made an interpretation of the contract which Loudoun had not understood; he affirmed that the contractors had to pay the costs of transport to any general storehouses which the commander in chief, on a three months' notice, designated, even to the frontier posts. Since the only general storehouses during Loudoun's career were at Halifax, New York, and Albany, some point was given to Townshend's assertion that the contractors sold at sixpence rations which cost them only threepence farthing. Townshend's enquiry was stopped both by the personal interference of Loudoun's friends,

21 Leake to Loudoun, April 4, 1757, LO 3282; Gage to Abercromby, April 29, 1757, LO 3503; HM 1717, vol. 3, April 16, 19, May 1, 6, 1757; Kilby to Webb, August 27, 1757, LO 3878; Kilby's memorial, December 12, 1757, LO 5002.

Argyll, Home, and Fox, and by the fact that his attack tended to drive Newcastle and Fox into closer union. But in 1760 a new provision contract, with Sir James Colebrooke, Arnold Nesbitt, George Colebrooke, and Moses Franks, set the price at fourpence three farthings a ration, all costs of interior transport to be borne by the Crown, and fresh provisions to be furnished by them, and not, as in Loudoun's time, by the army.[22]

To some extent, therefore, the fact that the army was stationed in the colonies complicated the business of paying and feeding the men, and adjustments had to be made to suit conditions.

Even greater adjustments were required in finding permanent and satisfactory transportation. Shirley's failure to make adequate arrangements in 1756, and Loudoun's own difficulties in impressing wagons, led the British army to find a transport service that would be independent of colonial whims.

Transportation in the frontiers of America was complicated. To carry a barrel of beef, weighing two hundred pounds, from New York to Fort Edward or to Fort William Henry required much handling and various kinds of vehicles and boats. The expense from New York to Albany was Baker and Kilby's, who hired sloops at the rate of £12 a trip. From Albany to the upper forts the expense was the Crown's. Loudoun found that if he hired or pressed wagons, the charge was 10s. 6d. New York currency a day for the fifty-mile trip to Fort Edward, over roads that were fairly good but narrow, each wagon carrying but four or five barrels, and the trip taking, one way only, about four days. In 1756 the province of New

---

[22] 27 *Commons Journal* 683, 696, 706, 724, 752, 754, 760, 761, 762, 768, 778; Additional MSS. 35,909, f. 241; Baker to Kilby, March 16, 1757, LO 3071; September 8, 1757, LO 4421; Argyll to Loudoun, March 12, 1757, LO 3028; W.O. 34: 72, f. 86.

York charged the army 29s. a barrel from Albany to the lake, nearly half as much as the food was worth. Oxteams were cheaper; they could be hired at 12s. a day, could carry seven barrels a load, and could cover the sixty-six miles to the lake in five days. Transportation by oxteam cost therefore about 17s. a barrel. Where batteaux could be used, they were still cheaper, but there were rifts in the Hudson between Half-moon and Stillwater over which laden batteaux could not pass, and at the Little and Great Falls above Saratoga a portage was necessary. Batteaux, which carried from seven to eight barrels a load, could be hired at 8s. for the ten mile trip from Albany to Half-moon, or could be purchased at about £5 apiece, and batteaux men hired at 3s. a day. Cheaper still were larger boats, which had to be built to order, as they were not available on the Hudson. A scow fifty feet long by fourteen feet amidships could carry 150 barrels, but required seven men to work it, at 3s. a day; a scow of thirty-eight feet by twelve would carry sixty barrels, and need five men to row and steer.[23]

By the spring of 1757 Loudoun had made his arrangements for the transportation of provisions, stores and baggage, with the minimum of aid from the local inhabitants. Acting on Christie's suggestion, he authorized the purchase of fifty wagons with horses at a cost of £2500, the building of a wagon house and stables, and the forming of an establishment for the drivers, with directors and sub-directors, at a fraction over £6 a day. By the end of the summer Christie estimated that the wagons, at a cost of £1021 over and above the initial cost, had

[23] Memorandum of Robert Livingston, LO 1504; Account with Province of New York, June 1, 1756, LO 3759; Account of Joshua Loring, July 26, 1756, LO 1356; Articles of agreement for oxteams, December 10, 1756, LO 2328; St. Clair's report on roads and water carriage, July 24, 1756, LO 1342. HM 1717, vol. 2, November 25, 1757.

done work which would have amounted to £2500 at the old rates. Loudoun contracted also with Sam Spencer and John Brown of Hartford county and John Hitchcock of Wallingford to furnish a hundred oxteams, at 12s. a day, with 48s. for expenses in coming to Albany. He commissioned Nathaniel Meserve of New Hampshire as captain of an independent company of carpenters, numbering a hundred men at from 6s. 6d. to 6s. 9d. New York currency a day, about £500 sterling a month. They were employed, partly in New York, and partly at Halifax, in building barracks, storehouses, scows, and boats, and in general repair work. During the summer the transportation to the lake was standardized; twenty to thirty batteaux were employed between Albany and Half-moon; oxteams and wagons carried goods on to Stillwater; between Stillwater and Saratoga four scows were used; and to Fort Edward land carriage was resumed. Goods going up the Mohawk went by wagon to Schenectady and by batteaux to points beyond. In the autumn Loudoun was entertaining suggestions from such men as Colonel Pearson of Connecticut and the fertile Bradstreet for improving the navigation of the Hudson, by reducing the rifts above Half-moon so that laden batteaux could pass over, and by constructing quays upon which wagons could drive. Bradstreet was positive that he could cut the cost of transport from Albany to Fort Edward to 7s. a barrel.[24]

All such transportation was extremely slow. When in 1758 the commander in chief was faced with the problem of supplying transport for the twenty thousand provincials whom Pitt had called into service, Bradstreet was

[24] Proposals for buying wagons, LO 1723; Christie to Cunningham, March 29, 1757, LO 3210; Scheme for the establishment of wagons, LO 3214; Abstract of state of the King's horses and wagons, November 1757; HM 1717, vol. 3, February 7, 1757.

asked what would be required to carry a month's provision for them from Albany to Lake George within the shortest space of time possible after the rivers and roads were open in the spring. He replied, in a careful estimate, that it would take three weeks for a thousand batteaux, eight hundred wagons, and a thousand oxcarts, to transport the 5760 barrels of provisions necessary, each barrel to be handled five separate times. Since so many vehicles were unavailable, Abercromby could not move his unwieldy army against Ticonderoga until the first week of July.

In the task of adapting the British army to American conditions, no problem was so important as that which concerned the art of war in the wilderness. The British regiments who came to America knew nothing of open-order or irregular warfare; they had been trained, as all troops in Europe, in the exacting discipline of the parade-ground. Cumberland prescribed that all recruits be taught that formal routine first, marching as directed in the "King's book for exercise", and loading and firing according to Cumberland's "new Platoon exercise".[25] They would have to meet the French regular soldier either in the open field or behind fortifications, and for such work European parade-ground discipline was best fitted. Irregular troops have seldom been able to carry an entrenchment in the face of artillery fire, or stand their ground before a bayonet advance. But in addition to formal manoeuvres, the British regiments learned something of the methods of brush warfare. For the new Royal American regiment Loudoun copied suggestions made by Haldimand; "they are then to fire at Marks, and in order to qualify them for the Service of the Woods, they are to be taught to load and fire, lyeing on the Ground and

25 Robert Napier (Adjutant-general), Exercises for the American Forces, approved by His Royal Highness, April 18, 1756, LO 1060.

kneeling. They are to be taught to march in Order, slow
and fast in all sortes of Ground. They are frequently to
pitch & fold up their Tents, and to be accustomed to pack
up and carry their necessaries in the most commodious
manner."[26] Such tactics were put into practice. British
soldiers acting as a covering party learned to march in
single file; if they fell into an ambush the command "Tree
all" was given, and every man found a tree and looked
out for himself.[27] Various suggestions were offered from
time to time to make the regular troops better fitted for
the American war. George Scott devised a plan to lighten
equipment and reduce firing motions; James Prevost,
who in common with other Swiss officers had a penchant
for "la petite guerre", went so far as to advocate the
formation of strictly American regiments, clothed for the
wilderness, armed with short, light guns, trained to swim,
run, and leap obstacles in obedience to the blasts of a
whistle, and to be accompanied by dogs for chasing the
Indians.[28] But such schemes Loudoun could not put into
practice; he never forgot that his raw men had first of all
to be trained to meet regular soldiers, themselves fighting
in close order.

He expected, moreover, that the provincials themselves
could serve as irregular troops, until he discovered that

[26] Loudoun to the Commanding Officers of the 62d or Royal American
Regiment, December 28, 1756, LO 2421.

[27] This command appears in evidence in several court-martial records,
July 9, 1757, Fort Edward, W.O. 71: 130. Such evidence offsets Wolfe's
strictures upon Loudoun's drill-school methods: "My Ld Loudoun, whose
management in the conduct of affairs is by no means admired, did adhere so
literally and strictly to the 1-2-3 firings by the impracticable chequer, etc.,
that these regiments must necessarily be cut off one after another unless they
fall into some method more suited to the country." Wolfe to Sackville, May
24, 1757, Historical Manuscripts Commission, *Report* on Stopford-Sackville
MSS., II, 257.

[28] Mémoire de Colonel Prevost Sur La Guerre d'Amérique, Cumberland
Papers.

the average provincial soldier knew less what to do if he
fell into an ambush than a British regular, for he had
never been trained, either in the discipline of arms or in
frontier warfare. There were some exceptions: a few
companies from New Hampshire and western Massachusetts, and men with long military service in Maryland and
Virginia, were fitted to meet the Indian on his own
ground. Loudoun's problem, therefore, became one of
finding enough men who understood Indian customs to
bear the brunt of scouting service, to act as advance
guards, to procure intelligence of enemy movements, and
to protect working parties or baggage trains from surprise attacks.

For such purposes Indians, if they could be trusted,
were most valuable, but the Six Nations were never suffi-
ciently dependable during Loudoun's career. He found
that Shirley, whose diagnosis of the situation was the
same as his, had arranged with the Stockbridge Indians,
in May, 1756, to form a company of fifty men, with one
captain, Jacob Cheeksaunkun, one lieutenant, Jacob
Naunauphtaunk, and one ensign, Solomon Uhauamvaumut; this company he continued, at a cost of more than
£2000 New York currency a year. Early in 1757 he was
considering the possibility of forming an Indian regiment
of five hundred men with field officers, to cost the Crown,
including provisions, over £30,000 a year. The scheme fell
through because Indians either would not enlist—the
Stockbridge Indians could raise only their fifty men—or
would not remain in service after they joined.[29]

In place of Indians, Loudoun placed his chief reliance

29 Instructions for Captain Cheeksaunkun [LO 1679], directing him to put
himself under Burton's command, and proceed wherever convenient for annoying the enemy, taking prisoners and scalps, intercepting enemy convoys,
destroying their cattle, burning their barns and magazines, £5 sterling to be
given for any Indian or French prisoner or scalp.

on rangers, about whom he had collected information as early as January, 1756. He followed Shirley again by maintaining and increasing the ranging companies that Shirley first ordered Winslow to form in May, 1756, out of the two thousand New Englanders who returned from the 1755 campaign in Nova Scotia. Shirley planned for three companies of sixty men each; officers to be paid as officers in the regular army; privates to receive the same wages as the provincial troops of Massachusetts Bay; each man to receive six dollars bounty money, out of which he was to buy a blanket, to be armed with the king's arms, to be fed with the king's provisions, and to be clothed by the king with a hunting coat, vest and breeches, Indian stockings, and shoes. For every Indian scalp he brought in he received £5 sterling. The 2d and 6th sections of the Articles of War were read to him, and he took the oath of fidelity.[30] The rangers therefore must be considered as independent companies attached to the British army, on an establishment of their own, a very expensive one, paid out of contingencies. Two of Shirley's companies did not take the field until August, 1756; the third, under Richard Rogers, began its muster roll on July 24. Captain Robert Rogers's original company, distinct from these three, had been a part of the Crown Point army of 1755. When that army disbanded, he continued his forty-three men in service, and Shirley gave him a commission on March 24, 1756.[31] Shirley likewise commissioned William Lampson as captain of a ranging company, but no man ever joined it, and in August Loudoun authorized Lampson to raise a hundred men, on a somewhat less extravagant establishment than Shirley's. The following spring, when the terms of enlistment

[30] Orders to Winslow, April 3, 1756, Winslow's Letter Book, Massachusetts Historical Society.
[31] W.O. 34: 76, p. 18.

of the original three companies expired, he re-raised them on the new basis of a hundred men each for the duration of the war. He gave them ten dollars bounty money, out of which they were to arm and clothe themselves, and he paid the privates 1s. 5½d. a day. Throughout the summer of 1757 there were four ranging companies in service, under Robert Rogers, Richard Rogers—who, dying of smallpox in July, was succeeded by John Stark—John Shepherd, and Charles Bulkeley. The following January four new companies of rangers were raised, and one new company of Indian troops from the Connecticut Mohegans under Moses Brewer. These were on a still cheaper establishment, the ten dollars bounty money being deducted from their first month's pay. But in spite of all these deductions, these nine companies cost the Crown nearly £35,000 sterling a year, £15,000 more than the cost of a regular regiment of ten hundred and forty men.[32]

In spite of the money spent on them, the rangers scarcely justified themselves by results. Unaccustomed to discipline, they were sometimes unreliable, and even disobedient. Rogers, for instance, undertook in August, 1756, to go off with his company without orders, and excused his action by the men's unwillingness to stay behind when other parties were out. In 1757 they were blamed for stealing provisions; and according to the account of Captain James Abercrombie, the general's aide de camp, they even rebelled against their own officers. He accompanied them on an expedition; "all I could doe or say to the officers they could not prevent firing on our march." They slept one night near Ticonderoga, and when the next morning a few of them were seen as they were about to take a prisoner, "Captain Stark who was with me set

---

[32] Beating Orders to Robert Rogers to raise five additional companies, January 11, 1758, LO 5391. The muster rolls of the ranging companies are attached to the duplicate of the warrants for their pay.

up the Indian hollow, upon that the whole party jumped up and yelled as if Hell had broke loose and all fell afiring at a few men running away. I did everything in my power to make them hold their tongues and behave as they ought to doe I even knocked several of them down and damned their Officers for a set of Scoundrels.'' A month later, the rangers encamped on the island off Fort Edward began a riot in an effort to rescue two of their number who had been imprisoned by their own officers, cut down the whipping post which was to them the chief emblem of the discipline they detested, and dispersed only after Captain Shepherd confronted them with a firelock in his hands. After that they began to desert. The whole affair shows that frontier spirit which the British army called ''levelling''; the rangers refused to take orders, or to perform any duty but that of scouting. If Webb is to be believed, they were not above lying and sleeping on an island in Lake George during one whole fortnight in July, 1757, when they were supposed to be surveying the enemy position. Loudoun had to bear with their humors, for he could not get along without them.[33]

But at the same time he took steps to supplant the rangers by more trustworthy scouts, and to improve their ideas of discipline. He encouraged British officers to accompany them on their trips; Rogers gives a list in his *Journals* of fifty-five British volunteers and a few officers who learned woodcraft from his men.[34] The lieutenants of some of the new ranging companies of 1758 were British officers. Loudoun had a definite purpose in thus training

[33] Rogers to Loudoun, August 11, 1756, LO 1467; August 16, 1756, LO 1501; Abercrombie to Loudoun, November 29, 1757, LO 4915; Abercromby to Loudoun, December 30, 1757, LO 5159.

[34] *Journals of Major Robert Rogers* (1765), p. 52. Of these fifty-five men, five were given ensigncies in Gage's regiment, and eighteen commissions in other regiments by the end of 1758.

regulars, for he meant to turn two companies out of every regiment of a thousand men into ranging companies, and to form a distinct corps if necessary. In December, 1757, he substituted for this plan the organization of a regiment of light-armed infantry. The scheme was proposed by Lieutenant Colonel Gage of the 44th, as a device whereby he might get a colonelcy. He offered to raise and clothe at his own expense a regiment of five hundred, to be reimbursed if his plan met with approval in England. Loudoun fell in eagerly with the plan, and permitted Gage to draft a nucleus of sergeants, corporals, and "good active healthy young men" from the other regiments. He left the choosing of officers to Gage, though he recommended that men who had gone out with the rangers be given preference. The importance of this move in the history of irregular warfare is very great; it was the natural and inevitable outcome of the failure of the provincial rangers to fulfill the function of acting as irregular troops. Gage's regiment constituted the first definitely light-armed regiment in the British army; the firelocks issued to them were "cut shorter and the stocks dressed to make them lighter." Composed as far as possible of woodsmen, it was officered by men who knew something of Rogers's methods and were also trained in regular discipline. After two years experiment with local devices, the British army took partly into its own hands the function deemed to be most peculiarly American.[35]

In all the aspects of army organization thus far discussed, conditions in America made some adaptation

---

[35] Gage's proposals are in LO 5065, 5072, 5074, 5075. HM 1717, vol. 2, November 22, December 11, December 23, 1757; vol. 5, January 7, 1758. Gage's regiment was approved in England; he was allowed £3500 as purchase money for his lieutenant colonelcy, of which £2000 came out of the off-reckonings of his new regiment, and £1300 out of the contingencies, Barrington to Abercromby, July 8, September 11, 1758, W.O. 34: 72.

necessary, whether it was colonial disunion, as in the case
of pay, colonial inadequacy, as in the case of provisions,
colonial disinclination, as in the case of transport, or colonial independency, as in the case of rangers. During the
nineteen months that Loudoun commanded in America,
he made arrangements, with comparative success, for all
of these major branches of administration. Under his direction troops never suffered for want of pay, justly distributed among them, nor for want of provisions, both
salt and fresh, nor for lack of transportation. These were
no small achievements in such a country as the new world.

The other aspects of British army administration have
little to do with the colonies; they belong rather to the
curious and involved system which the army brought
from England, and could not be changed by any mere
commander in chief. The problem of personnel, under
which can be conveniently included such branches as the
ordnance, is the most important, though various miscellaneous aspects deserve attention.

The quality of the men who officered eighteenth-century
British armies cannot be understood without some appreciation of the purchase system and of the attitude of
the commander in chief towards it. The purchase system
has had its share of blame, and if it meant that an incapable younger son could buy his majority or colonelcy
without seeing any service while grizzled veterans twid-
dled their thumbs in poverty-stricken despair at the bottom of the ladder, it deserves the opprobrium cast upon
it. But in the eighteenth century it never meant quite that.
Opportunities for the investment of a small capital were
not many for a gentleman, and putting one's money into
the army, or into a church living, or into some civil office,
was almost the only safe investment, promising a sure return, that a young man could make. His profits would

increase if he devoted himself to his duty. There were any number of men in Loudoun's army who had bought their first commission, had thus attained a ranking in the army, and had made thorough and keen officers of themselves, in the hope of getting the vacancy above them, not by purchase, but by promotion through rank or merit. For this is the second point in regard to the purchase system, that not every commission in the army could be bought. When a regiment was augmented, or when a new regiment was raised, as the four battalions of the 60th or the two new Scottish battalions of 1757, the new officers did not get their steps by purchase, and could not dispose of their places by selling. As long as the men in charge of promotions, either in the War Office in London or in the field in America, set themselves against the practice, the commissions in these new regiments remained forever outside the purchase system. This leads to the third point, that the extension of the system depended to a considerable extent upon the attitude towards it of the men who signed commissions. If they commanded in the field, they realized as a matter of course that officers would give most to a service in which promotion rested on merit and not on wealth. Finally, a young man of means could not immediately set about buying increasingly higher and higher rank; he had to wait his turn. If a captain who had bought his commission wanted to sell, and the commander in chief approved, his place might be offered to all the captain lieutenants in the army according to their rank in the service, and if none of them wanted to buy, to all the lieutenants according to their rank. A man might wait long before he could buy. Moreover, in the American service, where many vacancies made advancement by promotion possible, a commission was not worth as much as during peace in England, and men who might have got permission to sell hesitated to accept the loss.[36]

By his commission, Loudoun was authorized to fill up posts that became vacant through death, court martial sentences, or resignation, "having regard to the Merit of such Officers, as well as to their Seniority; Which last is to give way to the good of the Service, if you can give a sufficient reason for setting the same aside. . . ." Such authority extended to and included the rank of lieutenant colonel; Loudoun could not appoint colonels. Cumberland supplemented the formal instructions of the commission by urging Loudoun to set "bad men" aside, to appoint younger officers for particular merit, and to follow as far as convenient the seniority in the regiment rather than in the army. Loudoun took pains to become acquainted with the character, history, and abilities of every officer in his command; there were never more than five or six

[36] The following table compares the prices established in England, and those customarily followed in America. The latter were finally standardized by Amherst in 1759 (W.O. 1: 5, f. 144).

Commissions	In England		In America (Amherst's list)	
	Prices	Difference	Prices	Difference
Lt. Col.	£3400	£ 900		
Major	2500	1000		
Captain	1500	700	£1200	£ 600
Capt. Lt.	800	250	600	300
Lt.	550	150	300	100
Ensign	400	400	200	200
		3400		1200

The figures under "Difference" are the amounts, which, if a lieutenant colonel sold, every officer who bought and moved up in his respective rank would contribute to the total £3400. For example, when Captain David Kennedy of the 44th resigned, Lt. William Hervey paid him £900 for the captaincy, the new lieutenant £100, and the new ensign, £200, HM 1717, vol. 3, April 16, 1757. Captain Cunningham wanted to sell, "saying he bought for £1300 the capt. lt. 650, eldest lt. 300, eldest ensign 100, Vollunteer for the ensign 250," HM 1717, vol. 2, December 8, 1757.

hundred of them. But he was somewhat limited in his power of promotion by the recommendations of his political and military superiors and of people in America whom he had to oblige. Though no commissions under the rank of colonel were signed in England for any officer under Loudoun's command—Barrington maintained a strict adherence to that principle—a letter from him or from the secretary of state came to virtually the same thing. Such a young man as William Hervey of the 44th, a brother of the Earl of Bristol, was assured of his captaincy when Cumberland and Barrington wrote in his favor. As highly recommended, if perhaps more discreetly, was the natural son of Thomas Hervey, George Bartman of Shirley's, for whom Fox asked promotion as no common favor; "make his duties consistent with a tender Constitution."[37] As soon as Holderness got back into office in 1757, he urged advancement for a relative of his, Captain Milbank of the 28th, as "a particular Favour done to myself." Holburne got the post of brigade major for Captain Spittal, a relative; Captain Hussey had the support of Sir John Ligonier and H. B. Legge. In Loudoun's first promotion list, of November, 1756, nine officers had been recommended by such people at home as Lord Cathcart, Sackville, Grafton, Fox, and Marlborough; two by Sir Charles Hardy; two by Webb, and two by Abercromby.[38] There was another limitation upon Loudoun's free exercise of his power of promotion, and it too helped to undermine the feeling he tried to create among his officers, that every able man would have justice done him. When his army was augmented by drafts from Ireland, new officers came out from home,

---

[37] Both William Hervey and George Bartman wrote diaries which have been printed in the *Suffolk Green Books*, XIV.

[38] Loudoun's promotion lists, with annotations in his own hand, are in the Cumberland Papers.

and when Shirley's and Pepperrell's regiments were reduced, Loudoun was asked to make room for all the half-
pay officers before he filled places with men of his own
choice.[39]

Vacant ensigncies were filled from a group of young
men, who, as "volunteers", accompanied the army in no
official capacity, but were expected to perform whatever
duties offered, whether sergeant's or private's tasks in
the companies, or scouting service with rangers. Since the
rules of seniority did not apply to them, they were for the
most part conscientious. Some of them, even at this distance, were unusually attractive: young Lutterell (Luttrell), for example, worth £5000 a year, educated at
Westminster and Oxford, pressingly recommended by
Lord Home, the son of the M. P. for Mitchell, refused his
father's offer of a commission in the guards, and chose
to come to America as a volunteer, to carry arms, and to
get a commission if he deserved it.[40] William Henry Fairfax, son of Colonel Fairfax of Virginia, also educated in
England, refused Barrington's offer of an ensigncy in
London and preferred to follow Loudoun's army as a
volunteer. William Byrd of Westover, supported by Lieutenant General Pulteney; John Wilson, son of the Chief

---

[39] Both Shirley's and Pepperrell's regiments had their full quota of forty
officers. Those captured at Oswego, and exchanged in England, were provided
for in England, and many returned to America in the drafts. In America
Loudoun was forced to put off people to whom he had promised places in
favor of such men as Thomas Jocelyn, John Billings, John Bradstreet, James
DeLancey, John Foxon, for whom he signed commissions dated March 8, the
day after the regiments were broken in America, so that they never went on
half-pay.

[40] Lutterell, it is needless to say, got his ensigncy in the 48th five months
after his arrival. He fulfilled the promise of his youth and estate, succeeded
his father in the Irish peerage as Earl of Carhampton, was Member of
Parliament for Bossiney and Middlesex, Plympton Earls and Ludgershall,
and became master general of the Ordnance, *Dictionary of National Biography*, Henry Lawes Luttrell.

Justice of St. Kitt's; Thomas Pinckney, son of the treasurer of South Carolina; these were other colonials who served as volunteers.[41]

There were, of course, countless other recommendations from all kinds of people in England and America. Among the most amusing was one from Calcraft, who recommended an Archibald McAully, brother to Donald McAully, "about whom I told your Lordship I did not care sixpence"; a Chaplain Brooke, about whom he knew nothing, "but was sollicited to write for him by those I could not refuse"; a Mr. John French, mentioned by a "Miss Plunket, a Bath acquaintance, so pretty that your Lordship would not have refused her—I know nothing of him"; and a Mr. John Christopher, recommended by a "Lincolnshire gentleman, whom I hoped to make a Convert and did for a little time, but the Dog is gone back again." Miss Christiana Ramsay recommended Will, her brother, "though I cannot say in the legall way." David Baillie wanted something done for his son, a lad of sixteen. Governor Dobbs of North Carolina recommended his son Arthur, and Governor Tinker of the Bahamas his son, a lieutenant in Shirley's grenadiers. Sophia Beckers pleaded for a commission in the Royal Americans for her husband, captain lieutenant in the Jersey regiment. Governor Hopkins of Rhode Island asked a lieutenancy for Joseph Whipple, "a native of this colony, once possessed of a fair Estate", for two years deputy governor, a former midshipman of H. M. *Intrepid* and in the naval engagement off Minorca. Stanwix recommended Lieuten-

[41] Fairfax was commissioned in the 28th in November, 1757, LO 5525. Colonel William Byrd, III, had apparently the same ambition as Fairfax, to serve in the British army until he got a lieutenancy, and then, still holding his regular commission, to enter the Virginia regiment (HM 1717, vol. 3, February 26, 1757). This was not uncommon; Parker of New Jersey, Beamsley Glazier of New York, Major Babcock of Rhode Island, all held both the regular and provincial commissions.

ant Clapham of the Pennsylvania provincials, serving
with the Royal Americans as volunteer; and William
Penn, three Pennsylvanians who wanted the king's commission. Belcher asked a captaincy for his son-in-law,
Lieutenant Lyde of Boston. Besides such letters, there
were many memorials from men in the service. Washington presented a petition from the officers of the Virginia
regiment who had served since 1754, in which they re-
counted their services, though such recounting was "re-
pugnant to the Modesty becoming the Brave". He la-
mented that the best of Kings had raised six battalions
of regular troops in America and not provided for a
single Virginian, and begged that Loudoun might "give
them a Soldier's Reward."[42] Duke Butler, having once
been broke from his earlier rank, solicited permission to
serve as a private soldier, to convince Cumberland of his
honor. François DeRoy had served in a Swiss regiment
since 1722, and had fought under Saxe at Fontenoy. Caleb
Grainger of North Carolina, with "the oldest provincial
commission in North America", wanted a post in the
60th. Andrew Crotty, a volunteer in the 22d, had served
as quartermaster, ensign, and lieutenant in the East India service. Lieutenant Alexander Johnstone of the 47th
put in a plea for all Nova Scotia officers, who never got
preferment and were "stuck" forever in distant posts.
Captain Dagworthy of the Maryland provincials and
Lieutenant Colonel Angell of the Rhode Islanders wanted
regular commissions. François Sigismund Ebergeny
asked for employment as a "hussar". Lieutenant William Cook of the 51st had seen service in the Russian
Guards, had been imprisoned by the Swedes, had served
with Prince Golitzen in Prussia, and in 1752 had accompanied Lord Hyndford to Vienna.

[42] Memorial of Officers of the Virginia Regiment, LO 5296.

Such letters serve to show the cosmopolitanism of Loudoun's forces, and the many demands made upon him. Many of them were from his own Scottish friends, who regarded him as their sole patron; Abercromby and Webb had similar friends, while a due respect for the wishes of the colonels helped to keep the field officers in good humor. It is clear that it was no easy business for Loudoun to promote men without arousing criticism. In general, he kept a wise balance. He discouraged the purchase system as much as possible; "I am glade of every excuse to stope selling." Out of eighty-eight commissions granted by him from December to April, 1757, only sixteen were purchased. But it was difficult to refuse an officer permission to sell, especially when the field officers of the regiment agreed that a change would serve the regiment's interests. One such case is worth telling, not only because it shows the details of an army purchase and illustrates Loudoun's attitude, but also because it deals with that mysterious and tragic figure of Highland legend, re-told in Stevenson's *Ticonderoga,* Major Duncan Campbell of the Black Watch. On recommendation of Lieutenant Colonel Grant, Loudoun gave Campbell permission to sell. He then allowed Captain Gordon Graham, the eldest captain, to pay £200 for the majority, James Cockburn, "the 5th lieutenant in the regiment but the eldest that can purtches", £900 for the captaincy, Ensign Duncan Campbell, the eldest ensign, £100 for the lieutenancy, and some volunteer £200 for the ensigncy, making in all £1400 to the major. The captain lieutenant and the four elder lieutenants protested that such permission to Cockburn altered the natural course of preferment, and asked that Major Campbell and Captain Graham fulfill their share of the agreement, that the major be permitted to retire on the full pay of a captain, and that "your memorialists have their due course of promotion.''[43] Since Barrington and Cumberland frowned upon any officer's retiring on full pay,[44] Loudoun could not follow the suggestion, but he finally refused to permit the purchases to be made, and so left Campbell to meet the fate prophesied for him, according to the tale, before the lines of Ticonderoga the following July. On a par with this story, as revealing something of the character of British officers, was the request of Lieutenant Colonel Rollo of the 22d that his sergeant major, William Neale, be given the adjutancy of the regiment, which Captain French, who paid £250 for it, was willing to sell for £200. He (Rollo) and the sergeant made up a hundred between them, and the captains were so satisfied with Neale's merit that they were willing to bind themselves for the other hundred.[45]

"Proper instruction imparted with Gentleness" was in Loudoun's opinion the object towards which young officers should strive. They should ask themselves what the words in their commissions meant: "You are . . . carefully and diligently to discharge the duty of [ensign, etc.], by exercising and well-disciplining, as well the inferior Officers, as Soldiers", and they were to leave nothing un-

[43] Memorial of Captain Lieutenant John Campbell, Lieutenants William Grant, Robert Gray, John Campbell, and George Farquherson, LO 2551. HM 1717, vol. 2, November 25, 1757. The commissions of these four lieutenants were dated before 1751, a unique phenomenon in the British army in America in November, 1757, for with the exception of the three Nova Scotia regiments, the 48th was the only corps with lieutenants whose commissions antedated 1750.

[44] Loudoun permitted Lieutenant Colonel Chapman and Captain Mulloy to retire on full pay because they were incapacitated for service. Cumberland approved, though an exception to the rule, and Barrington drafted to Loudoun an unnecessarily severe letter condemning any such future acts. Cumberland to Barrington, August 28, 1757, Cumberland Papers. Shute Barrington, *William Wildman, Viscount Barrington*, p. 32.

[45] Rollo to Loudoun, October 28, 1757, LO 4708; HM 1717, vol. 2, November 21, 1757.

performed that might conduce to well-disciplining. They "are to inform the ignorant, encourage the willing and by their advice and Example engage all who are under them to bestow their whole Time and Attention, in fitting the battalion for the Field."[46] He demanded from all officers strict obedience, and the tone of finality he could assume on occasion appeared in a letter to Major Charles Craven of the 51st, who disobeyed Loudoun's order to return the subsistence money of his regiment into the paymaster's hands. "These things may seem very extraordinary to you, but I do assure you they cannot seem more so to you, than the Freedom you are pleased to use both on this Occasion, and a former one with my orders; as that Manner is totally new to me in any Service I have seen, I will endeavor to prevent its creeping into any part of the Army where I command."[47]

Over the commanding officers of a regiment, and over his own staff, Loudoun could exercise but little control as long as they performed the letter of their duties and did not flagrantly disobey. Majors he could promote, but he signed only two commissions for lieutenant colonels, one to his closest friend, "the creature of his goodness", John Young, the eldest major in the Royal Americans, and the other to Henry Fletcher of the 35th.[48] Lieutenant colonels

[46] Loudoun to Prevost, March 20, 1757, LO 3108. General Orders to the Commanding Officers of the Royal American Regiment, LO 2421.

[47] Loudoun to Craven, November 3, 1756, LO 2146.

[48] Loudoun recommended Young to Halifax for the lieutenant governorship of Virginia, and Young was so confident of getting the post that he asked Montcalm to release him from the capitulation of Fort William Henry, lest in some way it hinder his civil advancement. Montcalm graciously acceded, and Loudoun as graciously expressed his thanks, a pretty example of the chivalry still common. But Pitt's control of affairs spoiled Young's chances; in December, 1757, Calcraft wrote that Halifax, approached again on the subject, had replied that *now* there were no thoughts of making a military government out of Virginia by giving it a good officer. Young to Loudoun, March, 1757, LO 3234; Loudoun to Halifax, June 3, 1757, LO

he could recommend for promotion, but during his command only one lieutenant colonel of his army got a regiment; vacancies were filled from England, and it quite broke John Calcraft's heart "to see everything go from your army so." Pitt's promotion of all the lieutenant colonels to be colonels in America only, encouraged them to think that they were not forgotten at home. Loudoun could neither reward nor punish them. The case of Lord Charles Hay involved a flagrant disobedience of orders, and Loudoun's only remedy was to ask permission for him to return to England. Webb gave no such opportunity.

The havoc that an incapable field officer could raise with a regiment was demonstrated by the same Colonel James Prevost who had conceived the idea of the Royal Americans. He was a thorn in the flesh to Loudoun, Abercromby, and Amherst. He made himself agreeable to no one except Lord Charles Hay. His major and captains accused him of failing to preserve that "certain delicacy" necessary between officers to permit them to live happily together, and so antagonizing his subalterns. He was plainly no gentleman, according to the British pattern. Bouquet and Haldimand, seeing that his conduct reflected upon all foreign officers, warned him in vain not to show "those haughty airs he is accused of". His attitude towards his soldiers was that of an ignorant Continental officer; he seems to have sanctioned the cruel punishment of beating men "tyed neck and heels". Two of his corporals who had beaten a man to death in that fashion were court martialled and broken, but when Loudoun informed him that men were not so punished in the British army, he denied all knowledge of the affair. He chose the men for

3785; Montcalm to Loudoun, August 9, 1757, LO 4182; Loudoun to Montcalm, November 8, 1757, LO 4786; Calcraft to Loudoun, December 29, 1757, LO 5140.

his battalion out of all the recruits in the regiment, and got it into the worst shape of any corps in the army; he then proudly wrote that the 4th battalion was fit for any service. He discharged as invalids thirty men, some of them with full equipment, though two surgeons of the general hospital found that only seven were incapable of service. His returns of arms, equipment, and troops were never accurate. He followed no rules in issuing provisions, but let his quartermaster knock in the heads of barrels, dump the contents on dirty blankets, and leave the men to help themselves. He behaved to Loudoun with such disrespect and insolence that witnesses agreed that a court martial would have broken him for it, but Loudoun contented himself with using the harshest language he ever employed to an officer: ''I told him I had suffered more from him than I ever had from any man or ever would again. Not on his account but of those who brought him into the service. That from his behaviour I should never have guessed he had been in any service, for I am sure there was no pressident in any service of such behaviour as his . . . My door was open to every man from morning to night, but he had abused it, no day having passed that he was not in 2 or 3 or 4 times, more than I can spair.'' Prevost bewailed the scant authority a colonel exercised in a British army, and considered that he merited Loudoun's rebuke only because he had failed to exercise sufficient prudence and circumspection in dealing with the commander in chief. Wolfe in 1758 summarized the general opinion: ''He is most universally detested by all ranks of people, and ministers cannot do worse than to let him serve in the army. He is fit for no sort of command, and does not know how to obey.''[49] The case of

[49] Representation of officers of the 4th battalion, March 15, 1757, LO 3041; Bouquet to St. Clair, April 12, 1757; Loudoun to Cumberland, April 25, 1757; Prevost to Cumberland, May 12, 23, 1757, Cumberland Papers; Re-

Prevost shows two things: the sanctity of a colonel's rank in the army; and the influence of political considerations, for had Loudoun demanded that Prevost be recalled, he would have seemed to be criticizing Cumberland, who was responsible for the appointment.

Other branches of the army served to complicate the command. The engineers, for example, were under the Ordnance Board, who kept in their hands the control of pay and personnel, acting upon letters and reports from America six months after they were written. But they were also under the commander in chief's orders, and therefore a part of the army. Early in 1756 James Montrésor, the chief engineer in America, complained that "his poor, abandoned branch" had no rank in the service as such, and that therefore engineers could not receive public orders by the hands of orderlies, could not advise in councils of war, and did not share equitably in the distribution of provisions or quarters. It was not that engineers had no rank in the army, but that their rank did not correspond to their rank as engineers; Montrésor was a lieutenant in the 14th foot, and William Eyre, rated as engineer extraordinary, was a major in the 44th. They drew army pay in their regiments, and from the Ordnance Board, which had a paymaster of its own in America, as engineers. In 1757 they were given the rank they asked: the chief engineer as colonel of foot, directors as lieutenant colonels, sub-directors as majors, engineers in

port of Richard Huck and William Russell, LO 3468; HM 1717, vol. 3, March 3, 15, 29, May 20, 21, 23, 24, 25, June 16, 1757; HM 1717, vol. 2, December 29, 1757; vol. 5, January 4, 1758; Wolfe to Sackville, July, 1758, Historical Manuscript Commission *Report*, Sackville-Stopford MSS., II, 257. In 1758 Abercromby gave him permission to leave the army until orders from England arrived; in 1759 Prevost left for England; in May, 1760 he arrived again in America expecting to take part in the campaign, but Amherst refused him permission to join the army. Cumberland Papers; W.O. 1: 5; G.D. 8: 31.

ordinary as captains, engineers extraordinary as captain lieutenants, sub-engineers as lieutenants, and practitioner engineers as ensigns.

At no time did the British army in America have the service of as many engineers as it needed. In 1756 it contained only six men so rated in England, and two others, Lieutenants John Montrésor and George Bartman, who served as assistants. When the Royal American regiment was being planned, an effort was made to include among the foreign officers enlisted in Germany a number of men who might serve as engineers, and Bouquet reported that ten were qualified. These men, of whom Wetterstrom and Hollandt were the most prominent, were paid by Loudoun in 1756 out of the contingencies whenever they served as engineers, but in 1757 by the ordnance paymaster. He complained of their general lack of ability to Cumberland, who gave him scant comfort by answering that he must not expect Vaubans among the Swiss officers in an American service. By the summer of 1757 the number of engineers was increased to ten, including Dugal Campbell, who ranked Montrésor as chief;[50] William Green, who was called down from Newfoundland; Matthew Clarke, who gained unenviable fame in advising the frontal attack on the lines at Ticonderoga in July, 1758; and William Brassier, draughtsman.

In spite of their limited numbers, the engineers performed valuable work, and demonstrated their importance by constant advice upon the technical details of siege work, fortifications, and buildings. Eyre, for instance, told Loudoun at Halifax that the general proportion of besiegers to besieged was usually deemed to be four to one, but that in the case of Louisbourg it ought to be at

[50] Campbell died at sea of a bilious fever on August 28, 1757, and was replaced by Montrésor as chief, with Eyre as second. HM 1717, vol. 4, August 28, 1757.

least six to one, because of the difficulty of landing supplies. Wetterstrom was indefatigable; his remarks upon the fortification of Fort Edward, based upon the "latest developments of the art" in Europe, left that poor provincial fortress, the strongest the British possessed in North America, with few points in its favor. If Wetterstrom could have had his way with Schenectady, he would practically have razed the town, partly diverted the Mohawk from its course, and erected an elaborate fort with stone-faced bastions.[51] All newly-arrived engineers were impatient with what passed in America for forts; there was an impassable chasm between their vision and the reality. Those who had been longer in the American service, as Montrésor, Mackellar, and Eyre, understood the difficulties of building European defenses. Montrésor, to whom Loudoun felt he did not dare entrust a siege, spent £10,000 upon the works in New York in the fall of 1756 and estimated that another £7000 would complete them.

Since the Royal Regiment of Artillery, with everything that appertained to it, was also under the direction of the Ordnance Board, a complete establishment had to be maintained in America, consisting of a comptroller at 11s. a day, a storekeeper and paymaster at 7s., a clerk of stores at 4s., and two armorers at 3s. each. Its headquarters were at Boston, although assistant clerks were in charge of branch storehouses elsewhere. No other office in America required as much bookkeeping as this one. For the issuing of any kind of stores there was an elaborate procedure. The commanding officer or quartermaster of a regiment submitted a memorandum of his needs to the commander in chief, who, in a brief note, informed the comptroller, who in turn instructed the store-

[51] Manuscript maps by such engineers as Wetterstrom, Richard Gridley, John Montrésor, William Brassier, are in the Huntington Library.

keeper to issue the articles. The storekeeper took an indenture from the person who received them, and entered them on duplicate forms and in a ledger. Such paper work was entailed by the numerous separate articles with which the office dealt. For fifty rounds of regimental practice with a single six-pounder there were required, in addition to the round shot, 400 tin tubes, 30 portfires, and match, flannel cartridges, fine paper, corned powder, sheepskins, sponge tacks, and worsted in proportion. Ordnance lists contain such various items as tarpaulins, handspikes, leather buckets, bellows, iron crows, hair cloths, "Grape shott with wooden Tampeons and pins compleat for Howitzers", tanned hides, iron melting ladles, lanthorns, linstocks with cocks, padlocks, white rope, drag ropes, Hambrough line, packthread, sets of weights, priming wires, tallow candles, fuzes, files, needles, brass quadrants, copper nails, rasps, scales, scissors, flax, and funnels. Some conception of the paraphernalia collected to serve a single train on the march is afforded by an estimate of the number of horses the expedition of 1757 would have required for its ordnance and stores if it had attempted to transport the whole by land; for the artillery, 571 horses, and for the whole train, including forty-two tons of musket balls, a thousand wagons and 3623 horses.[52]

In spite of this array of artillery, there were not enough pieces of the quality or caliber recommended by engineers for American needs. Not that there were not extraordinary numbers of guns in the colonies; from 1720 to 1755 the Ordnance Board shipped to continental colonies alone 649 pieces, ranging from 3-pounders to 42-pounders, all iron except sixteen light brass twelves

[52] There were at Halifax but thirty-one horses, and twenty oxen, and of these eighteen horses were for the use of the general staff. HM 1717, vol. 3, April 21, 1757.

and sixes.[53] But many of these, through exposure to the
weather or improper care, were rendered useless; the
reports of the various governors to Loudoun in 1756 are
a procession of honey-combed and unfit cannon, and when
the Board of Trade in 1755 asked governors what was
necessary for their defense, they all included ordnance
and stores as a primary necessity.[54]

When an engineer recommended a distribution of guns
for a fort, it was often impossible to accommodate him.
Late in 1757 Montrésor estimated what ought to be done
for the defense of Fort Edward; he recommended for the
four bastions four eighteen pounders, nine twelves, seven
nines, and seven mortars; the fort, though it boasted
thirty-nine pieces altogether, had of the larger calibers
eight eighteens, no twelves, six nines, and four mortars.
The iron guns, which during a siege were estimated to
fire only three rounds an hour, were not dependable; at
Fort William Henry the largest and most serviceable
pieces of artillery burst. Brass guns, especially light
twelves, were rare.[55]

[53] Ordnance, Mortars, Small Arms and Gun Powder sent to America from
1720 to 1755, Cumberland Papers. The list includes Newfoundland, Nova
Scotia and the continent, Bermuda, the West Indies, and the Mosquito shore,
and totals 1467 cannon and mortars, 22,028 small arms, of which 15,569
were muskets, and 8,822 barrels of powder.

[54] Fitch to Loudoun, August 2, 1756, LO 1393; Lyttelton to Loudoun, June
13, 1757, LO 3672; Reynolds to Loudoun, July 23, 1756, LO 1334; Dobbs to
Loudoun, July 10, 1756, LO 1305; Denny to Loudoun, November 10, 1757,
LO 4793; Belcher to Loudoun, February 21, 1757, LO 2883. Such statements
are summarized in a report of the Board of Trade on the defenses of the
colonies, May 11, 1756, LO 1137 and W.O. 34: 101. The answers to the ques-
tionnaire of the Board of Trade are printed in part in Connecticut Historical Society *Collections*, I, 282; *Maryland Archives*, VI, 352; *North Carolina
Colonial Records*, V, 570; *New York Colonial Documents*, VII, 2; *Dinwiddie
Papers*, II, 338.

[55] The difference in weight between a light brass twelve pounder and a
heavy brass twelve was over a ton, the former weighing nine cwt., the latter
twenty-nine cwt. and two quarters.

The ordnance department in America was likewise responsible for the repairing and issuing of small arms and stores. All small arms came from England; between 1739 and 1755, 11,536 muskets were shipped to continental colonies, sixty-five hundred of them to southern colonies, and in 1756 Shirley issued to provincials 8450 stand of arms out of ten thousand shipped from England. Powder and shot also came from England or Holland, though in the early spring of 1757, before he knew what proportions were accompanying Holburne, Loudoun contracted with various dealers and forges in Boston for both. Thomas Hancock furnished powder at £7 6s. 8d. lawful money a barrel, and Joseph Scott and Peter Oliver were recommended by Gridley to supply ball and shells from the furnaces at Hanover, Plimton, and Middleborough at £2 sterling for a 13-inch shell, 16s. for a 10-inch, and £14 a ton for round shot. The small arms issued to Shirley's and Pepperrell's regiments in 1755 were decidedly inferior; they were described as "musquets with Single bridle locks, nosebands, and wooden rammers," half of them old Dutch arms; whereas those issued to the 44th and 48th were "musquets of the King's pattern without nosebands [and] with Steel Rammers."[56] Those issued to the Royal American regiment were also of inferior quality. But according to a list in Cumberland's papers, there were in England in 1755 only 52,707 muskets for land service.

[56] Cumberland Papers. This list includes among the stores for the engineers the item of armour, back-pieces, breast-pieces, and head-pieces. They were the only men in Loudoun's army so attired, unless the officer's gorget may be counted the residue of an earlier breast-plate. The standard musket for land service, with steel rammer, had a barrel 3 ft. 10 inches long, a bore of .76 inches, and weighed complete 12 lbs. 4 ozs.; it shot lead balls numbering 14½ to the pound. The wall-piece, a rare small-arm used over parapets, had a barrell of 4 ft. 6 in., a bore of .91, weighed 35 lbs. 2 ozs., and shot balls numbering 6⅔ to the pound. From a descriptive table of small arms in use in 1756, September 4, 1757, (signed) George Williamson, LO 6683.

If one can judge from an undated proposal for augmenting the artillery, the detachment of the Royal Regiment of artillery was never as large as the American service demanded. In June, 1756, the detachment at Albany under Captain Ord numbered complete, including officers and such civil members as the staff, conductors, and artificers, only one hundred and forty-one, while under the "scorbutic dropsical" Captain Brome[57] at Halifax were one hundred and two. The suggestion was made that men be drafted from the Royal Americans to make up a total of three hundred in New York, and that officers be appointed from among those regimental officers who possessed a knowledge of artillery to make up to twenty-two, both officers and men to have additional pay for their services. The pay was not great enough to appeal to army officers, however. The various regiments continued to use their own men for the service of such field-pieces as were assigned to them, and in the following year, after an additional detachment arrived from Woolwich, under Lieutenant Colonel Williamson, the total in North America reached only three hundred and thirty-nine, including officers. This seems a small proportion for distribution among various forts and expeditions, and much of the artillery must have been served by men without great experience. Yet Montrésor's proportion of artillerymen for his twenty-nine pieces at Fort Edward was only forty men. Officers of the Royal Artillery had enjoyed army rank since 1751.[58]

The hospital service in the British army during the Seven Years' War, especially in comparison with that in

---

[57] "Captain Broom of the train asks leave to go home . . . I have flattered the old man and persuaded him to stay to defend the place in case of they should happen in my absence which he is pleased with." HM 1717, vol. 4, July 16, 1757.

[58] Royal warrant, April 30, 1751, C.O. 324: 38, p. 293.

the navy, was of a high standard, for Cumberland paid particular attention to this necessary branch. A distinction must be drawn between the general hospital, with a staff of its own paid in England after certificates had been signed by the commander in chief and the director of hospitals that they were serving in their respective capacities, and by the deputy paymaster general that he had himself advanced them no part of their salaries; and the regimental hospitals, attended by surgeons and mates attached to the regiments as regimental officers, and paid from the regimental establishment. By the summer of 1757 the general hospital comprised a staff of a director and chief surgeon, James Napier, a physician, Richard Huck, four surgeons, three apothecaries, twelve surgeon's mates, ten apothecaries' mates, and a matron, Charlotte Brown, who had come over with Braddock's army. The government of the general hospital was vested in the physician and chief surgeon, who, when not on duty at general headquarters, were instructed to visit the sick, prescribe diet and medicines, give directions for lodging in uncrowded wards, with free circulation of air and clean beds, see that instruments were kept clean, with plenty of lint and bandages, and assign duties to inferior officers, whom they could suspend temporarily until the hospital board met. This board consisted of the director, physicians, chief and master surgeons, who passed sentence on incapable men, but the commander in chief made the final decision. Nurses could be dismissed without application to the board. The physicians and chief surgeon recommended men to fill vacancies, or to be appointed as additional mates.[59] In the summer of 1755 Napier had recommended that the general hospital be broken up, and the surgeons and mates divided among the regiments,

[59] This board was inaugurated in 1756, at Cumberland's suggestion, W.O. 26: 23, pp. 57, 179.

since the forces were so scattered that a general hospital
seemed of little use. The suggestion fortunately was not
followed; there continued to be general hospital buildings
at New York, Albany, and Halifax, but the problem of
reaching scattered regiments was partly solved by the
installation of a "flying hospital", as in Flanders during
the previous war.[60] General hospitals were fitted with
lock beds and bolsters, six feet by three, with blankets,
sheets, and necessary utensils. The nurses in attendance
probably came from the ranks of the women who followed
the army, six to a company, sometimes one to every
twenty-five men; these women usually had their hands
full in preparing food, washing linen, and in general assisting "in keeping the men clean".[61] Some of the surgeons knew their business; Richard Huck (Huck-Saunders) served later in various London hospitals and was a
Fellow of the Royal College of Physicians before his
death. A true "original", Huck brought to everything
he did the rarest wit in Loudoun's army; his private

[60] The high quality of the hospital in Flanders can be deduced from a
manuscript report in the Cumberland Papers, entitled The Oeconomy of the
British Hospital in the Low Countries, in all its Branches, drawn up by Mr.
James Pringle, Comptroller, 1748. The index refers to such main headings as
Nurses' Tickets, Daily Abstract, Table of Diets, Diet Book, Steward's Re-
turn of Provisions, Register of Provisions, Daily Entries and Discharges,
Subsistence Receipts, Register of Stores, Rules to be observed by Servants
and Nurses, Register of Servants and Nurses' Wages, Register of Incidental
Charges, Cash Book—showing altogether a well-organized and complicated
system in practice.

The Forces in Germany in 1758 likewise made use of "flying hospitals."
Historical Manuscripts Commission *Report*, Various Collections, VIII, p. 452.

[61] Report from the *Strafford* to Loudoun, asking for an allowance of
women, April 20, 1756, Gravesend, LO 1065. Provisions were allowed for only
six women to a company; they were not permitted to ride on wagons, General
Orders, September 19, 1756, LO 1538. Provisions were issued only to women
in the field, where they could not maintain themselves in any other way; in
garrison they could so maintain themselves, HM 1717, vol. 4, August 14,
1757.

letters are mixtures of classical quotations and pert common sense criticism; while even his official communications are couched in a language unusual enough for the army: "I hereby certifie, that Captain William Morris of His Majesty's forty eighth Regiment of Foot labours under such a Complication of Diseases, as will render him forever incapable of performing the Duties, and supporting the Fatigues of a military Life."[62]

The regimental surgeons and mates were neither as skilled nor as well equipped with buildings and supplies as those of the general hospital. The customary regimental staff contained but one surgeon and one mate, though Loudoun had permission to appoint an additional mate to each battalion, to be paid out of contingencies. He made a further allowance to the regiments to cover hospital expenses, of £6 10s. a muster, "occasioned by a demand from the 2d battalion of the Royal or 1st regiment of £295 for a regimental hospital in Nova Scotia."[63] This considerable reduction in what appears to have been a justifiable demand is evidence that the regimental hospital service was none too well supported. The mates were often scattered; wherever one went in America, he might find a surgeon's mate. There was one with Johnson's Indians, another with the provincials at Number Four.

In the fall of 1757 there were few regiments that did not have from fifteen to twenty men in the general hospital, and forty to forty-five sick in their tents or quarters. At the beginning of that campaign Loudoun's eleven regiments averaged thirty men sick in quarters, and thirty-five in the general hospital. That was about seven per cent

---

[62] May 16, 1757, LO 3640, with a note in Loudoun's hand, "He tells me that besides his bad State of health he has Rupter will nearly fill his Hatt."

[63] Memorial of John McColne, surgeon to the 2d battalion of the Royals, LO 4728; HM 1717, vol. 2, December 25, 1757.

of the total number of effectives. Not only were men liable "to the inveterate fluxes they have in this country", but they suffered from the excessively salt meat, even though that diet was relieved by fresh greens and fresh meat, or by spruce beer as an anti-scorbutic. Men suffering from the scurvy were regularly sent to the Jerseys, where they might enjoy abundance of fresh vegetables. Prevost's battalion, which was, one hopes, an exception, had men with "fitts", consumption, ruptures, ulcers, men who were blind, sciatic, asthmatic, and rheumatic. Men with venereal diseases were usually compelled to keep their places in the line; smallpox patients were isolated.[64]

The chaplains in Loudoun's army, who were attached to the regimental staffs, deserve a word. Even though the commander in chief and his aides might consider it diplomatic to attend church and occupy the governors' pews at their invitation, the army in general reflected the spiritual apathy of some parts of the eighteenth-century Church of England. Of twenty-one regiments in the winter of 1757, but seven chaplains were present, though six more were officiating by deputy, on Sundays, Wednesdays, and Fridays. Chaplains are marked absent on the returns either by the leave of Loudoun himself, or of the "Governor of Ireland", or sometimes simply "not joined", or "absent", or "left behind".[65] But a regimental chaplaincy was a plum worth having, 6s. 8d. a day, and Loudoun had numerous applications from which to fill vacancies. He often chose men for the service they might render in addition to their calling; on Sir William Johnson's recommendation he appointed John Ogilvie, who preached to the Indians in their own language and was especially useful among the Mohawks, to be a chaplain in the Royal Ameri-

<hr>

[64] General Orders, August 2, 1757, LO 3576.

[65] Not until 1760 did the War Office refuse pay to absent chaplains unless they were represented by deputies, W.O. 1: 5, p. 276.

cans; four years later Amherst singled him out for especial praise. Michael Schlatter, the leading clergyman among the Germans in Pennsylvania, recommended by Penn, likewise became a chaplain in the 60th. Loudoun went to considerable pains to find a place for Michael Houdin, a missionary and parson of Trenton, because his knowledge of Canada, and his ability to continue to acquire such knowledge, rendered him of unique value. The chaplaincy of the 48th was bought for Houdin at a cost of £300, the deputy paymaster general paying that sum out of the contingencies, and making it up by stopping three shillings a day from the four absent chaplains. The more typical applicant was the sincere and pompous provincial clergyman, such a man as Theodorus Freelinghous, who declared that in spite of his name he was an Englishman born, that he admired the English language and the English constitution above any other, that he wanted to be an Englishman by office as he was by birth and inclination, "And that the great God of Heaven lift up the Light of his Countenance on your Lordship, that his gracious Presence be with you everywhere, especially in the High Places of the Field and of the Wilderness, to fight for you and to save you, to lead you on conquering and to conquer, prospering and to prosper, and that having done great and valiant Things in this, you may in the eternal World shine as a Star of the first Magnitude in glorious Immortality, is the sincere and most hearty Prayer, My Lord.''[66]

Of the various miscellaneous problems with which Loudoun had to deal, none was as annoying as that arising out of the establishment of the four independent companies of New York. That establishment, which was dated in 1700, permitted a ten per cent deduction from the pay of the men to provide for two surgeons and a chaplain.

[66] October 20, 1756, LO 2054.

The privates therefore received less than those in regiments. Since the companies had existed for half a century with no effective supervision from British offices, they had become simply a source of profit to their officers, who pocketed the entire subsistence and did not trouble to recruit. When Loudoun arrived, the companies lacked forty to sixty of their full complement of ninety-nine men each, and were badly trained and equipped. He saw no way to get them completed and put into order except by making them into a marching regiment of foot, with a new and proper establishment; but though he urged the scheme on Barrington, the Treasury refused to approve a change. Loudoun changed the officers and improved the discipline, but could not fill the ranks, and in January, 1758, the four companies numbered but two hundred and fifty-three men.[67] The three independent companies of South Carolina had been formed out of Oglethorpe's regiment when it was reduced in 1748, with officers who had served with him,[68] and they were therefore in better condition than the New York companies. Bouquet found them nearly complete, but "in indifferent shape", and their arms, which had been issued to Oglethorpe's in 1738, almost worn out.[69]

As the legal channel through which the military law, as described in the Mutiny Act, reached British troops in America, Loudoun issued warrants for the holding of general courts martial, which tried officers, acted as a court of first instance in cases such as theft, mutiny, desertion, and sleeping on guard, for which the penalty might be

[67] S. M. Pargellis, "The Four Independent Companies of New York," in *Essays in Colonial History.*

[68] List of Officers in Oglethorpe's, with remarks, S.P. 44: 181, f. 371.

[69] Muster rolls of the three independent companies in South Carolina, August 25, 1756, LO 3034, 3057, 3099; Bouquet to Loudoun, June 23, 1757, LO 3871.

death, and heard cases on appeal from regimental courts martial. Loudoun, or the commanding officer of a district, passed upon all sentences, exercised the royal clemency if advisable, and signed death-warrants. The provost marshal, the police officer of the army, acted with his assistants as executioner; in camp or garrison the provost made his rounds and arrested all violators of general orders as well as the articles of war, and confined them either in a military prison or in a special room of a civil prison turned over to his use by a civil officer. The severest punishment for enlisted men, short of death, was whipping, on the bare back with a cat and nine tails. Samuel Leach of Rogers' Rangers got five hundred lashes for refusing to proceed on a scouting expedition until he had had his allowance of rum. A soldier who stole from a sutler was given two thousand lashes and drummed out of the regiment with a halter and a label on his breast. John Anderson of Connecticut refused to turn out with the guard, and when his captain drew a sword called out to his mates to stand by him; he got a thousand lashes. At Halifax a soldier drunk and asleep on sentry duty received a like number. Sergeant Robert Beckett went beyond the limits of the camp to shoot ducks, was captured by Indians, escaped; he was reduced, given a thousand lashes, and drummed out of camp. James Derwood of the 44th got a thousand for stealing a greatcoat from one of the Connecticut officers; and Thomas Hopkins of the 60th, for stealing two ten-dollar bills from his dead master. John Burney of the 60th got a thousand lashes for stealing a pound of butter from the stores, which he was guarding as sentry; and John Alexander a like number for stealing a shirt from the line. John Thomas of the Rhode Island regiment got five hundred lashes for trying to pass counterfeit dollars, which he had made himself, having first borrowed a dollar with which to form a mold.

Whipping was the usual punishment for desertion. James Grayer of the 45th received five hundred of his thousand lashes the day after sentence was passed, a hundred at the head of the 22d, a hundred at the 2d battalion of the 60th, a hundred at the 48th, a hundred at the 17th, a hundred at the 55th, "and the rest of his punishment when the Surjean of the regiment think him able to bear it." In other cases corporal punishment was inflicted "as far as the men can bear". But often Loudoun reduced a sentence by five hundred or a thousand lashes, and sometimes remitted it altogether.

For officers the only severe penalty was dismissal from the service. Lieutenant Nathaniel Williams of the 51st was broken for disobeying Craven's orders, for behaving in a scandalous manner unbecoming the character of an officer and gentleman by selling rum, and for not transmitting regular accounts of the pay of his detachment. Ensign David Roche of the 47th and Volunteer Alexander McAllaster of the 2d battalion of the Royals began a dispute over gratuitously-rendered advice at a billiard game and went on to employ swords, cudgels, canes, pistols, and fists; the former was discharged from the service for conduct unbecoming an officer and gentleman, and the latter, a young man of good character who had been but six months in the service, made public acknowledgment of his bad behavior at the head of his regiment and received public reprimand. Ensign Charles Sherriff of the 45th was adjudged guilty of breaking the 2d article of the 7th section of the articles of war by sending Ensign Witherhead of the 47th a challenge to fight a duel, but the court realised that he had received such abusive treatment from Witherhead that if he had not acted as he did, he would have been guilty of conduct unbecoming the character of an officer and a gentleman, and liable to a breach of the 23d article of the 15th section. Both of them were discharged the service, but in consideration of Sherriff's good character Loudoun reinstated him. Lieutenant Samuel Knowles of the Massachusetts regiment, for saying that no one at Fort Edward had a right to command the Massachusetts soldiers to remain there, had his sword broken over his head at the head of his regiment, was banished from the camp, and dismissed the service. Captain John Pickering of the New Hampshire regiment was cashiered for "absolutely refusing to do his duty, speaking words tending to mutiny, and defaming his superior officer."

Deserters were seldom shot or hanged; they were too precious. When recruits cost from five to seven pounds apiece to acquire, the army hesitated to put men to death. Courts martial usually took into account the offender's age, length of service, degree of "simplicity", and excuses. Some of the latter, such as being captured by Indians when easing one's self, seem to have become quite standardized. Philip Steers of the New York regiment was acquitted of desertion; he had sent his Indian stockings home to his mother at Schenectady to be mended, and had no other way of getting them except going after them. Of twenty-six cases of desertion tried before a general court martial at Philadelphia in January, 1757, four were acquitted, four condemned to death, and the rest given from two hundred to a thousand lashes by the court; of these sentences Loudoun remitted twelve, including two of the death sentences, and abated the punishments of five others. Sometimes condemned deserters were reprieved at the last moment. "I have ordered Wm Richards to be shott whom I pardoned last year for the same offence, and have pardoned Roswald Brown as it appears to be his first desertion but the pardon not to be intimated to him till he comes to the place of execution and sees the other shott." At Halifax Loudoun pardoned all deserters except one, a notorious offender. In Pennsylvania in the summer of 1757 Stanwix's Germans in the 60th found the temptation to run away too great to resist; he lost fifty by desertion, recovered eighteen, and hanged only four. But at times the penalty of death was exacted, always attended with as much publicity as possible; the 35th, the 42d, and the 1st battalion of the 60th stood at solemn attention when Edward Jaffreys of the 35th was hanged. After one such execution the general order appeared: "His Lordship hopes and expects that the example of yesterday will effectually prevent the reigning vices of desertion and theft so very unbecoming soldiers, his Lordship being resolved not to pardon such as shall be convicted of the above crimes. . . ." Loudoun was well aware that the attitude of the inhabitants encouraged desertion. He praised coöperation from them, as when the Schenectady justices fined local inhabitants for hiding deserters' plaids and giving them sailor's jackets; and he denounced the deliberate neglect of civilian officers, as when, at Bristol, he told Justice Morris that if he caught any man whom the jailers had let escape on sham debts, he would hang him in the middle of the town and let him hang there for a month.[70]

Loudoun drew the line, as distinctly as it was drawn in England, between civil crimes committed by soldiers and breaches of the articles of war. The former were tried by civil courts. James Smith of Schuyler's New Jersey regiment was turned over by a court martial to a civil court for a murder at Schenectady. On the same day that Lou-

[70] The separate facts above are from the general court martial records, in W.O. 71: 44, 127, 128, 129, 130, 131, 132; General Orders, September 16, 1756, a general pardon of all deserters serving in other corps, LO 1538; Stanwix to Loudoun, September 1, 1757, LO 4372; September 26, 1757, LO 4534; Stanwix to St. Clair, September 10, 1757, LO 4444; Abercromby to Loudoun, December 20, 1756, LO 2373. HM 1717, vol. 3, March 28, April 18, 1757.

doun issued his warning to Judge Morris at Bristol, four soldiers lay in jail there awaiting trial by civil courts. A plea from Ensign Skinner of the 35th to save his servant, a soldier in the regiment, confined "for ravishing the landlord's daughter of 7 years of age and giveing her the French disease", met the reply that the law should take its course, and that no officer should interfere. At Halifax, in a somewhat similar case, Lieutenant Colonel Rollo of the 22d confined three soldiers in his regiment for ravishing the wife of a civilian. James Monk, the justice of the peace, went at once to Loudoun, who "was pleased to declare that he was come here to protect all His Majesty's Subjects and would not suffer any injuries to be done them, but that all offenders should be resigned to the ordinary Course of Justice." Monk thereupon issued his warrant for their arrest, and asked Rollo for a file of soldiers to assist the constable in conducting the men to his house for trial.

Out of this varied mass of information regarding manifold aspects of army administration the figure of Loudoun emerges with a certain clarity. No genius in war, and wedded by temperament and training to the lessons of the European school, he took over a command in which men were untrained, improperly armed, sometimes unfed and unpaid, and in which officers did their duty as it pleased them, and he succeeded in the course of a year in producing a force that knew the fundamental duties of the soldier, and that could not complain of its equipment, of its supply, or of the spirit of its officers. Loudoun never forgot that he was first of all creating an army, and that whatever hindered the smooth operation of an army had to be changed for the better. Sometimes he was unsuccessful in soliciting ministerial support for his proposals, as in the case of varied rates of pay and of the independent companies; sometimes the ministry failed to support him, as when it left him with inefficient officers. Such matters he could not remedy. But in his general supervision of the distribution of provisions, his concern for an adequate transportation service, and his care in providing the scouting or ranging forces, he made beneficial and in some cases permanent changes. Under him the British army came to resemble an army encamped on alien territory, for it was practically complete in itself, and relied as little as possible upon the abilities or whims of the countryside. To the management of the personnel and to the welfare of the troops he brought a stern sense of justice and a high conception of the meaning of duty. The general results of his administration cannot be minimized; this army, reinforced by nine regiments in 1757, which came to a service prepared to receive them, won Canada within the next two years. Whether or not Loudoun might himself have led it to victory is not the question; it was an instrument fit for victory, and its preparation under conditions that were nearly always discouraging is a fair monument to Loudoun's patient pertinacity.

CHAPTER XII

LOUDOUN AND PITT

THE reasons for Loudoun's recall were largely political. Though Pitt returned to office in July, 1757, with the support of Newcastle's majority in the House of Commons, he considered that as long as his chief antagonist, the duke of Cumberland, held independently the command of the army, he would never be able to exercise over it that plenitude of power which a civil minister ought to possess. This opinion became with Pitt more than a conviction, it was rather an *idée fixe*. He seemed to see the whole of the army and navy leagued with Cumberland against him, willing to go to any lengths to discredit him politically and to reinstate in civil power their military leader upon whom in large measure their advancement depended.

When Loudoun and Holburne abandoned the Louisbourg expedition, in the face of his direct orders and in spite of the opinion of the council of war, and when Loudoun's brief explanatory letter gave inconclusive reasons for such conduct, Pitt leaped to the conclusion that "some Hints" had been sent to America from another source. The opinion of the rest of the ministry was divided. Halifax thought Loudoun's conduct "not only irreproachable but Highly judicious"; Lord George Sackville blamed the phrasing of the letter, but believed the decision a proper one; Mansfield had exactly the same opinion; Devonshire was clear on every point but the council of war; Fox thought Loudoun had "done right and acted sensibly".[1]

1 These opinions were either expressed directly by various ministers to

Newcastle and Anson thought that Loudoun should have
gone to Louisbourg and taken the chance, while Hardwicke, saying that he had never seen such a "papier
raisonée" as Loudoun's letter in his life, went on to recall
what was said of Loudoun at his appointment, that he
"might be a very good Colonel, but was absolutely unfit
for chief command." "What could he mean [said Hard-
wicke] by taking a final Resolution in direct contradiction
to the unanimous opinion of the Council of War: and
That, upon a single letter from the Admiral, without even
advising and deliberating with that Admiral, who was but
in Halifax Harbour, and could have met him as easily as
going to the next door. Much Stress is laid on the advanced Season of the year; but they had lost almost a
month at Halifax in doing nothing, except repairing a
mast or two, and such Trifling damages, as must happen
in all Voyages. I don't find that Sr Charles Hardy was
consulted in the last instance. There are some obscure
passages in the letter. What had the Council of War done
to give offence? And what is meant by the *Construction of
words,* and *difficulties arising from thence?* These are
mysterious to me, as it is also why our Fleet might not
have made their passage as soon as M^{on} de Bois la Motte
from Brest. I presume the same wind would serve both
squadrons the greatest part of the way. . . . But in short,
it seems to me that they all proceed upon the *Byng-
Principle,*—that Nothing is to be undertaken where there
is Risque or Danger."[2] But in spite of these unworthy

Captain Cotterell, whom Loudoun sent to England to present his reasons
(Cotterell to Loudoun, October 8, 1757, LO 4606), or transmitted to John
Calcraft through his patron Fox (Calcraft to Loudoun, October 8, 1757, LO
4611).

[2] Hardwicke to Newcastle, September 5, 1757, Additional MSS. 32,873,
f. 469. He added a characteristic query: "According to these Gentlemen's
accounts, what a Country are we throwing away all this Blood and Treasure
about? It is unapproachable either in Summer, Autumn, or Winter."

strictures, Hardwicke saw no grounds for Pitt's suspicions of Cumberland's interference: "It don't occur to
me what purpose it could answer in that quarter of the
world." Nevertheless Pitt would have insisted upon Loudoun's recall in September if there had been anyone else
to replace him. Cornwallis seemed to be the only available
general, and no high opinion was entertained of his abilities.[3]

Early in October the failure of Sir John Mordaunt's
expedition against Rochefort added fresh fuel to Pitt's
indignation. From the moment that he planned that enterprise, in opposition to the opinion of his cabinet, he
had entertained doubts of the willingness of land and sea
officers.[4] The reasons for its disastrous outcome he therefore imputed "to a prevailing opinion, that neither the
King, nor the Duke, wish'd Success to this Expedition,
treated it as a Chimera of Mr. Pitt's: which must mis-
carry, in order to shew, that the only practicable thing, to
be done, was to employ Our whole Force in *A German
War;* and this he combines with Lord Loudoun's late conduct in North America.'"[5] Unless the army acted in support of the measures of the administration, he did not see
how things could go on.

At this point the unexpected occurred. Cumberland,
who had commanded an army in Germany that summer
for the defense of Hanover, under instructions from the
king which handicapped his independence of action, found
himself confronted with a superior French force and

[3] Newcastle to Hardwicke, September 3, 1757, Additional MSS. 35,417.

[4] Business with Ld. Mansfield, September 7, 1757, Additional MSS. 32,997,
f. 233. "Pitt grew warm, and said, He would defend the measure of the Expedition, at the Hazard of his Life; that the Country was in the Way to be
undone, But that he would do his utmost to save it." Jones to Hardwicke,
September 5, 1757, Additional MSS. 35,417, f. 45.

[5] Newcastle to Hardwicke, October 8, 1757, Additional MSS. 32,874, f.
473.

signed in accordance with the latitude given in those instructions the inglorious convention of Klosterzeven, by which his German troops were disbanded. Favorable as the treaty was under the circumstances, the king had to repudiate it to save his name and laid the whole blame upon his son. Cumberland made no defense, but resigned his military employments and retired to private life. That he should so long have retained the king's support in an age when "the law of conflict between successive generations of the Royal Family", as Namier calls it, inevitably drove princes into opposition, is in itself a tribute to his high sense of loyalty and filial duty.[6]

Pitt considered that his opportunity had come. In choosing Cumberland's successor who would direct and control all purely military affairs within the army itself, Pitt was emphatic that he should have no voice whatsoever in determining policy. Newcastle's suggestion that Sir John Ligonier be given the supreme command of the army "in Great Britain and America" delighted him: *"He concludes that a Com^n of Commander in Chief in Great Britain and America revokes Lord Loudoun's Comm^n under the great Seal,* and He wished and desired it might.'' But when the question was discussed in a cabinet, Mansfield objected strongly to the insertion of *America* in Ligonier's commission, for it would make Ligonier responsible for all occurrences abroad, and "in the Ticklish situation of the Colonies, nobody could tell what effect it might have over there." Newcastle himself thought that Loudoun's recall ought to be treated as a distinct question and not be confused with Ligonier's appointment, and said that he had suggested the wording simply to ensure a *real Command in Chief* over the army

---

6 Charteris, *Cumberland and the Seven Years' War;* Ilchester, *Henry Fox, First Lord Holland,* II, 97-103; L. B. Namier, *England in the Age of the American Revolution,* p. 63.

and had never meant it to convey a power to the Commander in chief in England to send orders to America independently of the civil minister. The cabinet finally agreed to give Ligonier a commission as general and commander in chief of the army in Great Britain only, revoking Cumberland's commission as captain general, and to instruct the commander in chief in America to correspond with him upon the *"State of the Army only."*[7]

As far as Loudoun was concerned, this breach between Cumberland and the king meant that his most powerful supporter had no longer the influence to save him. Cumberland himself had no doubts of the wisdom of Loudoun's conduct. After telling of his resignations, he acknowledged the receipt of Loudoun's latest letters, and added, "I have read them all with that Satisfaction your Dispatches have always given me, as these latter ones have afforded me fresh Proofs of that Diligence, care, Prudence & Zeal with which you have all along exerted yourself in His Majesty's Service, Since you have been in North America".[8] But Loudoun's other friends still had influence, and perhaps more important still, the opinion of the press and of the London streets, in October and November, turned in his favor. A mezzotint print of his portrait sold "prodigiously" and was copied in the *London Magazine* for October.[9]

In November it seemed to be the general opinion that

[7] Newcastle to Hardwicke, October 23, 1757, Additional MSS. 35,417, f. 127; Hardwicke to Newcastle, October 16, 1757, Additional MSS. 32,875, f. 144; Memorandum for the king, Additional MSS. 32,875, f. 191; Hardwicke to Newcastle, October 24, 1757, Additional MSS. 32,875, f. 253.

[8] Cumberland to Loudoun, November 26, 1757, Cranbourn Lodge, received March 12, 1758, LO 4907.

[9] Calcraft to Loudoun, October 8, 1757, LO 4611. This portrait, painted by Allan Ramsay in 1747, was engraved by J. Faber in 1755. Winsor in *Narrative and Critical History of America*, V, 506, reproduces a mezzotint of the same portrait by Spooner, from J. C. Smith, *British Mezzotint Portraits*, p. 1343.

Loudoun would remain in America, though the command of the projected expedition against Louisbourg would be a separate and distinct one. Ligonier's list of forces for 1758 divided the army in America into two parts: one, of 11,401 men, including a reinforcement from England of two regiments, was to be destined for Louisbourg, under the command of Amherst, with Howe, Lawrence, and Wolfe as brigadiers; the other of 12,568 men for the campaign in New York, was to remain under Loudoun, with Abercromby, Webb, and Hopson. Ligonier added the instructive note: "The Earl of Loudoun to avail Himself of as many Provincials, as possible, in order to defend the Colonies, and to act Offensively, if He finds it practicable, —the Concert of which Operations to be left entirely to His Lordship, as He best knows the Country, and must proportion His Attempts to the Strength He can draw from the different Provinces."[10]

But Pitt during this time was collecting all the information he could about American affairs and finding justification for his distrust of Loudoun. The sources of his information are suggestive. Shirley was in London, still defending himself from the charges of mismanagement. He may have been the author of the suggestion which Pitt entertained, that an army of seventeen thousand provincials attack Quebec by the Kennebec river route—a suggestion not adopted because the country about the Kennebec was unknown, and far from any base of supplies. Craven, who had been kept in North America from May to October in the *Herriott* packet which Loudoun detained, arrived early in December, full of bitterness.[11] Webb's letters justifying his inaction at Fort William

[10] Received, December 7, 1757, from Marshall Ligonier, Additional MSS. 33,047, f. 108. A fuller series of remarks, unsigned, but ending with the same note as above, is in G.D. 8: 96.

[11] Craven to Pitt, February 1, 1758, G.D. 8:96.

Henry by the scanty forces at his disposal were sent off in August.[12] Lord Charles Hay, still under arrest at Halifax, was writing to the secretary at state: "I shall say nothing at present of what is going on here, only that I am a melancholy witness of such a scene as I believe no age can parallel."[13] Of far greater importance, because less prejudiced, were letters from John Bradstreet to Sir Richard Lyttelton, pointing out the immense value of the fur trade, denouncing the policy which conducted the war in America with so scanty a force when so many men were available, and urging that forty-six thousand men be employed in 1758, thirty thousand against Louisbourg and Quebec, ten thousand against Ticonderoga, and six thousand against Montreal by way of Lake Ontario.[14]

Probably of more significance still in shaping Pitt's opinions were the file of letters from General Abercromby or his aide de camp to James Abercromby, the Virginia agent. They contained no direct criticism of Loudoun, on the contrary high praise, but their general effect was to suggest that desirable changes could be made. Such a passage as the following, for instance, was capable of two interpretations: "There is no foundation for any coolness betwixt Lord L——n and Mr. Webb— those who are eyewitnesses of the pains and application his Lordship gives to the publick concerns, would be highly to blame if they did not coöperate in rendering his burthen lighter in place of clogging the wheels—that single article of writing is too much for one man, which

12 Webb to Barrington, August 17, 1757, W.O. 1: 1.

13 Hay to Pitt, February 26, 1758, Chatham Papers, State of North America, 1758-1763. Richard Bulkley to Cunningham, October 6, 1757, LO 4599, with the information that Hay was writing long dispatches to Pitt.

14 Bradstreet to Lyttelton, August 15, September 5, 1757, G.D. 8: 95. Bradstreet asked for the government of New Jersey, or for the colonelcy of a regiment of rangers, or for the command of the third expedition he suggested.

he does all with his own hand, trusting his Secretary only
to copy, committing the common orders of detail to M G
Abercromby and sometimes admitting him to answer a
letter relative theretoo. As he is supposed to have no
great aversion to writing of which his correspondents
have often reason to complain that gentleman might be
easily prevailed upon to take some part of that task,—so
would his [Loudoun's] aide de camp Cunningham who is
very capable, but his Lordship's great anxiety makes him
take all on himself from morning to night, in so much,
that it's surprising how he holds it out.''[15] Whether General Abercromby was the author of this letter or not, he
must have had cognizance of it, and knew that Pitt
would see it. These letters partly explain why Abercromby was chosen as Loudoun's successor. It was apparently this highly unethical procedure of Abercromby's
that prompted Calcraft to write of his ''dirty behavior''
later in 1758, when he was recalled; his ''cunning has not
done him much good.''[16]

Finally Sir Charles Hardy, who arrived in London
early in December, spent much time with the ministry,
and especially with Pitt. His remarks were as vivid as
they had been two years before, when he criticized Shirley. The troops in America, said Hardy, ''can't stir without their curling irons and brown paper; the French
make winter expeditions, why can't we?'' Loudoun all too
clearly put military power above civil, had not explored
the country, was exerting too much authority over the
inhabitants, was not treating provincial troops as they
deserved, put slights on governors by writing to others in
their provinces, interfered in the government of the Jerseys, had no boats on Lake George, had given the governor at New York but two roughs of the drum and not

15 To Mr. James Abercromby, May 30, 1757, G.D. 8: 95.
16 Calcraft to Loudoun, September 14, 1758, LO 5921.

three, had left Webb too weak, and had committed a New
York baker to the provost's.[17] From such information
Pitt drew his conclusions: that the war in America could
not be won unless large bodies of provincial troops took
the field, and that Loudoun's conduct, instead of unifying, had further separated and antagonized the colonies.

Early in December Loudoun's dispatches of October
arrived. They gave Pitt fresh grounds for dissatisfaction.
Loudoun enclosed no plan of operations for 1758—the result of his hasty and ill-advised decision of August.[18] But
at the same time Pitt learned of Loudoun's letters to
Cumberland, which, together with copies of his letters to
the ministry, were sent to Calcraft in an open box so that
Fox too could read them. In his private letter to Cumberland Loudoun told of his scheme for a winter expedition
against Ticonderoga, and added that he was not mention-
ing it to the ministers, because so many people read their
mail that it could not be kept a secret.[19] It was a tactical
error; Loudoun's greatest mistake was to attach himself
too closely to the political fortunes of his patrons. Pitt
interpreted it as additional evidence of Loudoun's unwillingness to obey his commands, and of a conspiracy of his
political enemies.

One further episode contributed to Pitt's fears of military interference. The court martial of Sir John Mordaunt, on the charge of disobeying the orders from the
king and the secretary of state, began on December 14.
Pitt was called to testify. In answer to at least one question, whether expert opinion at the ministerial council
which planned the details of the expedition thought a cer-

[17] Calcraft to Loudoun, December 29, 1757, LO 5140; Hardy to Pitt, December 14, 1757 [G.D. 8: 95], enclosing his thoughts "upon the conversation I had the honour of having with you the other morning."

[18] See *ante*, p. 252.

[19] Loudoun to Cumberland, October 17, 1757, LO 4642.

tain fort could be taken by sea, he launched forth a long-winded reply,[20] and according to Cotterell's version was stopped by General Cholmondeley, the president, from speaking "a little more than was consistent with the nature of his testimony."[21] Such a direct affront from the military fanned Pitt's indignation to the extreme, and when he spoke in the house two days later, a place where civil authority reigned supreme, he let himself go. There was a determined resolution, he declaimed on this "very solemn Occasion," both in naval and military commanders against any vigorous exertion of the national power in the service of their country, and no man could be found to execute a plan; in North America there was one gentleman from whom the nation had great expectations who had done nothing from July 9 to August 5, who would do nothing in the future, who had expressed the greatest contempt for the civil power by virtue of which he held his office, in neglecting to send either letters or plans.[22] Sometime between the 14th and the 16th of December Pitt decided upon Loudoun's recall.[23] The official reason was for not properly corresponding with the secretary of state and neglecting to send plans for 1758. When Loudoun arrived in London, he learned the reasons from Pitt's own lips: "Went to Mr Pitts had a very Gratious reception Then told me that the objection he had to me was that I had given my information in on other Quarters that he found I did not choose to correspond with the Civil Ministers of the King That he had been very fully informed that I was offended with his letter that I received at Halifax and had taken a resolution of not sending them any plan for future opperations that he had

---

[20] W.O. 71: 45.   [21] Cotterell to Loudoun, January 9, 1758, LO 5374.

[22] J. Almon, *Review of Pitt's Administration*, p. 42.

[23] Hardwicke to Newcastle, December 17, 1757, Additional MSS. 32,876, f. 321.

very patent [?] information of that That the want of a
Plan had putt him to great Difficultys and he was obliged
to do the best he could that on finding I would not correspond with him it was impossible to go one and that in this
situation eather he must not be minister or I could not be
General. For that reason he had given the King the advice he did about recalling me . . . That as to the Milli-
tary Part whether it was right or not to attack Louisbourg he was not a Judge of it that must be left to the
Judgement of the People of the Tread He likewise mentioned that Frase in my letter to the Duke where I sade
I should not mention that to the ministers.'' To which
Loudoun replied that he corresponded with the office, and
not with the person, and his August letter was begun to
Holderness, though finished to Pitt; that Pitt was certainly well informed on his decision to send home no plan,
for he had the information from the same person [Sir
Charles Hardy] who gave Loudoun the advice; and that
he would not justify his decision, being wrong in it; that
he thought in August and still thought Pitt's orders
harsh, in that they left no discretionary power to the
commander; ''that since he saw those things in the light
he did I thought he was in the Right to give the advice he
did of recalling me.'' Pitt assured him he bore him no personal ill will; ''I told Mr. Pitt Sir I have not the Honour
to be known to you personally or you would not have had
the opinion of me you have had . . . And so we parted
seemingly good friends.''[24]

From all this evidence it is possible to understand the
various factors contributing to Pitt's point of view in the
autumn of 1757. He was jealous of Cumberland personally and distrusted anyone under Cumberland's influence.
As he feared the possible constitutional effects of the con-

24 HM 1717, vol. 5, London, June 6, 1758.

tinuance in high military office of the most capable member of the royal family, who could not be removed by ordinary parliamentary means, so he sympathized with that American opinion which saw in Loudoun's command the supremacy of military over civil power. Since he considered himself alone capable of saving England by winning the American war, he could not work with a general who visualized his post as one of initiative and responsibility. Finally he convinced himself that victory could be gained only by utilizing provincial aid, which could not be had except by giving to the colonies what they desired.

As matters stood at the end of 1757, some change was necessary in the conduct of American affairs. Loudoun could scarcely have gone on without further support from England, and perhaps some increase of power. He had too much to do. It was during this period that he was corresponding with the northern colonies over the voting of rangers for the winter; with Pownall over quartering; with Sharpe over Maryland's challenge to his authority; with Fitch over the New London recruiting fracas; with Wentworth about the Portsmouth riots. For a month he was in upper New York; and from between the dull lines of Montrésor's journal a characteristic picture of him emerges, incessantly busy and precise, demanding plans of forts and returns of engineers, sending back incomplete returns, making a hurried trip to Fort Edward, soundly condemning—being "excessive angry"—an inadequate storehouse at Saratoga, giving orders for improvements in the road, and for surveying the water transportation on the river.[25] He planned during that period a winter expedition against Ticonderoga, but the pressure of provincial business later compelled him to turn over to Lord Howe complete charge of preparations.

[25] Montrésor Journals, New York Historical Society *Collections*, 1881, p. 47.

Had it succeeded, he could have retired with better grace, for it would have redeemed the failures of the summer. Unfortunately, when in February the sledges were ready for the howitzers, the scaling ladders finished, the cream of the troops selected by Howe, a heavy snow, five feet at Fort Edward, and two on the lake itself, put an end to the scheme. For there were no snowshoes. The wood for them was lying at Fort Edward, and Rogers had been entrusted with their construction. Rogers excused himself for his failure by saying that two hundred rangers with snowshoes could open a path for any number of troops, but when Howe and his men reached the lake, they found it impossible to follow the rangers. Rogers set off gaily alone, to meet the superior force collected by the French, who had learned of the plan, in his unlucky but dramatic fight at Rogers' Rock.[26] During this same period dissatisfaction arose among some of Loudoun's officers. It was secretly fomented by Webb, who insinuated that since Loudoun, Abercromby, and Forbes were Scots, Englishmen stood no chance of promotion, and that under a less frugal commander officers could increase their perquisites. When Monro of the 35th died, Loudoun planned to promote to the lieutenant colonelcy Major Fletcher of the same regiment, but Webb encouraged all the majors in the army whose commissions antedated Fletcher's, though by a few days only, to ask the post for themselves. In the "party" he was thus forming, Burton and Gage were inclined to join. On at least one occasion, Captain Lee, swearing that the army was a parcel of Scots, and that Forbes had got his battalion by drinking the pretender's health with the duke of Bedford, proposed in the presence

26 Matthew Clarke to Loudoun, January 23, 1758, LO 5449; Loudoun to Howe, February 2, 1758, LO 5523; Report of Lieutenant Leslie, February 8, LO 5553; Abercromby to Loudoun, February 8, LO 5561; Howe to Loudoun, February 14, LO 5584; *Pitt Correspondence*, I, 193-4.

of Gage, Burton, Proby of the 55th, and several younger officers, his own toast, "A Head to the Army".[27]

Loudoun saw no way out of these difficulties except by the removal of those individuals who were working in opposition to him. He turned as a last resort to Argyll, the "Viceroy" of Scotland, the most powerful of his remaining supporters. In an extraordinarily frank letter he stated his difficulties: "My Sittuation is that, I am more a Slave to Business than any man alive by having not only the affairs of the Army as a Soldier to manage and that being divided in three or four places and each to provide for without one man to assist me but M. G. Abercromby or to consult with but him and he very often at a Distance from me in the time when I want his Advice most.

"Besides which I have an Eternal Negotiation to carry on with Governments 1500 miles in length where every Day Produces not only New Plans, which effect the carrying on the Service but likewise meet with all sorts of opposition in it. So that my Business Begines every Day the moment I am out of Bed and lasts from that time to Dinner and from then till nine at night and this from day to day without Intermission or even allowing myself an hower for any Amusements and this for want of propper Assistance under me.

"I have showed you in my other letter how matters go with Mr. Webb and what I imagine Mr. Pownel is about . . . Mr. Pownel is the vainest man alive and the most Ambitious but I may add to that the wrongest headed and the Falsest man I ever mett. His Plan is to be putt at the Head of all the Colonies in North America and he lookes on me as a Rival and from there Springes his Actions

[27] Loudoun to Argyll, February 14, 1758, LO 5599. HM 1717, vol. 2, October 29, November 26, December 15, 16, 1757; vol. 5, January 25, 1758.

altho I have told him I not only never had proposed any thing of that Kind but that I never had any such plan.

"But how I am to be Supported in carrying thro the Kings affairs in this country is more than I yet know . . . If [his criticism of Dinwiddie] had been published I should have had no more trouble with Governors and if I am not to be supported against Officers who shall endeavour to Rais Partys in an army at this Distance 'tis greatly better both for the King's Service and I think for me that some one that will be supported should have the Command and I be recalled. . . ."[28]

In that plan of conducting the war in the colonies by forming them into a union under a commander in chief, which had begun with the appointment of Braddock and had been strengthened by the powers given Loudoun in 1756, the next step in development would have been what Loudoun suggested, further support of his authority from England. By recalling him, Pitt put an end to that plan as completely as the Glorious Revolution of 1689 in England put an end to Andros's governor-generalship of New England, which also lasted but three years. Pitt broke the slow evolution towards a greater unifying and drawing together of the colonies; after his fall from office that evolution was resumed, when it was too late to have full effect. In its stead Pitt substituted the requisition system, the first time during this war when that commonly used term ought to be applied, for in 1755 and 1756 provincial troops took the field on their own initiative, and in 1757 by virtue of arrangements of commissioners or governors with the commander in chief. In later years of the war Amherst was enabled to reduce his correspondence with the governors to a minimum. Pitt wrote the letters to the governors asking for men and promising

28 Loudoun to Argyll, February 16, 1758, G.D. 8: 48.

financial assistance; the assembly voted them, and then
notified the commander in chief that they were on the
march; Amherst sent warrants for victualling them while
on the road at the usual fourpence a day, and named the
rendezvous; the assembly then collected from parliament
its reimbursement for the expenses of the campaign.
There was no pleading, no cajoling, and few threats.
Amherst's correspondence with Governor Hopkins of
Rhode Island, for instance, dwindled at times to two or
three letters a year, most of them only half a page or a
page in length, and dealing in cold and perfunctory fashion with matters of routine.[29] His letters to Wentworth
concern similar points: the raising and dispatching to the
rendezvous of provincial levies requested by Pitt; maintaining a proportion of them during the winter; the recruiting campaign of the regular army in 1762. A mere
hint, as on June 9, 1762, that New Hampshire would not
share in the next allotment of specie from England unless
recruits were raised, was enough to call forth fervid
protestations of eagerness.[30] With Fitch his correspondence was somewhat greater, for Fitch raised questions
concerning the conduct of regular regiments quartered
in the colony, and for three successive years urged in vain
parliamentary reimbursement for the expenses of the
Connecticut militia in marching to Fort Edward in 1757.[31]

The reason why this requisition system in the northern
colonies in the last part of the war ran so smoothly is not
far to seek. For the five campaigns after 1757 the colonies
received as reimbursement from Great Britain sums ag-
gregating £866,666 sterling. Those sums permitted the
colonies to do two things. In the first place they could be
as extravagant as they pleased in the raising of provin-

[29] W.O. 34: 24.

[30] Amherst to Wentworth, June 9, 1762, W.O. 34: 24, f. 237.

[31] W.O. 34: 28.

cial troops, serene in the knowledge that they would receive back a sum in proportion to the amounts they spent.
In 1758, for example, Massachusetts voted 6925 men, of
whom 6500 took the field for a period of five months; for
raising, clothing, and paying those men she put in a claim
of £103,809 sterling.[32] For that amount the Crown could
have raised, clothed, and paid for the same period of time
a thousand more men than did Massachusetts. In 1758
some twenty-one thousand provincials were in service at
one time or another during the campaign, though it would
be difficult to say just how many might have been counted
in September or October. For the £200,000 which parliament allotted to the colonies for their expenses in that
year the Crown could have kept up for five months twenty-
seven thousand regular troops, or for the whole year,
some ten thousand. The difference in cost was caused by
the exorbitant pay and the high bounty of eight pounds
sterling a man which many provincial assemblies offered.
In the second place, the specie or credit received from
Great Britain enabled the colonies to put their own financial structures in order, and to emerge from the war
which saddled Great Britain with an enormous debt comparatively free from obligations. Connecticut, for example, was able to keep taxation during the war itself down
to a low figure, to pay off practically the whole of her war
debt before 1763, and to lay up a credit in London banks
which permitted her to meet without taxation the ordinary expenses of civil government for some years after
the war was over.[33]

The only justification which could be advanced for
Pitt's destruction of a responsible commandership in
chief and for his reckless increase in the costs of the war

[32] G.D. 8: 96.
[33] L. H. Gipson, ''Connecticut Taxation and Parliamentary Aid,''
American Historical Review, XXXVI, 721-739.

was that the war could not have been won without a large
provincial army in the field and amenable provincial assemblies supporting it. But considerable doubt can be
thrown upon such a statement. By the end of 1757 the
French *troupes de la terre* and *de la Marine* were reduced
to seven thousand, and the whole number, including *milice*
and Indians, could not have been more than twenty-four
thousand.[34] Canada was suffering from a provision shortage. The British army, on the other hand, had in 1758
some twenty thousand regulars, well equipped, well disciplined, and well fed. They were nearly independent of
provincial aid in provisioning, transport, and scouting—
an efficient and mobile force, according to the standards
of the day. By 1758 the chief tactical problem in the interior was one of transportation, either across country to
Fort Duquesne, or by combined water and land carriage
to Fort Frontenac, Ticonderoga, Crown Point, and Montreal. Mobility was the primary necessity, and regular
troops stationed in northern New York could have been
on the march, with the batteaux and wagons belonging to
the army, as soon as the lake and rivers were free from
ice in the spring. Alone, they could have utilized the British advantage in the matter of climate, for French troops
could not leave their winter quarters in Montreal or
Quebec until two weeks after the British left Albany.
When Pitt encumbered Abercromby with some sixteen
thousand provincials, that advantage was lost. The provincials did not appear at Albany until after the middle
of June; by June 29 there were only 5960 of them at
Lake George,[35] and Abercromby's flotilla finally put out
from the lower end of the lake before the New Hampshire
regiment had arrived. This increase in the number of
forces rendered previous arrangements for transporta-

[34] W. Wood, *The Fight for Canada*, p. 63.
[35] Returns in the Abercromby Papers.

tion and provisioning insufficient; Howe was engaged in May and June in carrying supplies with far too few wagons.[36] Abercromby had to appeal to all justices of the peace to impress batteauxmen to take provisions to Stillwater. When finally his army invested Ticonderoga, on the 8th of July, the French had concentrated their forces to meet him. The provincial troops had been of no value up to that time, and the brunt of the attack itself was borne by Abercromby's eight regular battalions, a total of less than six thousand rank and file. Of the 1945 casualties, 1610 were regulars, and 335 provincial; 1429 of the regular rank and file were killed or wounded, 281 of the provincial.[37] Even if Abercromby had succeeded in taking the fort, he could not have moved his large and undisciplined army against Montreal.

These remarks are not meant to detract from the valuable services which provincials in small numbers undeniably rendered in 1758 and later years of the war. Lyman's advance party distinguished itself at the landing place at Ticonderoga, where Lord Howe was killed; Bradstreet's tiny force, which took Fort Frontenac in August, was composed largely of provincials accustomed to batteaux. Provincials fought at Niagara in 1759, and on Amherst's voyage down the St. Lawrence in 1760. For the most part they acted as workmen, repairing and building forts and roads, or as wagoners and batteauxmen, transporting provisions and supplies. These were useful and necessary services, but they scarcely justified the enlistment of fifteen to twenty thousand men at high rates.[38]

36 Abercromby to Howe, May 29, 1758, W.O. 34: 76, f. 125.

37 Return of Killed, Wounded, and Missing at Ticonderoga, W.O. 1: 1, f. 339.

38 Correspondence between Amherst and Lyman, W.O. 32: 43; Bradstreet to Amherst, W.O. 34: 57, f. 45; Amherst to Bradstreet, February 22, 1760, W.O. 34: 58, f. 95; J. C. Webster, ed., *The Journal of Jeffery Amherst* (1931), pp. 114, 125, 142, 153, 203, 247.

In framing his plans for 1758, Loudoun took into consideration the wisest disposition that could have been made of provincial troops.[39] He would have asked for only seven thousand men, and bent every effort towards getting them into the field by May. Half of them, the New York and New Jersey troops, he planned to send with Bradstreet, for he had accepted Bradstreet's proposal to pay the charges of an expedition from his own pocket, to be reimbursed if successful, and recommended for promotion; by February Bradstreet had selected batteauxmen and was building boats. The other half of the provincial forces, those from New England, Loudoun planned to send to Nova Scotia to assist the regulars stationed there, and any reinforcements from England, in an attack on Louisbourg. He was well aware that after a landing had been forced—and only as many men could take part in that manoeuvre as the boats of the fleet could hold—the real work of the expedition would be in constructing roads or passageways over the rocks and morasses, and in dragging up artillery. For such work provincial troops were better fitted than regulars.

Loudoun's plans for the 1758 campaign were based on the experience that his study of the American situation had given him. He designed four expeditions, and during the winter he moved the quarters of his troops with an eye to the campaign. He concentrated eight regiments in and around Albany, two at New York and Long Island and one in Connecticut. These eleven regiments, together with Gage's which was being raised, were all within a short distance of the New York frontier, and he meant to get them on the move against Ticonderoga by the end of May, before the enemy could reinforce it. He planned that at the same time Bradstreet should proceed to Fort

Frontenac, so that the road to Montreal might be open in two directions and Bradstreet's attack cause the French to detach men from that post. On the other hand Pitt ordered four of the regular regiments in New York to Nova Scotia, added to those left for Ticonderoga the unwieldy and comparatively useless provincial army, made Bradstreet a quarter master general in Pennsylvania, and included no plan for Fort Frontenac. Loudoun's third expedition was to be against Fort Duquesne, and in preparation for it he had quartered the 35th at Philadelphia, and part of the 1st battalion and the whole of the 2d battalion of the 60th, in Lancaster, York, and Reading. These forces, under Stanwix, who was familiar with western Pennsylvania, were to have been aided by six hundred Cherokees, whose services Byrd engaged early in the spring. Pitt ordered Stanwix to Albany, sent the two battalions of the 60th to Louisbourg, and the 35th to Albany, while he called in for the Fort Duquesne expedition Montgomery's, then in South Carolina, Prevost's in New York, and a mixed force of southern provincials. By the time the two regiments had reached Philadelphia, the Cherokees, who had arrived in Pennsylvania in good time to begin the campaign, wearied of waiting and went home. Forbes reached Fort Duquesne, to find it in flames and the enemy retired, on November 26. Loudoun's two regiments and the Indians could conceivably have made as good time as Braddock's, who were within eight miles of the fort on July 8; they could then have gone on against the French posts to the northward. Loudoun's fourth expedition was against Louisbourg, the only one in which he needed the support of a fleet. He designed for that the six regiments wintering in Nova Scotia and the New England provincials, who could have taken ship near the places where they were raised and could not have deserted from Cape Breton. The nucleus of a fleet was at

Halifax under Lord Colvill, nine of the men of war which had wintered there after Holburne's ships were shattered in September, 1757. Pitt sent to Louisbourg fourteen regiments and a handful of workmen. They made their landing on June 8, and from then until the 17th of July, with the exception of Wolfe's activities near Lighthouse Point and occasional skirmishes, they worked on roads and the transportation of artillery and stores. The actual siege lasted but ten days, and it was then too late in the year for further operations. Loudoun's provincial troops would have shortened the time spent on the works; "here every labouring man was worth two Soldiers, here any Number could be easiely supply'd with Provisions. With General Abercrombie's Army, every Man but a good Soldier was an unsupportable Burthen."[40] While all of Loudoun's plans might not have succeeded, certainly on paper there was no comparison between them and Pitt's. If they had succeeded, the surrender of Canada would have come a year sooner at least, for all of the French outposts would have been in British hands early in the summer. Pitt's expeditions, because precious time was wasted in preparing for them, could not have been set in motion any earlier than they actually were.

Even if Pitt had recalled Loudoun, at the moment when his hard work with the army was bearing fruit, he should have given to a successor that leeway and discretion which any commander in chief, far removed from civilian oversight, ought to have in the field. Loudoun's successor should have been allowed to coördinate preparations and plans already undertaken with the reinforcements and the fleet from England. But Pitt in 1758, even more markedly than in 1757, determined at home the details of all campaigns. Amherst had a separate command for Louis-

---

[40] James Robertson to the Earl of Morton, December 19, 1758, Cumberland Papers. HM 1717, vol. 2, October 29, 1757.

bourg, which he was obliged to attack; the only matter left to his discretion was whether, after taking Louisbourg, he should proceed against Quebec, other French settlements in the Gulf of St. Lawrence, or Mobile, or whether he should await orders from Abercromby.[41] Forbes also had an independent command, and Abercromby was at considerable loss to know just what authority, if any, he could exercise over the other two commanders.[42] Pitt's instructions to Abercromby fill sixteen printed pages.[43] He was ordered to send six hundred rangers, Meserve's company of carpenters, and the artillery train at New York to Halifax; to take up six thousand tons of transport; to lay an embargo; to employ batteauxmen—all the details, in short, that Loudoun had arranged the previous year on his own initiative. Moreover, the supervision of the building of the boats on Lake George was entrusted, not to Abercromby, but to the governor of New York. Captain Loring was given charge from England; and DeLancey ordered to act in accord with Abercromby and "give all proper and necessary Directions, Assistance and Encouragement to Mr. Loring."[44] The Ordnance Board in London sent its chief engineer instructions for preparations for the 1758 campaign, and such instructions took precedence of any Abercromby might have given him. All this was the logical carrying to completion of Pitt's efforts in 1757 to direct matters, even in their details, from England.

Such evidence tends to show that the great changes of policy which Pitt inaugurated, detraction from the commander in chief's exclusive and responsible authority in military affairs and surrender to the demands of provin-

41 Instructions to Amherst, March 3, 1758, G.D. 8: 96.
42 Abercromby to Appy, June 24, 1758, W.O. 34: 76, f. 141.
43 *Pitt Correspondence*, I, 143-151, 157-160, 167-169, 200.
44 Pitt to Governor of New York, December 30, 1757, W.O. 34: 72, f. 38.

cial assemblies in order to get a larger provincial force in the field, were neither of them necessary for victory, but on the contrary contributed to the postponement of victory. It is some extenuation of Pitt in 1758 that his plans had to be based upon insufficient information; he had before him in December the winter quarters of the troops as they were determined in the autumn of 1757, and not as Loudoun moved them during the course of the winter.[45] But the very fact that it took six months for an exchange of information and orders was an inherent weakness of Pitt's policy; half the year was lost. In later years of the war he still called into service large bodies of provincials and he still gave precise orders. Even though thoroughly sympathetic with Pitt in most matters, Pownall, when collecting information for a second edition of his work on the colonies, questioned the wisdom of Pitt's orders to Wolfe. "If it be not improper [he wrote], as I hope in this view it is not, may I ask a question which otherwise would be impertinent, Whether the Commanding Officers on the Quebec Expedition were not as to the Particular Dispositions left to their own Discretion so as to take up with them the whole or Part of the Fleet to Quebec or to leave Part in the Atlantic to cover the Sea Line of the Colonies as they themselves on the Spott should find and judge proper?"[46] It is likewise the best of excuses for Pitt's destruction of the military union of the colonies which was slowly evolving under Loudoun that such a union, based upon the prerogative and held together, in the last instance, by force, was opposed to the whole trend of constitutional development within the colonies themselves. Sooner or later it would have come

---

[45] Distribution of Forces in North America in the winter of 1757-1758, G.D. 8: 97.

[46] Pownall to Pitt, January 24, 1765, G.D. 8: 53. No such latitude had been given, *Pitt Correspondence*, I, 444; II, 2.

to grief, as did the centralizing and imperialistic policy
of the British government in the twelve years after the
close of the war. But Pitt, in abandoning this effort
towards colonial union, failed to substitute anything in
its place. He left unchanged the constitutional structure
of the colonies, the nature of the commissions and instructions to royal governors, the whole atmosphere of
royal government in the colonies, with its bitterness,
jealousies, and constant opposition from provincial assemblies. A statesman intent upon the best interests of
the British empire, and aware, as Pitt was keenly aware,
of the temper of colonial encroachments upon the prerogative, would scarcely have let matters slide in that
critical period when the dangers of the war provided
sufficient justification for setting them right.

As for Loudoun, one can regret that he was not given
the opportunity to gain the reward that he deserved. He
was not a great man and not a great general, but he certainly deserves none of the opprobrious epithets show-
ered upon him. He was neither cowardly, lazy, incompetent, dishonest, nor a bully. The worst that can be said of
him is that he was encrusted with the code at once of the
professional soldier and of the eighteenth century aristo-
crat, a man of high station in the army and in life. The
former made him impatient with all civilian bickerings
which injured the best interests of the soldiers under his
command; even in 1762, when he commanded the British
forces in Portugal, his great anxiety for the welfare of
his troops raised such a coolness between him and the
Portuguese ministers that the British ambassador was
forced to intervene.[47] The latter characteristic made him

---

[47] Loudoun was appointed second in command of the Portuguese expedition, under Lord Tyrawley, and from February to June remained in London
concerting necessary measures for supplying and equipping the British force
of 6000 men. When Tyrawley resigned in July for reasons of health, Lou-

unsympathetic with the colonial point of view, as when he insisted that letters franked by him as a peer should not have postage charged.[48] Even when he tried to bridge it by tact and polite words, the chasm between him and the colonials was always there; and when he deliberately undertook to gain his point by a show of temper, he left an impression which sunk so deep into the minds of contemporary American observers that it has been magnified out of all proportion to the relatively few times that he let himself go. He aroused the bitterest of oppositions, for in supporting his aims he had the threat of armed troops at his back; but when one remembers that every royal governor who tried to obey his instructions to the letter likewise aroused bitter opposition, Loudoun's relations with the colonies assume a proper place. He was not unique, but one of a long line.

The confidence of his own army, in spite of Webb's double-dealing, Loudoun in large part retained. The letters of his officers, seeing him leave them, carry a pang that the lapse of years does not destroy. They can stand as testimony for him. "It has shock'd me excessively [wrote Stanwix when he heard of Loudoun's recall] for I always believed and believe so still that your Lordship is the likeliest General to reduce the enemys of this Country and bring this immense Continent into order. It don't

doun became commander in chief of the British contingent, though the whole mixed force of Germans, British, and Portuguese was under the supreme command of the Count de la Lippe, a German prince. The Franco-Spanish advance was checked, but in the only action of importance in which British troops played a part, at Villa Vilha, Burgoyne commanded the detachment. Loudoun was at Soubreira Formosa, a short action won by British artillery, and in the latter part of the campaign commanded a mixed force of eighteen regiments at Portalegre. Letters to Secretary of State from Edward Hay and Generals in Portugal, 1762, S.P. 89: 57; Correspondence of Lord Tyrawley, Additional MSS. 23,635.

[48] Loudoun to Mrs. Deborah Franklin, January 24, 1758, W.O. 34: 76, f. 100.

become me to say much more and from the fullness of my
heart could not say less, knowing how much your Lordship has had the general service at heart and carried it on
with so much judgment and indefatigable pains and at the
same time made every officer happy who has had the
honour of being under your command.''[49] John Forbes,
who died a year later at Philadelphia, wrote: ''I shall not
say how I found myself, or how I find myself yet, but I
see well who are pleased or displeased and I am happy
to find you have a number of Friends . . . particularly
the DeLanceys . . . I assure my dear Lord, I wish the
Government well, and that all their Servants may with
the same zeal and assiduity be their humble servants is
my reall wish. But I can say nothing upon a Subject that
if you believe there is faith in Mankind, you must know
is distressing to me to the outmost, but God be thanked, I
hope to laugh and eat Collops with you at Loudoun, spite
of all this treatment. I am quite impatient to see you. So
God Bless you.''[50] ''If I am not much deceived,'' wrote
Sir John St. Clair to Governor Sharpe, ''I may rank you
amongst the number of those who regret our General
Loss, if you do not you will be one of few and in damn'd
bad company to the bargain.''[51] Sir Henry Seton of
Fraser's Highlanders said that he would have accepted
no commission except for service under Loudoun, nor
would his men have enlisted so readily. James Robertson
wrote to Calcraft of Loudoun's ''unblemished upright-
ness, unwearyed diligence, uncommon spirit and capacity
joined to every amiable value . . . when qualities like his
bring disgrace, I shall not be over anxious for preferment.'' Two years later, in December, 1759, Richard Huck
gave his opinion of Amherst, and added: ''How often

[49] Stanwix to Loudoun, March 14, 1758, LO 5756.
[50] Forbes to Loudoun, March 4, 1758, LO 5692.
[51] *Maryland Archives*, IX, 155.

. . . have your Friends wished that your Lordship had
. . . had equal Advantages in the command . . . Fortune
drops her favors into some men's laps, nor can merit always secure her Smiles . . . Amherst came a propos to
reap innumerable Advantages from the labours of a Loudoun, he profited by the miscarriages of Abercromby, and
all the world sees what easy work the enterprising spirit
of Wolf made for him, nor do I think the death of that
brave man an unlucky circumstance for him.''[52] In the
same year James Abercrombie summed up his own conclusions: ''I assure your Lordship upon my honour, I
verrily believe were it put to the voice of the officers your
Lordship would be at the head of us here. They are now
convinced your Lordship never had it in your power to
effect any thing while in Command, and in general agree
if your Lordship had not meddled so much with provincial matters, you would have been the best General they
could have had . . . This is the sentiment of the thinking
people here and I am certain your Lordship has more
friends on the Continent than you at present imagine.''[53]

Such evidence, most of it from Loudoun's own Scottish
friends, must be taken for what it is worth. His active
enemies, as St. Clair suggested, were not admirable men;
but it is some detraction of his paternal methods that
Lord Howe scrupulously remained outside the dispute,
and that Gage and Bradstreet, each capable in his own
way, were glad to see him go. There was always jealous
bickering in an army composed of independent units;
later years of the war were not free from it, and Loudoun
left his command without getting from England the support that would have stopped what was, after all, a small
affair. He left behind him no such recriminations as

[52] Huck to Loudoun, December 3, 1759, LO 6153.
[53] February 27, 1759, LO 6046.

Braddock[54] or Shirley had done; his successors could find more to praise than to criticize in his heritage. If he had had the same opportunities as they, which his own hard work had done much to create, there is no reason for supposing that he would not have had equal success.

[54] Daniel Dulany, Military and Political Affairs in the Middle Colonies in 1755, *Pennsylvania Magazine*, III, 11-41.

BIBLIOGRAPHY

MANUSCRIPT SOURCES IN THE UNITED STATES

The ten thousand documents on American affairs in the Loudoun Papers in the Huntington Library, San Marino, California, comprise the most important single collection on the early years of the Seven Years' War. About fifteen hundred of these concern the period before 1756; the remainder deal with Loudoun's term of office. They are a very full set. Loudoun was by nature a systematic individual with an eye for minute detail, and he was also fearful of an official enquiry into his conduct of affairs. He kept therefore every document which would illuminate even the insignificant phases of his administration. There is the usual run of commander in chief's papers: files of correspondence with the captain general, the principal departments in London, and the chief British officials in the colonies, such as the governors, superintendents of Indian affairs, naval officers, and military subordinates. In addition there are letters from private persons, letters of recommendation, returns of troops, provisions, and supplies, copies of warrants and receipts. Much of this material is duplicated in the letters and enclosures sent to England, and in the printed collections of colonial archives. I have first referred to the printed document where possible and then usually to the departmental papers in the Public Record, so that for the most part the LO references indicate that the only available copies are in the Loudoun Papers.

The Loudoun notebooks, sixteen in number, are also in the Huntington Library, listed as Huntington Manuscripts 1717. Five are memorandum books and diaries covering the period from January 1 to July 26, 1756 and from January 1, 1757 to July 15, 1758. They contain a day by day account of Loudoun's actions, including often reports of his conversations, and were used by him as the basis of his official letters to England. The other eleven notebooks are either indices or general memorandum books from February 14, 1756 to July, 1756 and from May 9, 1759 to March 31, 1760, the latter dealing with Lord Charles Hay's court martial. HM 1718 is the account book of Duncan Richmond, Loudoun's servant, from January 1, 1757 to July, 1758. I have described this collection at greater length in Huntington Library *Bulletin,* No. 3, 1933.

The Abercromby Papers in the Huntington Library, from March to December, 1758, are mostly made up of official correspondence with the ministry, provincial governors, and such officers as Forbes, Amherst, Stanwix, and Bradstreet. There are a few official documents such as reports and returns.

Of the formidable volumes in the Massachusetts Archives at Boston, those numbered 5 (Colonial), 55 (Letters), 75 and 76 (Military), 89 and 90 (Military Accounts), and 136 (Miscellaneous Pecuniary Military) are useful for the organization and supply of provincial troops, as are the volumes labelled ''War'' in the Connecticut Archives at Hartford. Additional information on New England provincial troops can be found in the Pepperrell Papers and Winslow Journals in the Massachusetts Historical Society, in the William Samuel Johnson Papers in the Connecticut Historical Society, in the valuable orderly-book and journal of Major Moses Deshon and the Ezekiel Price manuscripts in the Boston Athenaeum, and in the journal of Moses Dorn in the Widener Library.

MANUSCRIPT SOURCES IN ENGLAND

The Public Record Office

The following list of volumes, necessary for tracing the complex system of British administration as far as it concerned military affairs, includes all letters that passed between departments and all existing records of the action taken by each department from January to July, 1756.

State Papers, Domestic

Letters and Papers, George II (S.P. 36: 133, 134, 135, 136)
Secretary's Letter-Books (S.P. 44: 120, 121, 122)
Under-secretary's Letter-Book (S.P. 44: 148)

Entry-books, Military (S.P. 44: 177, 178, 179, 181, 184, 189, 192)

Entry-books, Naval (S.P. 44: 226, 228, 229, 230)

In-letters, Military (S.P. 41: 22)

In-letters, Naval (S.P. 42: 39)

Warrants (S.P. 44: 372, 373)

Admiralty Papers

In-letters from

Ordnance Board (Ad. 1: 4010)

Secretaries of State (Ad. 1: 4120, 4121)

Treasury Board (Ad. 1: 4285)

War Office (Ad. 1: 4322)

Orders in Council (Ad. 1: 5164)

Out-letters

Orders and Instructions from the Lords of the Admiralty (Ad. 2: 76, 78, 79)

from the Admiralty Board to Secretaries of State (Ad. 2: 219, 220, 221, 222)

from the Secretary to Public Offices (Ad. 2: 515, 516, 519, 520)

Secret Orders and Letters (Ad. 2: 1331)

Admiralty Board Minutes (Ad. 3: 64)

Papers relating to Transports (Ad. 49: 125, 126)

Miscellanea (Ad. 49: 1)

Navy Board Papers

Out-letters to the Admiralty (Ad. Navy Board 2188, 2189)

In-letters relating to Transports (Ad. Navy Board 242, 259, 246, 247, 274, 276)

War Office Papers

In-letters from

General Officers in America (W.O. 1: 1, 4, 5)

Secretary of state and Treasury Board (W.O. 1: 678)

Various Departments (W.O. 1: 857)

Miscellaneous (W.O. 1: 972)

General Out-letters (W.O. 4: 51, 52)

Embarcation Orders (W.O. 5: 43, 44)

Marching Orders (W.O. 5: 32)

Board of General Officers (W.O. 7: 25)

Registers of Military Establishments (W.O. 24)
Miscellany Books (W.O. 26: 22, 23)
Misc. Various (W. O. 30: 54)
Ordnance Board Papers
  Out-letters (W.O. 46: 8)
  Minutes (W.O. 47: 47, 48)
  Ledgers of Accounts (W.O. 48: 96, 97)
  Miscellaneous (W.O. 55: 283)
Treasury Board Papers
  In-letters (T. 1: 364, 365, 366, 367, 368)
  General Out-letters (T. 27: 27)
  Minutes (T. 29: 32)
  Warrants not relating to money (T. 54: 36)
  Public Disposition Book (T. 61: 16)

Volumes in the Series mentioned above, particularly useful for earlier military affairs, are the Establishment Registers (W.O. 24), the War Office Miscellany Books (W.O. 26), and the State Paper military and naval In-letters (S.P. 41 and S.P. 42)

For the study of ministerial policy towards colonial defense before the Seven Years' War, the minutes (S.P. 44: 273-322; S.P. 45: 6) and correspondence with Hanover (S.P. 43) of the Lords Justices are perhaps as valuable as any other single classification. These papers cover usually the six months from May to November in such critical years, among others, as 1720, 1740, 1743, 1748, and 1755. Colonial items are rare, but they reveal, sometimes unexpectedly, the degree of ministerial interest in general colonial matters. Information on this same subject can be found in those divisions of the great mass of Colonial Office Papers which deal with Plantations General (C.O. 5: 3-7, 9, 12, 21, 36, 41-48; C.O. 323: 7-13; C.O. 324: 10, 11, 37, 38; C.O. 325), and some representations, reports, warrants, and letters in occasional volumes of the C.O. 5 series relating to Virginia, New York, Georgia, and New England are valuable for ministerial policy.

Two especially useful classifications for army administration in America are the Declared Accounts in the Audit Office Papers (A.O. 1; A.O. 13; and A.O. 17) and in the Paymaster General's miscellany books (P.M.G., 14), and the General Courts Martial

Records in the War Office Papers (W.O. 71). These last reconstitute the intimate details of army life more satisfactorily than any other kind of document.

Three volumes on North America in the Chatham Papers (G.D. 8 : 95-97), and one on army affairs (G.D. 8 : 75) are indispensable, and if one knows the names of men primarily interested in the colonies, he can turn up important letters in earlier volumes of Pitt's original correspondence, which is arranged alphabetically. The Amherst Papers (W.O. 34) provide a convenient, and in some cases the only means of checking Amherst's relations with provincial governors and troops, and with various branches of army administration. I have not pretended to examine the whole of the fifty thousand documents. Many of Loudoun's drafts of letters in his own hand are in these papers.

The British Museum

In the rich collection of Newcastle Papers (Additional Manuscripts 32,686-33,057) the important volumes are those of Newcastle's home correspondence from 1753 to 1758, the three well-known volumes on American affairs (Add. MSS. 33,028-33,030), and especially the four labelled Memoranda (Add. MSS. 32,993-32,997), which contain notes of cabinet council meetings from 1696 to 1758. I have examined other volumes in critical years when either colonial or military affairs were being discussed, but in spite of the fact that Newcastle, as secretary of state for the southern department, had charge of colonial matters until 1748, there is less general material than might be expected. In the Hardwicke Papers (Add. MSS. 35,349-36,278) there are separate volumes on American affairs, some correspondence with Newcastle and with Lord Townshend in the 1720s, a few cabinet council notes and law officers' opinions. Besides these two chief collections I have used random volumes in the Carteret Papers (Add. MSS. 22,515-519), and in the Lansdowne, Kings, Egerton, Stowe, and Sloane collections.

The Royal Archives at Windsor Castle

From 1754 to 1757, when as captain general of the army the

duke of Cumberland was closely connected with American affairs, the Cumberland Papers have a special value. They contain unique material of which copies either were not made or have been destroyed, such as copies of private letters from American governors to Halifax, manuscript journals, letters of inferior officers to Cumberland or to Napier, his aide de camp, and returns of troops and commission lists. A volume of the material in the Cumberland Papers relating to North America, to be published under the Beveridge Fund of the American Historical Association, is being compiled.

PRINTED SOURCES

The well-known printed collections of colonial archives and official British material are, of course, indispensable, and need no detailed description. Of the *Army Lists,* however, which begin in their printed form in 1754, a word of caution is necessary. They cannot be taken as authoritative for their year of issue. They were often incomplete and incorrect for regiments serving in North America, and they do not show all the transfers and promotions during a single year, but only the status of officers, according to War Office lists, at the time they were compiled. Worthington C. Ford's compilation of *British Officers serving in America, 1754-1774* (Boston, 1894) is useful only as an index to the *Army Lists* themselves. A volume is badly needed to fill the gap between Charles Dalton's *George the First's Army,* 2 vols. (London, 1910-12) and the *Army Lists.* Of the *Reports* of the Historical Manuscripts Commission, the *Report on the Manuscripts of Mrs. Stopford-Sackville,* 2 vols. (1904, 1910) is perhaps the most useful, though it by no means represents the cream of that collection which is now known as the Germain Papers and is in the William L. Clements Library (*Bulletin* No. 18 of the Clements Library). Other valuable reports are the XIVth on the Dartmouth Manuscripts (1895), the XIth on the Townshend Papers (1887), vol. VIII of the Reports on Various Collections (1913), and the Diary of the First Earl of Egmont, 3 vols. (1923).

COLLECTIONS OF CORRESPONDENCE

There are six chief collections of correspondence for this period. Of these two pretend to some degree of completeness: *The Official Records of Robert Dinwiddie* (cited as *Dinwiddie Papers*), with introduction and notes by R. A. Brock, 2 vols., forming volumes III and IV of the *Collections* of the Virginia Historical Society, new series (Richmond, 1883-4); Correspondence of Governor Horatio Sharpe of Maryland, edited by William Hand Browne, in volumes VI, IX, and XIV of the *Maryland Archives* (Baltimore 1888-1911). Two are as complete as their editors could make them without the Loudoun materials: *The Fitch Papers, Correspondence and Documents during Thomas Fitch's Governorship of the Colony of Connecticut, 1754-1766*, edited by Albert C. Bates, volume XVII of the *Collections* of the Connecticut Historical Society (Hartford, 1918); *The Papers of Sir William Johnson*, edited by James Sullivan, 3 vols. (Albany, 1921-1922). Two works, edited under the auspices of the National Society of the Colonial Dames of America, contain selections from available manuscript material: *Correspondence of William Shirley, Governor of Massachusetts and Military Commander in America, 1731-1760*, 2 vols., edited by Charles Henry Lincoln (New York, 1912); *Correspondence of William Pitt when Secretary of State with Colonial Governors and Military and Naval Commanders in America*, 2 vols., edited by Gertrude Selwyn Kimball (New York, 1906).

Correspondence of less direct importance is found in *The Letters and Papers of Cadwallader Colden*, 7 vols., in *Collections* of the New York Historical Society, 1917-23 (New York, 1918-1923); *The Diary and Letters of His Excellency Thomas Hutchinson, Esq., B.A. (Harvard), LL. D. (Oxon.), Captain General and Governor-in-Chief of his late Majesty's Province of Massachusetts Bay in North America*, by Peter Orlando Hutchinson, 2 vols. (Boston, 1884); the Bouquet Collection, calendared by Douglas Brymner in the *Report on Canadian Archives*, 1889 (Ottawa, 1890); *Collection Des Manuscrits du Maréchal de Lévis*, publié sous le direction de l'abbé H.-R. Casgrain, especially volume VII, Journal du Marquis de Montcalm durant ses campagnes en Canada de 1756 à 1759 (Quebec, 1895); *The Writings of George Washington,* edited by John C. Fitzgerald (Washington, 1932); *Letters to Washington and accompanying Papers,* published by the Society of Colonial Dames of America, edited by Stanislaus Murray Hamilton, II (Boston, 1899); "Papers of the Lloyd Family of the Manor of Queens Village, Lloyd's Neck, Long Island, New York," edited by Dorothy C. Bark, in New York Historical Society *Collections* for 1927; "Correspondence with the British Government, 1755-58," in *Collections* of the Connecticut Historical Society, I (Hartford, 1860); "Calendar of the Emmet Collection," *Bulletin* of the New York Public Library, 1900; the intercepted letters to the Duc de Mirepoix, 1756, printed in full in the American Historical Association *Report,* 1896, I, 660-703; "The Military Letters of Joseph Shippen, 1756-1758," *Pennsylvania Magazine of History and Biography,* XXXVI, 367-378 and 385-463 (1922); *The Works of Benjamin Franklin,* edited by Jared Sparks (Boston, 1836-44); *The Correspondence of the Colonial Governors of Rhode Island,* 1723-1775, edited by Gertrude Selwyn Kimball under the auspices of the National Society of the Colonial Dames of America, 2 vols. (New York, 1906); *The Northcliffe Collection* (Ottawa, 1927), which contains the papers of Robert Monckton presented to Canada by Sir Leicester Harmsworth in memory of Lord Northcliffe; *The Correspondence of General Thomas Gage with the Secretaries of State* 1763-1775, compiled and edited by C. E. Carter, I (New Haven, 1931); "Manuscript Records of the French and Indian War in the Library of the Society," *Transactions and Collections* of the American Antiquarian Society, XI (Worcester, 1909).

CONTEMPORARY JOURNALS

Six journals or diaries of officers serving in North America are valuable: *An Historical Journal of the Campaigns in North America for the Years, 1757, 1758, 1759, and 1760,* by Captain John Knox, edited by A. G. Doughty, 3 vols. (Toronto, The Champlain Society, 1914); *The Journals of Major Robert Rogers, containing an account of the several excursions he made under the Generals who commanded upon the continent of North America during the late war* (London, 1765); ''The Montrésor Journals,'' in the *Collections* of the New York Historical Society, 1881; ''Journals of the Honorable William Hervey, 1755-1814,'' *Suffolk Green Books*, XIV, (Bury St. Edmunds, 1906); ''Robert Orme's Journal,'' in *The History of the Expedition against Fort Duquesne in 1755 under Major General Edward Braddock,* edited by Winthrop Sargent (Publications of the Historical Society of Pennsylvania, Philadelphia, 1856); ''John Winslow's Journals in 1755,'' in volumes III and IV of the *Collections* of the Nova Scotia Historical Society (Halifax, 1883, 1885); and *The Journal of Jeffery Amherst,* edited by J. C. Webster (Toronto and Chicago, 1931).

Provincial military diaries are few in number and of little value. The best are the long diary of Jabez Fitch, in various numbers of the *Mayflower Descendant*, I-XV; and *The Journals and Papers of Seth Pomeroy,* edited by Louis Effingham De Forest and published by the Society of Colonial Wars in the State of New York (New York, 1926).

CONTEMPORARY PAMPHLETS AND HISTORIES

Pamphlets written by Shirley's supporters in his defense are worth reading, for they give a broad picture of the difficulties of campaigning in America: *A Review of Military Operations in North America from the year 1755 to the surrender of Oswego in 1756* (London, 1757), reprinted in Massachusetts Historical Society *Collections*, 1800 (Boston, 1801); *The Conduct of Major-General Shirley, late General and Commander in Chief of His Majesty's Forces in America, briefly stated* (1758). But those which attack Loudoun are political in tone' and the facts untrustworthy: *Remarks upon a letter published in the London Chronicle or Universal Evening Post N° 115, containing an enquiry into the Causes of the failure of the late Expedition against Cape Breton* (1757); Dr. John Shebbeare's *4th Letter to the People of England* (1756). The same is true of those pamphlets which defend him: *The Conduct of a Noble Commander in America impartially reviewed* (1758); *A full and particular answer to all*

*the calumnies, misrepresentations and falsehoods contained in a
pamphlet, called, a 4th letter to the People of England* (1756) ;
*An answer to the letter to two great men . . . vindicating the
character of a Noble Lord from inactivity* (1760). The first of
these last three, which is the ablest, was written by that professional title-collector, free-lance journalist, and quack doctor,
John Hill, whose career won him a place in the *Dictionary of
National Biography;* his letter to Loudoun of June 27, 1758 (LO
5865), admits his authorship. Descriptive pamphlets are more
useful, such as: Lewis Evans' *Geographical, Historical, Political,
Philosophical, and Mechanical Essays, No. 2,* and J. Huske's *The
Present State of North America* (1755).

Thomas Mante, who wrote the *History of the Late War in
North America* (London, 1772), served his military apprentice-
ship in Montgomery's Highland battalion, which was sympathetic with Loudoun; he estimates the value of Loudoun's career
better than any other contemporary historian. Neither *The Military History of Great Britain, 1756-1757* (London, 1757), though
apparently the work of an eyewitness, nor J. Entick's *The General History of the Late War,* 5 vols. (London, 1763-4), can compare with Mante.

Thomas Pownall, *Administration of the Colonies* (2d. ed., London, 1765), is the ablest contemporary survey of colonial governments. Thomas Hutchinson's *History of Massachusetts Bay,* vol.
III (London, 1828) was too cautiously written to be of great use
today.

SECONDARY WORKS: A SELECTIVE LIST

Three works bearing directly on the Seven Years' War in
North America stand in a category by themselves: Julian S. Corbett's *England in the Seven Years' War: A Study in Combined
Strategy,* 2 vols. (London, 1907), though primarily concerned
with naval strategy, surveys the whole war arena with breadth
and judgment. George Louis Beer's *British Colonial Policy,
1754-1765* (New York, 1922), if less inclusive than its title suggests, is particularly valuable for the commercial aspects of the
war and for one factor, colonial trade with the enemy, with which

Loudoun had no time to concern himself actively. Beer's was the first treatise to relate the war to Great Britain's whole colonial system. H. L. Osgood's *The American Colonies in the Eighteenth Century*, 4 vols. (New York, 1924) is built upon the framework of the four wars with France but deals rather with the colonial than with the British end. It is an invaluable repository of facts.

Two general works of outstanding merit are Leonard W. Labaree's *Royal Government in America: A Study of the British Colonial System before 1783* (New Haven, 1930), an authoritative pronouncement on the constitution of the royal colonies, and W. T. Root's *Relations of Pennsylvania with the British Government* (Philadelphia, 1914).

Of works upon the British army the two volumes of Charles M. Clode, *Military Forces of the Crown* (London, 1869) are still of primary importance for their breadth of treatment and close adherence to the documents. Sir John Fortescue's *The British Army, 1783-1802: Four Lectures delivered at the Staff College and Cavalry School* (London, 1905), is more useful than volume II of his *A History of the British Army* (London, 1910), which is rather a history of campaigns than of the army.

The most illuminating works on the practical workings of British politics and government in the eighteenth century are by L. B. Namier: *The Structure of Politics at the Accession of George III*, 2 vols. (London, 1929); and *England in the Age of the American Revolution* (London, 1930), the first chapter of which is a masterly summary.

Francis Parkman's two volumes on *Montcalm and Wolfe* remain the classic account, vivid and charming, of the last French and Indian war as the colonist saw it. Two other readable books are A. G. Bradley's *The Fight with France for North America* (London, n.d.) and W. C. H. Wood's *The Fight for Canada* (London, 1905). But no author since Bancroft has realised the importance of the commander in chief's office; his story of the "Viceroy," when stripped of its patriotic bias, remains essentially true in its main lines.

There are a great many secondary books dealing with special phases of the Seven Years' War and of the growth of British policy before it. I have found H. W. Richmond's *The Navy in the War of 1739-48,* 3 vols. (Cambridge, 1920) valuable in its details and its judgments. Lewis Butler's *The Annals of the King's Royal Rifle Corps,* I, "The Royal Americans" (London, 1913) is a good regimental history, and the appendix dealing with *Uniforms, Armament, and Equipment,* by S. M. Milne and Major General Astley Terry (London, 1913) is a specialised treatise that might well be duplicated for other regiments. Colonel J. F. C. Fuller's *British Light Infantry in the Eighteenth Century* (London, 1925) is a suggestive work, though neither Gage's regiment nor the rangers, the only true light infantry in Loudoun's army, are mentioned. Viola Barnes' *The Dominion of New England: A Study in British Colonial Policy* (New Haven, 1923), and Louise Phelps Kellogg's *The American Colonial Charter* (Washington, 1904) are the best accounts of early British efforts to unite the colonies.

Of many biographies I am most indebted to Evan Charteris' *William Augustus, Duke of Cumberland, and the Seven Years' War* (London, n.d.), a sympathetic study which gives Cumberland the credit he deserves; Lord Ilchester's *Henry Fox, First Lord Holland, His Family and Relations,* 2 vols. (London, 1920), in the writing of which both the Holland House papers and the Devonshire manuscripts have been used; Albert von Ruville's *William Pitt, Earl of Chatham,* translated by H. J. Chaytor assisted by Mary Morison, 3 vols. (London, 1907); Philip C. Yorke's *The Life and Correspondence of Philip Yorke, Earl of Hardwicke, Lord High Chancellor of Great Britain,* 3 vols. (Cambridge, 1913); Usher Parsons' well-worn *Life of Sir William Pepperrell, Bart.* (Boston and London, 1856); George A. Wood's *William Shirley, Governor of Massachusetts, 1741-1756,* I (New York, Columbia University Press, 1920), for whose second volume, which has not yet appeared, the Loudoun Papers will be indispensable; A. T. Volwiler's *George Croghan and the Westward Movement,* 1741-1782 (Cleveland, 1926).

ARTICLES AND SHORTER MONOGRAPHS

Six articles deserve special mention. E. I. McCormac printed in 1914 in the first volume of the University of California *Publi-*

cations a study of "Colonial Opposition to Imperial Authority
during the French and Indian War" which is the only attempt
made hitherto to deal with the subject; it is based wholly upon
the standard printed colonial sources. C. E. Carter has briefly
described the powers of General Thomas Gage, in "The Significance of the Military Office in America, 1763-1775", *American
Historical Review*, XXVIII, 475. Gage's authority was essentially a revival of Loudoun's, altered to meet new conditions.
W. L. Grant's "The Capture of Oswego by Montcalm in 1756:
A Study in Naval Power . . .", *Transactions* of the Royal Society of Canada (1914), series III, vol. viii, p. 193, is a splendidly
thorough application to inland waters of the principles of naval
strategy laid down by Corbett and Mahan. T. W. Riker's "The
Politics behind Braddock's Expedition", *American Historical
Review*, XIII, 742, connects the political situation in England to
American affairs. In "Some Attempts at Imperial Co-operation
during the Reign of Queen Anne", Royal Historical Society
Transactions, 4th series, X, 171, W. T. Morgan has drawn together widely separated varieties of material into a detailed narrative. Finally, L. H. Gipson, in his article on "Connecticut
Taxation and Parliamentary Aid", *American Historical Review*,
XXXVI, 721, has reinterpreted, by a close study of Connecticut
taxation, the significance of Pitt's large subsidies for colonial
military aid.

INDEX

Abercrombie, James, captain in 42d regiment and aide de camp to General James Abercromby, account of ranging company, 303-304; desires Loudoun's return, 364.

Abercromby, James, major general, suggested for 1756 command, 42; second in command, 74; assumes command in America, 83; forces dispute over rank, 89; comments on provincial troops, 99; learns of condition of Oswego, 161-163; settles rates of exchange, 286; writes to James Abercromby, 343-344; commander in chief, 344; hampered by provincials, 354; limitation of power of, 358-359.

Abercromby, James, colonial agent for Virginia, corresponds with Pitt, 229; with General Abercromby, 343-344.

Admiralty, Board of, arranges details of Braddock's expedition, 31; independence of judgment of, 45; orders given by, in 1756, 47, 69-70; clashes with Treasury, 48; relation of, to commander in chief, 80; activity of, in 1757, 236.

Albany, Abercromby assumes command at, 83; Loudoun arrives at, 90; rent of storehouses in, 137; quartering in, 195-198; Abercromby in command at, 218 n.; Loudoun's measures at, 262, 268; transportation to and from, 296-299; artillery detachment at, 324; hospital at, 326; troops at, in 1758, 356.

Albany Plan of Union, 28 n.

Albemarle, William Anne Keppel, Earl of, governor general of Virginia, offers to repair to Virginia, 28 n.; death of, 60.

Alexander, William (self-styled Earl of Stirling), secretary to General Shirley, makes bid as provision contractor, 73 n.; associated with Livingston, 135; secretary to Niagara expedition, 147; plans forts at Oswego, 149; assigns trading privileges, 154; hoodwinks Shirley, 155; disclaims responsibility for Oswego, 158; Shirley's right-hand man, 162; offers to supply provisions, 295.

Alexandria, meeting of governors at, 36; Shirley's journey to, 145 n.

Americans, recruited in 1740, 1746, 13-16; Balcarres' opinion of, 55; in British army, 104; inducements to, to enlist, 110; Cosnan's opinion of, 115; attitude of, towards British army, 125.

Amherst, Jeffery, commander in chief, attempts to recruit Americans, 110, 111 n.; explains failure of recruiting, 113; settles Oswego carpenters' claims, 139; borrows from New York assembly, 140 n.; warrants drawn by, 290; commands against Louisbourg, 342; relations with colonies, 351-352; limitation of powers of, 358-359.

Anderson, John, of Connecticut, 331.

Angell, Samuel, lieutenant colonel of Rhode Island troops, 312.

Annapolis, troops quartered in, 205; Loudoun plans to visit, 221.

Anson, George Anson, Baron, first lord of the Admiralty, 31.

Appy, John, Loudoun's secretary and judge advocate, 81, 168.

Apthorp, Charles, agent to money contractors, 137 n., 282; Shirley's warrant to, 142; Shirley's funds in hands of, 144.

Argyll, Archibald Campbell, Duke of, connection with Loudoun, 42; Loudoun's letter to, 350-351.

Arms, issued to 60th regiment, 66; to provincials, 217; discussion of, 323.

Army, British, in North America, financing of, 280-292; annual expense of, 290. See also Regiments, British.

Artillery, Royal Regiment of, 320-324.

Assemblies, provincial, Townshend defines character of, 27; place of, in Braddock plan, 33-37; raise independent army, 83-84; attitude of, towards recruiting, 115; Loudoun's opinion of, 170; attitude of, towards quartering, 195, 206; commissioners of, in Boston, 214-216.

Atkin, Edmund, superintendent of southern Indian affairs, 41; Loudoun's relations with, 258-259.

Atkinson, Theodore, secretary of New Hampshire, 214.

Augusta regiment of Pennsylvania, 224.

Avery, James, forcibly recruited, 126.

Ayrshire, Loudoun's activities in, 43-44.

Babcock, Henry, major of Rhode Island troops, assists Loudoun, 91 n.; lieutenant in 60th regiment, 311 n.

Baker, William, merchant of London, plan of, for permanent garrison, 19; contractor for Nova Scotia, 233; money contractor for Nova Scotia, 288 n.

Baker, Kilby, and Baker, appointed provision contractors in North America, 72-74; fresh meat clause in contract of, 138 n.; provisions furnished by, 291-296.

Balcarres, James Lindsay, Earl of, opinion of Americans, 55.

Barracks, at Nova Scotia, Rattan, and Georgia, 189; at Wills Creek, 190; at Castle Island, 190; at Albany, 191, 197; at New York, 200; at Philadelphia, 202.

Barrington, William Wildman, Viscount, secretary at war, 46 n.; orders for North American expedition, 47; for raising Royal American regiment, 63; draws up recruiting act for America, 116; forbids officers to retire on pay, 314 n.

Bartman, George, lieutenant in 50th regiment and Webb's aide de camp, Shirley's warrants in favor of, 142; recommended by Fox, 309; assistant engineer, 319.

Bas (bat) money, explained, 289.

Battalion, explained, 109 n.

Batteauxmen, raised by Livingston and Morris, 139; by Bradstreet, 139, 155.

Beaufremont, Sr. Chevalier de, sails from Martinique, 237.

Beckers, Sophia, 311.

Beckett, Sergeant Robert, 331.

Bedford, John Russell, Duke of, secretary of state, approves Shirley's schemes for union, 10.

Belcher, Jonathan, governor of New Jersey, deals with Loudoun's requests for troops, 173; asks Loudoun's assistance, 225; too infirm to serve actively, 263.

Bellomont, Richard Coote, Earl of, governor of New York, Massachusetts, and New Hampshire, 9.

Best, E., merchant trading to Oswego, 154.

Bills of exchange, sold by contractors' agents, 141.

Bladen, Martin, member of the Board of Trade, tax proposed by, 10.

Blair, William, lieutenant in 51st regiment, killed by Indians, 156.

Blakeney, William, colonel, adjutant general of Vernon's expedition, 13.

Board of Trade, representation of, in 1721, 9, 10 n.; Walpole fails to support, 11; forts and garrisons proposed by, 12; recommends ordnance for Virginia, 23; orders Indian conference, 23; draws plan for colonial union, 24; drafts Loudoun's commission as governor of Virginia, 61; reports on military state of colonies, 322 n.

Bollan, William, agent of Massachusetts, petitions against Royal American Regiment, 63; receives letter from General Court, 84 n.

Boston, recruiting in, 128-129; meeting of commissioners at, 214-215; Pownall arrives at, 246; meeting of independent commissioners at, 276; Loudoun at, in 1758, 276-277; headquarters of Ordnance Board in North America, 320.

Bouquet, Henry, lieutenant colonel of 1st battalion of 60th regiment, 63; in Philadelphia, 201; in South Carolina, 202, 219; relations with Prevost, 317.

Braddock, Edward, major general, appointed commander in chief, 30; meets governors at Alexandria, 36; permits enlisting indentured servants, 107; number of troops with, 108; forbidden to draw on non-effective fund, 122 n.; warrants drawn by, 290; quarrels among officers of, 365.

Braddock plan, defined, 31, 33; causes of failure of, 35-37; revised in 1756, 39-41, 67; revived in 1762, 111; failure of, 112, 114.

Bradstreet, John, lieutenant colonel, batteauxmen raised by, 139, 155; arrives at Oswego, 148; construction by, at Oswego, 149, 151; attacked at Oswego Falls, 157; fits transports, 236; advises attack on Louisbourg, 240; buys rum for army, 291; suggests improving Hudson navigation, 298; corresponds with Lyttelton, 343; captures Fort Frontenac, 355; proposes to lead expedition, 356; pleased by Loudoun's recall, 364.

Brassier, William, engineer and draughtsman, 319.

Brewer, Moses, captain of Mohegan company, 303.

Brintwood, New Hampshire, riot in, 129.

Broadley, Housman, captain, commands Royal Navy on Lake Ontario, 160.

Brome, Charles, captain of the Royal Regiment of Artillery, 324.

Brown, Charlotte, matron of hospital, 325.

Brown, John, of Hartford county, supplies oxteams, 298.

Bulkeley, Charles, captain of rangers, 303.

Burgoyne, John, brigadier general, in Portugal, 362 n.

Burney, John, of 60th regiment, 331.

Burton, Ralph, lieutenant colonel of the 48th regiment, relations with Shirley, 89 n.; in command at Fort Edward, 93; "a diligent, sensible, man,'' 234 n.; opposed to Loudoun, 349.

Butler, Duke, 312.

Byng, John, admiral, his fate a warning to Loudoun, 239.

Byrd, William, appointed special Indian agent, 259; informs against Dinwiddie, 267 n.; volunteer in British army, 310, 311 n.

Cabinet, meeting of, on American affairs, 20, 23, 24, 30, 39, 40, 77, 230, 232.

Calcraft, John, regimental agent, recommendations from, 311; opinion of Abercromby, 344; letters from, 338 n.; letters to, 345.

Campbell, Dugal, engineer, 319.

Campbell, Duncan, major of the 42d regiment, 313-314.

Campbell, Ilay, Lord Advocate of Scotland, 189 n.

Canada, early expeditions against, 3; proposed invasion of, in 1746, 14; French troops in, 354.

Carpenters, at Oswego, 139, 153.

Cartagena Expedition, colonials raised for, 13.

Castle Island, barracks in, 190.

Chaplains, 328-329.

Chapman, Russell, lieutenant colonel of the 60th regiment, 314 n.

Charlestown, South Carolina, regulars quartered in, 202, 220.

Charteris, Henry, captain in the 60th regiment, 128-129.

Cheeksaunkun, Jacob, captain of the Stockbridge Indian company, 301.

Cherokee fort, 219.

Cherokees, raised by Loudoun for 1758, 259, 357.

Chignecto Isthmus, 30.

Cholmondeley, James, lieutenant general, 42, 346.

Christie, Gabriel, captain in the 48th

regiment, assistant deputy quartermaster general, 291; suggests purchase of wagons, 297.

Christopher, John, 311.

Clapham, Lieutenant William, of the Augusta regiment, 312.

Clarke, Matthew, engineer, 319.

Claverack, troops quartered in, 196.

Clearances, 125.

Cleveland, John, secretary of the Admiralty, 47.

Clinton, George, governor of New York, conference with Mohawks, 23.

Cockburn, James, lieutenant in the 42d regiment, 313.

Coins, in use in America, 284-288. See also Provincial currency, Bills of exchange.

Coit, Daniel, justice of the peace in New London, 126-127.

Colden, Alexander, deputy postmaster at New York, 291.

Colebrooke, George, provision contractor, 296.

Colebrooke, Sir James, provision contractor, 296.

Collins, Thomas, lieutenant of the Royal Artillery, at Fort William Henry, 249 n.

Colonial defense, methods of providing for, 6-16.

Colonial merchants, buy bills of exchange, 288.

Colonial union, proposed by mercantilists, 6; effected under the Stuarts, 7-8.

Colonies, protected by Indians and by navy, 4; expected to provide own defense, 6; separatism of, 6; proposals to tax, 10, 37; troops raised in, 12-15; in schemes of colonial defense, 17; refuse to support Braddock plan, 35; granted reimbursement by parliament, 41,

352-353; military strength of, 105 n. See also Assemblies, Provincial troops.

Colvill of Culross, Alexander Colvill, Lord, 358.

Commander in chief, legal basis of appointment of, 9; powers of, 57-60, 79-80; relations with governors, 260-268; requires further support from England, 277-278, 351; powers lessened by Pitt, 340-342.

Common fund, as a part of the Braddock plan, 33, 114.

Cone, Daniel, captain of the Connecticut troops, 179.

Connecticut, provides men for 50th regiment, 114; troops quartered in, 205; militia in, 226.

Connecticut, assembly of, deals with Loudoun's request for troops, 176-177, 179; limits freedom of commissioners, 213.

Contingent men, defined, 124.

Contractors, see Livingston and Morris; Baker, Kilby and Baker; Thomlinson and Hanbury.

Conway, Henry Seymour, major general, 42.

Cook, William, lieutenant in the 51st regiment, 312.

Coram, Thomas, proposes to settle soldiers in Maine, 4.

Cornwallis, Edward, colonel, 42.

Cosnan, John, captain in the 45th regiment, remarks on Americans, 115.

Cotterell, William, captain in the 45th regiment, sent to London, 337 n.

Courts martial, British, treatment of provincial soldiers, 96-97; discussion of, 330-334.

Craven, Charles, major of the 51st regiment, paymaster, 144-145; builds forts at carrying place, 149; forts of, destroyed by Webb,

164 n.; reprimanded by Loudoun, 315; in London, 342.

Croghan, George, reputed author of intercepted letters, 77 n.; represents Crown at Easton conference, 255.

Crotty, Andrew, volunteer in the 22d regiment, 312.

Crown Point, Cumberland suggests operations against, 30, 34; Johnson's expedition against, 36.

Cruikshank, Charles, captain of the New York independent company, complains of rioters, 126, 250 n.

Cumberland, William Augustus, Duke of, captain general, feared by Hardwicke, 21-22; in inner cabinet, 26; proposes viceroy for North America, 28; proposes to recruit in North America, 30, 105; recommends Denny as governor of Pennsylvania, 57; responsible for Loudoun's powers, 79; settles rank of provincial officers, 86-87; draws up recruiting act, 116; refuses to allow warrant men, 124; recommends Shirley's court martial, 165; orders on quartering, 192; left out of Pitt's inner cabinets, 228; allows Loudoun latitude in orders, 230; alters Pitt's campaign plans, 232; Pitt's opinion of, 337; resignation of, 339-340; Pitt's jealousy of, 347.

Cummings, Archibald, collector at Boston, proposes permanent garrisons, 12.

Cunningham, James, captain in the 45th regiment, Loudoun's aide de camp, 167; wants to sell, 308 n.

Cuyler, Cornelius, assistant commissary of stores, 164 n.

Dagworthy, John, captain of the Maryland troops, taken into pay of the Crown, 221; asks regular commission, 312.

Dana, Caleb, of Boston, rescues recruits, 129.

DeLancey, James, lieutenant governor of New York, advises attack on Niagara, 35 n., 39; aids Loudoun, 262; in charge of boats on Lake George, 359.

DeLancey, Oliver, agent of Baker and Kilby, estimates New York troops in 1756, 100; reports on Shirley's contractors, 137 n.; checks provisions, 138; reports on supplies, 163 n.; agent of New York assembly, 184; troops quartered on, 199.

Demler, George, at Oswego, 149 n.

Denny, William, governor of Pennsylvania, 57; deals with quartering, 201; meets Loudoun, 218; forbidden to interfere in Indian affairs, 254-255; questions Loudoun's authority, 263.

DeRoy, François, Swiss professional soldier, 312.

Derwood, James, of the 44th regiment, court martialled, 331.

Desertion, 333-334.

Deshon, Moses, major of the Massachusetts troops, orderly book of, 95 n.

Desieure, John, report on roads in America, 35 n.

DeWitt, Charles, army trader, 154.

Dinwiddie, Robert, lieutenant governor of Virginia, builds forts on Ohio, 23-24; asks for British troops, 29, 39; pays Loudoun half his salary, 61; estimates military strength of colonies, 105 n.; supplies recruits, 114; meets Loudoun, 218; breaks embargo, 266; his recall asked by Loudoun, 278.

Discipline, military, 330-334.

Dobbs, Arthur, son of Governor Dobbs, 311.

Dobbs, Arthur, governor of North Carolina, meets Loudoun, 218.

Dominion of New England, 8-9.

Dongan, Thomas, governor of New York, 4.

Dreessen, H., Loudoun's landlord in Albany, 196 n.

Dummer, Jeremiah, writes pamphlet, 9.

Du Revest, 237.

Dusseaux, Joseph, colonel of the 2d battalion of the 60th regiment, 234.

Dwight, Joseph, brigadier general of Massachusetts, 100.

Easton, Indian conference at, 255.

Ebergeny, François Sigismund, soldier of fortune, 312.

Ellis, Henry, governor of Georgia, praises Virginians, 220 n.

Ellison, Robert, lieutenant colonel of the 50th regiment, ordered to America, 141.

Embargo, laid by Loudoun's orders, 265-267; by orders from England, 267 n.

Engineers, discussion of, 318-320.

Ernst, Matthew, supplies pork for army, 137.

Erving, John, contractor for Massachusetts troops, 84 n.; associated with Morris, 135; warrants drawn in favor of, 142-143.

Evans, Lewis, 54 n.

Exchange, rates of, in North America, 284-289.

Eyre (Eyres), William, major of the 44th regiment, engineer with Johnson, 88; promoted, 147; ordered to build fort at Oswego Falls, 164; engineer extraordinary, 318.

Fairfax, William, acting governor of Virginia, 265.

Fairfax, William Henry, volunteer, 310, 311 n.

Fairfield, 205.

Fairservice, James, appointed to command working party, 156.

Fawkener, Sir Everard, postmaster general, 120 n.

Fidele, Pierre, author of intercepted letters, 76, 77 n.

Fitch, Thomas, governor of Connecticut, connection with New London recruiting affair, 127-128; deals with Loudoun's request for troops, 176-177; divulges Loudoun's plans, 213; relations with Amherst, 352; appoints independent commissioners, 273.

Fletcher, Henry, lieutenant colonel of the 35th regiment, 315, 349.

Forbes, John, colonel of the 17th regiment, maligned, 349; at Fort Duquesne, 357; friendship of, with Loudoun, 363.

Forts,
Beauséjour, 34.
Bull, captured, 157.
Crown Point, 30, 34, 36.
Cumberland, 219, 221.
Duquesne, 34.
Edward, provincials at, 93-94; Wetterstrom's remarks on, 320; Loudoun at, 348.
Frederick, 219.
Frontenac, 149, 354-357.
George, New York, 264.
Le Boeuf, 23.
Loudoun, 219.
Ontario, 148-149, 151-153, 156, 159.
Oswego, 148-160.
Ticonderoga, 303, 345, 355.
William Henry, provincials at, 94-95; captured by Montcalm, 243-250; massacre at, 250 n.

Fox, Henry, secretary at war, 21; secretary of state, 38; contests control of House of Commons, 46; drafts commission for commander in chief, 53; out of office, 228.

Franklin, Benjamin, postmaster and assemblyman, on recruiting indentured servants, 120; in quartering dispute, 201; assembly spokesman to Loudoun, 223.

Franklin, Mrs. Deborah, 362 n.

Franks, Moses, provision contractor, 296.

Fraser, Simon, lieutenant colonel of the 2d Highland battalion, 205.

Freelinghous, Theodorus, 329.

French, Christopher, captain in the 22d regiment, 314.

French, John, recommended by Calcraft, 311.

Fry, Joseph, colonel of Massachusetts troops, 217; advises Monro to surrender, 250 n.

Gage, Thomas, lieutenant colonel of the 44th regiment, 89; "a good officer," 234 n.; proposes to raise light-armed regiment, 305; opposed to Loudoun, 349; pleased by Loudoun's recall, 364.

General Officers, Board of, 48.

Georgia, Virginia troops in, 220 n.

Gill, John, merchant trading to Oswego, 154.

Gilman, John, major of New Hampshire troops, 250 n.

Glazier, Beamsley, lieutenant in the 60th regiment, half-pay from Pepperrell's first regiment, and colonel of New York troops, 311 n.

Goffe, John, colonel of New Hampshire troops, 250 n.

Goldthwait, Benjamin, 176 n.

Gooch, William, lieutenant governor of Virginia, authorizes Ohio company, 18.

Governors, colonial, relations with

Loudoun, 260-268; forbidden to draw on paymaster general, 272 n.

Grafton, H.M.S., ordered to America, 76.

Graham, Gordon, captain in the 42d regiment, 313.

Grainger, Caleb, of North Carolina troops, 312.

Grant, Thomas, ensign in the 51st regiment, 158.

Granville, John Carteret, Earl, Lord President, 21; approves American troops, 32.

Grayer, James, of the 45th regiment, court martialled, 332.

Green, William, engineer, 319.

Greene, William, governor of Rhode Island, supports Loudoun, 273.

Gridley, Jeremiah, opinion on recruiting, 119; aids recruiting, 129; criticism of Pownall, 274.

Gridley, Richard, engineer, 320 n.

Haldimand, Frederick, lieutenant colonel of the 60th regiment, 63; advises on barracks in Pennsylvania, 202; suggests drill for Royal Americans, 299-300.

Half-moon, 297-298.

Halifax, George Dunk, Earl of, president of the Board of Trade, favors imperialist policy, 20; proposes to tax colonies, 27; proposed as viceroy in America, 28; scheme of, for 1756 campaign, 40; opinion of Loudoun's conduct at Halifax, 337.

Halifax, Loudoun at, 237-242; royal regiment of artillery at, 324; hospital at, 326; courts martial at, 331, 333; fleet at, 358.

Halifax, brigantine on Lake Ontario, 69.

Hall, Stephen, of Medford, Massachusetts, 84 n.

Hamlin, Jabez, agent for Connecticut, 184.

Hancock, Thomas, warrant to, for powder, 291, 323.

Hanover, Massachusetts, 323.

Hardwicke, Philip Yorke, Earl of, Lord Chancellor, 21; criticizes Board of Trade's plan, 26; disapproves Loudoun's conduct, 337.

Hardy, Sir Charles, governor of New York, quarrels with Shirley, 37; asks for British troops, 39; orders audit of Livingston and Morris's accounts, 139; criticizes Shirley, 162; familiar with Loudoun, 167; dilatory in quartering, 198-199; corresponds with Pitt, 231; advises against attacking Louisbourg, 242; assists Loudoun, 262; questions Loudoun's authority, 263; suggests embargo, 265; recommends officers, 309; criticizes Loudoun, 344-345.

Harriott packet, detained by Loudoun, 265 n.

Hartford, meeting of governors at, 272, 276 n.

Hay, Lord Charles, major general, sent to America, 234; at Halifax, 240-241; court martial of, 241 n.; writes to Pitt, 343.

Herkimer, John, 198.

Hervey, William, lieutenant in the 44th regiment, purchases captaincy, 308 n.; recommended by Cumberland and Barrington, 309.

Highlanders, recruiting of, suggested by Pepperrell, 16; recruited by 42d, 68; battalions of, raised by Pitt, 109; Montgomery's battalion of, at Charlestown, 202; Fraser's battalion of, quartered in Connecticut, 205.

Hill, John, major general, 13, 14.

Hill, John, author of pamphlet defending Loudoun, 375.

Hill, Ralph, captain lieutenant in the 45th regiment, court martialled, 89.

Hitchcock, John, of Wallingford, Connecticut, 298.

Holburne, Francis, rear admiral, at St. Helen's, 236; arrives at Halifax, 237; his fleet destroyed, 242.

Holderness, Robert D'Arcy, Earl of, secretary of state, orders independent companies to Virginia, 23-24; in charge of American affairs, 238.

Holland, troops of, requested by ministry, 52; powder and shot from, 323.

Hollandt, Samuel Jan, engineer, 319.

Holmes, Charles, captain of the *Grafton*, 76, 241 n.

Hopkins, Rufus, governor of Rhode Island, agent for Rhode Island, 184; defeated in 1757, 215 n.; Amherst's correspondence with, 352.

Hopkins, Thomas, of the 60th regiment, 331.

Hopson, Peregrine, major general, 234, 241.

Hospitals, discussion of, 324-328.

Houdin, Michael, missionary and chaplain, 329.

Howe, George Augustus, Viscount, 42; colonel of the 60th regiment, 235; arrives at Fort Edward, 250; suggested as brigadier against Louisbourg, 342; commands winter expedition, 348; death of, 355; not involved in party against Loudoun, 364.

Hubbard, Thomas, speaker of Massachusetts assembly, 84 n.

Huck (Huck-Saunders), Dr. Richard, physician, accompanies Loudoun to America, 81; one of Loudoun's

"family," 167; service of, 325-326; summarizes the war, 363-364.

Hunter, John, of Virginia, agent of Thomlinson and Hanbury, 138, 282.

Hunter, Robert, governor of New York, settles Palatines, 4.

Huntington, Hezekiah, agent for Connecticut, 184.

Hussey, John, captain in the 47th regiment, recommended by Ligonier and Legge, 309.

Hutchinson, John, sergeant in the 35th regiment, 118 n.

Hutchinson, Judge Eliakim, defrays expense of raising 50th regiment, 142.

Hutchinson, Thomas, heads Massachusetts commissioners, 214; distrusts colonial extravagance, 216; opinion of Pownall, 278 n.

Imperialism, not a motive of British policy, 1 ff.; Pitt's ideas of, 228-229.

Impressment of sailors, in London, 52, 71; in New York, 237.

Indentured servants, recruiting of, 107, 119-120.

Indians, British alliances with, 4; Mohawks break covenant chain, 18; conference with Governor Clinton, 23; under Braddock's supervision, 33; Shirley's trade with, 155; Loudoun's supervision of, 253-260; refuse to act as rangers, 301; ranging company formed of, 303; missionaries to, 328-329.

Intercepted letters, 76, 77 n.

Ireland, British troops in, 32, 49; provisions supplied from, 41, 47-48, 292; opposition to British government in, 49 n.; regiments sent from, 109.

Iron ore, quality of, in North America, 236 n.

Iroquois, alliance of, with Crown, 4; Shirley's opinion of, 256.

Jackson, George, merchant at Oswego, 154.

Jaffreys, Edward, of the 35th regiment, hanged, 334.

Jamaica, Long Island, 118.

Johnson, William, son of Dr. Johnson of King's College, 54-55.

Johnson, Sir William, at Crown Point, 1755, 36; sends Pownall to London, 54; causes of failure at Crown Point, 67; criticizes provincial troops, 97; commands militia in Albany, 177; relations of, with Loudoun, 253-257; payments to, 291.

Johnston, William, deputy paymaster general at Albany, 282; pays soldiers at 4s. 8d., 286.

Johnstone, Alexander, lieutenant in the 47th regiment, 312.

Keith, Sir William, governor of Pennsylvania, settlement proposed by, 4; garrisons proposed by, 12.

Kelly, William, merchant trading to Oswego, 154.

Kennebec river, Shirley's expedition up, 24; proposed as route against Quebec, 342.

Kennedy, Archibald, captain of brigantine on Lake Ontario, transport agent, 70.

Kennedy, David, captain in the 44th regiment, resigned, 308 n.

Keppel, Augustus, commodore, 148.

Kilby, Christopher, provision contractor in North America, 294.

Kinderhook, troops quartered at, 196.

Kingston-Goshen frontier, 263.

Kissam, Joseph, attacks recruiting party, 118.

Klosterzeven, Convention of, 340.

Knowles, Samuel, lieutenant of Massachusetts troops, cashiered, 333.

Lake George, boats on, 235 n.

La Motte (La Mothe), M. Du Bois de, 237.

Lampson, William, captain of rangers, 302.

Lancaster, Pennsylvania, 357.

Lawrence, Charles, governor of Nova Scotia, superseded by Braddock, 32; distrusts provincial officers, 88; dislikes American recruits, 116; reports on Shirley, 142 n.; questions Loudoun's authority, 264.

Leach, Samuel, of Rogers' Rangers, 331.

Leake, Robert, commissary of stores, complains of Livingston and Morris, 137-138; duties of, 292.

Lee, Charles, captain in the 44th regiment, 349.

Lee, Corbin, Maryland planter, 126.

Lescoet, Chevalier Barbier de, journal kept by, 237 n.

Levy money, defined, 123.

Lewis, Francis, commissary of stores at Oswego, 136, 153-154; refuses to pay soldiers, 158.

Ligonier, Sir John, lieutenant general of Ordnance, orders small-arms for the 60th regiment, 66; appointed to command army, 340-341; plans campaign of 1758, 342.

Listing money, defined, 123.

Livingston Manor, 196.

Livingston, Peter van Brugh, and Morris, Jr., Lewis, Shirley's contractors, 135 ff.

Livingston, Robert, 154.

Locke, John, proposes colonial union in 1696, 9.

Lords Justices, consider colonial defense, 10; instructions to, 19; appoint Shirley commander in chief, 39.

Loring, Joshua, captain of brigantine on Lake Ontario, appointed transport agent, 70; in charge of boats on Lake George, 359.

Loudoun, John Campbell, Earl of, appointed commander in chief, 42; title of, in North America, 43 n.; commission of, discussed, 52-60; nature of instructions to, 59; appointed governor of Virginia, 60-61; activity of, in London, 79; powers of, analyzed, 79-80; sails for America, 81; description of, 82; arrives at Albany, 90; meets Winslow, 91; analyzes ideal provincial army, 102-103; draws up recruiting act, 116; settles recruiting complaints, 118-119; meets Franklin, 120-121; forbidden to draw on non-effective fund, 122 n.; considers recruiting feasible, 130; opinion of, of Shirley, 132; relations with Livingston and Morris, 138-139; denounces Shirley's promotions, 147; sends Webb to Oswego, 164; life of, in New York, 167-168; opinion of, of provincials, 168-169; asks aid from assemblies, 172, 178; buys provincial provision stores, 183; recommends parliamentary interference, 185-186; policy of, in quartering, 193; threatens forced quartering, 203-204; dispute with Pownall, 207-208; plans for provincial troops in 1757, 212; arrives at Boston, 214; meets governors at Philadelphia, 218; takes Marylanders into Crown's pay, 221 n.; intervenes in

Pennsylvania government, 223; meets New Jersey assembly, 225; advocates parliamentary tax, 225 n.; arrives at Halifax, 238; determines to abandon expedition, 242; resents Pitt's interference, 251; relations of, with governors, 261-262; at Boston in 1758, 276; economizes in army management, 281, 291; settles exchange rates, 286; permits officers perquisites, 293; commits baker to jail, 294; attitude of, towards promotion, 308; portrait of, 341 n.; meets Pitt, 346; recalled, 346; at Fort Edward, 348; activities of, in 1758, 348-349; letter of, to Argyll, 350-351; plans 1758 campaign, 356-358; in Portugal, 361 n.; relations of, with officers, 362-364.

Loudoun, brigantine on Lake Ontario, 69.

Louisbourg, capture of by New Englanders, 7; British garrison at, 11; named by Pitt as 1757 objective, 232; attack on, abandoned, 242-243; Amherst at, 357-358.

Ludlow, Thomas, supplies provisions, 137.

Lunenburg, 196.

Lutterell (Luttrell), Henry Lawes, volunteer, 310.

Lyde, Byfield, half-pay lieutenant from Shirley's first regiment, 312.

Lydius, John Henry, colonel of Indians on the Niagara expedition, 154 n.

Lyman, Phineas, general of Connecticut troops, 94; explains provincial desertion, 184; at Ticonderoga, 355.

Lyttelton, Sir Richard, correspondent of Bradstreet, 343.

Lyttelton, William Henry, governor of South Carolina, captured at sea,

62 n.; fears invasion from South Carolina, 219.

Mackay, Sam, captain in the 40th regiment, 119 n.

Mackellar, Patrick, engineer *en second*, at Oswego, 149-161; journal of, at Oswego, 152 n.; as engineer, 320.

MacKinnon, Robert, lieutenant in the 1st regiment, cost of board of, 124; in New London recruiting affair, 126-128.

Mansfield, William Murray, Earl of, on Board of Trade plan, 27; proposes American troops, 29; opinion of, of Loudoun's conduct, 337.

Marlborough, Charles Spencer, Duke of, master general of Ordnance, 46 n.

Marshall, Samuel, captain of *Nottingham*, 75.

Maryland, enlisting of servants in, 107; raises recruits for the 44th and 48th regiments, 114; votes Loudoun £3000, 114 n.; troops quartered in, 204; troops of, taken into Crown's pay, 221 n.; militia in, 226.

Maryland, House of Delegates of, conflict with Loudoun, 220-221.

Mascarene, John Paul, lieutenant colonel of the 40th regiment, 87 n.

Massachusetts, assembly of, deals with Loudoun's request for troops, 175-176; sells provisions to Crown, 185-186; objects to quartering, 205-206; votes troops in 1757, 214 ff.; Pownall's management of, 269-278; troops raised in 1758, 353.

Massachusetts, troops of, with the 40th regiment, 87 n.; recruiting in, 119; militia in, 226.

Masson, Jean, Loudoun's mistress, 81.

McAdam, Gilbert, lieutenant in the 60th regiment, Loudoun's aide de camp, 167.

McAdam, Mrs. Gilbert, daughter of Christopher Kilby, at New London, 127.

McAllaster, Alexander, volunteer in the 1st regiment, 332.

McAulay (McAully), Archibald, complains of the justices of the peace, 118; lieutenant of the New York independent company, recommended by Calcraft, 311.

McColne, John, surgeon of the 1st regiment, 327 n.

Medical service, discussion of, 324-328.

Mercantilism, determines British policy, 2 ff.

Mercer, James F., lieutenant colonel of the 51st regiment, ordered to America, 142; at Oswego, 152, 153, 161.

Meserve, Nathaniel, colonel of the New Hampshire troops and captain of the company of carpenters, Loudoun's opinion of, 169; raises carpenters, 298; ordered to Halifax, 359.

Meyer, Elias, lieutenant in the 60th regiment, 202.

Middleborough, Massachusetts, 323.

Milbank, Alcomb, captain lieutenant of the 28th regiment, recommended by Holderness, 309.

Milford, 205.

Military discipline, in provincial army, 95-96; in regular army, 299-300; 314-315; 330-335; among rangers, 303-305; in Prevost's regiment, 316-317.

Militia, colonial, defined, 5; regiments in Massachusetts, 175; assembled at New York, 177; ordered by Loudoun to be ready, 225; account of, at Fort William Henry, 246-248; commander in chief's control over, 269 n.

Mobile, attack on, contemplated, 359.

Mohawk river, troops serving along, 144; transportation along, 155-156.

Mohegans, formed into ranging companies, 303.

Monckton, Robert, lieutenant colonel of the 47th regiment, captures Fort Beauséjour, 37; reports on recruiting, 108.

Monk, James, justice of the peace at Halifax, 335.

Monongahela, causes of Braddock's defeat at, 36; Braddock's losses at, 108.

Monro, George, lieutenant colonel of the 35th regiment, under Webb, 234; in command at Fort William Henry, 249-250; death of, 249 n.

Montcalm, Louis, Marquis de, appointed to command in Canada, 45; at Oswego, 158; captures Fort William Henry, 243-250; releases Young from capitulation of Fort William Henry, 315 n.

Montgomery, Archibald (Earl of Eglinton), lieutenant colonel of the 1st Highland battalion, arrives at Charlestown, 202; ordered to South Carolina, 251. See also Highlanders.

Montrésor, James, chief engineer, instructs Mackellar, 157; reports to Ordnance Board, 244 n.; opinion of, of Massachusetts militia, 248; reports on Fort William Henry, 252; complains of engineers' treatment, 318; estimates ordnance for Fort Edward, 324.

Montrésor, John, lieutenant in the 48th regiment, assistant engineer, 319.

Moore, Mrs. Frances, Loudoun's landlady in New York, 167.

Mordaunt, Sir John, suggested to command in America, 42; expedition to Rochefort, 339; court martial of, 345-346.

More, John, captain, in the 50th regiment, paymaster, 143.

Morris, Roger, captain in the 48th regiment, Webb's aide de camp, 167.

Morris, Staats Long, Shirley's agent in London, 54; marries Dowager Duchess of Gordon, 54 n.

Morris, William, captain in the 48th regiment, 327.

Morris, ——, justice of the peace at Bristol, 334-335.

Mortier, Abraham, deputy paymaster general at New York, 140 n., 282.

Mulloy, Terence, captain in the 44th regiment, 314 n.

Murray, John, affidavit of, supporting Shirley, 163 n.

Murray, John, of Rutland, 84 n.

Muster master general, duties of, 282 n. See Pitcher, James.

Mutiny Act, extended to provincial troops, 85-86; recruiting sections of, 106; recruiting sections of, extended to America, 116; quartering sections of, 188; various extensions of, to America, 189; never suspended in England, 193; quartering sections of, proposed to extend to America, 194; copied by Pennsylvania assembly, 201; for quartering in North America, 1765, 209.

Napier, James, a physician in the general hospital, 325.

Napier, Colonel Robert, aide de camp to Cumberland, 299 n.

Naunauphtaunk, Jacob, lieutenant of the Stockbridge Indians, 301.

Navy Board, 47; blamed for delay in

fitting transports, 50; conflict with the War Office, 71.

Navy, Royal, condition of, in 1756, 51; on Lake Ontario, 160.

Neale, William, sergeant major of the 22d regiment, 314.

Nesbit, Arnold, provision contractor, 296.

Newark, New Jersey, sick troops lodged at, 294.

Newcastle, Thomas Pelham-Holles, Duke of, secretary of state and first lord of the Treasury, plans Cartagena expedition, 13; plans Quebec expedition, 14; on French encroachments, 19; delays declaring war, 21; control of House of Commons by, 22, 46; fears colonial union, 27; opinion of, on Board of Trade plan, 27-28; approves American troops, 29, 38; economizes on American war, 32-33, 35; relations with Loudoun, 42; fears French invasion, 51; concern of, over Pennsylvania, 56; out of office, 228; opinion of, on American conquests, 229; arranges affairs with Pitt, 238; criticizes Loudoun, 338.

New Hampshire, assembly of, deals with Loudoun's requests, 174, 181; votes troops, 214-217.

New Hampshire, riots in, 129; militia in, 226; embargo not kept in, 266.

New Jersey, assembly of, deals with Loudoun's requests, 182; fails to vote troops in 1757, 225.

New Jersey, militia in, 226; fails to furnish horses, 262-263.

New London, recruiting affair at, 126-128.

New York, asks aid from neighbors, 7; riots in, 129; town council of, provides quarters, 198-200; jurisdiction of harbor of, 265.

New York, assembly of, furnishes troops, 182; provides for quartering, 198-200; provides rangers, 275.

New York, four independent companies of, 11-12; ordered to Virginia, 24; neglect of, 31; quartered by assembly, 189; proposal to regiment, 329-330.

Nicholson, Francis, colonial governor, 11, 14.

Nightingale, H.M.S., 81-82.

Non-effective fund, defined, 122.

North Carolina, four companies of, in New York, 171; assembly of, votes troops, 220; militia in, 226.

Norwalk, troops quartered at, 205; Loudoun at, 213.

Nottingham, H.M.S., ordered to North America, 75 n., 77.

Nova Scotia, encroachments of French in, 18; New Englanders in, 88; exchange rates in, 288 n. See also Halifax.

Number Four (fort), Indian attack on, 216; Pownall tries to provide for, 274; surgeon's mate at, 327.

Nurses, 326.

Officers, British, discussion of, 306-318.

Off-reckonings (stoppages), 101, 122, 123 n., 216, 281 and note, 283-284, 289 n., 293, 329.

Ogden, Jonathan, captain of rangers, 250 n.

Ogilvie, John, Indian missionary and chaplain, 328.

Ogle, Samuel, governor of Maryland, 12.

Oglethorpe, James, commander in chief of Georgia and South Carolina, proposes means of defense, 5; regiment of, 11, 330.

Ohio, region of, proposal to neutralize, 20.

Ohio company, 18; destruction of fort of, 20.

Ohio river, fort built at forks of, 22.

Ohio valley, fertility of, discussed, 19.

Oliver, Andrew, secretary of Massachusetts, 84 n.

Oliver, Peter, supplies ammunition, 323.

Ord, Thomas, captain of the Royal Artillery, 324.

Ordnance Board, objects to sending cannon to Virginia, 23; character of, 46 n., 73; engineers under, 318; royal regiment of artillery under, 320; artillery shipped to America by, 321.

Ordnance, taken to America by Loudoun, 69 n., 70; shipped in 1757, 233; discussion of, 320-322.

Orme, Robert, lieutenant (with captain's rank) in the Coldstream foot-guards, Braddock's aide de camp, 114 n.

Osborn, Sir Danvers, governor of New York, suicide of, 54 n.

Oswego, court martial at, 96 n.; carpenters at, 136; 50th regiment at, 143; account of, in 1756, 147-160.

Otis, James, of Massachusetts, account of, settled by Loudoun, 139 n.; sells whaleboats to army, 291.

Panmure, William Maule, Earl of, 42.

Paris, Ferdinand John, agent of Pennsylvania Quakers, 56.

Parker, John, colonel of the New Jersey regiment, 182; loses boats on Lake George, 244; lieutenant in the 60th, 311 n.; advises Monro to surrender, 250 n.

Parliament, funds voted by, for American war, 280.

Pay, of regular soldiers, 281-285.

Pearson (Payson), Colonel Nathan, of Connecticut, 298.

Pelham, Henry, first lord of the Treasury, 21.

Pemberton, Israel, of Pennsylvania, 73 n.

Penn, Thomas, proprietor of Pennsylvania, appoints Denny, 57; does not object to taxation of estates, 222 n.

Penn, William, recommended for regular commission, 312.

Pennsylvania, assembly of, on quartering question, 191, 200-202; conflict of, with Denny, 222-224.

Pennsylvania, factional dispute in, 56-57; plan to raise 60th regiment in, 61-62; enlisting of servants in, 107; militia in, 226; Indian affairs in, 254-255.

Pennsylvania Gazette, 119, 120 n.

Penobscot, Pownall wishes to build fort on, 272.

Pepperrell, Sir William, colonel of regiment, 15; suggests recruiting of Highlanders, 16 n.; complains of Shirley's tactics, 142 n.; opinion of militia, 248. Regiment of, see Regiments, British, 51st.

Philadelphia, recruiting in, 118; quartering in, 200-202; meeting of governors in, 218-220; complaint against embargo in, 266; court martial at, 333.

Philipse, Mary, 168.

Phips, Spencer, lieutenant governor of Massachusetts, deals with Loudoun's request, 178-179; death of, 216.

Pickering, John, captain of New Hampshire troops, 333.

Pinckney, Charles, of South Carolina, 251.

Pinckney, Thomas, volunteer in British army, 311.

Pitcher, James, muster master general, at Oswego, 143 n., 158.

Pitt, William, secretary of state, as paymaster general, 21; in opposition, 46; gives rank to provincials, 92-93; refuses to allow contingent men, 124; unwilling to court martial Shirley, 165; fails to settle quartering question, 194-195; campaign plans of, arrival of, 225; becomes secretary of state, 228; imperialistic ideas of, 228-230; plans of, for 1757 campaign, 231-232; decreases Loudoun's powers, 231-233; out of office, 238; gives reasons for failure of Louisbourg expedition, 251; opinion of Cumberland, 337; receives criticisms of Loudoun, 342-345; recalls Loudoun, 346-347; ends colonial union, 351; his plans compared with Loudoun's, 356-359; limits commander in chief's powers, 358-359; criticism of, 359-360.

Plimton, Massachusetts, 323.

Pownall, John, secretary of the Board of Trade, 55 n.

Pownall, Thomas, governor of Massachusetts, on importance of Niagara, 35 n.; early career, 54 n.; declines governorship of Pennsylvania, 57; Loudoun's secretary, 81; distributes recruiting act, 118; remonstrates against forced recruiting, 126; member of Loudoun's family, 167; scheme of, for quartering, 194; supports assembly in quartering, 207-208; relations of, with Pitt, 231; goes to London to present Loudoun's case, 231 n.; orders militia to Fort William Henry, 246-247; character of, 268-270; conflict of, with Loudoun, 268-278; arrives at Boston, 269; Loudoun's opinion of, 350-351.

Prevost, Augustin, major in the 60th regiment, 63.

Prevost, James, colonel of the 4th battalion of the 60th regiment, proposes raising regiment in America, 61; early career of, 62 n.; German planters of, 111 n.; unfit for command, 234; scheme of, for American war, 300; incompetence of, 316-318; later career of, 318 n.

Pringle, James, comptroller of hospital in Flanders, 326 n.

Pringle, John, 97.

Provincial currency, 281-289.

Provincial officers, rank of, 85-87; dispute over rank of, 89-90, 92-93.

Provincial troops, defined, 5; use of, not intended in 1755-56, 32, 41; raising of, asked in 1756, 67-68; effectiveness of, 94-102; American opinion of, 97; pay and perquisites of, 101-102; ideal form of, 102-103; Loudoun's plans for, in 1757, 212; raising of, in 1757, 216; distribution of, in 1757, 219; returns of, at Fort William Henry, 244-246; behavior of, at Fort William Henry, 249 n.; difficulty of finding transport for, 298-299; unfamiliar with woods, 301; disadvantages of, in 1758, 354-355; services of, 355.

Provisions, London contractor for, in North America, 67; selection of contractor for, 72-74; provincial allowance of, 101; furnished by Shirley's contractors, 137; purchased from colonies, 183; collected at Halifax, 233; furnished gratis to regulars, 284; discussion of, 291-296.

Purchase system, 306-308.

Quartering of regular troops, in West Indies, 189; in Virginia, 189, 190; in New York, 189; in Maryland,

190, 204; in Massachusetts, 190, 207; in Albany, 191, 195-198; in Pennsylvania, 191, 200-202; in New York city, 198-200; in South Carolina, 202-204; in New Jersey, 205; in Connecticut, 205.

Quebec, Loudoun plans to attack, 211.

Quotas, colonial, named by Crown, 7; named by Loudoun, 215; in south, 219; proposed alteration of, 273; settled by Hartford meeting, 276 n.

Ramsay, William, ensign in the 60th regiment, 311.

Rangers, provincial, requested by Loudoun, 275-276; discussion of, 300-305. See also Robert Rogers.

Reading, Pennsylvania, 357.

Recruiting, of New Englanders in 1746, 15; of British regiments, numbers proposed, 105; methods used in, 106; failure of, 110-112; regulations governing, 117; expenses of, 121-125; quartering of parties engaged in, 207.

Regiments, American, in British pay, 12-15, 34.

Regiments, British, stationed permanently in colonies, 11; plans for recruiting of, in America, 105; annual losses of, 108; sent to America in 1757, 109; distribution of, in 1757, 235 n.; training of, 299-300.

1st or Royals (St. Clair's), 109 n., 130.

17th (Forbes'), 109 n.

22d (O'Farrell's), 109, 111, 122, 199-200, 211.

27th (Blakeney's), 109 n.

28th (Bragg's), 109 n.

35th (Otway's), ordered to America, 47-49; recruited in England, 67-68; stores of, shipped, 69; recruiting funds of, 121; station of, in 1756, 172,

178; quartered in Albany, 196; in 1757, 211, 235 n.; in 1758, 357.

40th (Phillips', Hopson's), in Nova Scotia, 11; under Braddock, 31; station of, in 1755, 34; Massachusetts troops with, 87 n.; recruiting of, 105.

42d (Oglethorpe's), in Georgia, 11; broken, 330.

42d (Lord John Murray's), the Black Watch, proposal to send to America, 29; ordered to America, 47-49; recruited in Highlands, 67-68, 109; supernumeraries of, 111; recruiting funds of, 121; station of, in 1756, 171, 178; quartered in Albany, 196; in 1757, 211; embarks for Halifax, 237.

43d (Kennedy's), 109 n.

44th (Halkett's, Abercromby's), under Braddock, 31-33; plans for recruiting of, 34; on Irish establishment, 49; Shirley's plans for, 87; Americans in ranks of, 104-108; Loudoun's opinion of, 116 n.; recruiting funds of, 121; ordered to Oswego, 163; station of, in 1756, 171; quartered in Pennsylvania, 191; in 1757, 211; embarks for Halifax, 237; arms of, 323.

45th (Warburton's), in Nova Scotia, 31; station of, in 1755, 34; recruiting of, in America, 105.

46th (Thomas Murray's), 109 n.

47th (Lascelles'), in Nova Scotia, 31; station of, in 1755, 34; recruiting of, 104-108.

48th (Dunbar's, Webb's), under Braddock, 31-33; recruiting of, 34; on Irish establishment, 49; Shirley's plans for, 87; at Fort Edward, 93; Americans in ranks of, 104-108; Loudoun's opinion of, 116 n.; recruiting funds of, 121; station of, in 1756, 171, 178; in 1757, 211; embarks for Halifax, 237; arms of, 323.

50th (Shirley's), raised in 1746, 15, 141 n.; broken, 16; ordered re-raised, 31-33; Americans in ranks of, 104-108; men of, drafted into other regiments, 130; account of, 141-146; equipment of, 161, 323.

51st (Pepperrell's), raised in 1746, 15, 141 n.; broken, 16; ordered re-raised, 31-33; Americans in ranks of, 104-108; men of, drafted into other regiments, 130; account of, 141-146; equipment of, 161, 323.

55th (Perry's, Howe's), 109 n.

60th or Royal American Regiment (originally the 62d, Loudoun colonel in chief, Stanwix, Dusseaux, Jefferys, Prevost, colonels commandant), account of formation of, 61-66; clothing of, 64 n.; shipping of stores of, 69; Americans in ranks of, 104-108; composition of, 111-112; wealth of, 124 n.; station of, in 1756, 178; quartering of, 198-205; station of, in 1757, 211; training of, 299-300; officers in, 307; account of Prevost's battalion in, 316-318; station of, in 1758, 357.

63d (1st Highland battalion commanded by Montgomery; 2d Highland battalion commanded by Fraser), see Highlanders. See also Artillery; New York and South Carolina, independent companies of.

Rhode Island, raises men for the 50th, 114; difficulty of recruiting in, 130; assembly of, relations with

Loudoun, 172-173, 180; militia in, 226.

Richards, William, 333.

Robertson, James, major in the 60th regiment, in charge of recruits, 71 n.; sent to New London, 127-128; guest of Loudoun, 167; opinion of, of Loudoun, 363.

Roche, David, ensign in the 47th regiment, 332.

Rogers, Richard, captain of ranging company, 302.

Rogers, Robert, captain of ranging company, takes scalps, 98; appointed, 302; undertakes scout, 303; fails to provide snowshoes, 349.

Rollo, Andrew, lieutenant colonel of the 22d regiment, 234, 314, 335.

Rutherford, John, major in the 60th regiment, Shirley's agent, 54; gives information to Loudoun, 92 n.; opinion of, of indentured servants, 107.

Sackville, Lord George, 42; opinion of, of Loudoun, 337.

St. Clair, James, lieutenant general, 14-15.

St. Clair, Sir John, deputy quartermaster general, estimates wagons for Braddock's expedition, 35; estimates provincial troops, 100; ordered to prepare supplies, 163; accompanies Massachusetts militia, 248; recommends forage money, 289; opinion of, of Loudoun, 363.

Saltonstall, Richard, captain of Massachusetts troops, 250 n.

Saratoga, 90, 297-298; storehouse at, 348.

Saul, Thomas, Baker's agent in Nova Scotia, 233 n.

Schenectady, stores at, 163; fortification of, proposed, 320; justices in, 334.

Schlatter, Michael, German pastor and chaplain, 329.

Schuyler, Peter, colonel of New Jersey regiment, appointed lieutenant colonel, 88 n.

Scotland, recruiting in, 68; quartering in, 188.

Scott, George, captain in the 40th regiment, on Fort Beauséjour expedition, 88; suggests drill alterations, 300.

Scott, Joseph, of Massachusetts, 323.

Scudder, John, discharged from regular army, 118.

Seton, Sir Henry, of Fraser's Highlanders, 363.

Shackerley, Captain, transport agent, 237 n.

Shannon, Richard Boyle, Viscount, 13.

Sharpe, Horatio, governor of Maryland, appointed to American command, 24; superseded, 32; furnishes recruits, 114; meets Loudoun, 218; opinion of, of Loudoun, 278.

Shepherd, John, captain of ranging company, 291, 303.

Sherriff, Charles, ensign in the 45th regiment, 332.

Shirley, William, governor of Massachusetts and commander in chief in North America, proposes parliamentary tax, 10; appointed colonel, 15; proposes Kennebec expedition, 24; authorized to raise New England battalions, 34; quarrels with Johnson, 36; appointed to chief command, 39; Niagara expedition of, 67; recalled, 76; plans of, for 1756, 83, 87; encourages raising provincials, 83-84; misinterprets orders, 88 n.; approves courts martial, 97; makes loan to New England governments, 102; permits enlisting servants, 107; grants funds for recruiting, 123-124; meets Loudoun, 132; learns of recall, 133 n.; character of, 134; warrants drawn by, 136 n., 290; drains army chest, 140-141; raises 50th regiment, 142-143; luxury of, in field, 145 n.; objects breaking 50th regiment, 146; receives letter of demission, 146; reaches Oswego, 148; leaves Oswego, 152; refuses to supply funds for Oswego, 158; responsible for loss of Oswego, 160-161; Hardy's opinion of, 162; court martial of, recommended, 165; supplies wagons, 176; leaves for England, 177; fails to provide quarters, 190-191; issues arms to provincials, 217; appears before House of Commons, 295; forms rangers, 302; in London, 342. For Shirley's regiment, see Regiments, British, 50th.

Skinner, William Ann, ensign in the 35th regiment, 118 n., 335.

Slap-gelt, defined, 145; paid by Shirley, 191.

Smallpox, feared by colonial assemblies, 179; at Albany, 181 n.; at Philadelphia, 201; at Charlestown, 202.

Smith, James, of New Jersey regiment, 334.

South Carolina, difficulty of recruiting in, 130; quartering in, 202-204; assembly of, votes troops, 220; militia in, 226.

South Carolina, independent companies of, 24 n., 330.

Spencer, Sam, of Hartford county, 298.

Spittal, John, captain in the 47th regiment, 309.

Spruce beer, 283 n.

Stamford, 205.

Stanwix, John, colonel commandant of first battalion of 60th regiment, on recruiting, 103; commands in Pennsylvania, 219, 234; deserters from regiment of, 334; services in 1758, 357; letter from, 362.

Stark, John, captain of ranging company, 303.

Steers, Philip, of New York regiment, 333.

Stevenson, Visger, and Van Eps, New York merchants, 139 n.

Stillwater, 297-298, 355.

Stockbridge Indians, 256-257, 301.

Stoppages (off-reckonings), 101, 122, 123 n., 216, 281 and note, 283-284, 289 n., 293, 329.

Stratford, 205.

Subsistence, defined, 122.

Temple, Robert, Shirley's son in law, 142.

Thomas, John, of Rhode Island troops, 331.

Thomlinson, John and Hanbury, John, London money contractors, 137 n.; amount received by, 290 n.

Thomlinson, Hanbury, Colebrooke, and Nesbit, money contractors, 282 n.

Ticonderoga, rangers at, 303; winter expedition planned against, 345; Abercromby's attack on, 355.

Tinker, Jeremiah, lieutenant in the 50th regiment, 311.

Townshend, Charles, Viscount, Lord President, 10.

Townshend, Charles, lord of the Admiralty, objects to the Board of Trade plan, 27; proposes American regiments, 29; attacks Baker and Kilby contract, 295.

Townshend, Roger, lieutenant colonel, 1.

Transportation, discussion of, 296-299.

Transports, for the 35th and 42d, 49; for recruits of the 35th and 42d, 69-71; in North America, 236.

Treasury Board, conflict of, with Admiralty, 48; delays in connection with the 60th regiment, 64-65; times of meeting of, 73-74; settles exchange in America, 285-287.

Trumble (Trumbull), Jonathan, colonel of Connecticut regiment, 180.

Tyrawley, James O'Hara, Baron, lieutenant general, 42.

Uhauamvaumut, Solomon, ensign of Stockbridge Indian company, 302.

Utrecht, Peace of, 20.

Van Schaack, Henry, 291.

Vaughan, Thomas, lieutenant of the 45th, 128.

Vernon, Edward, admiral, 14.

Vickers, John, captain of the 50th regiment, 153.

Victualling Board, 47.

Virginia, Loudoun appointed governor general of, 60-61; raises recruits, 114; supplies provisions, 138; assembly of, provides quarters, 189; votes troops, 220; militia in, 226; Young recommended as lieutenant governor of, 315 n.

Walpole, Sir Robert, discusses colonial defense, 5; fails to provide colonial defense, 11; "system" of, destroyed, 46.

War Office, character of, 45-46; conflict of, with Navy Board, 71; suspects Shirley's promotions, 147; recommends Shirley's court martial, 165.

Warrant men, defined, 124.

Washington, George, ministry learns

of defeat of, 26; suspected as author of intercepted letters, 77 n.; meets Loudoun, 219; asks for regular commission, 312.

Watts, John, New York assemblyman, 97.

Webb, Daniel, major general and colonel of the 48th regiment, appointed temporary commander in chief, 74; instructions for, 75 n.; sails for America, 77; arrives at New York, 83; sends letter of demission to Shirley, 146; ordered to Oswego, 164; sickness of, in 1757, 234; conduct of, at Fort William Henry, 243-251; foments dissension in army, 349.

Wells, Edmund, captain of Connecticut troops, 94-95.

Wentworth, Benning, governor of New Hampshire, deals with Loudoun's requests, 174, 181; relations of, with Amherst, 352.

Wentworth, Thomas, brigadier general, 14.

West Indies, American troops in, 13-15; assemblies in, provide quarters, 189.

Wetham, Thomas, major general, 13.

Wetherill, John, assemblyman of New Jersey, 205.

Wetterstrom, Gustavus, captain in the 60th regiment, 319-320.

Whipple, Joseph, former deputy governor of Rhode Island, 311.

Whiting, Nathan, half-pay lieutenant from Pepperrell's regiment and colonel of Connecticut troops, 235 n.

Willard, Josiah, secretary of Massachusetts, 185.

Williams, Israel, colonel of Massachusetts troops, 248.

Williams, Nathaniel, lieutenant in the 51st, cashiered, 145 n., 332.

Williams, William, captain in the 51st regiment, 154.

Williamson, George, lieutenant colonel in the Royal Artillery, 323 n., 324.

Wills Creek, Braddock at, 108; barracks at, 190.

Wilmington, riot in, 125-126.

Wilson, John, volunteer, 310.

Winslow, John, general of provincial troops, 83; character of commission of, 84-85; colonel of New Englanders in Nova Scotia, 88; arrives at Fort William Henry, 90; meets Loudoun, 91; estimates wagons for provincials, 163; reports French attack, 178; reports on provisions, 183-184; ordered to form rangers, 302.

Witherhead, ensign in the 47th regiment, 332.

Wolfe, James, major general, disapproves provisioning of troops, 284; criticizes Loudoun, 300 n.; opinion of, of Prevost, 317; at Louisbourg, 358; Pitt's orders to, 360; death of, 364.

Woodward, of Stonington, forcibly recruited, 127-128.

Wraxall, Peter, captain of New York independent company and secretary of Indian affairs, describes Loudoun, 82; criticizes provincial troops, 97.

York, Pennsylvania, 118, 357.

Yorke, Joseph, British minister at The Hague, 65.

Young, John, lieutenant colonel of the 60th regiment, Loudoun's protégé, 81, 167; at Fort William Henry, 234; advises Monro to surrender, 250 n.; recommended as lieutenant governor of Virginia, 315 n.